NEW TOPICS IN POLITICS

THE CONGRESSIONAL POLITICS OF IMMIGRATION REFORM

JAMES G. GIMPEL

JAMES R. EDWARDS, JR.

ALLYN AND BACON

Boston • London • Toronto • Sydney • Tokyo • Singapore

For Veronica
and
for Linda and MacKenzie

Vice President, Editor in Chief: Paul A. Smith
Editorial Assistant: Kathy Rubino
Marketing Manager: Jeff Lasser
Editorial Production Service: Chestnut Hill Enterprises, Inc.
Manufacturing Buyer: Megan Cochran
Cover Administrator: Jennifer Hart

Internet: www.abacon.com
America Online: keyword: College Online

Between the time Website information is gathered and published, it is not unusual for some sites to have closed. Also, the transcription of URLs can result in typographical errors. The publisher would appreciate notification where these occur so that they may be corrected. Thank you.

Library of Congress Cataloging-in-Publication Data
Gimpel, James G.
   The congressional politics of immigration reform / by James
G. Gimpel and James R. Edwards, Jr.
     p.   cm.
   Includes bibliographical references and index.
   ISBN 0-205-28203-2 (pb)
   1. United States–Emigration and immigration–Government policy.
2. United States. Congress. 3. United States–Politics and
government–1945-1989. 4. United States–Politics and
government–1989- I. Edwards, James R., Jr. II. Title.
JV6483.G56 1998
325.73'09'045–dc21

                   98-3341
                   CIP

Printed in the United States of America
10 9 8 7 6 5 4 3 2 1 RRD-VA 03 02 01 00 99 98

CONTENTS

CHAPTER 3

Issues in the Contemporary Immigration Debate on Capitol Hill   60

CHAPTER 4

The Congressional Politics of Immigration Policy, 1965–1982   93

CHAPTER 7

Congress and the Future of Immigration Policy 297

PREFACE

For all its faults, the United States remains an attractive place to live. If it were less desirable, perhaps residence here would not have to be legally restricted. But in the closing years of this century, immigration levels are at historic highs, and the demand to move here is as great as it has ever been. The assumption behind U.S. citizenship and immigration law is that we cannot accommodate all who would like to make this country their home. There must be some standard for admission and exclusion. So whom do we admit? This is essentially the question of immigration law and policy. Although states have been clamoring to make their own policies governing immigrants' eligibility for public services, states cannot make their own policies on immigration admissions. Immigration policy is the overarching responsibility of the national government, chiefly that of the legislative branch. A search for knowledge about the politics of immigration policymaking must begin, then, with the U.S. Congress.

Our goal in *The Congressional Politics of Immigration Reform* has been to write a serious account of congressional action on immigration policy since 1965, the year in which the National Origins Quota System for selecting immigrants was repealed by a lopsided margin in both chambers of Congress. This reform of the U.S. immigration system, coupled with subsequent changes in the 1970s, 1980s, and 1990s, has led to noticeable changes in the immigrant population. Thanks to our generous immigration policies, the nation has a far larger Asian and Hispanic population today than it had in the 1960s. But the country is also more divided about immigration policy than it was thirty years ago. Although the 1965 law was passed by a consensus vote, in recent months Congress battled over this issue along pronounced partisan and ideological lines. At some point between 1965 and the end of the century, the consensus disappeared. How and why did that happen? One obvious answer—and we think the incorrect one—is racism. The country is more ethnically diverse today, and many members of Congress and the public are uneasy with this increasing diversity. From this viewpoint, the call for immigration restrictions may be a manifestation of racism. Indeed, the controversy over immigration policy reflects *sophisticated* prejudice, in contrast to the more bald-faced expressions of the mid-century. Since the culture frowns on open expressions of nativism and xenophobia, these sentiments are couched in a less obvious lingo today. We do not doubt that some opponents of expansionist immigration policy are racist, but uneasiness with ethnic diversity is not the main reason why immigration policy is more controversial now than in earlier times. What, then, has been the source of the disappearing consensus? This is the question we seek to answer in writing this book.

We began puzzling over the subject of immigration reform from two different standpoints, both personal and professional. James R. Edwards, Jr., approached the issue from the perspective of a congressional insider working as an adviser to a member of Congress who currently serves on the House Judiciary Committee. James G. Gimpel 's interest in the subject was stimulated by the fact that his spouse is a Hispanic immigrant and his in-laws may seek, at some point, to emigrate from the country where they now live. Gimpel began studying immigration policy at least partly to understand what changes in law and policy could mean to his family. For Edwards, the congressional politics of immigration reform involved making sense of a complex legal history in order to provide counsel and advice on the controversies of the 1990s as they were aired in the Judiciary Committee hearing room where he often worked.

Although we were differently motivated by this subject matter, it is difficult to sort out our separate contributions. While Gimpel conducted almost all of the personal interviews, Edwards contributed crucial eyewitness details on the workings of the legislative process in subcommittee, full committee, on the floor, and in the House-Senate conference. Edwards contributed important information about the nuances of immigration law and policy, while Gimpel did most of the data analysis. Edwards, trained in communications, made the book far more readable than it would have been had it been left to Gimpel, the political scientist. While knowing that no book can be all things to all people, we set several standards in writing this one: completeness, analytical rigor, and readability.

We owe great debts of gratitude to the members of Congress, the congressional staff, the policy experts, and the interest group representatives who granted interviews and supplied other helpful information. We are pleased to acknowledge the following:

Members of Congress: Gary Ackerman (D-NY), Bob Barr (R-GA), Ken Bentsen (D-TX), Howard Berman (D-CA), Randy "Duke" Cunningham (R-CA), Cal Dooley (D-CA), Bob Ehrlich (R-MD), Bob Filner (D-CA), Floyd Flake (D-NY), Barney Frank (D-MA), George Gekas (R-PA), Bob Goodlatte (R-VA), Steve Horn (R-CA), Peter King (R-NY), Jay Kim (R-CA), Zoe Lofgren (D- CA), Bill McCollum (R-FL), Patsy Mink (D-HI), Ed Pastor (D-AZ), E. Clay Shaw (R-FL), Lamar Smith (R-TX), Mark Souder (R-IN), and Esteban Torres (D-CA).

Retired Members of Congress: Peter W. Rodino (D-NJ).

Interest Group Representatives: Stuart Anderson (CATO Institute), Wright H. Andrews (FAIR), Jeanne Butterfield (American Immigration Lawyers Association), Jennifer Denson (FAIR), Jennifer Eisen (INTEL Corp.), Matthew Finucane (Asian Pacific American Labor Alliance), Michael Hill (U.S. Catholic Bishops Conference), Daphne Kwok (Organization of Chinese Americans), Bryan Little (American Farm Bureau Federation), Stephen Moore (CATO Institute), Kyle Rogers (U.S. English), Frank Sharry (National Immigration Forum), Linda Chavez Thompson (AFL-CIO), Georgina Verdugo (Mexican American Legal Defense and Education Fund), and Lisa Zachary (Council of Jewish Federations).

Staff and Others: Paul Donnelly and Susan Martin (U.S. Commission on Immigration Reform), Mary Ann Fish, George Fishman, Cordia Strom, and Ed Grant (House Subcommittee on Immigration and Claims), Nicholas Hayes (former AA to the late Congressman Hamilton Fish, Jr. (R-NY)), Raymond Kethledge (Legislative Counsel, Senator Spencer Abraham (R-MI)), David Lehman (Legislative Counsel, Congressman Bob Goodlatte (R-VA)), Peter Levinson (House Judiciary Committee), J. Michael Myers (Senate Subcommittee on Immigration), Richard Mereu (Legislative Counsel, Congressman Elton Gallegly (R-CA)).

There were more than a dozen others who preferred to remain anonymous.

We gratefully thank Congressman Ed Bryant (R-TN) for allowing us to use his legislative files and materials. And we thank Mike Freeman for lending Edwards his laptop computer, which greatly facilitated the completion of the manuscript.

A unique and special feature of this book is the photographs of the congressional policy makers responsible for the last thirty years of immigration reform. For these photographs we are particularly indebted to Bill McCollum (R-FL), Nicholas Hayes, Mary Ann Fish, Peter W. Rodino (D-NJ), Edward Roybal (D-CA), Lucille Roybal-Allard (D-CA), Daniel Lungren (R-CA), Lamar Smith (R-TX), Elton Gallegly (R-CA), Howard Berman (D-CA), Dianne Feinstein (D-CA), Mike DeWine (R-OH), Spencer Abraham (R-MI), Edward M. Kennedy (D-MA), the librarians of the photograph collection of the Library of Congress, the U.S. Senate Historical Office, and Pat Chisholm of *Congressional Quarterly Weekly Report*.

We want to thank our editor, Paul Smith, and production coordinator, Marjorie Payne, working for Allyn and Bacon, for patiently coaching us through the publication process and giving us helpful feedback along the way. Allyn and Bacon's reviewers, John J. Pitney, Claremont McKenna College; Daniel Tichenor, Rutgers University; and Rosanna Perotti, Hofstra University, provided thorough and insightful criticism that enabled us to greatly improve the manuscript. The authors also thank their colleagues at work who read parts of the manuscript or discussed it with us.

We thank our families for their support while we were working on the project. Finishing any book-length work under a deadline inevitably involves some pressure and stress that spills over onto those closest to us. Our book is dedicated to those who put up with us, knowing that there would be an eventual end to the business. Finally, God blessed us with incredible energy and focus as we undertook this task, while opening many doors that would have otherwise remained closed to our inquiries. For these undeserved blessings, we are very grateful.

IMMIGRATION TO THE UNITED STATES: POLITICS AND POLICY

In a 1996 debate, Congressman Lamar Smith (R-TX), the chairman of the House Immigration Subcommittee, glared across the floor at the members who were offering an amendment that would kill his efforts to curb legal immigration and said:

> We need to remember that immigration is not an entitlement, it is a privilege. An adult immigrant who decides to leave his or her homeland to migrate to the United States is the one who has made a decision to separate from their [sic] family. It is not the obligation of U.S. immigration policy to lessen the consequences of that decision by giving the immigrant's adult family members an entitlement to immigrate to the United States. (*CR* 3/21/96 H2590)

In proposing new restrictions on legal immigration, Smith argued that times had changed and with them the nation's interest in immigration policy. Newly arriving immigrants were not equipped to contribute to a nation as technologically advanced as the United States. In earlier times, legions of unskilled and illiterate immigrants could easily fit into an industrial economy that did not require many skills. According to leading economists, by the early 1980s, the United States had clearly turned the corner into the postindustrial age (Piore and Sabel 1984). Yet, to those on Smith's side of the debate, immigration policy had not kept pace with the nation's economic advances. The United States continued to import people as if its economy had an endless supply of low-skill and no-skill jobs. Smith argued that the mismatch between immigrant skills and labor market needs meant that immigrants were now costing the society more than they were contributing to it. And increasing costs were the frightening specter in Smith's immigration nightmares. By using the term "entitlement," Smith indicated his preoccupation with the fiscal burden of immigration. Over and over he cited figures showing that legal immigrants were entering the country only to take advantage of public benefits. He pointed to studies showing that unskilled immigrants compete directly with America's lower-skilled workers, taking

1

away jobs and lowering wages. Because unskilled immigrants were no longer fit to compete in a postindustrial economy, they often dropped out of the labor market altogether or caused unskilled native-born workers to drop out of it. U.S. immigration policy badly needed updating, and Smith's legislation was the instrument to that end.

To his opponents, however, Smith was doing the unthinkable. His bill combined controversial new limits on legal immigration with ambitious efforts to control illegal immigration. Many members did not believe the two should be handled in one bill. To reform legal immigration, Smith had proposed a new emphasis on employment-based immigration and less emphasis on family reunification as the basis of annual visa allocations. His bill would make it easier for immediate family members (spouses, children) of U.S. citizens and permanent residents to enter the country, but more difficult for more distant relatives, such as adult brothers and sisters. The point of this reform was to reduce the backlog of immediate relatives waiting in line for immigrant visas by cutting back on the number of visas granted to more distant relatives. Those visas that were once dedicated to adult brothers and sisters would be reallocated to more immediate family members, thereby shortening the length of time they would be required to wait to reunify with their loved ones. The long backlogs had been created by passage of a previous immigration law, the Immigration Reform and Control Act of 1986 (IRCA), which had granted legal status to more than two million illegal residents living in the United States (see Chapter 5). Naturally, the newly legalized residents were now petitioning to bring in their spouses and children, making for long waiting lists that delayed family reunification for years and understandably tempted families to reunify through illegal entry. Backlogs led people to break the law. The backlogs should therefore be eliminated.

Opponents were skeptical of Smith's motives. He had been typecast as a restrictionist, and nothing he said or did convinced the opponents of restriction that he had the best interests of immigrants in mind. If he was so concerned about family reunification, so the argument went, why not just increase the number of immigrant visas for all categories of relatives, rather than taking from one group and giving to another? Asian groups, in particular, were apoplectic about the attempt to eliminate visas for more distant relatives. In their cultures, adult brothers and sisters *were* close family members. Opponents charged that Smith's approach was antifamily. Even the Christian Coalition, an influential interest group firmly allied with Republican causes, dubbed it antifamily and lobbied against it at a crucial point in the debate (see Chapter 6).

In spite of public opinion polls that indicated widespread support for cutting immigration, many members of Congress remained deeply committed to the notion that the United States is a nation of immigrants. Cincinnati Congressman Steve Chabot (R-OH) seemed to sum up their views in stating:

...I deeply value the fundamental character of this Nation as a land of hope and opportunity and because I cherish our unique American heritage as a country of immigrants, united by shared values, a strong work ethic and a commitment to freedom. Let us not tarnish that heritage or ignore our greatest strength, which is our people. (*CR* 3/21/96 H2595)

Chabot and his allies went on to draw a sharp distinction between legal and illegal immigration. Legal immigration was legitimate and an unqualified source of all that is good in America. If negative consequences were at all traceable to immigration, it was *illegal* immigration that was the culprit. Member after member invoked America's immigrant heritage in declaring their opposition to Smith's new limits on legal immigration. America was built by hardworking, taxpaying, legal immigrants. Immigrants energize America, bring needed skills and talents, open businesses, revitalize urban neighborhoods, pay more in taxes than they consume in government services, and breathe life into the American Dream. How could anyone dare to slam the door? If anything, the door should be opened even wider. In everyone's history is the story of someone's coming to America from a faraway land. This was powerful symbolism and it was sufficiently strong to defeat the effort to change the laws governing legal immigration. In the end, most of Lamar Smith's proposals to control *illegal* immigration would be enacted, but the major battle on legal immigration had been lost, leaving Smith and his allies deeply disappointed.

The debate in 1996, then, hinged largely on this issue of the separability of legal from illegal immigration. On the one side, immigration restrictionists suggested that the difference between the two was overdrawn. Legal immigrants and illegal immigrants were part of the same migration stream and were sufficiently similar to address both at the same time. Proponents of restriction came to the debate armed with facts, statistics, and arithmetic. On the other side, a powerful but unusual coalition of high-tech businesses joined with the well-financed immigration bar, minority rights groups, and religious organizations heavily involved in refugee resettlement, to eliminate the restrictions on legal immigration and focus the legislation only on illegal immigration. These groups chose to argue primarily by anecdote, filling their testimonials with case histories attached to faces, emotions, and sad histories of family separation. Policymaking by anecdote often prevails in Washington, and it did again this time.

Restrictions on legal immigration had not been in vogue in previous rounds of immigration reform. In fact, the opposite was true. Congress had not passed legislation to reduce legal immigration since 1924. In recent times, all of the pressure seemed to move in favor of eliminating existing limits—to the point at which two million illegal residents were legalized with passage of the 1986 Immigration Reform and Control Act (IRCA). In 1990, the next major round of immigration reform, the focus was on legal immigration. The

1990 Act substantially increased the nation's annual immigration quotas. Restrictions on legal immigration were thought to be hostile to America's expansive immigration tradition. Public opinion polls indicated that a majority of Americans desired a less expansive immigration policy (see Chapter 2), but in most places Americans were not inclined to vote on this issue. Those favoring generous immigration policy had in their corner a strong interest-group coalition combining ethnic, business, and religious interests. The lobby for immigration restrictions was not nearly as well developed. By the 1990s, this coalition consisted mainly of a few population-control organizations that many legislators viewed as on the fringe. No group represented mainstream American voters who supported reasonable reductions in immigration levels. Because of this lopsided balance of interests, it had always been easier to lift legal immigration limits than it had been to impose them.

Proponents of restriction in Congress knew this history, of course, and the effort to combine proposals to control both legal and illegal immigration was clearly motivated by the desire to pass a more controversial proposal on the back of a less controversial one. Congress was frequently divided about how to control illegal immigration, but none of the members advocated illegal entry into the country. "What are we talking about? It's illegal!" the late Congressman Sonny Bono (R-CA) once declared in a campaign debate. Legal immigration, though, was a different matter. As New York Congressman Gary Ackerman (D-NY) put it with a touch of humor, "I'm in favor of everything legal. I'm for the law. Not only that, I'm in favor of legal immigration. I'm against things that are illegal!" (Ackerman interview 4/8/97).

It was easy to talk tough about controlling illegal immigration and how it should be stopped. Illegal immigrants, after all, had broken the law. But while illegal immigration was a no-brainer, legal immigration divided members between those favoring a generous policy and those who would restrict the number of legal immigrant visas; and these divisions did not always fall along party lines. A number of those supporting the effort to kill the restrictions on legal immigration, including Steve Chabot (R-OH), were Republicans. The coalition to kill Lamar Smith's proposals combined liberals who had long believed in open immigration as a humanitarian gesture, conservatives who believed in open markets, and libertarians who stressed individual liberties (see also Tichenor 1994). But partisanship played a much larger role in the 1996 debate than it had in earlier rounds of immigration reform. In the mid-1960s, major changes in immigration law were adopted by a strong bipartisan consensus. By the 1990s, that consensus had all but disappeared (Tichenor 1994). Republicans had emerged as the chief proponents of both legal and illegal immigration restrictions. A majority of Democrats favored generous immigration policy.

Like so many other issues Congress grapples with, immigration had been translated from a consensus issue into a fiercely partisan one. This book relates the evolution of this issue from consensus to cleavage. Before proceeding further, however, some background facts are in order.

Immigration Policy and Immigrant Admissions 1900–1996

It is a fundamental right of a sovereign state to control its borders, define who can legally reside and seek employment within its borders, and define those who are citizens and those who are not. Immigration policy is a nation's set of rules designed to govern this important aspect of national sovereignty. As such, immigration policy is inherently discriminatory. Immigration policy allows some people to enter the country, while keeping others out. So the question then becomes, on what basis does a nation choose to discriminate? A restrictive immigration policy will permit a few select immigrants to enter, perhaps on the basis of family ties, ancestry, wealth, skills, or education. A generous policy will permit many to enter, perhaps discriminating only against those whom governing authorities deem undesirable—say, people with criminal backgrounds. Most nations have very restrictive immigration policies, and some permit no immigrants at all. In recent years, France has even encouraged "foreigners" to leave by offering them bonuses to return to their countries of origin (Martin and Houstoun 1984, 37–38). These "foreigners" included people *born in France*. Few nations in Europe grant citizenship solely on the basis of having been born on that nation's soil, as the United States does.

The United States, Canada, and Australia have been among the more generous nations. In the United States, immigrants are granted status as legal residents as well as permission to remain and work by being awarded an immigrant visa. The United States has a visa preference system, which awards a limited number of visas each year primarily on the basis of family relationships and special skills needed, but in short supply, in the domestic labor market. Beyond legal resident status, citizenship requirements have been, by standards of other nations, quite minimal. Anyone born in the United States is automatically a citizen. When one is petitioning to naturalize, citizenship requirements have generally included a basic facility with English and an elementary knowledge of American history and government.

Figure 1.1 illustrates the trends in immigrant admissions to the United States over the course of the twentieth century. The trend line has been unmistakably on a steady upward climb since the 1940s. The sharp spike in the trend line in the late 1980s is the result of the legalization of two million residents who had illegally settled in the country, having either entered without an immigrant visa or overstayed the terms of a temporary visa. Under the 1986 Immigration Reform and Control Act (IRCA), these illegals were

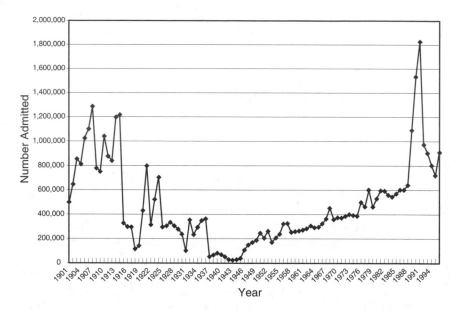

Figure 1.1   Legal Immigrants Admitted to the United States 1901–1996

granted amnesty and permanent resident status (for details see Chapter 5). Following the amnesty program, immigrant admissions declined from 1991 to 1995, but still remained well above pre-amnesty levels. In 1996, the United States admitted 915,900 immigrants, an increase of 28 percent over 1995. In the twenty years between 1975 and 1996, immigration has been a major source of population growth, adding approximately 17 million people to the nation's population.

The Changing Origins of the Legal Immigrant Population

Not only has annual immigration been on the rise since the 1940s, the composition of the immigrant population has changed (Keely 1971; Carlson 1994), and this too has been the result of immigration policymaking in Congress. Prior to 1965, immigration law was heavily biased toward European countries. Figure 1.2 illustrates the consequences of this bias for immigrant admissions. Approximately 53 percent of all immigrants entering the country between 1951 and 1960 were from European countries, compared with only 27 percent from North America (including Canada and Mexico) and 6 percent from Asian nations. A new immigration law was passed by Congress in 1965, eliminating a bias toward Northern European countries that many legislators considered racist (see Chapter 4 for details). The results were dra-

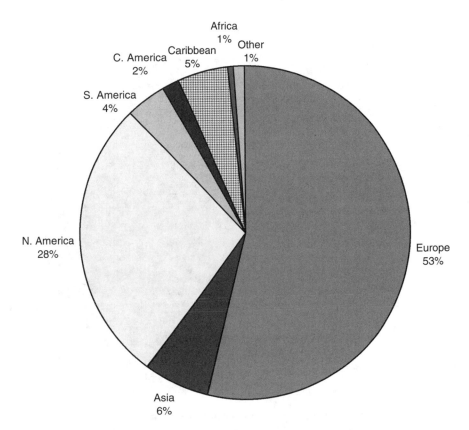

Figure 1.2 Origin of the Immigrant Population Entering between 1951 and 1960

matic. Figure 1.3 displays the regional origins of the immigrant population that entered the country from 1981 to 1990. By this time, a full decade after the 1965 Act took effect in 1968, 35 percent of the immigrant population came from Asian countries and only 18 percent from Europe. Eighteen percent entered from North America and 16 percent from the Caribbean island nations. A final comparison presents the origins of the immigrant population that entered the country between 1991 and 1996 *(see Figure 1.4).* During this four-year period, the Asian population comprised 29 percent of immigrant admissions, Europeans 14 percent and North Americans (primarily Mexicans) 34 percent. The Caribbean nations had dropped to about 10 percent.

The contrast between the first pie chart (Figure 1.2) and the third (Figure 1.4) are worth noting. Compared with the 1950s, the immigrant population is far less European now. The inflow of new arrivals is dominated by

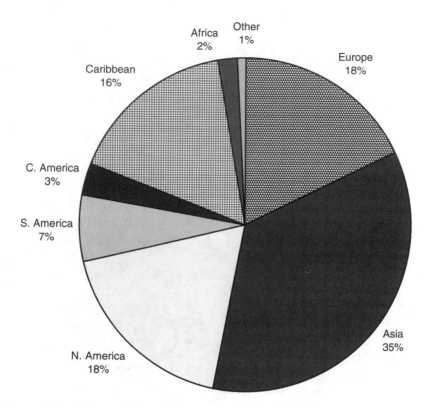

Figure 1.3   Origin of the Immigrant Population Entering between 1981 and 1990

those of Hispanic and Asian ancestry. Given current law, the ethnic composition of the newly arriving population is not likely to change. The demand to emigrate from impoverished Latin American and Asian countries will continue because economic disparities between industrialized and less developed countries are increasing (Rolph 1992; Hofstetter 1984). But commanding a living wage in the American economy increasingly requires skills and education, something many emigres from impoverished countries do not bring with them (Funkhouser and Trejo 1995; Borjas 1990, 20–21; Chiswick 1986). The low skill levels of recent immigrants have been of concern among many who worry about the capacity of the newer arrivals to prosper (Alba and Nee 1997; Zhou 1997; Schoeni, McCarthy, and Vernez 1996; Massey 1995; Borjas 1990; Borjas, Freeman, and Katz 1992). With economic and demographic disparities across nations increasing rather than decreasing, the skill levels of the new arrivals will continue to be much lower than what is necessary to support the standard of living that an average U.S. citizen enjoys.

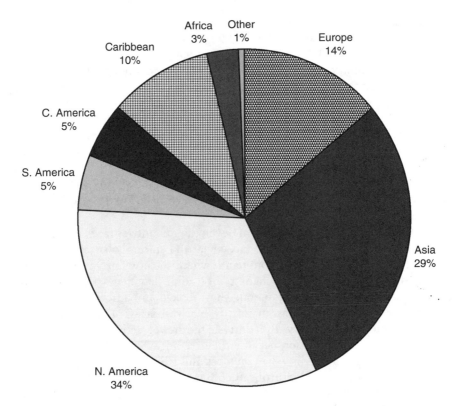

Africa 3%　Other 1%　Europe 14%
Caribbean 10%
C. America 5%
S. America 5%
Asia 29%
N. America 34%

Figure 1.4　Origin of the Immigrant Population Entering between 1991 and 1996

Some argue that immigrants have always arrived on the shores of the "new world" penniless and without skills—the new immigrants are no different from the old in that respect. There is a strong degree of truth to this, but it is also true that the society to which they are arriving has changed. In the 1890s, when Europeans arrived on American shores, they were not much different in their level of skills and education than most native-born Americans. Few immigrants had a high school education, but few natives did either. Immigrants could easily match the economic accomplishments of natives with a little hard work. Within a generation or less, immigrants were as well-off as the native-born. The new immigrants face a very different American economy than the old. And the newer wave of immigrants is starting with a far greater skill deficit, given the premium the national economy now places on education (Hout 1988; Levy 1995). As of the 1990s, the United States had a glut of unskilled laborers (Briggs 1992). The upshot of this oversupply of low-skilled workers is that newer arrivals may struggle just to remain employed, much less get ahead. The gap in earnings between immigrants and natives increased between 1970 and 1990, especially among those with little education (Schoeni, McCarthy, and Vernez 1996).

Data on immigrant consumption of public services bolster the point that many immigrants remain well behind natives. Conservative estimates by scholars at the Urban Institute suggested that 6.6 percent of the foreign born use AFDC, SSI (disability benefits), or General Assistance, compared with 4.9 percent of natives. These may seem to be modest differences, but the percentages conceal numerical differences in caseloads that run in the hundreds of thousands. Consumption of public benefits is particularly concentrated among foreign-born residents who have not naturalized, and of those, the elderly and refugees stand out as the neediest groups (Fix, Passel, and Zimmerman 1996).

While the new immigrants from developing countries face challenges to their economic progress, they also face racial and cultural obstacles to assimilation. America remains a predominantly white society. Early in the twentieth century, Europeans often had to overcome language barriers in the process of becoming American, but they looked no different from most native-born residents. The vast majority of native-born Caucasians are themselves of European ancestry. By contrast, the newer arrivals are potentially easy targets of discrimination because they are not white. There is considerably more distance between Asian cultures and white American culture than there is among the various European cultures or between European culture and American culture. When German and Irish immigrants first arrived in North America in the 1840s, for example, they were distinct ethnic groups. Decades of intermarriage eventually produced citizens of mixed parentage, and eventually the distinct ethnic backgrounds had little relevance (Massey 1995; Russell 1994, 184–185). This gradual disappearance of distinct cultural identity is what is usually meant by the terms "assimilation" and "melting-pot." Ethnic languages and cultures were lost by the second and third generations (Massey 1995; Wolfinger 1965; Glazer and Moynihan 1970). But some cultures assimilate more easily than others, a point that presidential candidate Patrick Buchanan clumsily made when he said on a national news program, "I think God made all people good, but if we had to take a million immigrants in, say Zulus, next year, or Englishmen, and put them in Virginia, what group would be easier to assimilate and would cause less problems for the people of Virginia?" The first slaves on the North American continent were, in fact, Irish indentured servants. When these slaves escaped, or were freed, they were indistinguishable from the rest of the population; not so with black slaves from Africa (Rothbart and John 1993, 56–57). The cultural distance between German and Irish immigrants, or, say, between Irish immigrants and American natives, is much shorter than the distance between—to take an example other than Buchanan's—Vietnamese immigrants and American natives. This very distance slows the process of assimilation. The cultural and ethnic differences between the newer arrivals and citizens of their host country may prove to be an obstacle to their achievement and prosperity in a society where the native-born are often heard chanting, with Patrick Buchanan, "Keep America American."

Illegal Immigrants

If there were no immigration policies restricting entry into the country, there would be no illegal immigrants. A nation with totally open borders has no illegal immigration. Some scholars are under the mistaken impression that the United States once had open borders. Recently, however, legal scholars have pointed out that movement across the borders of the United States has never been totally unrestricted (Neuman 1993). While there were no numerical quotas or national origin exclusions in the early years of the Republic, many states enacted laws imposing various restrictions on population mobility—aimed particularly at keeping out undesirables: convicts, vagrants, the physically disabled, people with diseases, and the mentally ill (Neuman 1993; Manheim 1995). The slave trade was also subject to numerous restrictions imposed mainly by states. Nevertheless, by the standards of the twentieth century, it is fair to say that Congress was inactive on immigration policy. Unrestricted immigration was encouraged for most of the nineteenth century as a means of populating a vast, empty continent (Schuck and Smith 1985, 92–95). Aside from needing human resources for the sake of westward expansion and industrialization, the national government avoided the issue because of the divisiveness of slavery. States had highly variable preferences on the importation and migration of slaves, and strong national immigration laws might have provoked a North-South confrontation, something many politicians wanted to avoid.[1] The Supreme Court did not extinguish state control over immigration policy and assert federal supremacy until the 1870s (Manheim 1995). Still, restrictions on immigration in the modern sense of imposing quotas and preferences were not enacted until the 1880s, in the wake of a national economic recession.

With the coming of ever more restrictive immigration laws in the twentieth century, the nation had to face a growing problem of illegal immigration. The Truman administration first took note of "wetbacks"—immigrants entering the country illegally across the southwestern border from Mexico—in 1952, and proposed legislation to impose sanctions on those who harbor illegal immigrants. However, serious efforts to penalize those who hire and

---

[1]The one exception to Congress's inactivity was the passage of the Alien and Sedition Acts, in 1798, which were shortly thereafter repealed.

harbor these illegal entrants were blocked by an influential group of Texas congressmen whose constituents included farmers who relied upon seasonal farm workers (Hill 1953). In 1964, the Johnson administration allowed a Mexican *Bracero* guest–worker program to expire, exacerbating the illegal entry problem. Since the 1940s, the *Bracero* program had provided temporary work permits to Mexican nationals holding jobs in the United States, mostly in agriculture and construction (Donato 1994; Reimers 1992). The *braceros* were a cheap and easily exploitable source of labor, and for that reason were never popular with American labor leaders who had long pressed for the elimination of the program. After it ended, employers who had once depended upon it turned to hiring illegal workers, primarily from Mexico (Corwin 1984, 225). There are no firm numbers on the number of illegal aliens who enter the country every year, but estimates in the mid-1990s put the figure at about 300,000. Estimates of the number of illegals residing in the country in the mid-1990s ran anywhere from three to 12 million, excluding the two million who had been granted legal residence through the provisions of the 1986 Immigration Reform and Control Act. An official INS report in October 1992 estimated the number of illegal residents to be 3,218,000.

By the late 1990s, stepped-up border interdiction had increased the risks involved with illegally entering the United States. Most illegal entries occur along the United States–Mexico border, sometimes aided by smugglers who charge fees to navigate safe passage through border patrol outposts. Smugglers are said to be notoriously untrustworthy—variously characterized as "thugs" and "rip-off artists"—who don't care about endangering the lives of their clients, whom they reportedly call "chickens." Border Patrol authorities have found that smugglers along the Mexican border have crammed their clients in all sorts of bizarre hiding places. In March of 1996, border patrol agents found 17 illegal immigrants crammed into a portable toilet being hauled behind a truck on a California interstate highway. Smugglers have abandoned their clients to die of exposure in the deserts of Arizona and the mountains of California, involved them in life-threatening, high-speed chases, and even held them for ransom (Associated Press 1996; Covarrubias 1996; Garlington 1997). While these stories attract headlines, a majority of border crossings are undetected, and while not quite "routine," are uneventful.

Of the 3.2 million illegal residents estimated to be in the country in 1992, one-third were reportedly from Mexico. The precise breakdown appears in Figure 1.5. This bar graph shows that Latin American countries are a heavy source of illegal immigrants. Nevertheless, a consequential proportion of illegal immigrants have entered from Canada and even Poland. Land border crossings are not the only source of illegal immigration. Some illegals are smuggled into the country aboard ocean-going vessels. Nearly half of all illegal residents are those who overstay student and tourist visas; in other words, they

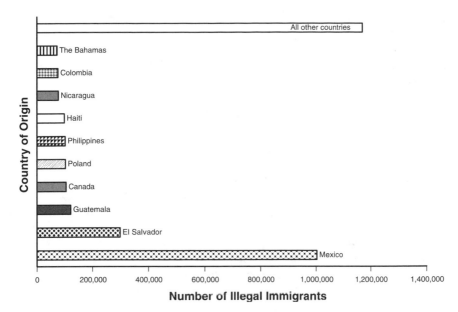

Figure 1.5   Origin of the Illegal Immigrant Population in the United States, 1992

enter the country legally, but remain after their temporary visas have expired. Once an illegal immigrant has entered the country and settled here, the chances of discovery and prosecution are quite low—somewhere about one to two percent are ever apprehended once they have entered (Espenshade 1994, 872). Most arrests occur along the border, where the Immigration and Naturalization Service (INS) has concentrated its resources.

To control illegal entry, Congress greatly increased the staff and resources of the INS and especially its border enforcement division, the U.S. Border Patrol. In 1994, Congress passed crime legislation that authorized the addition of 1,000 border patrol agents each year between 1995 and 1998. Between 1993 and 1997, the budget for the INS doubled from $1.5 billion to $3.1 billion. In October 1994, the INS launched Operation Gatekeeper in San Diego, an intensified effort to prevent illegal crossings along the southwestern border. The number of apprehensions increased sharply, but the effect was to displace smuggling activity to less traveled regions closer to the Arizona border. And the cost illegal aliens must pay smugglers has consequently increased. In spite of an impressive build-up of resources and personnel along the border, INS officials estimated that they still arrested only a small fraction of the total number of illegal entrants, perhaps as few as 15 percent. Recent studies have shown that the risk of being caught is so minimal that border enforcement efforts have not been an effective deterrent to illegal entry (Espenshade 1994; Kossoudji 1992). By 1996, a new study released by the INS estimated the illegal immigrant population at five million, a 28 percent increase over 1992. The continued breaches of the border have increased calls for the militarization of the U.S. border by citizens and members of Congress alike.

Immigrant Settlement Patterns and Native Reactions

The immigrant population, whether illegal or legal, is neither randomly nor uniformly settled throughout the United States (Bartel 1989; Carlson 1994). According to INS statistics, 38 percent of all legal immigrants reside in California. In distant second place is New York with 13 percent. Third is Texas with 9 percent. These three states are followed by Florida (8 percent), Illinois (4.5 percent), and New Jersey (4.2 percent). Thus, just six states are home to 77 percent of the legal immigrant population. Contemporary trends are reinforcing these patterns of concentration. Map 1.1 shows the intended state of

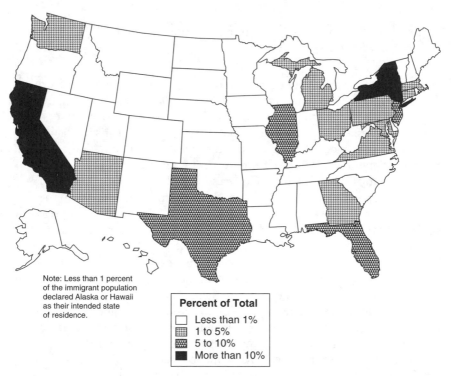

Note: Less than 1 percent
of the immigrant population
declared Alaska or Hawaii
as their intended state
of residence.

Percent of Total
☐ Less than 1%
▦ 1 to 5%
▨ 5 to 10%
■ More than 10%

Map 1.1   Intended State of Residence of Immigrants Admitted 1993–1996

Source: INS, Immigration to the United States in FY 1996

residence of the 2.4 million immigrants legally admitted in 1993, 1994, and 1995. The darkly shaded states were the most popular with the immigrants admitted in those years: 26 percent intended to make their home in California, 17 percent in New York, and 7.5 percent in Florida. Texas, Illinois, and New Jersey ranked as the fourth, fifth, and sixth most popular states among the immigrants admitted during this period.

The illegal immigrant population has taken up residence in these same states, particularly California, New York, Florida, and Texas. In 1992, INS estimates put the illegal resident population in California at 1,283,000—about 40 percent of the estimated nationwide illegal population. New York ranked second, harboring about 15 percent of the illegal population. The settlement patterns of illegal immigrants are determined largely by where they are able to find work. Farmers in southern and central California have long relied on an illegal-immigrant workforce to pick specialty crops. Other immigrants have gravitated to urban areas and found work in restaurants and hotels, manufacturing, and food processing. Just as the population of illegal residents benefits only a few economic sectors that exploit their labor, the fact that illegal immigrants cluster in high concentrations means that whatever burdens they place on society are not evenly distributed.

The consumption of public services by illegal immigrants sparked a widespread anti-immigrant movement in California in the early 1990s. It is important to point out that illegal aliens are prohibited from consuming federal welfare benefits, including AFDC (or TANF for "Temporary Assistance to Needy Families," as it became known in 1996), food stamps, Medicaid, Medicare, and Supplemental Security Income. But they do enroll their children in public schools and make use of indigent care medical facilities, such as county hospitals and clinics. Illegal immigrants who commit crimes are incarcerated in jails and prisons at considerable public expense. In 1994, a study done by the Urban Institute estimated the cost of incarcerating illegal residents at $474 million and the cost of educating the children of illegal residents at $3.1 billion—with most of this burden falling on California (Clark et al. 1994). Several studies have attempted to estimate the fiscal impact of illegal immigration by measuring both its benefits and its costs (Huddle 1993; Passel 1994; Clark et al. 1994; Romero, Chang, and Parker 1994; GAO 1994). While their estimates varied, all of these studies concluded that illegal immigrants do not contribute in taxes as much as they consume in public services. And to the extent that illegal residents pay taxes, these funds accrue primarily to the federal government, not to states and localities (GAO 1994). The taxes and fees of local governments are also among the easiest to avoid (Muller and Espenshade 1985). Several of these studies have also raised questions about whether *legal* immigrants contribute in taxes as much as they extract in public benefits. These results have been less conclusive, and the answer appears to depend on the immigrant subgroup, as some groups have more unfavorable fiscal implications than others (Espenshade and King 1994).

In response to these rising costs, and in the wake of economic hard times, there have been calls for the exclusion of illegal immigrants from social services, public schools and nonemergency health care. In California, Proposition 187 sought to achieve this goal through the referendum process in 1994. Supporters of the controversial measure were charged with racism, xenophobia, and cruelty to children. Governor Pete Wilson (R-CA), who supported the measure in his effort to win reelection, was frequently described as an opportunist whipping up racial tension for political gain. Nevertheless, by voting to pass the measure, 59 percent of Californians protested the use of taxpayer money to provide services for illegal immigrants. Several federal judges later prevented the state from enforcing the law's provisions governing social services, health care, and education. Their action raised important constitutional questions about what states can do to control immigration. Although the Supreme Court has ruled that immigration is a federal responsibility, clearly the burdens of immigration do not fall equally on all states. Several states, including Florida, Arizona, California, New Jersey, New York, and Texas, have filed lawsuits to seek reimbursement of costs from the federal government. As of this writing, the courts have been reluctant to act on these claims.

Politically, legal and illegal immigration will continue to be polarizing issues in the areas where the volume of immigration is especially high. It is in these areas where people will be more likely to attribute problems associated with population growth to the arrival of legal and illegal immigrants: overcrowded schools, the lack of affordable housing, the lack of jobs, and higher crime rates. That is not to say, however, that efforts such as Proposition 187 will spread. California's extraordinarily large immigrant population makes it unique among states. Movements similar to the one in California have failed to gain much momentum in Florida, Arizona, and Texas. Aside from the fact that these states have far fewer immigrants than California, they have had stronger economies. In Arizona, for example, booming growth and the lowest unemployment rate in the nation stunted the growth of the anti-immigrant movement in 1994 and 1995. Congressman Ken Bentsen (D-TX), from a racially diverse Houston district, summarized the difference between California and Texas in the following terms:

> Texas has a different viewpoint than California. I do have lots of constituents who believe that illegals are just coming here for benefits. But most Texans, both Democrats and Republicans, think it's a labor issue. They're coming here to work and they send money back. In California, though, the belief is that they just come here to receive benefits. I just don't think that's true in total. Some come here to take advantage of our public hospitals and get better health care along the border and to get their children citizenship. But mostly they come here to make

more money than they could in Mexico or Central America. (Bentsen interview 5/17/97)

Bentsen could well have added that Arizona and Texas do not have the liberal social benefits that California provides. And the expense of providing such public benefits to illegal and legal immigrants is not nearly so terrifying to residents in states that are less generous to begin with. Arguably, Arizona and Texas also had stronger economic ties to Mexico than did California. Arizona's former Governor Fife Symington even wrote letters to Justice Department officials defending the governor of Sonora when he was being accused of taking bribes from drug traffickers.

In New York, a state known to be an immigrant gateway, the population growth due to immigration has not been as overwhelming as in California. The immigrant population in New York is also highly concentrated in New York City and its suburbs and is not as diffused as in California. Distance from the southwestern land border also makes a difference. Immigrants to New York most often arrive by plane or aboard ships, and do not simply walk into the country. The burden New York's immigrants have imposed on social services has not been as great, either.

In other areas of the country, where residents have little contact with immigrants, the issue of costs imposed by legal or illegal immigration simply does not stir up much grassroots protest. As we will point out in Chapter 2, people are not reluctant to express opinions on immigration matters, but these opinions do not influence their candidate choices once other political characteristics are taken into account.

Immigration: The Evolution of an Issue

The foregoing pages have provided some background facts necessary for understanding the contemporary immigration debate. More background material essential for understanding the immigration policy debate in Congress will be presented in Chapter 3. We have not argued, nor do we intend to argue, that immigration should be either increased or reduced. For purposes of this book, we are agnostic on that subject. Our goal so far has been to update the reader on what is known about the immigrant population, its ethnic make-up, where it has concentrated, and why so many are alarmed enough about immigration to have made it a political issue. The major focus of the rest of the book is to understand the congressional politics of immigration policymaking between 1965 and the late 1990s.

We started this book from the vantage point of the debates of the late 1990s, wondering if immigration policymaking in Congress was always as divisive as it had become by then. One means of examining the lines along which congressional policy battles are fought is to look at recorded votes on the policies in question (Poole and Rosenthal 1997; 1991; 1984). If there are few recorded votes, and if the recorded votes that do occur are highly consensual, then it is a clear sign that there is not much controversy in Congress on a particular issue. If, on the other hand, there are many recorded votes, and those votes are highly divided, then this evidence suggests the presence of controversy. Consensus has broken down and members are demanding to be put on record. In such cases, one may well wonder what is generating the conflict. By examining which members are on each side of the votes, we may gain insight into the nature of the conflict. Perhaps the chamber is dividing along partisan lines. Alternatively, partisan divisions may be weak and perhaps some other dimension is polarizing the chamber—say, by region or constituency characteristic. Studying roll-call votes on immigration policy is not necessarily the only, or even the best, means for discovering the causes of policy disagreement (Van Doren 1990; Kuklinski 1979). In addition, we have read the content of every immigration debate on the House and Senate floor since 1965, we have read most relevant committee documents, and in a few cases we have gone to Congress and obtained permission to read the transcripts of committee markups (which are not made public). We have conducted numerous interviews with members of Congress, congressional staff, and interest-group representatives. All of this has been indispensable to writing a comprehensive book. The roll-call analysis was added in the interest of providing a complete and systematic account of the facts. We believe it is a useful tool to supplement our investigation and that it brings out aspects of the political behavior of Congress that might otherwise go undetected.

As we approach the new century, the most significant battle lines on immigration policy have formed in response to the question of costs. Are immigrants, legal and illegal, a net good or a net bad for society?—where "good" and "bad" are measured mostly in the economic terms of costs versus benefits. The consensus that has emerged on illegal immigration is that it is, and continues to be, more of a cost than a benefit. But the consensus is shallow. Politicians must take a stand against illegal immigration because it is, after all, against the law. As Congresswoman Patsy Mink (D-HI) indicated, "Nobody wants to support anything illegal" (Mink interview, 5/23/97). But some politicians are more serious about controlling illegal immigration than others. Some, such as Georgia Congressman Bob Barr (R-GA), would say that the country must spare no effort to stop it and that "it's a national security matter" (Barr interview, 4/8/97). Border enforcement efforts are popular, but many members of Congress would stop short of assigning the military to patrol the border or building an elaborate fence network. Other measures, such as denying public benefits to illegal immigrants, imposing penalties on employers who hire illegal residents, or implementing a national work eligibility card, are almost as controversial. While nearly every credible voice in Washington will admit that illegal immigration is wrong, disagreements about how to control it persist.

On legal immigration, there is no consensus on the question of costs, or on whether those costs are worth bearing. Political opinions on legal immigration, much more than on illegal immigration, are formed on the basis of loose impressions and interests bolstered by a selective reading of the available academic research. Led by Lamar Smith (R-TX) and Alan Simpson (R-WY), a majority of Republicans in 1996 argued that legal immigration needed to be controlled because of its runaway costs. Measures restricting the access of legal immigrants to welfare passed as part of the GOP's Contract with America and were signed into law by President Clinton. For the Republican members, such as Senator Spencer Abraham (R-MI), who were supportive of legal immigration, the chant became, "immigration yes, welfare no," showing that they too were concerned about the contributions of newcomers. The concern about the cost of immigration to taxpayers has converted the immigration issue into one that in the 1980s and 1990s came to divide Congress along party lines.

Cost as the Link between Partisanship and Immigration Policy

How an increasing obsession with the costs of immigration would transform the issue into one that divides political elites along party lines is easy enough to understand. Since the 1930s, the major cleavage between Republicans and Democrats has concerned government's role in the economy. New Deal Democrats created the welfare state as President Franklin D. Roosevelt marshaled major new social insurance programs through Congress to cover children, the unemployed, and the elderly. Republicans took up the opposing position, generally opposing efforts to expand national government programs and services (Sundquist 1983, 212–215). The major issue between the two parties became one of government spending, or the costs of government programs. In the mid-1960s, the Great Society deepened this already sharply defined cleavage between the two sides. Democrats became the party of civil rights, favoring federal government intervention to advance the position of minorities through efforts such as busing and affirmative action (Carmines and Stimson 1989; Mead 1992). As the champions of disadvantaged minorities, the Democrats became even more closely associated with urban areas and the poor than they had been before. In the years following passage of the Civil Rights Act in 1964, attitudes toward government efforts to achieve racial integration, the growth of the welfare state, and government regulation of the economy came to define both candidate and voter allegiance to the two major parties.

First-generation immigrants were natural Democratic constituents in the years during and immediately after the New Deal. A majority were working class, and they had settled in urban areas that not only bore the brunt of the Great Depression but also benefited from President Roosevelt's federal relief programs. Democratic support following the 1932 election was particularly high among Catholics and Jews, Italians, Poles and working-class Germans and Anglo-Saxons (Sundquist 1983, Chapter 10). Support for generous immigration policy following World War II would be most popular in the Democratic bastions of the urban North, where immigrants constituted a sizable percentage of the electorate. Democrats in the South, however, were not predisposed to favor expansive immigration policy. The South had not experienced a significant wave of immigrant arrivals since before the Civil War. The South's agricultural economy, reliant on exploitable black labor, was not attractive to European ethnics, who could find work much more easily in the industrializing cities of the urban North. Immigrants were also associated with bad memories of the Union Army and they were now part and parcel of the liberal Roosevelt coalition, something Southern Democrats were never quite able to accept. The division between Northern and Southern Democrats on immigration policy would prove to be an enduring one.

Republicans had their own proud immigrant roots, although, at the time of the New Deal realignment, they were more likely than Democrats to be second or third generation. Although immigration in Republican strongholds was not as fresh as it was in Democratic areas, Northern Republicans had no particular reason to oppose opening the door to new immigration. While the Republican Party formed its identity in opposition to the New Deal's big government agenda, there was no reason that immigration should be linked to these other policy concerns. First of all, as Figure 1.1 shows, few immigrants were entering the country during the 1930s and 1940s. Newly arriving immigrants were not a particularly noticeable population. Moreover, there was no evidence at the time that first-generation immigrants who had arrived in the 1910s and 1920s had been any more dependent on redistributive programs than many natives. And federal welfare programs were largely nonexistent before the New Deal. Republicans in Congress could not oppose immigration on the basis of its cost.

In the 1950s and 1960s, some opposition to immigration was occasionally voiced by conservative Republicans and Southern Democrats on the basis of Cold War politics. Exclusionary policies were often justified on the basis that immigrants could be Communists or lacked commitment to American values (Duncan 1997). But these objections never formed the basis of a broad party front on the subject of immigration policy. As of the mid-1960s, immigration was not yet an issue that cleaved the parties.

By the late 1960s, Republicans had become identified as the party that was hostile to federal intervention in the advance of civil rights. After major GOP gains in the 1966 House elections, liberal progress on civil rights policy stalled (Orfield 1975). In 1968, Richard Nixon campaigned against aggressive civil rights policy in order to win strong Southern backing. This approach continued to mold the party's image as one hostile to the interests of racial minorities.

At the same time, major changes in immigration policy had set the country on a new population trajectory. The repeal of the National Origins Quota System in 1965 would come to alter the ethnic composition of the immigrant stock in the ways that were described earlier: Immigrants would be increasingly Hispanic and Asian and come from countries with low standards of living compared with the United States. Many would gain economic ground relative to natives and successfully compete in the U.S. economy in spite of discrimination and other disadvantages. But the availability of newly enacted federal welfare programs would attract those who did not prosper. To the extent that they remained disadvantaged, these new immigrants would be additional fodder for Democratic party-building efforts. Worse still, Republicans eventually realized that the changes wrought by immigration policy in the 1960s had inadvertently led to the expansion of the welfare state they had despised since the 1930s. Immigration policy had become a tool to import both Democratic constituents and poverty. As Republicans woke up to that fact in the late 1970s and 1980s, votes in Congress on restricting legal immigration and controlling illegal immigration became increasingly easy to predict in partisan terms.

Constituency Influences on Congressional Decision Making

If partisanship did not always divide Congress into opposite camps on immigration policy, the question remains as to other sources of the divisions. Between 1965 and the mid-1990s, there are important exceptions to the generalization that immigration issues cleaved political elites along party lines (Tichenor 1994). Where would we expect to find those exceptions? To answer this question, we must consider how members of Congress make up their minds on important votes.

Scholars of congressional decision making have long noted the importance of constituency influence in the mix of strategic calculations that politicians consider when they cast their votes (Turner 1951; Clausen 1973; Fiorina 1974; Mayhew 1974; Kingdon 1981; Arnold 1990; Barrett and Cook 1991). Political partisanship is only one cue, albeit an important one. While members may very well be linked to parties through their constituencies (see Rohde 1991, 170), partisanship is not the only relevant aspect of a constituency a member considers when casting recorded votes. We have already discussed the difference that region can make. For years, Southern Democrats in Congress held a virtual veto over passage of liberal civil rights policies advanced by Northern Democrats. Southern Democrats have also been known to oppose liberal party leaders on defense, foreign policy, criminal justice, and redistributive issues. Regional voting has been sufficiently strong that expert analysts have developed a scorecard called the "conservative coalition" to identify how often the group of Southern Democrats votes with Northern Republicans in opposition to Northern Democrats (Brady and Bullock 1980). Southern Democrats were also hostile to generous immigration policy, voting as a bloc against the 1965 Act. While their numbers have dwindled in the 1980s and 1990s (Gimpel 1996), the persistence of these conservative Democrats in modern times leads to a straightforward prediction: Southern members, regardless of party, are likely to be opposed to opening the door to new arrivals.

A second constituency characteristic that may not correspond to party lines is the percentage of immigrants in a legislator's district. Many immigrants in large cities were developing Democratic loyalties in the 1920s. In the wake of the New Deal, working-class immigrants in cities turned overwhelmingly to support Democrats. But there are Republicans elected from areas that are quite aware of their immigrant roots. Many of these districts are comprised of older suburbs of large cities that experienced the out-migration of white ethnics in the 1950s and 1960s. The suburbs of Nassau County, New York, are an example. We would expect, therefore, that those with large foreign-born constituencies would be generally supportive of expansive immigration policy independently of partisanship. It is noteworthy that, of the Republicans who supported the effort to kill Lamar Smith's legal immigration reforms in the 104th Congress, most of them were from urban and suburban districts with self-conscious immigrant traditions—including Detroit, New York City, and Cincinnati.

Related to the distinctiveness of the Southern membership on issues such as redistribution and civil rights, we hypothesize that the border states have distinct interests on immigration-related matters and that members representing these states are likely to vote as a cohesive bloc. We identify as border states those along the southern border that have experienced the most significant waves of immigration since the 1960s: California, Arizona, New Mexico, Texas, and Florida. These states bear a large share of the costs of legal and illegal immigration. We predict that members from these states will vote against open immigration policy as the costs to their state and local governments increase.

Fourth, independent of whether a district contains a large foreign-born population, the ethnic composition of the member's district matters. Individuals need not be of the first generation in order to sympathize with the plight of immigrants. Because the bulk of the immigrant flow since the late 1960s has been from Latin America and Asia, we are suggesting that, in areas with large Hispanic and Asian constituencies, there will be support for open immigration policy independent of partisanship, region, and other influences.

We also hypothesize that the proportion of blacks in a congressional district will cause members to vote more often in favor of immigration restrictions than for open immigration. This expectation is based on the social scientific research showing that immigrants compete with native blacks for jobs in urban labor markets and have filled labor market niches that would otherwise have been filled by blacks (Waldinger 1996; Kposowa 1995; Muller 1993, 167–219). Thus, native minorities are more likely to be hurt by immigration because they compete for the same low-skill, low-wage positions that the new immigrants seek. We hypothesize that, as representatives of their community's economic interests, members from such areas will support restrictions on legal and illegal immigration in order to protect the economic standing of their black constituents.

Similarly, we anticipate that areas suffering from high unemployment and poverty rates will be represented by members who will favor immigration restrictions. The economic logic here is straightforward. Areas of high unemployment have a large proportion of unskilled workers who are least mobile. The last thing an area of high unemployment needs is an influx of additional unskilled laborers flowing across the borders to put additional demands on an overstressed labor market.

We suspect that agricultural employment may be relevant to a member's decision making on immigration policy. Since the end of the *Bracero* program in 1965, many agricultural areas have increasingly come to depend upon legal and illegal immigrants to harvest specialty crops, ranging from lettuce and strawberries in California to tobacco in Kentucky. Major farming-related interest groups such as the American Farm Bureau have repeatedly pushed for expansion of existing guest–worker programs, which permit the temporary entry of agricultural laborers. By the 1980s, immigrant employment in agriculture and food processing had gone national. From Midwestern meat-packing towns to chicken-processing plants in the mid-Atlantic region, immigrants of primarily Hispanic origin have been a reliable source of low-wage labor. While agricultural areas have often been known for their political conservatism on issues such as redistribution and race, we hypothesize that the economic interests of large agricultural employers may outweigh competing considerations and lead members from agricultural districts to favor generous immigration policy.

Committee and Caucus Membership

Finally, members of Congress are not only cognizant of the interests of their constituency but also face institutional pressures from within the legislative body. One of these is the pressure from committee leadership to vote for the committee's product on the floor. By participating in the framing of legislation in committee, members acquire a stake in advancing the legislation to the floor and passing it there (Poole and Rosenthal 1997, 204; Evans 1989; Smith and Deering 1984). Even legislators who find themselves in dissent on major portions of complex legislation are sometimes co-opted into supporting it because of a single provision or two that they authored in the committee. While expectations for specific floor amendments are less clear, we do hypothesize that members of the Judiciary Committee will favor final passage of immigration legislation.

In our coming analysis of the floor votes on immigration policy, we also control for the race of the member, knowing that the minority caucuses, particularly in the House of Representatives, have often been a source of cohesive behavior independent of the heterogeneous interests of the constituencies these members represent. These caucus groups can be powerful agents of socialization. In the 1980s and 1990s, the Hispanic and black caucuses, and to a lesser extent, the Asian-Pacific caucus, worked together on a wide variety of issues relating to civil rights, affirmative action, welfare reform, and minority opportunity. We might expect the institutional pressures produced by these informal groups to force conformity to a common agenda independent of partisan, regional, and constituency influences.

In our analysis of immigration policymaking in Chapters 4, 5, and 6, we occasionally comment on the position of the various executive branch administrations over time. Inasmuch as the president is the nation's chief policymaker, presidential positioning generally has some influence on policy (Clausen 1973; Kingdon 1981), particularly when the president has introduced his own legislation on a particular subject such as the annual budget or tax reform. In these cases, the president has powerful resources of persuasion on his side, and the Congress becomes more reactive than proactive. Immigration, however, has been one area that has been subject more to congressional than presidential influence. No administration in recent times has ever sponsored a bill seeking to address *legal* immigration—a fact that we believe justifies our consciously Congress-centric approach to this topic. Immigration remains very much a Congress-driven policy area, and the executive has been the reactive branch.

Immigration: Not Just a Single Issue

In the foregoing discussion, we have argued that the number-one issue that has riven the immigration debate with partisanship is that of redistribution. When the expenses associated with legal immigration, refugee admissions, and illegal immigration began to rise, fiscally conservative—primarily GOP—politicians began to propose restrictions. We have acknowledged that characteristics aside from a member's partisanship are relevant to their decision making on immigration policy. But we also acknowledge the reality that immigration policy has never boiled down to only the numbers of immigrants to be admitted and whether they take advantage of public assistance programs. There are important and complex subsidiary issues such as *how* illegal immigration should be controlled, and this has not always divided Congress along party lines. Some have favored imposing civil and criminal penalties on employers who hire undocumented workers. Employer sanctions have been opposed by a coalition of members who represent business interests opposed to such regulation, along with Hispanic and minority rights advocates (mostly Democrats) who fear that employer sanctions could lead to discrimination against the hiring of anyone who looks or sounds foreign. Although our emphasis in this first chapter has been on the fundamental questions of how many immigrants should enter the country, who they are, and to what extent the host society should provide for them, we will address other aspects of the debate in the pages to come.

The Plan of the Book

Before advancing directly to our analysis of the congressional politics of immigration reform, we believe it is necessary to understand public attitudes on immigration. In the next chapter, therefore, we examine public opinion on immigration policy. When asked in recent polls, most Americans oppose open, unrestricted immigration. Very small percentages favor any increase in immigration. Given this tendency, it is odd that immigration to the United States since the mid-1960s has been mostly unrestricted. Something has prevented the public will from being translated into public policy.

In Chapter 3, we lay out some of the terminology surrounding the immigration debate as it has taken place on Capitol Hill. Immigration law is a rather technical and complex subject. The goal of Chapter 3 is to provide readers with a convenient reference source to the topics that fall within the area of immigration policy. We also use Chapter 3 to sketch out what the issues and opposing arguments have been under each topic discussed. This chapter should be treated as a preface to the subsequent discussion of public policymaking in Congress in Chapters 4, 5, and 6. As readers study the chapters that deal with congressional action, they can turn back to Chapter 3 in order to recall certain terms and definitions that may be new or unfamiliar.

Chapters 4, 5, and 6 comprise the heart of our discussion of congressional policymaking. Our goal in these chapters is to understand how Congress changes and to evaluate how immigration policy changes along with it. If the costs of immigration were not always on the minds of policymakers, when did costs become a consideration? We are also careful to focus on the people behind the policy. Laws are not determined solely by impersonal forces. Members of Congress are not mere wind-up toys programmed with party and constituency information and pointed in the direction of Washington on Election Day. There is an element of will involved, along with the irrational and accidental happenstance whereby certain leaders are in a place rather than others. In a phrase, people matter. Alan Simpson, Peter Rodino, Lamar Smith, Romano Mazzoli, Barbara Jordan, Dan Lungren, Howard Berman, Spencer Abraham—each had a unique impact on immigration law such that, had they not been there, things would have probably been different. We begin in Chapter 4 by detailing developments in immigration policy from 1965 to 1982. Chapter 5 covers the period from 1983 to 1994, focusing particular attention on the major rounds of immigration reform that took place in 1986 and 1990. Chapter 6 is devoted entirely to a detailed analysis of action on immigration legislation in the 104th Congress (1995–1996).

Chapter 7 summarizes our study of immigration policymaking and speculates about the future. There are several alternative explanations for why immigration policy has taken a more partisan turn. The first is that Congress itself has become more partisan. Nothing in particular has happened to the nature of immigration policy or the composition and size of immigrant flows to make it so. As public policy in general has become less consensual, immigration has fallen victim just as have other areas of lawmaking. Restrictionist complaints about immigrants and pro-immigration apologetics are simply rationalizations used by partisan minds that are made up well in advance of any facts. A second explanation is that the demise of Southern Democrats and the rise of Southern Republicans are responsible for the changes observed since 1965. The political parties have become more ideologically homogeneous (Rohde 1991). If the Republicans from the South in 1996 had been Democrats, the voting patterns would have been the same as in earlier times. What has changed is simple: The Democrats have been shorn of their bloc of anti-immigrant voters and the Republicans have been shorn of their liberal, open-borders types. The third explanation is that something about immigration policy has changed as the result of the changing nature of immigrants. In other words, new arguments and evidence about the costs and benefits of immigration have surfaced to alter the debate. In some cases, old arguments against immigration that did not hold water 20, 50, or 100 years ago, are more credible today. Our conclusions will address these alternative explanations of political change and test them against available evidence.

C H A P T E R   2

PUBLIC OPINION AND
INTEREST GROUP INFLUENCE

In the opening chapter we pointed out that political elites are far more divided on immigration policy today than they were in the past. The substantial consensus that reigned in the 1960s has given way to a battle that reflects traditional partisan and ideological cleavages in Congress. At the dawn of the twenty-first century, nearly every aspect of immigration is fiercely debated, from the issue of overall limits on legal immigration to the treatment of illegal entrants and the employers who hire them. In this chapter we will examine public attitudes about the principal aspects of the immigration debate. To what extent is the public divided on the major immigration issues? What explains disagreements about immigration policy? How active are interest groups in immigration policymaking?

Like most other issues, immigration policy has not been a universal or constant concern of the public in the United States nor of the pollsters who study public opinion. For vast periods of American history, it is fair to say that the public has not given much thought to the issue. From the 1920s to the 1960s, public opinion favored restricted admissions and there were relatively few immigrants admitted (Harwood 1986; Simon 1985; Simon and Alexander 1993). Those who were admitted went mostly unnoticed, partly because they were overwhelmingly Caucasian, partly because their numbers were small.

With the repeal of national origins quotas as a criterion for distributing immigrant visas in 1965, the character and volume of immigration changed. Immigrant admissions mounted in the 1970s and 1980s (see Chapter 1), and with them the call for restrictions (Harwood 1986, 202–203; Simon and Alexander 1993, 39). By the early 1990s, the immigrant inflow was at historic highs. By the mid-1990s, it seemed that almost everyone had an opinion on the subject, particularly in the areas where the immigrants settled. Few were arguing for increased immigration, some favored the status quo, while sizable majorities favored cutbacks in legal immigration and tighter enforcement of laws against illegal entry.

Those wishing to analyze public opinion data on immigration are faced with the constraining fact that questions by pollsters occur only sporadically—at times and in places where the volume and character of immigration is of special concern. When and where does immigration become a special concern of the public and of pollsters? Beliefs about how immigrants will threaten the culture, economy, health, or safety of established communities have long been the source of public opinion about immigration policy. The times in the nation's history when anxiety about immigration has peaked have been associated with economic downturn and especially large immigration flows (Muller 1996; Perea 1996). These considerations lead to a simple prediction that immigration policy will capture the public's attention under three conditions: (1) when and where the extent of immigrant resettlement is particularly high (e.g., noticeable) due to its volume or concentration; (2) at times and in places where the public is especially uneasy about the state of the economy, particularly unemployment; and (3) when the public has come to question the potential contribution of immigrant groups, suspecting them to be more of a burden than a benefit to society (Muller 1996; Tatalovich 1995).

First, immigrants will have a more noticeable presence in some areas than in others. Since the late 1960s, the major immigrant-receiving states have included New York, New Jersey, California, Florida, Illinois, Texas, Arizona, and New Mexico. In areas where immigrants remain a small and unnoticed population, established residents are not likely to develop strong opinions about policy. Second, many U.S. residents, including resident noncitizens, express fear that high levels of immigration erode wages and threaten job security. When economic conditions sour, therefore, one can predict that anti-immigrant feelings will run higher than in times of economic prosperity. Third, certain immigrant flows have led many natives and established immigrants to doubt that national immigration policy is on the correct course. This is particularly true of refugee admissions. The Cubans of the Mariel boatlift of 1980 come to mind. The Marielitos were reputed to be criminals, homosexuals, and mental patients that Fidel Castro had set loose from the prisons and institutions of his island dictatorship. The prospect that these immigrants could take their place alongside Florida's established Cuban community seemed rather slim (Grenier and Stepick 1992). Similarly, the Haitian refugees who have fled poverty and political oppression throughout the 1980s and 1990s are typically uneducated and unskilled, while others were reputed to be carriers of the HIV virus. Many of these reports were undoubtedly exaggerated, but the average citizen, even if untainted by racial prejudice, is unable to confirm or disconfirm these rumors and comes to the understandable conclusion that refugee admissions will erode the quality of life in his or her community.

Positive and Negative Opinions about Immigrants

In spite of the fact that survey questions are easier to find when new arrivals are least likely to be popular, we find that many citizens have positive impressions of immigrants. Even though a majority of U.S. citizens favors cuts in current immigration levels, many fondly characterize their own immigrant ancestry as one of noble struggle stemming from the purest of motives. A 1986 CBS News/*New York Times* poll asked several open-ended questions about immigrants that provide insight into the source of public opinion on immigration policy. One question asked simply, "What's the first thing that comes to mind when you hear the word immigrant—that is, people who have come to live in the United States?" The tabulation of responses is reported in Table 2.1. Roughly equal numbers of respondents replied with positive and negative terms of affect. Among the leading positive remarks were "freedom," "opportunity," and that "the U.S. was the land of immigrants." Among the most commonly mentioned negative terms were "overpopulation," "take jobs and resources from natives," and "illegal aliens." Many had neither positive nor negative things to say but instead provided the interviewer with a definition of immigration or mentioned a specific immigrant group, such as Haitians, Hispanics, or Vietnamese.

There is an obvious discontinuity between vaguely warm references to America's immigrant heritage and the experience of contemporary immigration trends. A follow-up question in the 1986 survey asked respondents what came to mind when they thought of immigrants from Latin America. This time a majority (58.6 percent) of the open-ended responses were negative (table not reported). The most common responses were "overpopulation," "drugs," and "illegal aliens." A second follow-up question asked what came to mind when respondents considered Asian immigrants. Asians fared better than Hispanics in the public eye, with only 39 percent of the references having clearly negative or disparaging connotations. Asians were most often mentioned in connection with negative remarks about "overpopulation," "poverty," and "taking jobs from natives."

From the open-ended responses, it appears that negative remarks about immigrants are rooted in several overriding preoccupations of the public: (1) concerns about the economic consequences of immigration; (2) concerns about the social consequences of immigration; and (3) concerns about the character of the immigrants themselves, including their morality, work ethic, and capacity to assimilate. Some of the public's fears about how immigrants could threaten the economy, health, or safety of established communities are legitimate and reasonable. No one wants criminals moving into the neighborhood, no matter what country they are from. And it doesn't take an economics degree to realize that the arrival of immigrants will expand the pool of available labor, hurting the employment prospects of natives who have the

Table 2.1   Public Responses to Open-ended Question
about What Respondents Think of Immigrants

Positive Responses	Percentage
Freedom, opportunity	7.8
U.S. is land of immigrants	7.3
Came to better themselves	6.2
Immigrants built America	1.0
Ellis Island	5.3
Misc. other positive comments	4.3
Total Positive Responses	*31.9*
Negative Responses	
Take jobs, use resources	5.0
Too many, overpopulation	11.5
Crime	.2
Drugs	.1
Welfare	1.4
Can't speak English	.6
Needy, poor	4.0
Illegal aliens	3.6
Misc. other negative comments	4.8
Total Negative Responses	*31.2*
Specific Groups Mentioned	
Hispanics	6.7
Haitians	.4
Asians	.7
Vietnamese	1.6
Other groups	2.5
Refugees	1.9
Total Mentioning Groups	*13.8*
Gave Definition of Immigration	*12.7*
Other Type of Response	*10.4*
Total Responses	*103.0*
N	*(1393)*

Source: CBS News/*New York Times* Monthly Poll, June 1986.

least education and fewest skills (Filer 1992, 258–263; Camarota 1998). Having admitted these reasonable grounds for opposition to immigration, the additional role of racial prejudice in the formation of attitudes about immigrants should not be ignored. Since 1965, when the National Origins Quota System was repealed, the bulk of immigrants have entered the United States from Asian and Latin American countries. These immigrants are more noticeable than the European immigrants who dominated in earlier waves. Since they are more ethnically distinct from the native white population than

Northern European immigrants (Germans, Irish, Dutch, Norwegians, Swedes) were in earlier times, they are also easier targets of discrimination and prejudice. In this connection it is no surprise that recent opinion studies have revealed some ethnic polarization in opinion about admissions policy, with Hispanics and Asians less likely to oppose sustained immigration than whites and African Americans. Racial polarization is not necessarily an indicator of prejudice, though, and it is difficult to argue that all whites who oppose immigration are doing so because they dislike strangers. The sources of opinion on immigration policy are too complex to be reduced simply to racism.

As a prominent issue that has come to divide elites along traditional lines of political cleavage (see Chapter 5), we would expect immigration to divide the public along similar lines: by partisanship, political ideology, race, and economic position. Because the public acquires most of its information about politics from its attentiveness to elite discourse (Zaller 1990; 1992), we would expect that Republicans would be more likely than Democrats to limit immigration and pursue the prosecution and deportation of undocumented workers. In the late 1970s, Democrats translated their support for civil rights and their association with minority groups into an immigration policy that emphasized immigrants' rights and the extension of public assistance programs to impoverished new arrivals. Similarly, we would expect that those who are ideologically liberal would be more likely than conservatives to favor a generous immigration policy. Conservatives opposed both the civil rights movement and the expansion of federal public assistance programs and would be more likely to oppose the guarantee of immigrants' rights and their access to public aid. Conservatives are also more nationalistic than liberals, fearing that large-scale immigration is undermining the national character (Citrin, Reingold, and Green 1990; Brimelow 1995). We also expect that white and African American natives would be more opposed to the new immigration flow than Asians or Hispanics who more closely identify with the newcomers. Those in lower-income groups, and with less education, would be more likely than those with high incomes and skill levels to fear the labor competition posed by the post-1965 inflow of unskilled immigrants. We might also expect gender differences to emerge, as women generally make less money and have fewer skills than men and would therefore have more reason to fear the labor competition of immigrants. But what do contemporary polls tell us about attitudes toward immigrants and on immigration policy?

Attitudes toward Immigrants in the 1980s

The year 1981 began with Ronald Reagan taking office, having won in a decisive landslide over the hapless Jimmy Carter two months before. The Carter administration had been plagued with a number of domestic and foreign policy crises directly or indirectly related to immigration levels: high unemployment and inflation at home, the Iranian revolution and hostage crisis, revolution and violence in Haiti, an influx of Southeast Asian refugees in response to civil wars in Cambodia, Laos, and Vietnam, and the Mariel boatlift of Cuban refugees. Before leaving office, President Carter signed into law the Refugee Act of 1980 (see Chapter 4), which provided permanent resident status and generous governmental benefits to refugees, including Aid to Families with Dependent Children (AFDC), Supplemental Security Income (SSI), and Medicaid, along with a host of other social programs meant to promote self-sufficiency. It was in this atmosphere that ABC News and the *Washington Post* commissioned a public opinion survey in the spring of 1981 to evaluate the state of race relations.

This survey contained a battery of questions about immigration and particularly refugee admissions. One series of questions asked respondents if the federal government should encourage or discourage the entrance of a variety of refugee and immigrant groups, including Iranians, Vietnamese, Haitians, Cubans, Russian Jews, Northern Europeans, and Italians. Results from this survey are listed in Table 2.2. These figures show the percentage of respondents in each category who favored admitting each of seven foreign-born population groups. The results are telling and reveal considerable biases in favor of European origin groups and against others. Forty-one percent of respondents favored the admission of Northern Europeans, while only 17 percent favored admitting Iranians, 21 percent for the Mariel Cubans, 30 percent for Vietnamese, and 32 percent for Haitians. Closer inspection of the results reveals considerable racial differences in these figures, with whites heavily favoring the exclusion of the Third World refugees while being more accepting of the Europeans and Russian Jews. Blacks were less supportive of refugee admissions than whites overall and strangely enough gave their strongest support to the admission of Italian immigrants. Support for refugee admissions was strong among the better-educated respondents, those with liberal political beliefs, Jews, and those who reported that the national economy had improved over the last year. Opposition to immigrant and refugee admissions was strong among those from rural/farm areas, among those with less education, women, the poor, and those who believed the economy was performing poorly.

While these figures suggest that there is some class bias in attitudes toward immigration admissions in the early 1980s, Table 2.2 provides little evidence of party-based differences. The survey suggests that Republicans were about as likely as Democrats to oppose the admission of Haitians, Vietnamese, Iranians, and Cubans. Republicans were considerably more accepting than Democrats of Europeans and Russian Jews. Multivariate analysis clarifies the relationship between partisanship and attitudes toward the foreign-born, showing that Democrats are slightly more likely than Republicans to

Table 2.2. Percent Supporting the Immigration of Refugees and Other Groups to the United States, Spring 1981

Group	Haitians	Vietnamese	Iranians	Cubans (Mariel)	Russian Jews	Northern Europeans	Italians
Total	32.4	30.2	17.3	20.5	39.0	40.9	41.7
Republican	31.5	31.3	19.8	20.3	44.0	47.4	47.4
Independent	34.9	32.2	23.9	23.9	40.0	41.0	46.7
Democrat	31.5	29.0	17.3	20.0	34.8	36.6	41.7
Reagan voter 1980	30.4	29.2	17.7	18.1	41.1	45.4	45.5
Carter voter 1980	31.9	39.5	21.1	22.2	38.0	38.0	41.5
White	31.7	31.1	19.6	20.4	42.5	45.1	46.3
Black	30.5	26.3	17.5	19.4	26.2	27.0	36.6
Hispanic	48.9	38.8	14.3	34.7	36.2	47.8	57.4
Less than 8th grade	13.5	10.0	10.0	6.0	17.5	20.6	25.8
College	44.6	43.0	28.9	28.1	57.4	52.9	52.5
Postgrad	49.5	51.3	41.6	44.2	65.8	61.8	62.8
Liberal	35.4	34.6	20.6	27.6	42.7	45.2	47.5
Moderate	32.3	33.9	23.4	20.3	40.4	39.7	43.1
Conservative	29.5	27.2	17.7	18.3	36.2	38.5	42.4
Under $8,000	23.7	21.8	13.0	11.4	24.9	26.1	36.1
More than $50,000	36.3	42.0	26.9	30.5	61.5	57.3	52.6
Large city	37.7	35.0	23.7	24.6	42.3	42.9	48.3
Rural/farm	27.1	23.1	14.9	16.7	35.3	37.5	43.8
Labor household	32.1	29.5	16.9	21.3	37.0	41.0	43.8
Male	34.6	32.0	22.4	22.5	42.5	44.4	45.3
Female	29.7	28.6	16.1	18.8	35.5	38.4	43.5
Economic assessment better	36.7	35.7	29.4	24.6	48.1	55.6	58.5
Economic assessment worse	31.1	26.9	18.5	21.1	35.8	38.5	42.1
Catholic	36.4	34.7	19.7	24.1	45.5	50.5	52.6
Jewish	50.0	60.5	48.6	44.7	69.8	62.5	64.1

Source: ABC News/ *Washington Post* Race Relations Poll, February–March 1981.

oppose the entry of several of these groups when other relevant variables are held constant (see Table A2.1 in the chapter Appendix). Republicans, if anything, are ambivalent about immigrant admissions.

Similar results obtain when one considers the June 1986 poll on immigration taken by CBS News and the *New York Times* (Table 2.3). The results from this poll show that in the midst of the legislative action on immigration in Congress that year, support for increasing immigration was uniformly low, although not quite so low as in a similarly worded September 1994 study conducted by the same organizations. Partisan divisions are not at all prominent in the 1986 poll, but differences by education and income are pronounced, as are differences between Catholics and Jews. Catholics are far more supportive of decreasing immigration than Jews.

Table 2.3   Percent Supporting Decreases/Increases in Legal Immigration, June 1986 and September 1994

	June 1986		September 1994	
Group	decrease	increase	decrease	increase
Total	51.7	11.0	59.2	5.8
Republican	51.9	7.5	64.8	4.9
Independent	54.3	7.6	60.3	6.4
Democrat	50.9	9.2	60.3	7.2
Bush voter 1992	—	—	63.8	4.8
Clinton voter 1992	—	—	59.1	5.3
White	54.1	6.2	63.8	4.9
Black	47.5	9.3	49.0	12.5
Hispanic	35.6	24.8	59.5	21.4
Less than high school	55.9	12.1	73.6	3.3
College	41.1	9.8	49.1	7.4
Liberal	48.4	10.3	59.0	9.9
Moderate	49.0	8.2	62.0	4.1
Conservative	57.4	6.5	63.3	7.0
Less than $15,000	58.2*	9.2*	64.8	6.2
More than $50,000	44.2	11.0	54.1	7.8
Male	52.0	8.3	59.0	7.6
Female	51.1	8.5	64.7	4.9
Economic assessment better	—	—	55.6	6.4
Economic assessment worse	—	—	67.6	6.6
Catholic	44.4	10.6	62.4	6.9
Jewish	22.7	18.2	40.0	10.0

Source: CBS News/*New York Times* Monthly Poll, June 1986, September 1994.

The absence of partisan divisions reflects the considerable consensus in the 1980s that immigrant and refugee admissions should be kept to a minimum. In the 1981 poll, even a majority of liberals opposed the entry of the groups mentioned. The fact that the sharpest separation of opinion occurs across educational strata is probably a reflection of who is most economically threatened by expanding the pool of unskilled labor. The poor and uneducated are the ones most likely to find themselves competing for jobs with the new immigrants (Camarota 1998; Olzak 1992; Bonacich 1972; 1976). The class distinction in public opinion about immigration is enduring. Polls in the 1940s indicated that poor and uneducated respondents were least likely to favor an increase in admissions of European refugees following World War II. These patterns persisted into the 1950s and 1960s (Simon and Alexander 1993, 34–36).

In the mid-1990s citizens in the lower occupational and educational strata also found themselves competing for housing and other public services with immigrants. They are also more likely than the wealthy to be living next door to them and sending their children to public schools in which the children of these immigrants will make special demands on educational services and resources. While education has been found to be directly related to tolerance, it is the well-educated who usually find themselves living in the most upscale and racially homogeneous communities, where virtues such as tolerance are least required. Those who are too poor to live in neighborhoods beyond the reach of the new immigrants are confronted with all of the challenges of a changing ethnic milieu while lacking the virtues required to make the transition a smooth and harmonious one.

Attitudes toward Immigration Limits in the 1990s

The differences in attitudes by level of education are not an artifact of network studies conducted in a single time period. Table 2.4 presents results to a question about the level of immigrant admissions asked on the 1992 and again on the 1994 and 1996 *American National Election Study (ANES)*. Here respondents were asked whether the number of immigrants should be increased, decreased, or kept the same. In Table 2.4 we report only the percentage indicating a desire to cut or increase immigration, and the reader should note that the balance of the 100 percent favored keeping immigration at the same level. First note that, across all demographic and attitudinal categories, there is more support for decreasing immigration in 1994 and 1996 than in 1992, with the most support for cuts occurring in 1994. In 1994, even majorities of Hispanics and Asians support reduced immigration, along with liberals and those in nearly every other demographic group. In 1996, the proportion of Hispanics and Asians favoring cuts in immigration does drop from 1994. Among liberals, however, it remains as high as it was in 1994. Generally, however, the peak in anti-immigrant sentiment occurred in fall of 1994 and had somewhat subsided by 1996.

Evidence of differences across levels of education in attitudes toward immigration admissions persists across all three of the *ANES* surveys. In all three years, support for decreasing immigration drops 15 to 20 percentage points as one moves from those with less than an 8th grade education to those with postgraduate degrees. Economic assessments do not make a great deal of difference in 1992 and 1994. The role of economic evaluation appears to be more influential in 1996, as those who insist that the national economy has weakened in the last year are about 13 points more likely to favor a decrease in immigration than those who say the economy has improved. Religion makes a significant difference, with 57 percent of Catholics desirous

Table 2.4   Percent Supporting Decreases/Increases in Legal Immigration, 1992, 1994, and 1996

Group	1992 decrease	1992 increase	1994 decrease	1994 increase	1996 decrease	1996 increase
Total	48.8	8.1	65.3	5.3	57.6	5.3
Republican	52.1	6.0	67.4	4.7	60.1	4.6
Independent	48.9	7.7	64.4	5.2	60.5	5.0
Democrat	45.9	9.9	64.4	6.2	55.1	5.9
Bush voter 1992	49.8	5.2	62.7	6.3	63.0	3.7
Clinton voter 1992	43.2	11.9	61.5	5.2	55.4	5.8
White	50.4	7.1	66.5	5.2	58.6	4.9
Black	41.2	13.0	59.1	7.3	50.9	8.0
Hispanic	48.5	9.2	58.1	6.6	49.6	9.8
Asian	41.8	12.7	56.8	8.1	33.3	9.5
Less than 8th Grade	52.3	7.8	63.8	2.5	54.8	6.5
College	40.4	11.7	58.2	6.5	45.8	4.8
Post Graduate	31.9	15.0	44.4	14.8	40.7	8.0
Liberal	40.7	13.3	53.5	8.4	53.2	5.5
Moderate	51.1	7.7	70.6	3.5	57.2	7.2
Conservative	51.5	6.8	63.1	6.5	59.9	4.9
Less than $9,000	42.7	10.0	56.9	8.8	51.4	8.0
More than $50,000	46.8	8.6	60.9	6.6	51.8	5.6
Large city	49.9	10.9	60.3	9.2	54.2	7.3
Rural, farm	52.4	6.3	68.5	4.0	63.0	6.5
Labor household	52.6	6.4	65.2	3.8	62.0	5.3
Male	48.7	7.5	63.9	6.3	56.1	5.8
Female	48.8	8.5	66.5	4.7	58.7	4.8
Economic assessment better	44.9	5.1	64.6	6.8	52.5	6.0
Economic assessment worse	49.9	8.5	69.4	4.7	65.8	3.8
Catholic	46.2	8.0	64.8	5.5	56.7	5.5
Jewish	30.3	24.2	47.1	11.8	33.3	22.2

Source: American National Election Studies, 1992, 1994, 1996.

of decreases in immigration levels in 1996, compared with only one-third of the Jewish citizens polled. Partisan differences between Republicans and Democrats are not pronounced in 1992, 1994, or 1996.

Decreasing immigrant admissions is also the most popular position reported in a September 1994 poll by CBS News and the *New York Times* (see Table 2.3). This poll suggests that 59 percent of respondents favored a cutback, and only 6 percent an increase, with the remainder (35 percent) saying that immigration levels should be kept as they are. As in the other surveys, a decisive 25-point gap separates those with less than a high school education from those with a college degree, with the latter much less likely to favor decreases in immigration levels. Sixty percent of Hispanics and 64 percent of whites favor decreasing immigration, while only half of black voters do. There are strong religious differences as well as differences between those with optimistic and pessimistic economic evaluations. Party affiliation and ideology are not highly relevant, however, as clear majorities of Republicans, Independents, and Democrats favor decreasing immigration, as do liberals, moderates, and conservatives.

What does this evidence add up to? On the subject of reducing legal immigration, it seems pretty clear that the country moved toward consensus on the issue from 1992 to 1994. Divisions of opinion certainly were not forming along partisan and ideological lines in the early 1990s. Republicans are only slightly more likely to favor reductions in legal immigration than Democrats and Independents. The difference by party is not statistically significant in numerous multivariate tests. Nor was partisanship relevant to opinions about refugee admissions in the early 1980s. To the extent that partisanship mattered at all, Democrats were less likely to support the admission of refugees than Republicans. That Democrats were most uneasy about the admission of refugees reinforces the impression that immigration policy brings out class divisons in the American electorate.

Economic Insecurity and Public Opinion

Students of public opinion have repeatedly noted that attitudes about immigration have economic roots (Citrin, Green, Muste, and Wong 1997; Simon and Alexander 1993; Harwood 1983). We should not be surprised that differences emerge on the subject of immigration control along class lines, or between those with little education and those with college degrees. There are many reasons why those with little education and few skills would be opposed to increased immigration, the most obvious of which is economic. The unskilled have less job mobility than the well-educated and are more vulnerable to layoffs and joblessness in recessionary periods. People who fear for their jobs are more likely than others to demand limits on legal immigration. Those who are most fearful are almost always the unskilled. In the 1981 ABC News/*Washington Post* survey, respondents with less than a high school education were twice as likely to fear that immigrants were "taking jobs from Americans" than those with postgraduate degrees. Similarly, 74 percent of those in the lowest income bracket feared immigrants were taking jobs from Americans, compared with only 45 percent in the highest income bracket. A greater proportion of Democrats than Republicans feared this job competition. Differences in opinion on the economic threat posed by immigrants did not correspond to variations in political ideology. Race, however, played a role. Blacks, in particular, expressed fears about the economic effects of the new immigration. Seventy-eight percent of blacks reported that immigrants take jobs from Americans, compared with only 58 percent of whites and 38 percent of Hispanics. Whether these fears that immigrant labor supplants native workers are well-founded, of course, is subject to dispute (Borjas, Freeman, and Katz 1992; Muller 1993; Waldinger 1996; Jenkins 1978; Muller and Espenshade 1985). There is less dispute about the fact that the influx of low-skilled workers has eroded wages for unskilled work (Borjas, Freeman, and Katz 1992; Topel 1994; Muller and Espenshade 1985; Jenkins 1978). But a complete account of the facts rarely stands behind public opinion, and natives and established immigrants with less education, along with majorities or near-majorities of those with higher levels of education, certainly worry that the influx of immigrants may be injurious to their livelihood.

Again in the 1992 *American National Election Study*, respondents were asked if they believed that Hispanic and Asian immigrants took jobs away from native workers. Respondents were given the choice of responding "extremely likely," "very likely," "somewhat likely," or "not likely at all." Very small minorities were confident enough to say that it was not at all likely that immigrants took jobs away from those already here. Predictably, respondents differed by their level of education, with 89 percent of those with less than a high school education responding that it was at least somewhat likely that Hispanic immigrants cost natives their jobs, compared with 79 percent for those with postgraduate education. Partisanship and political ideology were irrelevant, with solid majorities in all categories reporting fears that immigrants could take the jobs of American workers. Race mattered less in this poll than in the early 1980s, with whites joining blacks in the belief that immigrants diminish the employment prospects of natives.

Immigrants as Social Burdens on Society

While some are fearful that immigrants will take their jobs or depress their wages, others believe that immigrants will fail to pull their own weight—that they will become public charges or a threat to public safety. These negative views are surprisingly widespread. The 1986 poll conducted by CBS News and the *New York Times* asked, "What is the biggest problem immigrants have caused in this country?" Eighteen percent of respondents associated immigrants with problems of crime, drugs, and welfare dependency. When asked what comes to mind when "you hear about immigrants from Latin America," 17 percent mentioned crime, drugs, or welfare. Asians fared better on this question, with only 4 percent associating them with crime, drugs, or welfare.

Immigrants are understandably upset when they learn that natives consider them to be a threat to public health and safety. Most of the time, the belief that newcomers constitute such a threat is not based in reality. But there are times and places where such beliefs are based on more than racist attitudes. The prison systems of several western states are increasingly crowded with criminal aliens. The Cubans of the Mariel boatlift were feared to be a public safety threat because many of them did have checkered histories of crime and mental disorder. Similarly, concerns about the health status of immigrants have prompted calls to restrict the entry of immigrants who are HIV positive for fear they could spread the disease. These concerns account for the differences reported in Table 2.2 between support for Northern Europeans and Russian Jews compared with the generally much lower support for Haitians and Cubans. Similarly, the controversy over the consumption of public services by undocumented aliens in California turns out to be a problem caused by the *legal* admission and concentration of immigrants in that state. Illegal aliens are a minuscule drain on public resources compared to the resources consumed by legal residents admitted under current immigration law. Established residents confuse the legally admitted population with the illegally admitted one, refusing to believe that such a vast number of foreign-born residents could be in the state on a perfectly legal basis due to the nation's generous admissions policies.

Racial Prejudice in Public Opinion

We have seen that the differences in the opinions of educated and less-educated respondents are reflected primarily in their relative fears of labor competition by new arrivals. The fear of such labor competition brings about a demand for protection. Admittedly, the opinion studies reported here were conducted at times when economic insecurity was at its peak—during the early 1980s and early 1990s. This timing undoubtedly contributes to the strong element of consensus among respondents about the unemployment threat posed by sustained immigrant admissions. Earlier polls from more prosperous times, however, report similar patterns, suggesting that even when economic conditions are mostly favorable, those in more fragile economic circumstances fear for their jobs (Simon and Alexander 1993). We have also argued that established residents may sometimes have legitimate concerns about the health and safety threat posed by legal immigration. But even in hard times, concerns for economic and social well-being are not the only sources of hostility to immigrants and open immigration policies. It is clear, for example, in Table 2.2 that not all immigrant groups are welcomed equally by the public. Nonrefugee immigrants from predominantly Caucasian countries are favored over groups of Latin American, Caribbean, and

Asian origin. In a poll conducted by CBS News and the *New York Times* in January 1994, citizens were explicitly asked if they would favor limiting immigration to only those of European descent. When put so baldly, 11 percent said they would limit immigration to Europeans only, with 86 percent opposing such limits and the remainder saying that limits should "depend on the country of origin." These differences in opinion about who should be admitted may not be attributable to economic judgments and fears, but may instead be the product of racial distinctions that respondents draw between groups.

For clues about noneconomic sources of opinion about immigration, we looked at several other questions available in the polls that would help us evaluate the specific role that prejudicial attitudes play in opinions about immigrant admissions. To enhance comparison, we were particularly interested in surveys that queried respondents about their attitudes toward a variety of immigrant groups. The 1981 poll conducted by ABC News and the *Washington Post* served this purpose best, for in addition to asking about whether seven different groups should be admitted, it also asked questions tapping into attitudes of racial prejudice, particularly the racist attitudes of white respondents. We used five of these questions (listed in the chapter Appendix) in designing an index of prejudice ranging from 0 to 10, with 0 indicating the fewest prejudicial responses and 10 indicating the most (for more detail on the validity of this indicator, also see the chapter Appendix). We then incorporated this indicator into multivariate regression models (see Table A2.1) to determine what influences opinions about admissions. Included in these models were variables for partisanship, ideology, economic position, belief about whether immigrants take jobs from natives, and the respondents' education, gender, and race. Table 2.5 presents results from this investigation, showing estimates of the percentage of respondents who oppose each group's arrival in the United States at various values of three key explanatory variables: level of prejudice, level of education, and beliefs about the employment consequences of immigration. The results clearly show that attitudes about whether immigrants take jobs from natives have the most dramatic impact on opinions toward all of the groups. For instance, among those who feared that immigrants do take jobs away from natives, 84 percent opposed Haitians and 92 percent opposed the Mariel Cubans. But for those who believed there were enough jobs to go around, only 44 percent opposed Haitians and 60 percent the Mariel Cubans. The effects of prejudice were most dramatic for attitudes toward admitting Haitians, Vietnamese, and Russian Jews, with those of high prejudice registering overwhelming opposition to the immigration of these groups. Predictably, those of high prejudice were least opposed to Northern European and Italian immigrants. Finally, as reported earlier, moving from low to high education dramatically reduced opposition to all seven immigrant and refugee groups, reconfirming the

Table 2.5. Estimates of the Percentage Opposing the Immigration of Refugees and Other Groups to the United States by Selected Characteristics, Spring 1981

Group	Haitians	Vietnamese	Iranians	Cubans (Mariel)	Russian Jews	Northern Europeans	Italians
Immigrants take jobs: no	44	46	67	60	58	38	34
Immigrants take jobs: yes	84	83	93	92	74	72	67
Difference	*40*	*37*	*26*	*32*	*16*	*34*	*33*
Prejudice: low	62	65	84	80	58	57	50
Prejudice: high	91	85	91	92	74	66	65
Difference	*29*	*20*	*7*	*12*	*16*	*9*	*15*
Education: less than HS	80	80	93	91	79	71	63
Education: Postgraduate	62	60	74	71	42	46	45
Difference	*–18*	*–20*	*–19*	*–20*	*–37*	*–25*	*–18*

Source: ABC News/ *Washington Post* Race Relations Poll, February-March 1981. Authors' calculations from multivariate logistic regression models in Table A2.1 in Chapter 2 Appendix.

notion that the unskilled are opposed to immigration even when prejudice and attitudes toward employment are taken explicitly into account. The prejudicial beliefs of white natives clearly do influence attitudes on immigrant admissions. However, prejudice is but one of several sources of opinion on these issues. Unskilled workers opposed even the immigration of European whites in the 1940s and 1950s (Simon and Alexander 1993). And many people who are not highly prejudiced believe that immigrants threaten their job security and wages.

Immigration: Not an Issue on Which People Vote?

Rita Simon and Susan Alexander conclude from their study of public opinion on immigration policy that "it is something of a miracle that so many immigrants gained entry to the United States between 1880 and 1990" (Simon and Alexander 1993, 244). The slant in public opinion has been decidedly anti-immigrant, not just in the 1980s and 1990s, but in earlier times as well. This opposition, however, has not prevented Congress from increasing the flow of legal immigrants. For some reason, public opinion has not dictated immigration policy. Why is that so? One explanation is that immigration is not an issue that motivates people to vote. In spite of the substantial consensus, the issue does not inform candidate choice. Support for this notion is hinted at by results in Tables 2.2, 2.3, and 2.4 showing that support for decreasing (increasing) immigration did not sharply distinguish voters for Reagan from those for Carter, those for Bush from Clinton voters or those for Dole from Clinton voters. And if opinions on immigration are not relevant in presidential contests, they are probably even less relevant in congressional races where voters have less information about candidates' issue positions.

We sought to evaluate the impact of opinions on immigrant admission on the 1992 and 1996 presidential votes and the 1994 vote for the U.S. House of Representatives, controlling for other variables generally considered responsible for vote choice—including race, party identification, ideology, gender, retrospective evaluations of the economy, income, and education. The results from our analysis in Table 2.6 indicate that attitudes on immigration

Table 2.6 Estimates of the Percentage Voting Democratic in the 1992 and 1996 Presidential and the 1994 House Elections by Selected Characteristics

Group	Bush vs. Clinton 1992	Perot vs. Clinton 1992	Republican vs. Democrat 1994	Dole vs. Clinton 1996	Perot vs. Clinton 1996
Immigration limits: Increase	72	79	59	81	88
Immigration limits: Decrease	63	63	55	80	90
Difference	*9*	*16*	*4*	*1*	*−2*
Economic evaluation better	31	54	54	86	95
Economic evaluation worse	72	71	57	72	86
Difference	*−41*	*−17*	*−3*	*14*	*9*
Partisanship: Non-Democrat	49	56	47	55	72
Partisanship: Democrat	87	84	72	95	96
Difference	*−38*	*−28*	*−25*	*−40*	*−24*
Partisanship: Non-Republican	78	75	67	84	86
Partisanship: Republican	27	46	27	74	93
Difference	*51*	*29*	*40*	*10*	*−7*
Ideology: Very liberal	94	81	76	94	92
Ideology: Very conservative	27	55	38	64	87
Difference	*67*	*26*	*38*	*30*	*5*
Ethnicity: Non-Hispanic	67	68	55	80	87
Ethnicity: Hispanic	50	73	69	88	98
Difference	*17*	*−5*	*−14*	*−8*	*−11*

Source: American National Election Studies 1992, 1994, 1996. Authors' calculations from multivariate logistic regression models in Table A2.2 in Chapter 2 Appendix.

admissions do not separate Bush or Dole voters from Clinton voters, nor votes for Republican and Democratic House members in the 1994 election. About 72 percent of those favoring increasing admissions voted for Clinton over Bush in 1992, but about 63 percent desiring decreased immigration also favored Clinton over Bush. This difference is not great enough to be statistically different from zero. Similarly, in the 1994 House races, about 59 percent of those desiring increases in immigration voted for the Democratic candidate, but about 55 percent of those favoring decreases also voted Democratic. Again, this slight four-point difference clearly indicates that opinions on immigration limits did not divide people by the party they voted for. There is a slight tendency for Perot voters to use this issue in selecting Perot over Clinton in 1992. Seventy-nine percent of those favoring increased immigration favored Clinton over Perot, compared with only 63 percent of those wanting cuts in immigration (see Table 2.6). Perot's stances on protectionist trade policy and border control obviously swayed some for whom immigration was an important election issue in the 1992 contest. Immigration may be an important issue for a few independent voters; however, it is not sufficiently salient to override traditional cues such as party, ideology, race, and economic evaluations for the vast majority of voting citizens.

What we learn from this analysis is that in most of the nation immigration is not like abortion, school prayer, gay rights, gun control, or civil rights—issues that elicit such strong feelings that attitudes about them override other influences. There are places like California, of course, where immigration does have the status of some of these controversies, and local polls revealed strong partisan and ideological cleavages on Proposition 187 in 1994 due to Governor Pete Wilson's strong endorsement of the measure (Wang 1996; MacDonald and Cain 1998). For most places in the nation, though, the issue of immigration limits does not divide voters by party or ideology to nearly the same extent. Most Americans still report not knowing any immigrants or not having any contact with them. In the 1986 CBS/*New York Times* poll, 70 percent reported that there was no significant population of immigrants in their community. While having contact with immigrants is not necessary to forming opinions about them, California's experience strongly hints that it is the presence and concentration of immigrants, and their consumption of public services, that has led to the politicization of this issue there.

We have suggested that immigration is not likely to become a political issue until the economy sours to the point where natives begin to blame newcomers for job competition and unemployment. In 1992, though, the economy was widely alleged to be in bad condition. But these negative assessments of the economy did not split voters according to their attitudes on immigration levels (see Table 2.4). Rather, it is in the 1996 election, when the economy was doing well, that one can detect a far greater difference in attitudes toward immigration by people's assessments of economic conditions (Table 2.4). At first, this seems paradoxical. Why would economic conditions make more of a difference to attitudes on immigration in good times than in bad? The answer may lie in what many people have learned as a result of the immigration debate that took place between 1992 and 1996. In 1992, immigration was a relatively new issue in many places across the nation. By 1996, however, voters had learned that there might be a link between immigration and the economy—that immigrants have potentially negative consequences for the wages and employment prospects of natives. So in 1992, only about half of those who expressed negative evaluations of the economy desired cuts in immigration, but by 1994 this had increased to 69.4, and by 1996 it stood at 65.8 percent. The changing figures for labor union households also bolster this interpretation that citizens may learn, over time, from the content of elite discourse. In 1992, only 52.6 percent of those living in labor union households expressed a desire to cut immigration. In 1994 and 1996, these figures are 65.2 and 62.0 respectively (see Table 2.4). It is hard to argue that economic conditions for labor union households were worse in 1994 or 1996 than they were in 1992 (although in certain specific regions that may have been true). Instead, the change is attributable to the increase in information in the voters' possession in the latter two election years as compared with 1992 (Citrin, Green, Muste, and Wong 1997). Many voters had to learn of the ostensible connection between the nation's economic health and immigration policy. The more voters learn to connect the two, the more we can expect attitudes toward immigration to hinge on attitudes about economic conditions.

We come back to the fact that in the early and mid-90s there is considerable consensus across party and ideological lines in favor of reductions in immigration. In the 1996 *ANES* study, a sizable majority favors reducing immigration (57.6 percent) or keeping it the same (37.1 percent). Only a minuscule 5.3 percent favor any increase in immigration. But our research also shows that a large majority of those voters simply do not care whether public policy reflects those preferences. When voting for members of Congress or the presidency, few stop to consider what positions the candidates have taken on immigration. Or at least immigration is not a decisive issue with voters.

The sources of public opinion on immigration policy are complex. In the 1990s, opponents of immigration reform have repeatedly suggested that opposition to open-border policy is traceable to "racist nativism" (Perea 1996). To be sure, there is an element of public opinion that opposes increased immigration out of just such sentiments. But a much larger element is fearful for their economic security. Our analysis indicates that economic anxiety among lower-income and lower-skilled workers plays a greater role than racial prejudice in shaping attitudes on immigration policy.

Why hasn't the considerable consensus in favor of cuts in immigration translated into policy? The answer is that the consensus on the issue is not supported by much intensity of feeling among opinion holders. A member of Congress can safely vote in accord with the preferences of a particular interest group without fearing retribution at the polls. Similarly, President Clinton can reject the recommendations of his own immigration commission without being noticed outside the Washington Beltway. Not knowing how the public will react, many members of Congress refuse to campaign on immigration reform. It is a technical and complex area of law and policy that is not easy to explain in town hall meetings. So even as the debate in Congress appears to be increasingly partisan, these partisan divisions have not yet translated into public opinion. The ambivalence of the public on the issue in many parts of the country has cleared the way for interest group influence in the policymaking process.

Interest Group Involvement in Immigration Policymaking

We have indicated that the public clearly has opinions on the immigration issue, but it is not especially activated to express them at the voting booth except in areas of the country where the issue has been highly politicized. The evidence previously presented shows that economic worries and racial prejudice figure into the formulation of attitudes about immigration policy, and also candidate choice, but attitudes on immigration policy do not seem to have an impact on voting independent of these related influences. There are elite segments of the public, however, who are highly informed and aware of their stake in the immigration debate. These activists have contributed to the formation of interest organizations in Washington that have waged hard-fought campaigns in the halls of Congress on each side of the issue.

Interest groups are especially influential in Congress under two conditions: (1) when the public is quiet on an issue, or (2) when public opinion is highly divided. When a legislator's constituency is of one mind and cares intensely about an issue, there is little likelihood that the member will vote against constituency opinion, regardless of interest group pressures. The interest in reelection is simply too strong to ignore clear and explicit directions from home (Mayhew 1974; Wright 1996). Members of Congress who face divided constituencies, however, may turn to favorite interest groups to help them decide. Groups provide information that can tip the balance. In other circumstances, constituencies may be silent on an issue and members may turn to groups because groups provide information on unfamiliar issues. In many instances, interest groups know more about an issue than either members or legislative staff (Hansen 1991; Wright 1996, 88). Members must take their decision-making cues from somewhere, and when constituency is not the source, a vacuum is created that an advocacy group can help fill. In the final pages of this chapter, we will discuss the major advocacy groups that have come to play a role in the immigration debate on Capitol Hill.

Labor Unions and Business Groups

Because immigration levels directly influence the size of the labor market, labor unions and business groups have been among those most involved in lobbying for protection of their interests. Labor unions were once fierce opponents of open immigration, fearing that expanding the labor force drove down wages and eroded working conditions for working people (Reimers 1992; Tichenor 1997). That pitted them directly against businesses that lobbied for unrestricted immigration for exactly the opposite reason: to keep production costs in check and enhance profitability. Businesses that rely upon immigrant labor, both skilled and unskilled, were especially active in the 1980s and 1990s in lobbying against immigration restrictions and the imposition of penalties for those who hire illegal aliens. In the 1970s and 1980s, labor union leadership began to change its views on immigration, realizing that newly arriving immigrants were becoming an increasing proportion of the unionized work force. By 1996, roughly 300,000 Asians were unionized workers, two-thirds of whom were estimated to be foreign born (Finucane interview 2/24/97). The growing number of Hispanics employed in service industries became a target for union organizing in the 1980s. As the demography of the labor movement changed, labor organizations began to herald immigration as a means of rebuilding their depleted rank-and-file. By the 1990s, union leaders began to fight as fiercely to maintain high immigration levels as they once did to slam the door. The one exception to this change in viewpoint was in the area of skilled or employment-based immigration, where unions continue to insist that businesses are importing skilled workers in order to maintain low wages.

The business interests that have been most active on immigration over the longest period of time are the farmers who have depended on low-skill immigrant labor to harvest crops. In the 1950s, the American Farm Bureau Federation emerged as the leading interest group representative for farming interests. The Farm Bureau has persistently lobbied against the imposition of penalties for hiring illegal aliens. Agriculture groups have also pressured Congress to enact an agricultural guest-worker program that would allow immigrants to enter the country on temporary visas during harvest time. Farm interests have been particularly influential in immigration policymaking since the mid-1980s.

High-tech businesses emerged in the 1990s as a potent influence behind generous and expansive immigration policy. Computer software companies, such as Microsoft, and hardware engineering firms, such as Intel, Motorola,

Sun Microsystems, and Texas Instruments, were active in 1996 as part of the American Business for Legal Immigration (ABLI) Coalition. The companies and interest groups that were part of this coalition fought to retain employment-based immigration preferences on the grounds that high-tech firms must be able to recruit talent in an international labor market. Faced with domestic labor shortages, if these firms could not hire engineers and technicians from abroad, their competitiveness in the marketplace would surely be jeopardized. The high-tech firms were joined by such traditional business groups as the National Association of Manufacturers (NAM) and the U.S. Chamber of Commerce in the effort to maintain open immigration for employment purposes.

The Immigration Lawyers

Another group whose influence is felt on Capitol Hill when immigration matters are considered is the American Immigration Lawyers Association (AILA). AILA is the official organization of the immigration bar—the attorneys who represent immigrants and their families in the labyrinthine immigration system. AILA's membership in the late 1990s stood at about 4,500. Much of AILA's mission is to educate practicing immigration lawyers about changes in immigration law. AILA's interest in immigration law is fundamentally economic. Immigrants are their clients, so any proposed policies that are threatening to immigrants and their families are threatening to the lawyers who represent them. In response to calls for immigration restriction since the early 1980s, AILA opened a Washington office oriented toward lobbying and advocacy. AILA opens doors on Capitol Hill with its expertise on immigration matters. In other words, AILA's access and credibility comes not from its numbers but from its expertise. It is also a link to individuals and companies in members' districts who have hired immigration lawyers to help them with the cumbersome and unresponsive immigration system. AILA believes strongly in working together with other groups and was instrumental in cementing the coalition of business, religious, and immigrants' rights groups that lobbied against passage of restrictions in legal and employment-based immigration in 1996.

Ethnic and Immigrants' Rights Groups

Ethnic interest groups seek to mobilize ethnic sentiments to achieve political purposes (Litt 1970; Vigil 1990). In recent years, groups that promote the civil and legal rights of Hispanics, Asian-Pacific Americans, and other minorities have taken an active role in lobbying against immigration restrictions. These include groups such as the National Council of La Raza (NCLR), the Mexican American Legal Defense and Education Fund (MALDEF), the

League of United Latin American Citizens (LULAC), the Organization of Chinese Americans (OCA), and smaller organizations in the Hispanic and Asian-Pacific communities. The mandate of these groups is to educate law-makers and others about who Asian-Pacific Americans and Hispanics are and where their interests lie in public policy. Aside from immigration, leading causes for these groups include health insurance reform, job training, youth training, and welfare reform. Representing 27 million Latinos and 8 million Asians is not an easy task because both the Asian-Pacific community and the Hispanic community are internally diverse. All of the national organizations confront regular charges that they do not truly speak for the communities they claim to represent (Skerry 1993; Johnson 1995). On very few issues is there unity among members of any ethnic group. And on some issues, grass-roots opinion is opposed to the positions taken by the interest group leader-ship. Tolerance for illegal immigration is an example in which leaders and followers part company. Leaders of the Asian groups admitted that most Asians living in the U.S. believe that the government should crack down on illegal immigration. The interest group leadership, however, has defended the rights of illegal immigrants, insisting that they should receive the same humane treatment and due process rights accorded U.S. citizens (Finucane interview 2/24/97).

The Organization of Chinese Americans is one of the better-organized Asian-Pacific groups based in Washington. In 1996, this organization had 41 local chapters and about 10,000 members nationwide. Reportedly, the OCA had its strongest chapters on the East Coast and in the Midwest (Kwok inter-view 2/4/97). The source of OCA's credibility is its grassroots support. Mem-bers of Congress are responsive to groups that have chapters and members in their congressional districts. In the 105th Congress (1997–1998), there were only seven Asian members, so OCA must work in coalition with other groups in the broader civil rights community. With a small staff of four people, the OCA depends on the work of other coalition organizations for information gathering. OCA does not claim to have expertise on immigration issues, thus fostering ties to the immigration bar and other groups helps OCA focus its message and develop its strategy for influence.

The Mexican American Legal Defense and Education Fund (MALDEF), the League of United Latin American Citizens (LULAC), and the National Council of La Raza (NCLR) are leading examples of groups that have liti-gated and lobbied extensively to protect the civil rights of Hispanics. Founded in the 1960s as nonprofit organizations dedicated to representing Latinos, both MALDEF and NCLR have steadily expanded their agendas to focus on employment law, immigrants' rights, and educational opportunity—including bilingual education, political access, and voting rights (O'Connor and Epstein 1984; Vigil 1990). While MALDEF and NCLR are run by a board of directors and neither is a membership organization, LULAC has a truly grassroots foundation. LULAC's history is older, too—extending back to 1929, when the first LULAC convention was organized in Corpus Christi, Texas, to unite the Hispanic community in the state to fight discrimination. A decisive victory came in 1946 when LULAC's Southern California chapter successfully litigated to integrate the Orange County School System. By the mid-1990s, LULAC had 110,000 members organized in 700 chapters in 24 states and Puerto Rico (Castaneda 1997).

All three of the leading Hispanic organizations have opened offices in Washington for lobbying purposes. All were active in the fight against passage of Proposition 187, as well as the 1990 and 1996 rounds of immigration reform in Congress. Litigation for Hispanic civil rights is a major part of each group's mission. It was MALDEF lawyers, for instance, who brought the *Plyler v. Doe* (457 U.S. 202 (1982)) case to the Supreme Court. In *Plyler*, the Court ruled that undocumented aliens did have a right to a free public education, in the absence of legislative action by Congress that would limit that right. As a result of *Plyler*, thousands of undocumented children were given access to free public education (Johnson 1995). Realizing that litigation alone is not enough, the three organizations lobbied against provisions in the Immigration Reform and Control Act, passed in 1986, that sought to impose penalties on employers who hire illegal aliens. The Hispanic groups insisted that employers under threat of sanction will discriminate against Latinos in order to avoid possible punishment. Since the legislation passed, MALDEF has been active in litigating against the discriminatory impact of the employer sanctions and work eligibility verification provisions. In 1995 and 1996, LULAC, NCLR, and MALDEF vigorously lobbied against new limits on legal immigration and against passage of an employer verification system.

The National Immigration Forum (NIF) is perhaps the leading immigrants' rights organization that is not directly tied to an ethnic group. The NIF started in 1982 as an organization dedicated to a generous immigration policy and fair treatment for immigrants. In the mid-1990s, the NIF was operating with a staff of 10 and a $1.2 million budget. The NIF came to be one of the more effective lobbying organizations in the 1995–1996 debate on immigration reform. It served as a coalition coordinator bringing business, labor, and ethnic interests together under one umbrella. The NIF's publications emphasize the contributions immigrants make and insist that the benefits of immigration far outweigh the costs. In the wake of the 1996 elections, NIF literature emphasized that the Republicans' anti-immigrant stance in Congress hurt them at the polls in the presidential election.

Environmental and Population Groups

An assortment of environmental organizations have expressed concerns about immigration policy on the basis that open borders threaten the nation with overpopulation. Prominent among these groups are Zero Population Growth (ZPG), Negative Population Growth (NPG), the Carrying Capacity Network (CCN), and the Federation for American Immigration Reform (FAIR). All four maintain active lobbying operations in Washington. ZPG, NPG, and CCN are concerned with population growth in general, and immigration is considered only one source of that growth. Along with immigration restrictions, they lobby in support of family planning programs, including abortion services. ZPG has called for a U.S. population stabilization policy that would include caps on annual immigration consistent with zero population growth targets. In other words, these groups are concerned about population expansion worldwide, and reducing immigration is seen as a means to this end.

NPG has a smaller membership than ZPG but is more aggressive in promoting immigration restrictions. NPG would set annual immigration admissions at 100,000 with the goal of reaching long-term reductions in the U.S. population. Like NPG, CCN points out that immigration is the main reason that the U.S. population is growing. CCN attributes a myriad of social ills to population growth due to immigration, including traffic congestion, air pollution, water shortages, school overcrowding, crime, joblessness, homelessness, and the national debt. CCN claims that current immigration levels are totally unsustainable and that immigration will cause a doubling of the U.S. population by 2050.

While FAIR would probably not say that its agenda is motivated by population and environmental concerns, clearly such concerns were the inspiration behind its founding. FAIR was founded in 1979 by Dr. John Tanton, a Michigan physician concerned about population's impact on the environment. Tanton was also a member of Zero Population Growth and helped start a ZPG chapter in Michigan (Reimers 1996). FAIR's influence on Capitol Hill is based partly on a grassroots membership that had reached 70,000 by the mid-1990s. FAIR is also a diligent producer of studies and reports designed to justify reduced immigration levels. FAIR was often a presence at hearings on the immigration issue in the 1980s and 1990s, offering expert testimony on behalf of restrictionist forces. The organization has built an extensive grassroots membership in California and Florida and maintains field offices in both states. FAIR activists circulated petitions to put Proposition 187 on the ballot in California as well as similar measures in Arizona and Florida, where their efforts were less successful.

Although the rising tide of anti-immigration sentiment has helped fuel contributions to both the population control organizations and FAIR, all of these groups have had to fend off charges of alarmism, nativism, and racism that have damaged their outreach efforts inside the Beltway. Naturally, the population control groups do not publicly rationalize immigration reductions on nativist or racist grounds, preferring instead to couch their arguments in claims about the negative economic and environmental impact of immigration. But their opponents regularly charge them with whitewashing xenophobia and racism. The controversy surrounding the issue has frightened some environmental groups away from taking stands on immigration. The Sierra Club, for instance, avoided taking a position throughout the 1990s, for fear that it would antagonize liberal interest groups that the Sierra Club often works with on other issues. Other organizations have taken positions but avoided lobbying on the issue for fear of antagonizing groups they find themselves allied with in other policy arenas.

Religious Groups

Of the religious organizations active in the debate on immigration reform, the most influential is the U.S. Catholic Bishops Conference. Together with the Council of Jewish Federations (CJF) and the Lutheran Immigration and Refugee Service (LIRS), the Catholic Conference lobbies for generous immigration policies and refugee resettlement assistance programs. For these groups, and others like them, immigration is a moral issue. While none lobbies for totally open borders, it is not clear where they would draw the line on immigrant and refugee admissions. From their viewpoint, providing comfort to strangers is a moral responsibility commanded of Jews and Christians in the Bible. Costs and benefits are not relevant. Refugees, asylees, and immigrants should be allowed entrance regardless of their capacity to support themselves.

The Catholic Church has always taken immigration very seriously, believing that Mary and Joseph were themselves refugees, or at least displaced persons. Between the World Wars, the Catholic Conference was organized to coordinate the Church's policy response to large refugee flows. The Conference has made its voice heard on immigration and refugee policy on Capitol Hill at least since the 1940s. The Migration and Refugee Services division of the Conference, with its nationwide network of local affiliates, provides legal services for poor immigrants and is engaged in refugee resettlement. By the mid-1990s, the Catholic Conference employed five full-time lobbyists in Washington, two of whom focused particularly on immigration legislation. The Catholic Conference is uniquely positioned compared with other organizations because its agenda is so broad. No one on Capitol Hill is a complete enemy of the Conference. Whereas the immigrants' rights groups can usually find a friendly audience only with liberal and Democratic members, the Catholic Conference has a wider circle of friends. On the abortion issue, and on some education issues, for instance, the Catholic Conference has many GOP allies. On welfare and human service issues, on the other hand, the Conference is firmly allied with the Democratic leadership. The Catholic Conference's influence is greatly facilitated by its huge grassroots base. There were 55 million Catholics in the United States by the end of the twentieth century.

The Council of Jewish Federations is a counterpart of the Catholic Conference within the Jewish community of faith. A second organization within the Jewish community dedicated to refugee resettlement is the Hebrew Immigrant Aid Service (HIAS). By 1996, CJF represented the policy arm of an association of 189 local Jewish social service providers. The service-providing arm of CJF is designed to provide cradle-to-grave services for the needy, including refugee resettlement assistance, vocational training, English language training, nutrition counseling, family counseling, adoption services, and mental health counseling. For many years, both CJF and HIAS have been involved in the resettlement of Jews facing persecution in Ethiopia, Iran, and the countries of the former Eastern Bloc. Clients of these resettlement programs, however, include both Jews and Gentiles. The philosophy of these organizations is that the Jewish community has a collective responsibility to care for immigrants, and particularly refugees in desperate circumstances. As a result, CJF and HIAS have taken strong stands on Capitol Hill against policies that would limit refugee admissions.

In Protestant circles, several pro-immigration groups have been prominent in the debate. The Lutheran Immigration and Refugee Services has been the most active for the longest period of time. From 1939, the date of its inception, to 1996, LIRS could boast of having resettled more than 170,000, including large numbers of Vietnamese, Laotian, and Cambodian refugees following the Vietnam War. Politically, LIRS is not as influential, by itself, as either the Jewish or Catholic groups, but it could open the doors of members of Congress from states where the Lutheran Church had large congregations, including much of the Midwest. LIRS's influence in the immigration debates of the 1980s and 1990s came largely as part of the broader pro-immigration coalition.

The Christian Coalition (CC), the nation's leading advocacy group for conservative Christian causes, played an important but perhaps only short-lived role in the immigration debate in 1995 and 1996. During the late stages of the debate on the bill to reduce legal immigration levels and eliminate preference categories for extended family members, Christian Coalition executive director Ralph Reed took a stand against the legislation, sending members of Congress a letter declaring the proposed changes to be hostile to family interests. It is not entirely clear how many legislators were persuaded by this correspondence, but players on both sides of the debate gave Reed's letter credit for defeating key measures in the original legislation (see Chapter 6). Because its grassroots constituency is divided on most immigration policy issues, the Christian Coalition has avoided taking prominent public stands on the issue. There is reason to doubt whether it will involve itself in future policy actions on a matter that divides the evangelical Christian community.

Think Tanks

Two think tanks deserve mention for their recent role in the immigration debate: the CATO Institute and the Center for Immigration Studies (CIS). The CATO Institute was founded as a nonprofit research institution in 1977 in Washington, D.C. Its charter is to advance principles of limited government and individual liberty through research and education. Essentially, CATO embraces a libertarian ideology. Immigration is seen by CATO experts and donors as an issue of freedom and individual rights. Throughout the 1980s and 1990s, CATO policy experts defended generous and expansive immigration policy on economic grounds, employing the late University of Maryland economist Julian Simon as a resident scholar and adviser. Working closely with the National Immigration Forum and other pro-immigration groups in 1995 and 1996, CATO produced pamphlets, working papers, and editorials attacking proposals to reduce annual immigration quotas. CATO did, however, go on record in opposition to welfare and the consumption of other public services for immigrants, adopting the slogan, "Immigrants yes, welfare no."

CATO's leading rival on immigration issues is the Center for Immigration Studies (CIS), a Washington-based think tank that specializes only on immigration-related policy research. Formed in 1985 with the support of FAIR, CIS publishes carefully documented reports and studies that generally support the conclusion that immigration is more of a burden than a benefit to the national economy. CIS scholars insist that immigration policy ought to reflect the national interest, and that too often, the existing research has been conducted at the behest of ethnic or business groups whose research is biased, selective, and narrowly focused. Naturally, pro-immigration interests typically dismiss CIS research as biased, selective, and narrowly focused.

It is difficult to assess how influential CATO and CIS have been. Much of the time they talk past each other to very separate audiences on rival sides of the issue. Immigration policy was so highly politicized in the 1980s and 1990s that the research was employed to bolster either restrictionist or expansionist viewpoints. Advocacy organizations are interested only in the facts that help make their case. Policymaking in Washington is almost never based on fully objective and sober research, but instead on the interests of the politicians and groups battling on both ends of Pennsylvania Avenue.

Conclusions: Public Opinion and Group Influence on Immigration Policymakers

For members of Congress from California, Texas, Florida, New York, and a few other high-immigration states, the position to be taken on immigration bills and amendments is made clear through the expression of constituency opinion. Because their constituencies have been so active and concerned, Southern California politicians have rarely been undecided in recent years about any aspect of immigration policymaking. When members have their minds made up, there is very little room for persuasion or interest group influence. Organized interests may be called upon for facts, figures, and arguments to support conclusions already reached, but the groups are only enriching the debate, not changing minds or helping members decide. In many areas of the country, however, the public is unaware of the issues. In some legislative districts where constituents have been vocal, views are shallow and without much conviction. In the absence of determined mass support for either immigration restriction or expansion, the interest group community has been a source of information for members of Congress who are deciding which policies to support.

There has certainly been an increase in the number of interest groups engaged in the immigration debate in the 1980s and 1990s. This proliferation has developed as a result of the breakdown of consensus on Capitol Hill on many aspects of immigration policy. In the 1960s and before, there were few groups that demanded immigration restriction, because immigration levels were low and the infrequent policy changes were subject to bipartisan consensus. The immigration restriction lobby, such as it was, consisted of a handful of groups concerned about the patriotism of new immigrants, together with labor unions that voiced arguments about the erosion of wages and working conditions due to immigrant competition for jobs. By the 1990s, however, the immigration restriction lobby had gained momentum and influence, given the historically high levels of immigration, the slowdown of the economy, and fears about the changing ethnic composition of the nation's population. Labor reversed itself and began supporting expansive immigration as a means of rank-and-file renewal.

On the pro-immigration side, the period before 1965 saw the presence of only a few religious and humanitarian organizations dedicated to generous immigration policy out of moral concern for the oppressed. These groups were active but not highly mobilized, because their interests were rarely threatened. In 1965, all of the momentum favored the elimination of the national origins quotas and expansive immigration policy. There were almost no civil rights or immigrants' rights organizations yet active on behalf of Hispanics and Asians. By the late 1980s, the long-standing religious and humanitarian lobbies had been joined by the small but vigorous Asian-Pacific interest groups and the more noticeable Latino organizations. In the early 1990s, businesses outside of agriculture that had come to rely on immigrant labor entered the ranks of the pro-immigration army. All of these groups, together with the converted labor movement, faced highly credible threats in 1990 and 1996 by proposals to restrict legal immigration and control illegal immigration. Together, they would form the substance of the left-right coalition that would win over enough fence-sitting members of Congress to defeat several determined attempts to shut the golden door.

APPENDIX TO CHAPTER 2

Questionnaire

Questions from ABC News/*Washington Post* Poll used to construct an indicator for racial prejudice:

1. Would you say that it is common sense or prejudice for whites to move out of a neighborhood when blacks begin to move in?

Prejudice	79.5%
It depends	5.6
Common sense	14.8

2. Would you say that it is common sense or prejudice for whites to change their child's elementary school when the number of blacks increases?

Prejudice	78.9%
It depends	5.6
Common sense	15.5

3. Would you say that it is common sense or prejudice for parents to prevent their children from dating someone of another race?

Prejudice	59.6%
It depends	5.2
Common sense	35.2

4. Would you say that it is common sense or prejudice for whites to avoid driving through large black neighborhoods?

Prejudice	39.6%
It depends	11.2
Common sense	49.1

5. Would you say that it is common sense or prejudice for an employer to expect whites to work harder than blacks?

Prejudice	88.9%
It depends	2.2
Common sense	8.9

Coding each response 0=prejudice, 1=it depends, and 2=common sense, we simply summed the total responses generating a ten-point scale with 0 indicating the fewest prejudiced responses and 10 indicating the most prejudiced responses.

To test the validity of this indicator, we examined its association with other related indicators, including (1) whether respondents believed that blacks have less in-born ability to learn than whites; and (2) whether respondents believed that blacks would rather accept welfare than work for a living. The results are as follows:

prejudice index and inborn ability question: χ^2=91.7, p<.00001; Cramer's V=.25

prejudice index and accept welfare question: χ^2=132.4, p<.00001; Cramer's V=.32

Coding of Variables in Table A2.1

Economic evaluation: 1=economy is better, 2=economy is same, 3=economy is better than a year ago

Immigrants take jobs: 1=enough jobs to go around, 2=immigrants take jobs from natives

Prejudice index: 1=nonprejudiced – 10=prejudiced

Asians: 0=non-Asians, 1=Asians

Blacks: 0=nonblacks, 1=blacks

Hispanics: 0=non-Hispanics, 1=Hispanics

Ideology: 1=very liberal, 2=liberal, 3=moderate, 4=conservative, 5=very conservative

Democrats: 0=non-Democrats, 1=Democrats

Republicans: 0=non-Republicans, 1=Republicans

Education: 1=less than 8th grade, 2=some high school, 3=high school, 4=some college, 5=college, 6=postgraduate

Sex: 0=male, 1=female

Urban/rural: 1=large city, 2=suburb of large city, 3=small city, 4=rural or farm

Table A2.1 Influences on Attitudes toward the Admission of Refugees and Other Groups to the United States, Spring 1981

Group	Haitians	Vietnamese	Iranians	Cubans (Mariel)	Russian Jews	Northern Europeans	Italians
Economic evaluation	−.04 (.11)	−.04 (.11)	.03 (.12)	−.22 (.12)	−.02 (.10)	.02 (.10)	.09 (.10)
Immigrants take jobs	1.91** (.15)	1.75** (.14)	1.81** (.17)	1.99** (.17)	1.66** (.14)	1.47** (.13)	1.39** (.13)
Prejudice index	.18** (.03)	.11** (.03)	.06 (.03)	.10** (.04)	.07** (.03)	.04 (.03)	.06** (.03)
Asians	.38 (1.25)	1.27 (1.13)	.51 (1.16)	.69 (1.15)	.20 (.89)	−.56 (.91)	.16 (.87)
Blacks	−.09 (.19)	.04 (.19)	−.32 (.22)	−.30 (.21)	.52** (.18)	.62** (.18)	.27 (.17)
Hispanics	−.15 (.40)	.40 (.40)	1.24** (.57)	−.16 (.41)	.90 (.40)	.27 (.38)	.11 (.39)
Ideology	−.01 (.06)	.06 (.06)	.008 (.07)	.02 (.07)	.08 (.06)	.09 (.06)	.03 (.06)
Democrats	.10 (.25)	.08 (.24)	.42 (.27)	−.01 (.27)	.16 (.24)	−.06 (.23)	.10 (.22)
Republicans	.30 (.27)	.11 (.26)	.39 (.28)	.14 (.28)	.02 (.25)	−.29 (.24)	.01 (.23)
Education	−.17** (.06)	−.20** (.06)	−.31** (.07)	−.28** (.07)	−.33** (.06)	−.21** (.06)	−.15** (.05)
Sex	.17 (.14)	.05 (.13)	.30** (.16)	.07 (.15)	.07 (.13)	.05 (.12)	−.12 (.13)
Urban/rural voters	.20** (.07)	.25** (.07)	.16** (.08)	.19** (.08)	.19** (.07)	.12** (.07)	.10 (.06)
Constant	−2.83	−2.41	−1.49	−.95	−2.25	−2.00	−2.23
N	1204	1260	1260	1271	1244	1250	1248
Model χ^2	287.6	263.8	1029.6	248.9	303.6	231.7	190.2
df	12	12	12	12	12	12	12
Significance	p < .0001	p < .0001	p < .0001	p < .0001	p < .0001	p < .0001	p < .0001
% Correctly predicted	74.2	73.5	81.4	78.9	72.7	69.5	68.4
Null model	68.0	70.0	81.0	80.0	61.0	59.0	56.0

Source: ABC News/*Washington Post* Race Relations Poll, February–March 1981.
Dependent variable: 0=encourage group, 1=discourage group.
Multivariate Logistic Regression; MLE Estimation; standard errors in parentheses
**p < .01; *p < .05.
Note: income was originally included in the model but later dropped due to its insignificance and relationship to other variables in the model.

Table A2.2   Influences on Presidential Vote Choice in 1992 and 1996 and the Vote for U.S. House Members 1994.

Variable	Bush vs. Clinton 1992	Perot vs. Clinton 1992	U.S. House 1994	Dole vs. Clinton 1996	Perot vs. Clinton 1996
Economic evaluation	.87**	.35	.06	−.39**	−.27
	(.21)	(.20)	(.13)	(.16)	(.19)
Limit immigration	−.21	−.40**	−.08	−.04	.07
	(.17)	(.15)	(.16)	(.21)	(.25)
Asians	−.18	.73	.24	−.71	5.11
	(.71)	(.84)	(.79)	(.82)	(12.39)
Blacks	2.44**	2.88**	1.04*	4.04**	2.85**
	(.54)	(.74)	(.44)	(1.11)	(1.08)
Hispanics	−.72	.27	.62	.67	2.05**
	(.47)	(.48)	(.46)	(.50)	(1.06)
Ideology	−.92**	−.32**	−.41**	−1.12**	−.23
	(.10)	(.09)	(.09)	(.16)	(.16)
Democrats	1.92**	1.41**	1.06**	3.40**	2.16**
	(.27)	(.22)	(.24)	(.47)	(.50)
Republicans	−2.24**	−1.27**	−1.68**	−.56	.74
	(.28)	(.30)	(.26)	(.44)	(.43)
Education	−.03	.19*	−.13	−.13	.11
	(.10)	(.09)	(.09)	(.09)	(.10)
Income	−.10	−.24**	−.14	.02	−.05
	(.08)	(.07)	(.08)	(.10)	(.10)
Sex	−.28	.45*	−.41*	.46*	.58**
	(.22)	(.20)	(.20)	(.25)	(.29)
Urban/rural voters	−.09	−.07	−.01	−.02	−.29*
	(.10)	(.10)	(.10)	(.16)	(.18)
Constant	2.59	1.03	3.14	2.57	.36
N	936	759	699	914	601
Model χ^2	709.3	267.0	308.5	760.6	81.0
df	12	12	12	12	12
Significance	p < .0001	p < .0001	p < .0001	p < .0001	p < .0001
% Correctly Predicted	87.1	79.2	77.9	90.3	89.2
Null Model	58.0	72.0	53.0	58.0	88.0

Source: American National Election Studies, 1992, 1994, 1996.

Dependent variable: 0=Vote for Republican
(H. Ross Perot in columns 2 and 5), 1=Vote for Democrat.
Multivariate Logistic Regression; MLE Estimation; standard errors in parentheses.
**p < .01; *p < .05.

Coding of Variables in Table A2.2

Economic evaluation: 1=economy is better, 2=economy is same, 3=economy is better than a year ago

Limit immigration: 1=increase level of immigration, 2=keep level the same, 3=decrease level of immigration

Asians: 0=non-Asians, 1=Asians

Blacks: 0=nonblacks, 1=blacks

Hispanics: 0=non-Hispanics, 1=Hispanics

Ideology: 1=very liberal, 2=liberal, 3=moderate, 4=conservative, 5=very conservative

Democrats: 0=non-Democrats, 1=Democrats

Republicans: 0=non-Republicans, 1=Republicans

Education: 1=less than 8th grade, 2=some high school, 3=high school, 4=some college, 5=college, 6=postgraduate

Sex: 0=male, 1=female

Urban/rural: 1=large city, 2=suburb of large city, 3=small city, 4=rural or farm

CHAPTER 3

ISSUES IN THE CONTEMPORARY IMMIGRATION DEBATE ON CAPITOL HILL

When we started our research into this area of public policy, we soon came to appreciate the complexity of immigration policymaking. Realizing that the issues are somewhat involved, we have designed this chapter to provide an introduction to themes that have framed the immigration debate since 1965. This overview is particularly useful for those new to the nuances of immigration policy. Our goal here is to provide an apprenticeship that will serve as a reference source for the more involved discussions in coming chapters. We introduce fundamental concepts, considerations, and terms that recur throughout the remainder of the book. This chapter will provide the reader with a sense of the policy options frequently discussed and the rationale commonly stated to support them. Subsequent chapters will describe the path Congress has actually taken when confronted with these policy choices.

The Immigration and Nationality Act, passed in 1952 over President Truman's veto, remains the foundation for U.S. immigration law, although it has subsequently been amended numerous times. Among the most far-reaching of those amendments, the 1965 Immigration Act, marked a sea change in U.S. immigration policy. From the 1920s until passage of the 1965 law, American immigration policy had operated on a strict per-country quota system. The 1965 law shifted that policy to a system that emphasized family reunification and employment or job skills needed in the U.S. labor market. Congress developed a preference system that ordered immigrants according to their relationship to U.S. citizens or permanent residents, or according to their training and expertise. Besides family-based and employment-based immigration, refugees also were expressly allowed to immigrate to the United States. The 1965 law contained a 170,000 annual cap on Eastern Hemisphere immigration, with a 20,000 per-country subcap, and a 120,000 cap on Western Hemisphere immigration without a per-country subcap. From this fundamental change in immigration policy (described further in Chapter 4) have stemmed many of the contemporary immigration debates about "preferences," "quotas," and "caps." But this is only the beginning of the obscure language of lawmaking on immigration policy. Following are the key concepts, one at a time.

Immigration Preferences

It is generally agreed that the United States cannot accommodate all of the millions of people around the world who would like to come here. Even the most generous immigration advocates do not support opening the doors without any restrictions. At the same time, the United States has a well-established tradition as a nation that has welcomed immigrants. The question becomes, then, on what basis does the country allow the admission of newcomers. On what basis do we grant immigrant visas?

Policymakers face a choice between awarding visas on a first-come, first-served basis or selecting visa applicants based on a system of preferences. The first-come, first-served system does not pit one petitioner against the next because of family relationships or because of employment skills. Two prospective emigres from the same country would receive immigrant visas from the United States government simply in the order in which their applications were received. It would not matter if the first applicant were a medical doctor, an unskilled laborer, or the child of a naturalized American citizen. The only preference shown would be on the basis of when the individual initiated the immigration process.

As an alternative to the first-come, first-served admissions basis, immigration policy may set certain preferences for determining which immigration visa applications may take precedence over others. A system of preferences must have a rational guiding principle. The guiding principle of U.S. immigration policy has always been to serve the "national interest," which has been defined differently over the years. Between the 1920s and passage of the 1965 Act, policymakers deemed immigration to serve the national interest when admission was based on the immigrants' national origins or ancestry. In recent times, however, the term has led to a policy based on family reunification, individuals with needed job skills, and humanitarian admissions. These were the principles adopted in the 1965 Act.

A related theme is the allocation of the numbers or percentages of visas among the preference categories. Lawmakers can choose to set hard numbers as a cap for visas to be issued under each of the three (or however many) main categories: family reunification, employment based, and humanitarian. They may choose to establish a maximum percentage of visas for each category. Policymakers may set a guaranteed minimum number or percentage of each kind of visa. For instance, policymakers may decide to set a minimum amount of family preference admissions in order to facilitate family reunification. Family preference categories allow certain close relatives of U.S.

citizens and permanent resident aliens to go to the "front of the line" in waiting for their immigrant visas.

Legislators may choose to raise or lower admission levels granted under one of the categories. For example, they may raise or lower the proportion of entrants immigrating on an employment basis. Employment-based entry may prioritize professionals and highly skilled individuals, or it may place a higher priority on low-skilled workers. One reason for placing a high priority on highly skilled and highly educated immigrants, for instance, is because such immigrants would promote economic growth and U.S. leadership in science, research, and technology. It is no secret that the United States space program benefited greatly in the post–World War II period from the know-how of German physicists and engineers who had fled Nazi Germany. By emphasizing job skills as a priority, legislators hope that American workers will be less likely to face job displacement because only those immigrants with skills that are in short supply in the domestic labor market are admitted. The other advantage to emphasizing employment-based immigration is that the immigrants who can easily find jobs in the U.S. economy are not likely to participate in welfare programs or seek other public assistance.

A preferential method of choosing among individuals differentiates among would-be immigrants on some basis. This system may be further refined than simply rank-ordering family ties, in-demand employment skills, and humanitarian needs. For instance, should all individuals having some familial relation to a United States citizen be admitted equally? And where do the relatives of lawful permanent residents stand in the queue? Are the married children of U.S. citizens to gain admission before the spouses and unmarried children of lawful permanent residents? Should some visa applicants with needed job skills be granted admission before certain relatives? To what extent is family reunification to take precedence over employment-based admission if it has been determined that family reunification outweighs filling employer needs as a policy matter? These complicated considerations are fundamental to the debate. Legislators have responded by ranking certain relatives of U.S. citizens higher in priority than those of permanent residents. Nuclear family members—that is, the spouses and children of citizens and permanent residents—have been awarded a higher preference than more distant relatives such as adult brothers and sisters. As of this writing, Congress has set the family preference hierarchy as follows:

Family-Sponsored Immigrant Preferences

1. Immediate relatives (spouses/minor children) of U.S. citizens (no annual limit on visas)
2. Unmarried adult children of U.S. citizens (limited visas)
3. Spouses and unmarried children of permanent residents (limited visas)

4. Married adult children of U.S. citizens (limited visas)
5. Brothers and sisters of adult U.S. citizens (limited visas)

A consequence, and therefore a subissue, of the preference system has become waiting lists, or *backlogs*, for immigrant visas. Currently, immediate relatives (spouses/children) of U.S. citizens have gained admission without being subject to annual numerical limits. But the other categories listed above are limited by an annual quota. With a system of several preference categories, inevitably some people who are admissible under certain priority categories end up waiting longer for permission to enter the country than other persons who qualify under some other category, depending on the demand for various types of visas in a given country. Furthermore, crafty immigrants (or their petitioner's astute immigration lawyer) have discovered ways to game the system (Abrams and Abrams 1975). The result has been lengthy backlogs. Those seeking immigration visas under various categories and under various preferences "stand in line" awaiting the next available visa allotted to their country for their circumstances.

As an example from within the family category, a higher proportion of annual visas could be awarded to spouses and minor children of permanent residents in order to facilitate the speedy reunification of nuclear families. The high proportion of visas awarded to extended family members, such as adult children and adult brothers and sisters, has caused many nuclear family members to wait for years in a backlog pending admission into the United States. Therefore, such a policy adjusting the preference system to give more visas to nuclear family members would speed their reunification, although it would also delay the reunification of families whose more distant relatives have been waiting in line. These adjustments, just as adding or eliminating preference categories, are policy options that have been recently recommended.

Policymakers may seek to ensure *ethnic diversity* among the national origins of immigrants. Almost any immigration policy, whether based on preferences or first-come, first-served, or on national origins or equal distribution, will result in some countries sending more immigrants than other countries. This is due to the fact that immigrants tend to come from places that have previously sent others to pave the way in the new country (Yang 1995). Those with more recent ties are more likely to come. Significant policy changes may adversely affect the number of visas available for certain countries that, under a previous system, received more immigration visas.

Making visas available to individuals in low immigrant-sending nations based on a lottery is one policy solution. The argument is partly based on fairness to those from low-migration countries. Lawmakers may establish either a temporary or a permanent "diversity" program to ensure the admission of immigrants from underrepresented source countries. Those arguing against introduction of a diversity visa program might suggest that the nation values immigrants from only certain countries and that only those desiring to emigrate from those countries should receive immigrant visas (this follows the controversial argument favoring a national origins admission policy discussed in the next section). Alternatively, they might argue that in a previous era a country may have had its turn to send immigrants and now it is the turn of other countries.

Related to immigrant visa qualification is the concept of *admissibility*. People desiring to immigrate to the United States must prove that they fall into one of the preference categories. They must also demonstrate to American officials that they are admissible, that no reason exists for rejecting them from consideration as immigrants. That is, prospective immigrants must show that they don't have a criminal record, don't pose a public health or national security risk, and are unlikely to become a public charge. The public charge standard means that the immigrant must not become dependent on the government for support (Vialet 12/3/96). The policy grounds for inadmissibility have generally been noncontroversial.

National Origins or Equal Visas for All Nations

Admitting immigrants of only certain nationality or ancestry groups presents one basis for immigration policy. The rationale is to control immigration flow based on racial and ethnic background. Under this scheme, preference is awarded to immigrants from certain cultures (*Immigration and Nationality Act* 1995). People from some nations and races may be considered more adaptable to American culture and values than are people from other ethnic backgrounds. The idea is to admit immigrants who are similar to the majority of Americans, because this policy would ensure cultural consistency—for example, a firm commitment to values such as democracy and free enterprise (Suro 1996). Driving the national origins position have been attitudes of racial supremacy and the faddish theory of eugenics (*Immigration and Nationality Act* 1995; Suro 1996). Also present has been the view that certain characteristics, such as intelligence, are immutable within certain groups (Suro 1996).

Alternatively, granting immigration visas on an equal basis among countries emphasizes a more equitable arrangement than national origins. Rather than preferring immigrants from certain parts of the world over others, the equal-visas-for-all-nations policy regards all nations as equals. Thus, at least in theory, British immigrants are treated equally with Korean immigrants as with Brazilian immigrants. The driving force behind this position has been the egalitarian attitude that rejects making policy decisions on the basis of skin color or nationality (Suro 1996; Abrams and Abrams 1975).

Worldwide Quotas

Immigration brings change—demographic, cultural, religious, and so forth. The speed and types of change depend on the level and character of the immigration flow. More immigrants usually mean greater change, especially if large numbers of immigrants arrive from nations that are culturally and economically different from the country of destination.

Societies, like people, vary in the extent to which they welcome change. Given that the population of a nation has many ramifications for its economy, polity, and culture, most countries in world history have given at least some thought to the meaning of national borders. One policy question, therefore, becomes whether to limit immigrant admissions. Should a quota be set for the number of immigrants admitted each year? If policymakers deem a worldwide cap desirable, then at what level should it be set? Should that annual quota be firm or flexible?

Those who argue for a restrictive immigration policy with low annual quotas often argue that immigrants make demands on social and governmental institutions, not only on the federal level, but also on the state and local levels; not only in the public sector, but also in the private sector. Immigrants tend to impose certain costs on labor markets, particularly at the local level. Increasingly, immigrants have participated in federal public assistance programs. Children entering public schools while lacking English language proficiency have overwhelmed some schools (CIR Report 1995). Moreover, the cultural differences between those arriving from non-Western and undeveloped countries and those enculturated in baseball and Yankee Doodle can clash harshly, as is evident by the struggle of Indochinese refugees to gain acceptance in Midwestern towns such as Appleton and Wausau, Wisconsin. Furthermore, immigrants have often concentrated in certain areas to build their own ethnic communities. This has raised concerns among the native-born that the immigrants are not seeking to assimilate, to "Americanize," to become immersed in the culture of their new homeland. Immigration should be limited in order to ensure that the host society capably "absorbs" the newcomers.

Of course, immigrants also benefit the country. Immigrants are more likely to settle in the inner city, where they often regenerate declining housing stock, open new businesses, and revitalize forgotten commercial areas. Many immigrants demonstrate a strong work ethic; they bring a deep commitment to family, and many value education (CIR Report 1995). Arguably, immigrants may import values that are "better" than those of many natives. Those who see immigrants as, on balance, beneficial may favor relatively open borders and high annual quotas. Advocates of this policy option argue that in an increasingly global economy, the United States benefits from a large and growing labor pool, from which American industry may draw the best and brightest, in order to maintain its international competitiveness (Briggs and Moore 1997).

Libertarian proponents of open immigration policy, such as the scholars at the CATO Institute, a Washington, D.C., think tank, argue from their foundational principle: Maximize individual liberty. Other open-borders advocates may compare recent immigration rates with those early in the twentieth century, showing that while the absolute number of immigrants is at historic highs, the number of immigrants relative to the U.S. population is lower than in times past (Briggs and Moore 1997). They may argue that immigrants do not increase American unemployment or tax the system inordinately, and that population growth fuels economic expansion (Abrams and Abrams 1975; Briggs and Moore 1997).

Some of those most focused on the growing economic costs and cultural clashes associated with immigration have called for a complete moratorium. They argue that the remarkable assimilative capacity of American society is so strained that the country cannot peaceably accept additional newcomers. They point to the education systems in high immigrant-receiving areas and insist that they are overburdened by the needs of immigrants who either are not proficient in English, or are illiterate in their own language, or both. Some moratorium supporters are seeking an immigration "time out" (Brimelow 1995). Others are motivated by a fixation on Malthusian overpopulation fears and are calling for a permanent halt to immigration (Abrams and Abrams 1975).

Still others support continued immigration, at either higher or lower levels under a worldwide cap. The worldwide ceiling is based on the belief that immigration should be controlled. This stems from the fact that the decision to grant a foreigner entry is tantamount to the meaning of sovereignty. A sovereign nation has the right, and perhaps the duty, to control its borders and ports of entry. Immigration is a privilege a country extends to an individual; immigration to a particular nation is not an individual right. A worldwide quota enforces control of permanent admissions.

The cap may be made *flexible* if certain entrants are treated as numerically exempt. That is, aliens granted permanent residence under some categories may not count against the numerical cap (*INS Statistical Yearbook* 1996). Congress may determine that certain entrants should be admitted or status adjustments made regardless of the availability of immediately available visas. Therefore, the worldwide numerical limits may be exceeded because policymakers value a degree of flexibility in the system. This flexibility allows for quick response to emergency situations and sudden changes in other countries. The determinations of which groups to hold harmless with respect to the caps are also policy decisions. For instance, Amerasians—the children of U.S. servicemen who served in the Vietnam war—have been exempt from the numerical cap on annual admissions (*INS Statistical Yearbook* 1996).

Per-Country Quotas

A *per-country quota* is the maximum number of preference visas any one country may receive in a single year. The question of whether to establish a per-country quota is a policy decision. In practice, the limit does not always guarantee that a country shall receive the maximum amount of yearly visas. The INS reports that most countries do not get the maximum number of visas allotted by law because of the combination of the preference system and the per-country quotas (*INS Statistical Yearbook* 1996).

The key policy choice here is whether there should be a per-country quota or whether immigration should be on a first-come, first-served basis. The rationale for establishing a per-country quota is to try to achieve some fairness among countries and diversity in visa allocation. The reason for adopting first-come, first-served, even if all U.S. immigrants during one year came from a single country, would be to sever any attention to country of origin and instead to focus on fairness to individuals who were admissible and who arrived in line first.

A related issue is the matter of why countries should have the same quotas. For years, American immigration policy gave each nation the same number of annual visas. Why shouldn't some countries have higher quotas than other countries? Should Lebanon, with a population of four million people, have the same quota as Nigeria, with 160 million? Perhaps countries should have quotas in proportion to the size of their population. In spite of the inherent fairness of this approach, Congress has never chosen to enact such a system into law. As of this writing, current law has established a maximum percentage of visas that may be issued to immigrants from any given country each year (*INS Statistical Yearbook* 1996).

Hemispheric Limits

An issue related to per-country quotas is that of *hemispheric ceilings.* Rather than simply setting a worldwide cap on immigration, the overall quota may be divided between the hemispheres of the world. The issue is whether a distinction should be made between countries close to the United States and those farther away. For foreign policy and trade reasons, the United States may consider its relationship with Canada and Mexico as unique and especially valuable, therefore granting these two countries special treatment. Alternatively, policymakers may determine to distribute equal visas to each hemisphere or they may set different ceilings for the hemispheres (which was the case in the 1965 Act: 170,000 for the Eastern Hemisphere with a per-country cap, 120,000 for the Western Hemisphere with no per-country cap). One rationale for distinguishing between the hemispheres in the 1965 Act was to allow Congress to justify placing per-country limitations on Eastern Hemisphere nations, but putting Western Hemisphere immigration on a first-come, first-served basis (Abrams and Abrams 1975; *INS Statistical Yearbook* 1996). Congress eventually abolished the distinction in the 1970s.

Family Reunification

Family-sponsored immigrants are those admitted for purposes of *family reunification*. Visas allotted to the family-based preference categories are issued on the basis of an individual's relationship to a U.S. citizen or permanent resident. The reason for establishing family-based preference categories is for the purpose of reuniting family members separated because one family member led the way to America, presumably with the intention that his family members would follow afterward. U.S. citizens and permanent residents may petition for close relatives to immigrate.

Family reunification was intended by the authors of the 1965 Act to enjoy top priority among reasons for admitting immigrants (Abrams and Abrams 1975). The largest proportion of immigrants seek to enter the country on the basis of family relationships; nearly two-thirds of the immigrants in fiscal year 1995 entered because they had a close family member already in the country (Vialet 12/3/96).

The policy choices concerning family reunification visas include determining the proportion of family-based versus employment-based visas to be allocated, as well as how the family-sponsored preference categories should be ordered and how many visas should be allotted to each category.

Some have argued that the preference system should be adjusted in order that it admit more skilled, professional, and business-oriented immigrants and fewer family-relation immigrants. The rationale is that the country would benefit more, in terms of its economic competitiveness, by gaining exceptionally skilled immigrants than from placing so much emphasis on family reunification. Others say the primary focus on family reunification flows from America's humanitarian tradition and that reuniting family members in itself benefits the country economically and socially (Abrams and Abrams 1975; CIR Report 1995).

With the current emphasis on family-based immigration, the phenomenon of *chain migration* has drawn the attention of legislators. Chain migration refers to use of the immigration preference system in order to reunite not only spouses and minor children with the initial immigrant, but also that immigrant's adult children and members of her extended family. The system is open to chain migration through the confluence of per-country quotas, the preference system, and supply and demand for certain visas in various countries. Potentially, the chain may include parents, adult brothers and sisters, and eventually each of those immigrants' spouses and children and parents. The number of chain migrants connected to a single family at the root of the migration tree may vary markedly, depending on the fertility rate and average family size in the country of origin. Whether immigrants decide to naturalize also affects the length of any given chain (since citizens are given special status in the visa queue).

A policy question may be raised as to whether it is desirable, given the limited number of visas allotted each year, that more distant relatives gain admission under preference categories that permit their application while the much closer relatives of other citizens and permanent residents have to wait in backlogged queues. The consequence of the present immigration system leads to fundamental policy questions regarding the number and order of family preferences. The options include preserving the existing familial categories, creating still more family categories or eliminating some present categories.

Employment-Based Immigration

Employment-based preferences aim at filling business needs that otherwise would go unmet based on available domestic labor resources. The point of opening the door on the basis of immigrants' skills and education is to enhance American economic competitiveness. The U.S. business community has long supported both long-term and short-term employment visas in order to gain access to sufficient labor pools, as well as to the world's best and brightest. Competition is the engine of the global market economy, and America clearly benefits from maintaining a labor force that is highly skilled.

Employment-based immigrant categories have included professionals, individuals with exceptional ability, and skilled and unskilled workers. Certain *nonimmigrants* may enter the country as temporary legal residents for business purposes. Nonimmigrants gain temporary admission as visitors for one of a number of reasons: to conduct business, or as diplomats, tourists, or foreign students. This is discussed more fully later in this chapter. The point is that under U.S. law foreign workers may enter the country, either temporarily or permanently, for the purpose of filling certain employment needs.

Some have argued that the admission of foreign workers presents a way for business to obtain cheap labor. Employers seek to maximize profits and minimize costs. With a larger labor supply, the demand for jobs rises, which tends to depress wages—one of the employer's most significant costs. When jobs go unfilled due to the presence of fewer people in the labor market, wages and benefits rise in order to attract workers. Policymakers who are closely aligned politically with labor unions argue that employment-related foreign workers take jobs away from American workers and drive down their wage rates. These political leaders harbor a deep distrust of business management and regard many business decisions as detrimental to the working conditions and living standards of U.S. workers. Generally, the legislators who have favored restricting employment-based immigration have been close political bedfellows with labor unions.

The policy question here is whether the national interest in maintaining economic competitiveness outweighs the prospect of potentially displacing certain segments of the American workforce. Some believe that certain workers lack the skills or education to retool and set out in new directions dictated by technological advances in production (CIR Report 1995). Skilled workers must be brought in from the outside because the cost of retraining unskilled domestic workers is just too high.

The magnitude of any threat of foreign workers to the native born ought to be explored in determining the answer to this policy question. It is naive to think that every immigrant deprives a citizen of a job. The 1995 U. S. Commission on Immigration Reform Report stated, "The magnitude of natives' job displacement from legal immigration are [sic], again, not well established from empirical data, but the weight of evidence implies that real and significant costs can take place in local labor markets" (CIR Report 1995, 29).

Nevertheless, the case can be made that the nation has a higher duty to protect its native-born workers from displacement than to provide jobs for noncitizens. Americans should be given the opportunity of job training or education so that they might adjust to shifts in the economy, that they might compete for the new jobs being created in related—or other—fields as their jobs disappear in the wake of economic progress. An analogy might be that while society enjoys a net gain switching from whale oil lamps to electric lights, the American whale fishermen whose jobs just disappeared should get the first opportunity to retrain as electrical technicians instead of allowing a crop of foreign electricians to get the jobs in the hot new growth industry. Policymakers must weigh the moral imperatives, the duty of a nation to its citizens, in just these kinds of changing economic conditions.

A policy option implemented by the 1965 Act seeks to balance the interests of native-born workers and American business interests. This is a *labor certification* requirement. Certain employment-based immigrants and temporary nonimmigrant workers must obtain the Secretary of Labor's certification that not enough U.S. workers are available to fill particular employment needs. The secretary must also declare that the foreign workers' admission and employment will not adversely affect the wages and working conditions of similarly employed American workers (*INS Statistical Yearbook* 1996). Abrams and Abrams (1975) cited two key shortcomings of the labor certification program: family-based immigrants, who comprise the largest proportion of immigrants, are not subject to labor certification, and therefore constitute a significant labor pool without regard to skills or impact; and labor-certified immigrants may change jobs or careers once in the United States. Of course, one policy option is to extend labor certification to family-based visa applicants. If the goal is to protect American workers, this choice should be seriously considered. If, however, family reunification is determined to outweigh the family members' impact on the national labor market (apparently the prevailing mood), then labor certification should remain limited.

Agricultural Workers

Policymakers have recognized that many agricultural employers require temporary workers to help plant and harvest their crops in season. The need for migrant farm workers is especially great in California. From the beginning of World War II as American recruits answered Uncle Sam's call as soldiers until 1964, the *Bracero* program allowed the entry of between four and five million temporary foreign agricultural workers, principally from Mexico, to fill the farm labor shortage (*Immigration and Nationality Act 1995*). Since the termination of the *Bracero* program, some farmers have relied on illegal aliens to harvest produce each season. The policy question is how to balance the labor needs of agriculture against the interest of the nation in controlling the border and upholding the law.

The agricultural workers issue becomes complicated by the low-skill and temporary nature of much agricultural work (Martin 1996). The work is labor-intensive, hard, and menial. These jobs pay low wages and do not include fringe benefits. Some agribusinesses have exploited the unskilled laborers, realizing that their illegal status makes them vulnerable. Many illegals cannot speak English and are unaware of even their most basic rights under U.S. labor laws. Because they are here illegally, they may fear taking legal action against exploitative work practices. Labor unions are perplexed about illegal immigration. On the one hand, these illegal workers, once legalized, would be ideal fodder for union-building efforts. Indeed, the AFL-CIO's membership has undergone significant demographic change as the ranks of blue-collar labor have increasingly been filled with immigrants from Asia and Latin America. On the other hand, most illegal immigrants are reluctant to pay attention to union organizers precisely because they are illegal and fear being discovered.

In the face of these problems, Congress has sought ways to control illegal immigration, yet provide an agricultural workforce. The policy options fall into two categories: law enforcement and a tightly regulated influx of foreign farm labor. Law enforcement challenges include such issues as cracking down on smugglers who help illegals to cross the border, document fraud (bogus Social Security cards and numbers), the presence and apprehension of undocumented workers, deportation of illegals, and border interdiction efforts. Employers could be sanctioned or fined for knowingly hiring illegal residents.

Regulating the flow of needed laborers touches issues such as the admission of temporary or permanent agricultural workers. Labor-related matters also come into play, such as the appropriate wage rate for these workers as well as the regulation of their hours and working conditions.

One policy option would be to allow undocumented workers to freely cross the border. However, this would seriously call into question any hope of controlling the flow of illegal entrants. Another option would be to admit aliens through a nonimmigrant visa program, with a class of visas dedicated to agricultural needs (see *INS Statistical Yearbook* 1996). These are also known as *guest-worker* programs. Yet another option would admit permanently immigrants for the purpose of performing farm labor, which strikes some as amounting to little more than importing indentured servants or slave laborers.

Whether the foreign-born enter as guest workers or as immigrants, it is important that the employer establish the need for laborers from outside the country. That is, policymakers must decide whether employers should be required to demonstrate that not enough native workers are available to fill the available positions. Such a determination could come through either labor certification, as discussed earlier, or by attestation of the employer. The tough part is balancing protection of American workers with the needs of the farmer to harvest his crop on time.

On one side, ethnic advocacy groups decry the exploitation of undocumented workers. Labor unions charge that foreigners displace native-born workers and provide a source of cheap labor. On the other side, agricultural employers complain that Americans will not take the jobs, which involve long, hot days and relatively low wages. They complain that current temporary worker programs are cumbersome—that the government has erected barriers too high to obtain legitimate guest workers on time and that many of their workers are illegal aliens but are using counterfeit documentation that is so well copied it is difficult to verify work eligibility without going to heroic efforts. Congress faces a messy set of circumstances, and advocates on all sides will struggle with the issue of farm labor for years to come.

Refugees

Admitting refugees and granting asylum are humanitarian gestures. These immigration categories have a long tradition in the United States. They represent means for aiding and relieving persecuted peoples from around the world based on changing political and economic conditions. Allowing refugees to enter a country and escape conditions at home is a privilege extended by the host country; it is not an individual's right to force himself on a nation where he desires to settle. Refugee admission may be either temporary or permanent, depending on the laws of the host country.

Refugees are those who are found to be fleeing persecution or to have a well-founded fear of persecution because of their race, religion, nationality, membership in a particular social group, or political opinion (*Immigration and Nationality Act* 1995; *INS Statistical Yearbook* 1996). Refugees are processed from abroad (Vialet 12/3/96). They must seek admission into the United States, and the decision to grant admission rests solely with the host country. Refugees have included those who fear persecution in situations of "special humanitarian concern" to America, such as fleeing communism. Refugee admission decisions are sometimes related to U.S. foreign policy goals. For example, one Cold War policy priority was to contain communist expansion. The United States therefore adopted refugee policies favorable toward those escaping communism in Cuba, Eastern Europe, and the Soviet Union. During the 1980s, as U.S. foreign policy supported the insurgent Nicaraguan Contras in their fight against the Sandinista regime, the United States admitted thousands of escaping Nicaraguan refugees. The traditional practice in U.S. law has been to allow the president to set annual refugee admission levels in consultation with Congress. Refugee admissions may be adjusted to respond to emergency situations.

The policy decisions relating to refugee entry frequently involve the volume of refugee admissions and the extent of resettlement assistance offered to this special class of immigrants. How many refugees should the U.S. admit? Should fixed limits be set on refugee admissions, or should admission levels be flexible year to year? What should the process be for determining admission levels; to what degree should Congress and the president each be involved? Some have argued that refugee admission should be permanent provided the refugees' desire to remain in the country. Others suggest that refugee admission should be strictly temporary—until the threatening conditions in the home country have subsided.

Some insist that the United States should allow for a steady flow of refugees who may be fleeing for a broad range of economic and political reasons, as well as retain the flexibility to respond to emergency situations. This policy preference is based on the belief that the United States, as a land of freedom and opportunity, should provide a haven of rest to all the oppressed of the world. Some holding this position seem almost apologetic for the blessings America has enjoyed and the wealth Americans have created through their ingenuity and effort. Others may bear a deep conviction of caring for the needs of the afflicted, often from a religious motivation.

Another, more restrictive view supports admitting only those refugees who are escaping persecution in a situation of special humanitarian concern to the United States. For instance, in the wake of the Vietnam War many believed the United States bore a special responsibility toward Vietnamese refugees.

Still another option concerning refugee policy would involve routing refugees to safe third countries as a first resort rather than admitting them directly into the United States. The rationale for such a proposal is that other nations also have a humanitarian duty to fulfill. U.S. refugee admissions have historically been higher than those of virtually every other nation, and America ought to have company in the effort to help refugees.

The length of time refugees are permitted to stay in the host country is also a matter of debate. Length of stay may be based on the home-country situation that precipitated the person's becoming a refugee. That is, the policy may admit a certain number of refugees, giving them a place of respite until the conditions in their home country are again normal. Then the refugees would return home. Alternatively, the admission could be more open-ended. Once refugees gained admission into the United States, if after a specified period of time things had not settled down at home, the refugees could adjust their status to that of a permanent resident. Such permanent admissions might result from the seemingly permanent or at least long-term home country situation, such as the expansion of Soviet influence in Eastern Europe following World War II.

Major disputes have also arisen on the issue of refugee resettlement. Some argue that the federal government should provide public assistance to help assist refugees in their adjustment to a new way of life, to help them get their feet on the ground. This policy position is founded on the rationale that refugees are fleeing their homes and homelands with very few material possessions. It also follows the logic of granting legal resident status. Instead of expecting refugees to gain admission and then be left on their own, advocates of this view argue that the country's humanitarian duty extends beyond merely admitting refugees to meeting some of their material needs.

Other policy considerations related to refugee resettlement include whether the resettlement costs are paid principally from public funds or from private funds. Refugee policy is a government policy, but the extent to which taxpayer funds should be used to fund resettlement is a controversial matter. It may be argued that the private sector—especially churches and philanthropic, charitable organizations—are best equipped to meet these needs; thus, the policy should be more focused on removing government obstacles to private assistance and perhaps even adopting policies that encourage private efforts, such as giving tax credits for individual and corporate contributions to organizations involved in resettlement.

Similarly, the length of time refugees should remain on public assistance is a resettlement-related question. On one hand, it may be argued that a certain level of public welfare assistance is proper in order to resettle refugees. On the other hand, some lawmakers may be concerned about the unintended consequence of nurturing dependency if the welfare benefits continue for too long. It is easy to see how this crosses paths with other policy questions, such as terms and length of refugee stay, immigrant status, and the number of refugees admitted in a given year.

Asylum Policy

An asylum is a sanctuary or a place of refuge. *Asylum* in immigration law is an immigrant status granted to certain refugees either who have been previously admitted into the country or who arrive at a port of entry. Asylum status is awarded on a case-by-case basis. The person seeking asylum must meet the definition of refugee within the meaning of the law. That means the asylum seeker must seek protection from persecution or have a well-founded fear of persecution on the same grounds as a refugee.

Because of the circumstances under which refugees and asylees come to the United States, they have often benefited from generous public assistance. That is, refugees and asylees have received more government benefits upon admission than other categories of immigrants.

A number of key issues related to asylum have arisen in recent years. We will consider three here. First, should those arriving without documents or with fraudulent documents and no credible asylum claim receive the same level of due process as those who can demonstrate a well-founded fear of persecution? Second, should restrictions be placed on asylum seekers? In other words, what should the process be for adjudicating asylum claims? Most notably, restrictions might shorten the period for filing an asylum claim and send asylum seekers to other countries where they would not face persecution. Third, should asylum be allowed on the basis of fleeing coercive population control policies? Essentially, this question involves mainland Chinese who face persecution due to their opposition to forced abortion or forced sterilization policies at home.

Regarding documentation, foreigners who arrive at the United States border or at a port of entry must possess passports and visas or other valid documentation—attesting that the entering person is legally eligible to enter the country. The foreign-born must undergo inspection by immigration authorities to ensure they have proper documents or that the alien qualifies as a refugee or asylee. Those seeking entry without documents or a credible asylum case may be detained and held in custody.

Some seek entry using fraudulent documents. There may be good reason to use fraudulent documents, such as the quite real possibility that secret police back home would whisk the individual away in the middle of the night if the previous afternoon the person was observed entering the U.S. embassy and going through the normal process of visiting with the consular officer and obtaining a valid visa. People flee their homeland due to coups or other sudden, threatening changes. However, presenting fraudulent documents and making a case for fleeing persecution differs markedly from presenting fraudulent documents and simply desiring to settle in the United States.

Other foreigners enter the country without entry documents, walking across the border or securing the services of an alien smuggler. These illegal entrants can buy false documents on the street once inside the country. How to ensure the validity of immigration documents is a problem that will not be easily solved. Proposed solutions have ranged from increasing the penalties for trafficking in fraudulent documentation, to limiting the number of documents issued or accepted, to making the documents harder to reproduce illicitly.

The processes for dealing with "excludable" and "deportable" aliens may differ under the law (deportation is covered later). Excludable aliens would be those denied entry. A process for quickly determining whether such an arriving alien is excludable has been considered and is known as *summary exclusion*. Under a summary exclusion process, these aliens have fewer due process rights than deportable aliens. The reason for this difference would be that aliens already having entered the country are generally considered to have passed an initial inspection and are presumably admissible. Excludable aliens may be considered as not "present" in the United States—that is, they haven't been admitted officially.

A key issue has become, how much due process are excludable aliens constitutionally due? And if these aliens have not technically "entered" the country, may appeals of immigration inspectors' decisions regarding their cases be tied up in court? Policymakers may argue that because excludable aliens have never been admitted, they have no or very limited constitutional rights. These aliens, no matter what grounds they claim for wanting to enter, have no right to enter, so they should not be able to tie up U. S. courts in lengthy appeals processes. Others may argue that, because of America's humanitarian tradition and ideals of liberty, opportunity, and justice, every individual should have a right to a full hearing and full, or at least broad, access to the judiciary.

A related matter involves false asylum claims. The asylum system has been subject to abuse. False applications have glutted a backlogged system, which has granted work authorization to most asylum seekers upon application for asylum status even though their cases may not be heard for years (INS 2/97). Many people have filed false applications in order to obtain the work authorization. False applicants have enjoyed rights to the full appeals process. The glut of asylum claims and the lack of punishment for filing false applications have served to keep those with valid claims at risk, while allowing the unscrupulous to game the system.

One point of view is that it is better to extend the benefit of the doubt and thus grant full rights to all aliens, regardless of the apparent merits of their case, than to chance sending anyone home to face persecution. In other words, this is the same argument used in connection with capital punishment—that it is better to let a thousand guilty men go free than to execute one innocent man. Those holding this position in the context of immigration policy would support a more involved process with more layers of appeals so that valid asylum claims would not slip through a more streamlined administrative process.

Other policymakers hold a view that seeks to balance interests—those of asylees, taxpayers, and the national interest in having a credible asylum process that is not a laughingstock and openly exploited for illicit purposes. This position would favor a streamlined asylum process to ensure that asylum claims are weighed in a timely manner. It would perhaps support a limited process of appealing decisions against the applicant. This is based on the view that aliens whose cases fail at the initial hearing stage probably do not have valid claims. This view also might advocate penalties for filing false asylum applications or withholding work authorization until a later time.

With regard to asylum for those facing population control policies in their home countries, the question has been whether to grant asylum on this basis. The People's Republic of China, a communist regime, has been the most notorious enforcer of coercive and cruel population control policies, though it is hardly alone in the world. The United States has to decide whether to allow aliens to make asylum claims on the basis of fleeing persecution associated with these harsh policies. Policymakers favoring the addition of this ground would add it to the list of reasons refugees and asylees are fleeing persecution or harboring a well-founded fear of persecution. Their argument rests on the principle of the inherent right of self-determination, including the right of parents to have children—this is not and should not be a government decision. The right to form a family is regarded as a fundamental human right by these policymakers. Forcing abortion, imposing sterilization, or adopting any other coercive population control measure is deemed a violation of human rights. Therefore, people fleeing persecution because of their opposition to such policies should be considered refugees and made eligible for asylum. In other words, these population policies are inherently illegitimate, so fleeing from persecution on this basis is no different from fleeing persecution due to religion or nationality.

Opponents to this addition note the abuses of asylum laws and thus fear giving unscrupulous aliens any more opportunities to exploit the system. They argue that this ground for asylum gives an incentive to millions of Chinese and others to take the chance to reach the United States and file an asylum claim. Given the backlog in the system and the instant work authorization that is granted while claims await adjudication, millions more aliens could clog the nation's already strained immigration system, even if many of the individuals held no personal convictions opposing their nation's coercive population control policies and had faced no persecution personally.

Diversity Visas

The pre-1965 national origins law favored immigration from countries in Northern and Western Europe. This changed markedly with the 1965 law repealing the national origins system. In the late 1980s, some members of Congress began to worry that a type of unintended "reverse discrimination" was occurring. Repeal of the national origins system opened up immigration to Asian nations for the first time. As the pie charts in Chapter 1 indicated, Europeans constituted a distinct minority of new arrivals in the 1980s and 1990s. In order to ensure a higher level of immigration from those nations "adversely affected" by the change in policy in 1965, some legislators favored creating a program to set aside a certain number of immigration visas for these countries. Such a program would diversify the mix of yearly immigrants, making it more European than it had been in the years since 1965.

The reason the 1965 law had an adverse impact on European immigration was that new priorities were set in place dictating that family reunification would be the cornerstone of immigration admissions. With the rise of chain migration from other parts of the world and the absence of the required family ties to the United States, the Northern and Western Europeans lost standing under the new law (CIR Report 1994).

Those advocating a diversity visa program complained that the 1965 law resulted in this unintended consequence and that it would only be fair to the nations that traditionally sent immigrants to set aside a certain number of visas for them. They pointed out that the country benefits from a diverse immigrant population that includes Caucasians, not just Asians and mixed race Hispanics. Opponents of this new program responded that the people coming to the United States ought to have close family ties—that family reunification remains the guiding principle in immigration policy—or essential job skills. They are less impressed with the diversity argument and instead favor limiting immigration to the three primary grounds for granting permanent admission.

Public Benefits for Legal Residents

When a U.S. citizen or permanent resident alien petitions for a family member to receive a family-sponsored immigrant visa, the sponsor must pledge that the prospective immigrant will not become a *public charge*. A public charge is anyone who cannot provide for himself or herself and has no one to provide support, and thus must depend on government assistance programs to survive. Immigrants who become public charges may be deported.

The public charge doctrine has been part of American immigration law for more than a century. It is intended to ensure that those admitted as immigrants contribute to rather than burden society. Nevertheless, even honest, hardworking immigrants may experience life's trials through no fault of their own. For instance, a drunk driver might strike any pedestrian at random, permanently disabling that person. This could happen to citizen or immigrant alike. In such instances, it is arguable that the welfare "safety net" should be equally available to legal residents. Beyond that, some argue that permanent residents pay taxes and even fight wars as members of the U.S. military and, therefore, that legal residents should qualify for public benefits on a par with U.S. citizens.

Others see abuses of the welfare system by recent immigrants. They note huge increases in immigrant use of public benefits. They believe access should be limited because of the strain on taxpayers and the fact that recent immigrants have not contributed to the system—particularly elderly parents of newly arrived immigrants. To illustrate their rise in welfare participation, immigrants represented 3 percent of the Supplemental Security Income (SSI) caseload in 1982. This had increased to 12 percent by 1993 (CIR Report 1994). The aged portion of the SSI caseload rose from 6 percent to 28 percent over that same period. Only a fourth of legal immigrants on SSI were refugees and asylees. Three-fourths were likely to have citizen or permanent resident sponsors. One-third enrolled in the program in the year after the sponsor's legal responsibility to provide for them had ended (CIR Report 1994). Further, in 1997, a National Academy of Sciences study found that immigrant-headed households are poorer than native households and receive more government-funded income transfers (Smith and Edmonston 1997, 6–30).

These figures are taken as evidence that contemporary immigrants are more likely than immigrants of the past to participate in welfare programs. Concerned legislators see a link between current immigration policy, especially family reunification and the escalation of chain migration patterns, and the growth of public assistance programs. They believe that immigrant sponsors increasingly fail to fulfill the financial obligations they freely took on in order to reunify their families. Policymakers on this side of the issue argue that, just as welfare for natives has engendered a culture of dependency and sloth, so immigrant sponsors manipulate American immigration policy to take advantage of the nation's generosity. Sponsors increasingly have turned the welfare safety net into a retirement program for the elderly and disabled of the world, all at taxpayer expense—and this has occurred precisely by the dereliction of the sponsor's pledged obligations to keep immigrants from becoming public charges.

Two primary issues related to sponsor responsibility have developed in recent years: first, sponsor-to-alien "deeming," and second, sponsor affidavits of support. Both matters have to do with ensuring that immigrants not become public charges and that sponsors be held accountable for fulfilling their commitments.

Deeming refers to accounting for the combined incomes of both sponsor and alien for purposes of determining the alien's eligibility for means-tested public assistance programs. That is, in order to qualify for a means-tested benefit, the income of the sponsor is "deemed" to be available to the alien, as pledged in the affidavit of support. Deeming is designed to ensure that admitted aliens won't become public charges.

The principal issue related to deeming involves the level of income an individual must earn in order to qualify as a sponsor. The question has become how much sponsor income is sufficient. Those advocating liberal immigration levels believe sponsor income requirements should be low enough that all have an opportunity to petition for a relative and reunite their families. Those supporting sponsor responsibility and strong measures to avert public dependency believe the sponsor income should be higher in order to help reverse the trend toward immigrant welfare enrollment and to enforce sponsor obligations. They determine that protecting taxpayers out-weighs the privilege of sponsoring immigrants.

An *affidavit of support* is simply the sponsor's pledge to provide for the new immigrant. In the past, these documents have not been legally binding. If the sponsor failed to fulfill the responsibilities agreed to, this pledge was unenforceable and the sponsor could not be sanctioned. Who is eligible to sign an affidavit of support has developed into an issue, as well as what the affidavit's contents should be. Open immigration advocates argue that family reunification outweighs the concern of who pays for the well-being of immi-grants. They would let individuals with more distant relations sign affidavits and would be less concerned with the enforceability of the document. Those favoring stricter ties between immigrant and sponsor seek to uphold the pub-lic charge doctrine and protect taxpayers. They believe sponsors should bear the primary responsibility for the immigrant's they pledged to care for. Ful-filling a pledge of support is a matter of integrity and honor.

Nonimmigrant Visas

Whereas immigrants are admitted for permanent U.S. residence, nonimmi-grants are temporarily admitted as visitors. Nonimmigrant visas are granted to officials of foreign governments, students, exchange visitors, and temporary workers, for example (Vialet and Forman 7/23/96; *INS Statistical Yearbook* 1996).

No numerical restrictions are placed on annual nonimmigrant admis-sions (*INS Statistical Yearbook* 1996). However, the terms of nonimmigrant admission are regulated concerning grounds for coming, length of stay, and travel and employment restrictions. Most nonimmigrants are expected to return home at the end of their visa term.

One policy issue related to nonimmigrants involves the admission of temporary workers (see the previous discussion on agricultural workers). Concerns are voiced about the possible displacement of native workers by foreign hires. On one side, policymakers favor the admission of the very best, most talented individuals in the world. This view is premised on giving the

United States a competitive edge. It upholds the free market as the means of raising the most talented and determined to the top. Every individual has an equal opportunity to compete, regardless of station in life or nation of origin. Further, businesses claim that they find it hard to fill certain low-skill jobs and need people who are willing to perform these menial but important tasks. Businesses report difficulty finding Americans who are willing to do menial labor or to work for low wages, particularly in some locations.

The opposite position holds that U.S. workers should be protected in their jobs. Businesses should not be allowed to fire an American and hire a temporary foreign worker in his or her place. It would place a hurdle before foreign workers who might perform jobs currently held by Americans. It would place burdens of proof on businesses that might prefer to replace American workers, whether from the motive of tapping the world's talent pool or from the motive of driving down wages and sacrificing native employees on the altar of the bottom line.

Another issue concerning nonimmigrants is related to illegal immigration. This is the situation known as *visa overstay*. Some estimate that half the problem of illegal immigration results from visa overstays—those who enter the country with a perfectly legal but temporary visa but who then stay in the country beyond the visa expiration date (Congressional Task Force Report 1995). Their status under the law makes these aliens as illegally present as someone who illicitly crossed the border or stowed away in a boat or airplane.

Couple the fact that these illegal immigrants arrived legally with the incredible difficulty of tracking them down, and the solution to this problem is elusive. The policy options range from searching them out with law enforcement personnel, to raising the priority for deporting overstayers, to restricting the issuance of visas that go to visitors from countries and in admissions categories that tend to overstay.

This issue of preventing visa overstays raises civil rights, privacy, and law enforcement concerns. Civil libertarians fear that severe measures to catch visa overstayers will move the country toward a police state, invade the privacy of legal nonimmigrants and others, and increase discrimination against anyone who appears or sounds foreign. At the same time, Congress recognizes that visa overstayers in effect thumb their noses at U.S. law: The law is only as good as its enforcement. Therefore, prevention, deterrence, apprehension, and punishment relating to visa overstays become a matter of restoring credibility to the underlying policy.

Deportation

Deportation is the removal of an immigrant from the United States. Immigrants may be deported for a number of offenses, such as dealing drugs, committing certain crimes, or becoming a public charge (*Immigration and Nationality Act* 1995). Deportation rules apply to those who have entered the country (as opposed to exclusion, previously discussed). Under deportation procedures, immigrants have enjoyed greater due process rights than those apprehended at the border or port of entry and turned away under exclusion rules.

The deportation system has come under heavy criticism as granting immigrants excessive due process and, perhaps even worse, as being inefficient. Many aliens against whom the INS has entered into deportation proceedings never show up for their hearings, and those judged to be deportable often never leave the country. Such a loose system encourages contempt for the process and undermines the laws the process is supposed to uphold. The policy issues include whether or how much to streamline the deportation process, whether or how to restructure the process, and the degree to which courts may review deportation decisions, which are administrative in nature.

On the matter of whether and how to expedite or restructure the process, one view holds that because deportation is an aspect of administering immigration policy, noncitizens have more limited rights than do citizens. Therefore, policy options that would change the process seek to speed the time for adjudicating cases, reduce the ways in which the alien can game the system, and limit court jurisdiction to review the immigration judge's decision to issue an order of deportation. Others argue that because immigrants have been admitted into the country, they should have a greater range of rights extended to them. They may argue that the 14th Amendment to the Constitution requires equal treatment of citizens and noncitizens under the law (although citizens cannot be deported). Opponents of such changes put deportation proceedings almost on a par with a criminal trial; they favor high hurdles for the government to win a removal. Policymakers holding this view also tend to hold civil libertarian positions. Policymakers seeking to streamline the deportation process tend to hold stronger law enforcement views.

Aliens with criminal histories or who commit certain crimes are subject to deportation. Congress has steadily expanded the offenses for which an alien may be deported, which include drug and firearms offenses, espionage, document fraud, and terrorism. Each of these is a policy decision.

Nobody believes that dangerous criminal aliens should remain in the country. The question becomes how much due process criminal aliens are due. Liberal immigration advocates argue that aliens, regardless of their status as criminals, deserve broad due process rights—much along the lines of criminal court proceedings, complete with thorough judicial review of the deportation decision, as mentioned before. Others argue that criminal aliens pose a threat to the public, they aren't U.S. citizens, and thus the government should be able to deport them expeditiously.

Illegal Immigration

Illegal presence in the United States is not condoned by government authorities, although efforts to put a halt to it have varied in their intensity. Still, it is generally considered indefensible. No credible policy player defends criminal conduct. The policy issues, therefore, revolve around how best to deter illegal immigration in a manner consistent with the important political values of freedom and due process. For example, illegal border crossings could be virtually stopped by militarizing the border, laying down fields of land mines, and manning machine-gun nests along the border. Border Patrol agents could be ordered to shoot illegal entrants on sight. But besides the foreign policy issues this would raise, the American public would not support such extreme measures.

In 1981, the Select Commission on Immigration and Refugee Policy, known as the Hesburgh Commission, concluded that, in order to continue immigration policies that serve the national interest, the "back door" of illegal migration should be shut so legal immigrants could come through the "front door." The key to locking the back door, the commission said, was to demagnetize the "job magnet." That is, the commission determined that the attraction of jobs drew aliens into the country illegally. This report set the stage for the 1986 immigration bill, which focused partly on imposing penalties on employers who hire illegal immigrants. A number of employment and enforcement issues flow from the Hesburgh Commission's framework for dealing with illegal aliens.

Clearly among the first things the public considers when the subject of illegal immigration arises is border enforcement. If government agents can turn away would-be illegal entrants at the border or ports of entry, taxpayers are saved the costs of tracking down, prosecuting, and deporting illegal aliens after they have entered the country.

Border Patrol personnel, barriers such as fences, and cracking alien smuggling rings all receive strong popular and political support. The nation's war on drugs has enjoyed public support, as well, and is closely associated with illegal immigration because large quantities of illicit drugs, including cocaine and heroine, are smuggled into the U.S. via the Mexican border. The challenge of border enforcement stems from the sheer size of the U.S. border. The U.S.–Mexican border alone stretches 2,000 miles. And the U.S. Border Patrol is responsible for policing 8,000 miles of border and 200 ports of entry. Of course, a much smaller proportion of the land border is practicably passable.

An additional complication is that a sizeable number of nonimmigrants live in Mexico and work in the United States legally. Many of them drive across the border at key crossing points. Consider also that vast miles of border are desolate. And remember that the U.S. Border Patrol had only about 4,000 officers in the field in the early 1990s. Immigrant smugglers and drug traffickers know that the terrain, the remoteness, and the vastness of the border are on their side; the odds of successfully entering the United States undetected are on the side of the illicit crossers. It is easy to understand why the back door remains ajar.

The issue with respect to deterrence is how to allocate human and other resources effectively in order to stem the tide of illegal border crossings. Policy options relating to border enforcement range from increasing Border Patrol personnel and its resources, to coordinating efforts among law enforcement agencies, to mandatory penalties for illegal entry, to mandatory prosecution for illegal immigrants who reenter the country, to making alien smuggling a racketeering offense under federal law (Congressional Task Force Report 1995; CIR Report 1994). Again, the debate rages over the extent of enforcement action.

Then there are the millions of illegal aliens already present in the United States. Some of these illegal residents have been present for years. One controversial policy option is to grant amnesty to those illegal aliens present in the United States who would come forward and file for legal permanent-resident status. The effect of such a legalization program on present illegal aliens, prospective illegal aliens and the nation has to be taken into account. The impact of three million suddenly legal aliens—such as the sheer paperwork and manpower costs to process these people—would profoundly affect the states and localities, as well as cost the taxpayer. Policymakers must consider this impact. Will an amnesty set a precedent and send a strong signal to those considering illegally entering America? If the U.S. Congress granted three million illegal aliens amnesty once, it may well do it again, would-be illegal entrants might reason. Therefore, it's worth the risk to cross the border— once in, you may well get away with it and be able to stay, even eventually receiving the blessing of the U.S. government.

Another policy option is to hunt the illegal residents down and undertake a massive deportation effort. This would be quite costly, and the public may not want massive regiments of INS enforcement officers searching for illegals in every neighborhood. Instead, policymakers might set priorities for the categories of illegal aliens that should face deportation. This policy choice has the advantage of upholding the law without turning the country into a police state. Yet another policy option entails disregarding the illegal residents with established ties in the country, doing nothing. This policy recognizes the roots these out-of-status aliens have put down, that many of them otherwise abide by the laws, and that many contribute to the nation's economy, albeit the underground economy. Acceptance of the status quo focuses deportation efforts on the worst cases and allocates resources to other priorities, perhaps border interdiction efforts.

Employer Sanctions

Many migrants enter the country illegally for one reason: to find work. If American jobs create an incentive for aliens to sneak into the United States, then impunity for hiring illegal aliens fails to give employers an incentive to hire native-born or legal immigrant workers. One policy option is to impose penalties on employers who hire illegals. Such actions are what is meant by the term, *employer sanctions*. Worksite enforcement may entail immigration agent's raiding suspect workplaces and rounding up the undocumented workers for deportation. If employer sanctions are enacted, then employers who knowingly hire unauthorized workers face fines and perhaps even jail time.

Should employers face sanctions as a deterrent to hiring illegal aliens? Some policymakers have supported employer sanctions in order to achieve a sense of fairness or balance by placing some responsibility on employers. They do not think illegal workers should bear the full responsibility or the brunt of consequences, while their employers get away without being penalized. These policymakers argue that employers have a duty to screen their workforces. Many have decried the exploitation of illegal immigrant labor. The practice of employing low-wage workers in squalid sweatshop conditions is surprisingly common in certain low-profit-margin businesses. The illegitimate employers routinely dodge wage and labor laws because they know the illegal workers they employ will not go to the authorities out of fear of being discovered and deported. The insularity of some immigrant communities makes labor exploitation possible. Many new arrivals are vulnerable to exploitation because they cannot speak English. They are dependent upon their employers to relate everything going on around them because only the employers are bilingual. Since employers have most of the bargaining power in the relationship, employers should be penalized for attracting the unlawful workers in the first place.

The policymakers opposed to employer sanctions have argued that any process for screening employees can be beaten. They point out that, in many parts of the country and in certain industries, illegals are not even likely to apply for work. Therefore, it would be an overreaction to require every single employer in America to screen documents in order to keep from hiring illegal residents. Such measures would cost every employer time and effort to comply with the bureaucratic paperwork. In other words, the costs of these requirements far outweigh the benefits in terms of illegal aliens deterred or caught, and they undermine the competitiveness of U.S. businesses. Furthermore, such requirements turn private citizens into police agents—every employer hereby becomes an INS agent and is forced to do the job of the INS. Opponents of sanctions argue that the federal agency should do a better job of keeping illegal workers out of the country in the first place, rather than forcibly requiring every employer to be a part-time government agent. Civil libertarians have expressed concerns about the loss of liberty associated with employer sanctions policies. They fear that such a policy represents a step toward an authoritarian police state, where informants cooperate with police agents.

Beyond the question of whether to adopt employer sanctions policies lie a number of policy options that relate to worksite enforcement of immigration laws. Many argue that some method of verifying the work eligibility of job applicants must be devised. This raises the issue of document verification (covered in the next section). Another option is to send agents regularly to inspect workplaces and enforce the sanctions; this could be joined with enforcement of labor standards. Yet another option would prioritize enforcement efforts against employers and business sectors known to hire illegal workers. Criminal penalties for such activities and stiffer penalties for flagrant conduct could be adopted (Congressional Task Force Report 1995; CIR Report 1994; *Immigration and Nationality Act* 1995).

Employment Verification

In order to ensure a job applicant's eligibility to work in the United States, an *employment verification* system must be established. The idea of such a system is to provide employers a surefire way of determining whether applicants are being truthful about their work eligibility. Naturally, an employment verification system may place additional paperwork burdens on businesses. Employers may be required to maintain records on each employee's work eligibility. Alternatively, a verification system may use government agents to perform the check.

The immigration issues surrounding employment verification involve whether to implement an employment verification requirement, what the verification system will require and the process for verifying eligibility, to what degree employers should have discretion in the verification process, how the integrity of documentation should be ensured, and whether a national identification card is needed. A host of thorny problems appears at every juncture, mostly pertaining to discriminatory practices, privacy, and claims of liberty over law enforcement.

Assuming that policymakers adopt some requirement to check employment eligibility, every boss in the country may have to check every new hire's documents. Otherwise, immigration agents would need to be present in every business to process new hires. A third alternative would require every person hired to appear at a government office and verify his or her employment eligibility in person. This latter requirement would apply not only to those hired for their first job, but to everyone changing jobs. The argument for having employers perform the process of verification claims that this method would put the onus on those subject to sanctions for hiring illegal workers. It would give law enforcement additional grounds for prosecution of violators. If an employer hires an unauthorized worker, the government's case is stronger if the employer was supposed to check the new hire's identification documents and complete paperwork on the employee. Also, having the millions of U.S. employers share the workload would spread the costs more widely than hiring hundreds or thousands of additional enforcement agents to do the checking.

Those arguing against requiring employers to verify work authorization claim that the costs imposed by such a regulation would undercut U.S. competitiveness. It could cost small businesses operating on narrow profit margins their very existence. For larger businesses, the cost of compliance would also come at the cost of other investment opportunities, including investment in new job creation. Again, such a requirement would effectively turn every employer into a government agent, enforcing immigration laws that the authorities should be carrying out. And depending on the complexity of the regulations, employment verification requirements could easily trip up employers in honest mistakes that lead to sanctions that sully these people's reputations. It would expose employers to lawsuits or prosecution for honest mistakes.

Relying upon immigration agents to perform the verification could entail either officers going to job sites or having new employees go to government offices. Either way, additional government personnel are needed. Either more tax dollars must be allocated to this effort, or employers or employees must pay a fee or hidden tax to cover the costs. Having agents visit job locations would be labor intensive and perhaps disrupt the workplace. Having new hires appear at a government office would take these employees away from their new jobs, disrupting their training. It also imposes logistical challenges, depending on where the closest immigration officers may be stationed in relation to each store and plant and office in the country. And if the employee in fact is illegal in status, the employee could circumvent the process and lie to the employer. It would be wrong to sanction an employer who gave his new employee time off and directions to the INS office, only to have the undocumented worker mislead the employer, who would think all along that the worker had complied with the requirements of the law.

A more promising means of verifying employment authorization would entail the use of technology—the telephone or the computer. Advocates say a system that allows employers to place a telephone call and the government operator to check employee information against a computer database would cut time, costs, and inconvenience. They argue that a national computer verification system would yield accurate results quickly. Opponents say such a system would certainly contain clerical errors, thus leading to wrongful treatment of innocent, law-abiding individuals. They also point to the potential for invasions of privacy and the threat to individual liberty posed by having a central government computer record of every single American worker. Such a system raises the spectre of Orwell's Big Brother.

Two things would need to be checked by any complete work eligibility verification system: (1) that the person hired honestly identified herself or himself, and (2) that that person is authorized to work in this country. Policymakers would have to determine the documents acceptable for identification and verification purposes. The documents could range from Social Security cards to driver's licenses to birth certificates to "green cards" to passports.

Some have forcefully argued that employers, instead of going to the trouble of checking the documents of all new employees, would simply refuse to hire anyone who looks or sounds foreign, regardless of his or her legal status. These policymakers, therefore, would argue that a verification system must also be accompanied by new laws imposing penalties for discrimination. To lessen the likelihood of discrimination, the law would have to require verification of every single new hire, rather than allowing employers to pick and choose among new employees as to whose documents should be checked. This regulation may apply equally to the small business owner in a rural American town hiring his long-time family friend or the daughter of a fellow elder at his church as to the Fortune 500 personnel director hiring 25 new employees for various jobs throughout the firm. Congress might prohibit employers from questioning the validity of the documents an employee shows if each document appears valid. Perhaps the policy would prohibit employers from asking for additional documents. Or employers might be given the discretion to request as many documents from the list as it took to satisfy each employer on a case-by-case basis.

Those policymakers most concerned about discrimination would limit the employer's discretion. Additionally, they might seek to give employees strong legal recourse against employers who question the validity of their documents or discriminate against them because of race, ethnicity, or some other immigration-related reason. Policymakers believing that most businesses would comply with the law in good faith would argue that employers are not government agents and therefore should enjoy some discretion in the verification process. They would say that government policy should not criminalize their attempt at compliance with a requirement that is very likely to involve some prudential judgments with respect to discerning the validity of numerous types of documents.

Of course, employment verification and discrimination raise another issue: the validity of documentation. With employers' hands tied as they walk the tightrope with employment verification required on one side and the potential charge of discrimination on the other, some people may profit illicitly by running through the gaps. A huge black market may develop that traffics in fraudulent documents. If the threshold for employment discrimination sanctions is low, a half-decent fake "green card" or birth certificate or Social Security card will become easily attainable on the street. Many of the documents that may be used to verify employment eligibility may be easy to counterfeit, and thus shield illegals from the law.

This added complication means that policymakers have to consider ways to deter document fraud. The policy options here include limiting the range of documents that will satisfy the document-checking requirement; setting standards for documents that would make it harder to counterfeit them; imposing strict penalties for producing, possessing, using, or trafficking in false documents; and dedicating enforcement resources toward document violations (Congressional Task Force Report 1995; CIR Report 1994; *Immigration and Nationality Act* 1995). Another policy option remains, which is highly controversial: requiring all legal residents and citizens to carry a *national identification card.*

The standardization of acceptable documents or the imposition from the federal level of state-issued document specifications raise questions about federalism. The federal government is constitutionally restrained from becoming entwined in certain areas of jurisdiction reserved to states and localities. Moreover, overreaching by the federal government has sparked renewed commitment to preserving states' rights to set their own policies in countless areas of the law. Any document-related immigration policies must take this constitutional balance into account.

One document-related proposal has been the issuance of a counterfeit-proof Social Security card. Every U.S. citizen and lawful permanent resident receives a Social Security number and card. Proponents of counterfeit-resistant Social Security cards say it makes the most sense to upgrade these cards already possessed by everyone eligible to work. Opponents of the proposal say it moves too close to a national identification card, again jeopardizing individual liberties and representing, again, shades of Orwell's *1984.*

Public Benefits for Illegal Immigrants

Whereas legal immigrants may qualify for certain public benefits, depending on the policies adopted setting qualifying standards and the primacy of sponsorship, illegal aliens have generally been excluded from receipt of public benefits. On this subject, the U.S. Commission on Immigration Reform wrote, "Except in limited circumstances where humanitarian principles prevail, benefits policy should not reward aliens who enter or remain illegally" (CIR Report 1994, 112). Most citizens and legislators would agree with that principle. However, drafting the policy into law is much more complicated.

The complexities originate in the determination of exactly what constitutes humanitarian necessities, as well as cases of so-called "mixed" households. Mixed households have some members who are legally present, either as citizens or legal residents, and some who are illegal aliens (CIR Report 1994). The legal residents are harboring their illegal relatives or providing a hideout for nonrelatives. Determining how to extend eligibility to the legal foreigners who meet the qualifications while keeping the benefits from the illegal residents presents a tough challenge in these cases.

Humanitarian principles, according to the U.S. Commission on Immigration Reform, compel the provision of services in an emergency or to guard public safety and health or to conform with constitutional requirements (CIR Report 1994). Even these instances are debatable when it comes to specific types of assistance.

Some policymakers would regard school lunches, immunizations, housing, and free education as meeting these humanitarian guidelines. These people not only would define humanitarian duty broadly, but also would place the provision of such benefits above law enforcement in importance. Other policymakers would say that illegal residents have no right to any public benefits, but on humanitarian grounds may receive emergency medical treatment en route to deportation proceedings, and a bunk and meals while they are being jailed and punished—just as would any other lawbreaker. Those holding the latter view would equate illegal aliens with others who break the law. These lawbreakers should be punished, which, in the case of illegal residents, generally means detention and deportation.

In the midst of this debate, the provision of public education to illegal residents arises. This issue raises states' rights and federalism issues, concerns about the economic impact of large school-age immigrant populations, and constitutional questions about the separation of powers. Conservatives and strict constitutionalists have long decried the encroachment of the federal judiciary on political questions, most of which, they argue, rightly should be resolved at the state and local levels. Of particular relevance to immigration policy is the 1982 Supreme Court decision in *Plyler v. Doe* (457 U.S. 202). In the *Plyler* case, the Court ruled that states may not deny public schooling to illegal immigrants. Those who believe that the Constitution limits the federal government's jurisdiction find such rulings exasperating, viewing them as examples of interference in state jurisdictional matters. Therefore, these policymakers would regard the *Plyler* decision as wrong and illegitimate. They would view the choice of whether to provide free public education to illegal residents as a decision that properly should rest with states and localities. They may distinguish public education as a more long-term benefit and therefore outside the proper definition of humanitarian circumstance.

Those agreeing with the court decision in *Plyler v. Doe* broadly construe the idea of humanitarian necessity. They tend to accept the Court's rulings as writing the passages of the Constitution as an evolving document, rather than fixed law. They take no issue with the reinterpretation of the Constitution, even when it means overturning longstanding legal precedent or stepping across the boundaries of state jurisdiction. Post-*Plyler*, policymakers have contended with the issue of whether to restore state jurisdiction over education. The question is whether Congress has the ability to give states the power to decide for themselves if they want to give illegal residents public education benefits (Congressional Task Force Report 1995).

The question of public benefits for illegal residents came to a head in California in the 1994 election. Californians cast votes on the Proposition

187 ballot initiative that proposed to deny most benefits to the undocumented. The initiative passed overwhelmingly before meeting legal challenges in U.S. courts (Suro 1996). Other policy options under consideration include requiring verification of eligibility before someone receives assistance, requiring illegals who have benefited from public services to repay the costs of the benefits and pay fines, and ending automatic U.S. citizenship at birth for children who are born here to illegal entrants.

Federal Reimbursement of Costs to States

As we indicated in Chapter 1, the impact of illegal aliens falls most heavily on a handful of states, especially California. The costs those states incur for providing unauthorized migrants with emergency medical care, education, criminal justice, and other services are viewed by many as unfairly tapping limited taxpayer resources. Furthermore, the costs have risen dramatically because the federal government has not gained control of its borders. Because border control is a distinctly federal responsibility, California cannot hire its own border patrol agents or enact its own immigration quotas. Moreover, legal immigrants usually settle in a few states, adding to the weight of demands on and the use of public services borne by those states and local governments. The National Research Council (Smith and Edmonton 1997) concluded that California's native households each pay $1,178 each year to cover the net fiscal costs imposed by immigrant-headed households in the state.

As these costs have risen, heavily affected states have increasingly clamored for *federal reimbursement* of unrecouped expenses for services provided to the undocumented population and to legal aliens. The issue is whether the federal government is liable for these costs. Should taxpayers in Nebraska be responsible for paying services used by a foreign population that has settled mostly in California?

Some policymakers may object to federal reimbursement of costs associated with immigration because reimbursement would place a drain on federal resources and additional pressure on the federal budget. Most would likely argue against open-ended reimbursement but would accept a short-term reimbursement. Such considerations would include whether the reimbursement was of the full costs or some lesser proportion of those costs. Should conditions be placed on the reimbursement? That is, will reimbursement follow on the condition that certain records be provided to document the claim that services were in fact provided to foreign-born residents? Perhaps one condition for reimbursement is that the care provider must notify immigration officials that it has provided services to medical patients who are illegally in the country. If reimbursement is determined to be appropriate, then a process for filing and paying claims must be established.

Conclusions

The 1965 immigration law shifted America's immigration policy to emphasize family- and work-based priorities. Subsequent changes have built on the fundamental features of this law's worldwide immigration caps and preference categories. In the years since 1965, the United States has accepted great responsibility for refugees. Illegal entry has brought new and complex problems, and the costs associated with U.S. immigration policy have become an important issue. Much of the contemporary immigration debate is focused on the costs and benefits of immigration—often quantified in terms of taxes paid versus public services consumed. This interest in the contribution of immigrants has been the result of the incapacity of Congress and the executive branch to make government revenues match expenditures. As budget expert Alan Schick has written, "For the foreseeable future, one issue looms above all others: the huge federal deficit." (Schick 1995, 3). While the bipartisan Balanced Budget Act of 1997 and a strong economy hold promise for a budget without deficit, the nation still owes nearly $6 trillion in debt in the late '90s. The key budgetary concern is the growth in entitlement spending, something that is not governed by discretionary spending decisions but instead hinges on the population of eligibles. "Population" is the key term in the previous sentence. Immigration policy is one means of controlling the nation's population, and therefore the pool of those eligible for costly entitlement programs.

Perceptive readers may have noted that we have not discussed the issue of "English only" legislation. Laws to make English the official U.S. language have never been closely tied to immigration reform, but have instead come up in Congress and in state legislatures as separate measures. While we acknowledge the relevance of the English-only debate to the changing composition of the nation's population, we have left the subject to other scholars.

The measure of a good policy is not necessarily how simple it is. Many complications are introduced by the fact that immigration is an ongoing process, with people being processed through the system over a period of months and years, and that it affects and is affected by changes in other policies, such as foreign affairs. Proposing reforms requires the policymaker to think retrospectively and prospectively, to look at people's situations as they are in different stages of the process. As in other areas of policy, attempts at reform and simplification create unanticipated problems that must be addressed later. Arguably, some cures are worse than the disease they are intended to treat. In evaluating immigration policy, one should not attack current policy simply because it is multifaceted, but rather should ask how well the system functions given that it addresses so many different circumstances. The system may well be broke, but adopting a simpler one is not necessarily the pathway toward fixing it.

C H A P T E R   4

THE CONGRESSIONAL POLITICS OF IMMIGRATION POLICY, 1965–1982

In Chapter 2 we showed that partisanship and political ideology do not define attitudes on immigration policy among the mass public. Even when there are political cleavages in attitudes toward immigration levels, it is not clear that people vote according to their views on the issue, except perhaps in California. In Chapter 3 we introduced the major issues framing the immigration policy debate in Washington. If the material presented there makes immigration policy sound rather involved—as well as political—we have conveyed the correct impression. The immigration debate on Capitol Hill has never boiled down simply to the numbers to be admitted. Legislators have usually distinguished legal from illegal immigration, arguing that the United States has a strong tradition of legal immigration but that illegal immigration should be stopped. Refugees and asylees are treated differently under the law than either legal or illegal immigrants. Refugees have never been subject to congressionally mandated numerical limits.[1]

Legal immigration is subdivided by policymakers into two general areas: family-based immigration and employment-based immigration (see Chapter 3). Legal immigration, whether employment- or family-based, is subject to numerical limits, but these limits can be legally circumvented by numerous provisions of U.S. law. U.S. citizens, for example, can bring in immediate family members (spouses, children) regardless of the numerical caps. Permanent residents, at the time they receive their work permits (green cards), can also bring in their immediate family members without regard to the numerical limits. Numerical limits apply to more extended relatives (adult brothers and sisters, adult married children) and immediate family members who do not enter the country at the time the original immigrant enters. The numerical limits, which were increased in 1990, are quickly reached as a result of

---

[1]Although, Congress has periodically awarded the president the capacity to set annual numerical limits on the number of refugees to be admitted.

the incredible demand among family members to immigrate. This demand has created the lengthy backlogs for visas described in the previous chapter. By the mid-1990s, immigration policy had become a complicated mess of preferences, exceptions, exclusions, and restrictions that took the debate far beyond the simple discussion of numbers. To comprehend the origins of this system, a review of legislative history is required.

Immigration Law before 1965

The origin of this intricate immigration system extends back to the passage of the first quotas in 1921, limiting the number of immigrants on a per-country basis. This law defined the per-country cap as 3 percent of foreign-born persons of a given nationality living in the United States as of 1910 (Hutchinson 1981, 179–181). For example, if a particular country had 200,000 émigrés living in the United States in 1910, its cap would be set at 6,000 visas per year (3 percent of 200,000). The effect was to reinforce previous patterns of immigration from Northern and Western Europe. The total world visa quota was set at 350,000 per year.

In 1924, there was a successful push by the House of Representatives to reduce the cap to 2 percent of foreign-born persons living in the United States in 1890, which had the effect of further restricting immigration from Southern and Eastern Europe and lowered the total worldwide annual quota to 164,667. Under this plan, annual quotas for Germany, for instance, were reduced—from the 1921 legislation—by about one-fourth from 68,000 to about 51,000, while the quotas for Southern European nations such as Turkey and Greece were reduced by 97 percent. This modification provided quotas for all countries, setting a minimum quota of 100 visas. In 1929, an amendment based visa distributions to nations on the percentage of persons from a given country residing in the United States as of 1920. So if 12 percent of the U.S. population was of Irish origin in 1920, Ireland would receive 12 percent of immigrant visas annually. No quota was to be smaller than 100 visas. The effect of this law was to further reduce the annual worldwide visa limit to about 154,277 (see Table 4.1).

In all of these laws, an important exception was provided for nations of the Western Hemisphere (nations of North and South America). Persons born in these countries could enter the United States not subject to the overall ceiling. The quota for Asian countries, however, was available only to white people from those nations (*CQ Almanac* 1965, 466; LeMay 1987). Only Filipinos were exempt from the Asian exclusion, because of the U.S. colonial presence there. Economic crises in the 1930s brought about renewed calls for immigration restrictions (Fitzgerald 1996, 152). In 1934, Filipinos were stripped of their status as nationals, and the Philippines became subject to a

Table 4.1   Major U.S. Immigration Legislation in the Twentieth Century

Legislation	Provisions
Immigration Act of 1924	Established a national origins quota system, limiting immigration mostly to Northern and Western European countries; put in place the first numerical immigration limits.
Immigration and Nationality Act of 1952	Continued national origins quota system; set a quota for aliens with needed skills.
Immigration and Nationality Act Amendments of 1965	Repealed the national origins quota system; established a seven-category system for allotting visas, based on family reunification and skills; set a Western Hemisphere quota and a 20,000-per-country limit for Eastern Hemisphere countries.
Immigration and Nationality Act Amendments of 1976	Extended the 20,000-per-country visa limit to Western Hemisphere countries.
Refugee Act of 1980	Established systematic procedures for admitting refugees; removed refugees from the seven-category preference system; established a refugee resettlement program.
Immigration Reform and Control Act of 1986	Imposed employer sanctions for hiring illegal aliens; established an amnesty program for long-time resident illegal aliens; increased border enforcement.
Immigration Act of 1990	Raised legal immigration levels; tripled employment-based visa numbers; established a diversity visa program.
Illegal Immigration Reform and Immigrant Responsibility Act of 1996	Streamlined removal process; increased border enforcement; established a pilot electronic employment eligibility verification system; limited immigrant access to welfare benefits.

numerical quota of 50 visas, half as many as any other country, even though it was not granted independence as a nation until 1946 (Hing 1993, 33).

The laws excluding Chinese immigration that had been on the books since 1882 were repealed in 1943, as a foreign policy measure designed to warm relations with a war ally (Reimers 1992, 11; Riggs 1950; Torok 1995). The annual quota for China was set at 105 visas. A major amendment in 1952, the McCarran-Walter Act, abolished the Asian exclusion but still kept immigration from Asian countries at very low levels, setting it at 2,000 per year from the entire "Asia-Pacific Triangle": nineteen Asian countries extending from India and Pakistan in the East to the Pacific Islands (except Australia and New Zealand) and Japan in the West. The quotas for Asian immigration were based not on country of birth, as for the Western nations, but on race (Eckerson 1966; Bennett 1966). For instance, thousands of Chinese ancestry born and living outside of China would be charged to the quota for China, not to the nation of their origin. For the first time since the 1920s, Asians were permitted to naturalize. Otherwise, the national origins quota system remained intact, limiting per-country annual immigration according to a formula of one-sixth of 1 percent of the persons of a given nationality in the United States as of 1920.

The principle of family reunification has been part of immigration law since the original quota law passed in 1921. Congress made family unity the basis of exceptions to country quotas first for minor children of U.S. citizens, and, in 1924, for their spouses and unmarried children between the ages of 18 and 21 (Bennett 1963, 277). The 1952 McCarran-Walter Act codified a four-tier preference system that awarded some immigrants a higher status or position in the queue for visas based on employment and family reunification. Fifty percent of each country's quota was set aside for "first preference" immigrants—those with special skills or education deemed important to the U.S. economy. Thirty percent of a nation's quota was set aside under "second preference"—visa applicants who are parents of adult U.S. citizens. The remaining 20 percent of each quota was awarded to "third preference" applicants, who are spouses and children of legal resident aliens. Finally, any portion of a nation's quota not used by the three primary preferences was made available to remaining immigrants, and up to 25 percent of these remaining visas were designated for "fourth preference" immigrants—brothers, sisters, and adult sons and daughters of U.S. citizens (Bennett 1966; Hutchinson 1981). President Truman vetoed the McCarran-Walter Act, complaining that the legislation did not sufficiently depart from the restrictive spirit of existing immigration law but rather intensified and reinforced those restrictions (Reimers 1992; Bennett 1963). His veto was decisively overridden by the House on a 278–112 vote (40 abstentions) and by the Senate by a narrower 57–26 vote (13 abstentions).

Mexican immigrants were noticed as early as the 1920s by members of Congress such as Representative John Box (D-TX), a member of the House Immigration Committee, who characterized them as "illiterate, unclean, peonized masses" (Divine 1957; LeMay 1987). But as scholars of the period have indicated, proposals to limit Mexican immigration ran into strong and organized opposition from farmers, cattle ranchers, miners, and sugar and railroad interests from the Southwest (Fitzgerald 1996; LeMay 1987, 90; Divine 1957). As World War II stripped American agriculture of its needed labor supply, growers increasingly put pressure on Congress to admit foreign workers to work as field hands. A temporary guest-worker program, also known as the *Bracero* program, was established in 1942 over the objections of labor unions (Reimers 1992; Craig 1971). More than 70 percent of these temporary workers were Mexicans, but workers from the Bahamas, Barbados, and Canada were also invited (Reimers 1992, 41). The *Bracero* program continued through the 1950s and was ended in 1964 by the secretary of labor. The 1952 McCarran-Walter Act also created a small guest-worker program administered by the Department of Labor known as H-2 (referenced to the section of the U.S. Code where it is detailed). As a result of labor union pressure, however, the H-2 program has never been popular with the Labor Department or with Congress and has not been widely used by employers.

Undocumented immigration, particularly from Mexico, was first "officially" noticed by the Truman administration in a report concluding that "wetbacks" were having a negative impact on the U.S. economy and may pose a threat to public health (Reimers 1992, 49; Fitzgerald 1996, 219). In response, President Truman asked Congress in 1951 to enact legislation penalizing those who smuggle in and otherwise harbor undocumented workers. Pressure from agriculture interests that take advantage of the low wage rates generated by the illegal immigrant flow has been sufficiently strong that attempts by Congress to stem the tide of illegal aliens have often been halfhearted. Generally, two types of solutions have been proposed to eliminate the illegal flow: stronger border enforcement, and punishment for employers who hire undocumented workers. Congress has preferred the former strategy, and the House of Representatives tried to give INS border patrol agents the power to conduct warrantless searches as early as 1952. The Senate, however, refused to go along with this proposal (*CQ Almanac* 1952, 160). Later in the decade members introduced the first bills to criminalize the hiring of illegals, but these proposals were repeatedly rejected in committee and on the floor. The employment of undocumented workers was not outlawed until 1986, when a weak system of employer sanctions was imposed establishing fines for those who knowingly hire undocumented workers.

Refugees have usually been provided for under legislation separate from immigration law and without regard to the usual per-country numerical limits. Following World War II, Congress passed the Displaced Persons Act in 1948, allowing over 400,000 refugees—principally from the European theater—to become permanent U.S. residents (Eckerson 1966). Six other refugee acts passed from 1953 to 1960, admitting 284,000 immigrants as political or economic refugees or as victims of floods and earthquakes. Perhaps the most significant turn in refugee policy came in 1959 with the Castro revolution in Cuba. A majority of those fleeing Castro's dictatorship entered the United States without visas and registered later with immigration authorities. By the end of 1961, the year the United States broke diplomatic relations with Cuba, over 100,000 refugees had fled the island, with three-fourths of those settling in the Miami area. Between 1959 and 1980, Cubans benefited from an unprecedented open-arms policy and were granted permanent residency as political asylees (Zucker and Zucker 1987).

The political forces lobbying to maintain immigration restrictions on Asian and Latin American immigration such as the major American labor organizations, such as the American Federation of Labor (AFL) and the earlier Knights of Labor (Fitzgerald 1996). The labor unions argued that cheap foreign labor was injurious to workers and undermined the union movement. The American Legion, Veterans of Foreign Wars, the Regular Veterans Association, and the War Veterans Association of America were particularly influential in lobbying for the exclusion of Asians. Veterans groups made political arguments about the possibility that the Western states might be dominated by China and Japan and that immigrants from these countries brought with them imperialist attitudes and traditions that were hostile to liberal democratic institutions (Riggs 1950). Nationalist and patriotic organizations, such as Sons and Daughters of the American Revolution, made cultural arguments about the inability of Asians to assimilate and expressed doubts about the political views of the potential newcomers, fearing that they might be Communists. European immigrants, it was argued, had a cultural and political background similar to that of most United States natives and should be preferred for these reasons. During House hearings for passage of the 1924 Act, the House immigration committee heard extensive testimony from prominent university biology professors from prestigious institutions such as Harvard and Yale about the dangers of race mixing (LeMay 1987, 88). Sentiment favoring Asian exclusion ran particularly strong on the West Coast states, where Chinese and Japanese immigrants had settled in the nineteenth century. In California, opposition to immigration came largely from the more populated central and northern parts of the state and from organizations such as the American Federation of Labor, the Grange, and veterans groups. Once their major rail lines had been constructed the California railroads were silent about immigration issues. By the 1880s, Chinese "coolie" labor was no longer needed, and the first Chinese exclusion law was passed in 1882 with little railroad protest.

Members of Congress from Nevada, California, Oregon, and Washington were nearly unanimous in their desire for exclusion of Asian immigrants until the 1940s. By the mid-40s, commercial elites in San Francisco and Seattle were beginning to recognize the potential benefits of trade with Pacific rim countries after the war. Repealing restrictive immigration laws could be seen as an instrument of warming relations between the United States and these future trade partners. Because of his West Coast origins, Congressman Warren Magnuson (D-WA) was one of the most influential and credible spokespersons in favor of liberalizing immigration policy. Northern members from urban areas with a long and self-conscious history of immigration were generally more receptive to opening the doors than were members from rural areas. These included representatives like Walter Judd (R-MN), Fiorello LaGuardia (R-NY), Samuel Dickstein (D-NY), Adam Clayton Powell (D-NY), Emanuel Celler (D-NY), Philip Hart (D-MI) and later Michael A. Feighan (D-OH), Edward M. Kennedy (D-MA), Peter Rodino (D-NJ), and Edward Roybal (D-CA). While most of the leading reformers were Democrats, partisanship was not a strong predictor of most floor votes. Eighty-three percent of Republicans voted for the 1924 law, and they were joined by 81 percent of Democrats. Instead, voting cleavages separated members by region. Members opposing restrictions came from states with a large foreign-born population, including New York, Connecticut, New Jersey, and Rhode Island (Spengler 1958). Members from Southern states were sympathetic to exclusion and formed a strong coalition with westerners against early attempts to liberalize immigration law. All of the Southern members voted for the 1924 national-origins quota system, compared with only 76 percent of representatives from Northern states (Tatalovich 1995; LeMay 1987). But unlike the West, Southerners, led by prominent members such as Judiciary Committee Chair Senator James Eastland (D-MS), remained staunchly opposed to open immigration policies—even as they employed cheap alien laborers on their own plantations (Corwin 1978; 1984). The Old South's opposition to immigration dates to the Civil War, when the North was associated with high immigration levels and immigrants were recruited to fight in the Union Army. Opposition to Asian and Latin American immigration by Southern members is also attributable to the history of racial divisions in Southern society.

The Coming of the 1965 Immigration Act

Between 1924 and 1965, the national-origins quotas became increasingly difficult to defend. A significant group of liberal politicians, including Hubert H. Humphrey (D-MN), Warren Magnuson (D-WA), and Herbert H. Lehman (D-NY), voted against the 1952 McCarran-Walter Act because it did not eradicate what they considered to be the arbitrary and discriminatory nature of immigration policy. The feeling among many leading liberals at the time was that an anti-Communist foreign policy must go hand-in-hand with open immigration policy (Reimers 1992, 62). A spate of legislative activity after 1952 continued to punch large holes in the original restrictive wall set in place by the 1921 and 1924 laws. Pressure to open the doors to immigrants and refugees was so successful that Congress enacted 32 separate laws to modify the national-origins system between 1953 and 1964 (Bennett 1966). The coalition pushing for a more open immigration policy included religious organizations: Protestants from mainline denominations, Catholics, and Jewish groups, all of whom eventually went on record in favor of repealing Asian exclusion. These were joined by liberal organizations, such as the American Civil Liberties Union, and influential independent citizens of liberal political inclination. Business interests such as the National Association of Manufacturers, the Associated General Contractors, the U.S. Chamber of Commerce, and the National Industrial Conference Board had originally opposed the 1924 restrictions on the grounds that closed immigration would deny their industrial constituents a workforce (LeMay 1987, 81). These same groups lobbied to liberalize the national-origins system in subsequent years. Western opposition to Asian immigration slowly waned, and five of the eight California representatives favored repeal of Chinese exclusion laws by 1943 (Riggs 1950). While Franklin D. Roosevelt was instrumental in repealing Chinese exclusion, Presidents Truman, Eisenhower, and Kennedy were against the national-origins quota system but could not muster sufficient support in Congress to completely overturn it (Hing 1993, 39). While successive efforts to build loopholes into the system had effectively nullified the original 1924 Act, pressure continued to build in the 1960s for a decisive repeal. Both political parties incorporated policy statements favoring more open immigration into their 1960 platforms. President Kennedy made repeal a central goal of his administration and had even written a lengthy well-known essay on the subject—*A Nation of Immigrants*, published in 1958—which served as the foundation of his subsequent legislative efforts. Racial arguments that had undergirded part of the restrictionist argument were discredited in the wake of the civil rights movement. Favorable employment trends undercut the economic arguments against immigration. Proponents of a more open immigration policy could point to the successful assimilation of hundreds of thousands of previous immigrants as they were successfully stirred into the melting pot. Conservative business interests could argue that they had benefited from immigration. Liberals could argue that past immigration policies had been unfairly discriminatory. In this climate, nativism was isolated to just a few areas of the country, including the Solid South. Outside the South, public opinion was not especially favorable toward liberal immigration policies, but the public was not inclined to punish politicians who sought to open the doors wider (see Chapter 2). This gave policymakers great freedom to jump on the pro-immigrant bandwagon that swept Congress toward enactment of the most open and egalitarian immigration law in the twentieth century.

Provisions of the 1965 Immigration Act

In 1963, President Kennedy introduced legislation to phase out the national-origins quota system and increase the quotas on immigration from the Asia-Pacific Triangle nations. The president's legislation still placed heavy emphasis

Box 4.1

James O. Eastland (D-MS) chaired the Senate Judiciary Committee in the 1960s and 1970s. Eastland is shown here (on the right) at a 1968 committee hearing with a young Senator Edward M. Kennedy (D-MA). Credit: Library of Congress

James O. Eastland (D-MS)

Senator James O. Eastland chaired the Senate Judiciary Committee and its immigration subcommittee from the mid-1950s until his retirement in 1978. From those positions he was able to cast a long shadow upon immigration policy-making during that period. Eastland was a conservative, Southern Democrat, generally opposed to open immigration policies.

Eastland temporarily gave up the subcommittee chairmanship after the 1964 election, opening the door for the landmark 1965 bill to move through the legislative process. In the 1970s, however, Eastland repeatedly prevented the Judiciary Committee from considering immigration reform measures, permitting limited action only on refugee-related matters.

Eastland was born in Doddsville, Mississippi, November 28, 1904. He attended Ole Miss, Vanderbilt, and the University of Alabama. He studied law and was admitted to the bar in 1927. He practiced law in Forest, Miss., beginning in 1927. He also farmed cotton and served in the state legislature from 1928 until 1932. He went to the Democratic National Convention in 1928 as a delegate. In 1934, Eastland moved to Ruleville, Miss.

When U.S. Senator Pat Harrison died, Eastland was appointed to fill the vacancy from June 30, 1941, until September 28, 1941. Eastland did not run in the special election.

In 1942, Eastland ran for the U.S. Senate and won his election. He won reelection until he retired in 1978. He chaired the Senate Judiciary Committee from 1955 until his retirement. He was President Pro Tempore of the Senate from 1971 through 1978.

Eastland also served as a delegate to Democratic National Conventions from 1944 to 1960. He retired to Doddsville, Miss., and died February 19, 1986.

(Sources: *Biographical Directory of the American Congress 1774–1971*; *Biographical Directory of the U.S. Congress 1774–1989*; *Political Profiles: The Nixon/Ford Years*)

on preferences for those with special education and skills but also wanted to add parents of U.S. citizens to those granted nonquota status. Opposition in Congress by key committee leaders delayed action on the Kennedy reforms. Lyndon Johnson had a history that predicted he would take a view opposite from President Kennedy on immigration issues, but as in other areas such as civil rights, education, and urban policy, he became more liberal once he assumed the presidency. Johnson's landslide election of 1964 seemed to open the door for major legislative reform on a broad array of fronts, including immigration. The 1964 election saw the departure of older antireform members from influential posts on Capitol Hill, including Senator Eastland (D-MS), who temporarily stepped down from his position as the immigration subcommittee chair, and Congressman Walter (D-PA), who died in office. Reform-oriented members enlarged their margins on the House and Senate Judiciary Committees and took control of both immigration subcommittees (Reimers 1992, 66).

As introduced by Congressman Emanuel Celler (D-NY), chair of the House Judiciary Committee, and Senator Philip Hart (D-MI), the legislation that would become the 1965 Immigration and Nationality Act made sweeping amendments to the 1952 McCarran-Walter Act. The idea that admission should be based on national origins was completely scrapped and replaced by a preference-only system. First preference would be maintained for those who are highly skilled. The remaining three preferences were to be the same as in the 1952 legislation. The Asia-Pacific Triangle limitations were to be stricken from the books.

Soon into 1965, however, the new chair of the immigration subcommittee, Michael Feighan (D-OH), introduced his own bill in the form of a substitute that would explicitly deny preference on the basis of race, sex, or national origin. The Feighan bill suggested seven preference classes that were distinct from the Hart-Celler legislation in that employment-based immigration was given sixth preference rather than first. This reversal of priority signaled Feighan's alliance with labor union interests that had long been opposed to employment-based immigration. The Judiciary Committee reported out a bill on August 6, 1965, that appeared much more like Feighan's substitute than Celler's original (Hutchinson 1981, 371). Annual immigration limits of 170,000 were to be imposed, about one-third lower than Feighan's initial proposal of 225,000. Not to be charged against this total were natives of Western Hemisphere nations, their immediate families, and the parents of U.S. citizens. Rather than per-country quotas, applications for visas were to be processed by the INS on a first-come, first served basis. A citizen's nation of origin was not to be considered except that no more than 20,000 of the 170,000 annual admissions could come from a single country. The national origins quotas were to be phased out entirely by 1968. The strict limits on Asia-Pacific Triangle nations were to be repealed, and particularly the provision determining that nonwhite persons from Asia be charged to the country quota of their racial ancestry rather than their nation of birth (*CQ Almanac* 1965, 461). The bill proposed seven preferences that have had a lasting impact (Hutchinson 1981, 371–372):

1. Twenty percent (of 170,000) for unmarried adult sons and daughters of U.S. citizens
2. Spouses and unmarried sons and daughters of resident aliens—next 20 percent, plus any unused portion of the first preference
3. Members of professions, scientists, and artists—next 10 percent
4. Married sons and daughters of citizens—next 10 percent, plus any unused portion of the first three preferences
5. Brothers and sisters of citizens—24 percent, plus any unused portion of the preceding preference categories
6. Skilled or unskilled persons capable of filling labor shortages—next 10 percent
7. Refugees from Communist governments or from certain Middle Eastern countries—next 6 percent

As a bow to the AFL-CIO, Feighan's bill also demanded that the Secretary of Labor certify that admitted immigrants would not displace native workers. Exempt from this requirement were those entering under the family reunification categories as parents, spouses and minor children of citizens, and resident aliens. Family reunification was clearly the priority in this legislation, as it has been in subsequent rounds of reform. Several Republicans, including Clark MacGregor (R-MN), opposed the nonquota status granted to North and South American nations on the basis that it discriminated in favor of those nations and against all others. MacGregor and his colleagues argued that if supporters of the bill were really intent on eliminating the biases in immigration law, annual immigration from these nations should be capped as it is for all other nations. MacGregor was unsuccessful in committee in pushing for a Western Hemisphere ceiling of 115,000. On an overwhelming 27–4 vote, the Judiciary Committee sent the bill to the floor where it came up for consideration on August 24.

House Floor Debate on the 1965 Act

Reflecting their key roles on the Judiciary Committee, representatives Feighan (D-NY) and Celler (D-NY) led the debate on the House floor and made strong arguments against the national-origins quota system. They repeatedly pointed out that the current law was discriminatory and made family reunification more difficult for most immigrants than it would be under the new law. To those who raised the objection that immigration would pose an economic threat to native workers, Celler offered the reassurance that the Secretary of Labor would guarantee that Americans would not be displaced (*CR* 8/25/65, 21758). Representative Clark MacGregor (R-MN) objected to the absence of restrictions on Western Hemisphere immigration, making the same argument that he had in committee that nonquota status for these countries effectively discriminated against the remaining countries. MacGregor offered the same amendment that had failed in committee to cap Western Hemisphere immigration at 115,000 per year. MacGregor noted that immigration from these countries had increased dramatically between 1959 and 1964 and that the figures for 1965 suggested an increase well above 1964 levels. Were these trends to continue, Latin American immigration would soon overwhelm the U.S. economy. Celler (D-NY) parroted the Johnson administration's line that the cap would lead to complaints from Western Hemisphere nations and muddy foreign relations with Latin American countries and Canada. Celler also countered that Western Hemisphere immigration had been at higher levels in the past and that economic growth and prosperity had not suffered for it. When the MacGregor Amendment came up for a vote it was defeated 218–189.

Those speaking in favor of the bill on the floor were preponderantly from immigrant-receiving states in the Northeast, particularly New York, New Jersey, and Connecticut, and from the urban industrial areas in the Midwest, including Ohio and Illinois. Typical of the comments made in favor of the legislation were those of Judiciary Chairman Celler:

> If you go to my district you will find people of all nationalities. And to give you an idea of the pluralistic character of my district, which is symptomatic of many, many districts in the Nation, I would like to tell you a story.
>
> A man goes into a Chinese restaurant, and there, to his amazement, he sees a Negro waiter—a Negro waiter in a Chinese restaurant. And he says to the waiter, "What is the specialty of the house?" and the Negro waiter says, "Pizza pie."
>
> "Pizza pie in a Chinese restaurant?"
>
> And he said, "Yes, this is the Yiddish neighborhood."
>
> That gives you some idea of what is happening in this country and what is happening is good for the land because all those races are amalgamated and they are here for a good, common purpose, the weal and the welfare of our Nation, to which all these diverse races make a contribution (*CR* 8/25/65, 21757).

Others, however, were less than enthusiastic about the diversity the new legislation would encourage. Among them Representative O. Clark Fisher (D-TX), whose 21st district encompassed approximately the same territory that Representative Lamar Smith's (R-TX) 21st district would thirty years later, when he became Congress's leading proponent of restrictions. Like Smith after him, Fisher opposed liberal immigration policy on the ground that the immigrant flow would come much too fast for the United States to absorb

Box 4.2

Emmanuel Celler (D-NY), right, chaired the House Judiciary Committee in the 1960s at the time the 1965 Immigration and Nationality Act passed on a largely consensual vote. Credit: Library of Congress

Emanuel Celler (D-NY)

One of Congress's longest-serving members, Representative Emanuel Celler chaired the House Judiciary Committee in the 1960s and sponsored the 1965 Immigration Act. Celler was a strong force in advancing the 1965 bill to do away with the national-origins quota system.

Celler was born in Brooklyn, N.Y., on May 6, 1888. He graduated from Columbia College in 1910 and from Columbia University's law school in 1912. Celler practiced law in New York City from 1912 until 1922. During World War I, he was a government appeal agent on the draft board.

In 1922, Celler won election to Congress, where he served through 1972. He chaired the House Judiciary Committee from 1949 till 1952, then again from 1955 till 1972. He also served on the Special Committee on Seating Adam Clayton Powell in 1967 and 1968. Celler lost his bid for renomination in 1972 to Elizabeth Holtzman, who was later elected to his seat.

Celler was a delegate to the New York Democratic conventions from 1922 to 1932. He also served as a New York delegate to Democratic National Conventions from 1942 through 1964, where he was a member of the Platform Committee.

After Congress, Celler resumed his law practice and served on the Commission on Revision of the Federal Appellate Court System from 1973 till 1975. Celler died January 15, 1981, in Brooklyn, N.Y.

(Sources: *Biographical Directory of the American Congress 1774–1971*; *Biographical Directory of the U.S. Congress 1774–1989*)

capably while changing the composition of the U.S. population. Those opposing the Hart-Celler Act recognized that the demand to emigrate from Asian countries was far greater than that from European countries. By eliminating the Asia-Pacific Triangle limitations, the door was being thrown open to a much larger pool of potential immigrants than under the old policy, which favored Western Europe. Other arguments against liberal immigration reform that were voiced in the debate—such as the threat to national security posed by inviting in immigrants from Communist countries—seem less plausible today.

Those like Fisher who expressed reservations about the 1965 reform were from the rural Midwestern states and from the South. These divisions foreshadowed the floor division on the legislation as reflected in the roll-call vote.[2] Table 4.2 provides evidence of the cleavages that divided members on this legislation—the MacGregor Amendment, the House passage of the final version of the legislation (the conference report). The statistical model on which the results in Table 4.2 are founded is anchored in the theory that members of Congress take cues from their constituencies as well as from their political party. Thus, the demographic composition of each member's district may figure into important decisions about immigration policy. Naturally we would expect districts with large numbers of immigrants to elect legislators who favored expansive immigration policies. Similarly we hypothesize that, as the proportion of black, Asian, and Hispanic voters rises across districts, support for a less racially discriminatory immigration policy will also rise. Along similar lines, we hypothesize that members who are themselves members of racial minorities are likely to vote as a bloc in supporting a less racially discriminatory, more open immigration policy, independent of the nature of their constituency. Variables to test the presence of regional voting blocs have also been introduced: one for Southern states and a second for "border" states—those states along the country's southern border that have received the most immigration from Central America in recent times: California, Arizona, New Mexico, Texas, and Florida. Briefly, our expectation is that members from the South will be more likely to oppose generous immigration policy than members from Northern states, regardless of their party. For the border states, we anticipate that these delegations will, on average, be more opposed to reforms that loosen immigration restrictions owing to the disproportionate burdens placed on these states from population growth caused by immigration. Finally, knowing that committees attempt to work together, harmoniously, to produce legislation to which all of their members can agree, we have included a variable to capture membership on the House Judiciary Committee with the expectation that members of this committee are likely to vote as a bloc on immigration policy votes coming up on the floor.

The results in Table 4.2 shed considerable light on the floor divisions on immigration policy in the mid-1960s. Partisanship is important on the

---

[2] Complete logistic regression models for each vote are included in the chapter Appendix.

Table 4.2   Estimated Probability of Voting Yes on Aspects of the 1965
Immigration and Nationality Act Amendments, Given
Values of the Independent Variables, 89th Congress, U.S.
House of Representatives

Variable	MacGregor Amendment	House Passage	Conference Report
Democrat	.11	.90	.93
Republican	.93	.87	.96
White member	.39	.89	.95
Non-white member	.01	.94	.51
Non-South	.28	.94	.97
South	.59	.63	.68
Nonborder state	.37	.90	.95
Border state	.29	.86	.94
Not Judiciary	.36	.88	.94
Judiciary Committee	.30	.95	.96
Foreign born = .12	.66	.68	.87
Foreign born = 28.9	.01	.99	.99
Agriculture = .05	.30	.92	.96
Agriculture = 36.01	.64	.67	.69
Black = 0.0	.31	.92	.95
Black = 87.1	.22	.46	.89
Asian/other = .02	.37	.90	.94
Asian/other = 67.3	.01	.70	.97
Unemployment = 1.6	.51	.82	.93
Unemployment = 13.2	.12	.97	.97

Values represent the estimated probability of a Yes vote at the lowest and highest value of the
independent variables, with all other variables held constant at their sample means.

MacGregor Amendment, with roughly 93 percent of the GOP members
supporting limits on Western Hemisphere immigration compared with an
estimated 11 percent of Democrats. Southern members were highly supportive of the MacGregor Amendment, regardless of their party. As predicted,
members from districts with a high proportion of foreign-born residents
voted against MacGregor's attempt to extend annual limits to Canada and
Latin America. It is not clear that local economic conditions had much relevance to member decision making. Indeed, those in areas of high unemployment were more likely to vote against limits on Western Hemisphere
immigration than those in more prosperous areas.

As for House passage of the 1965 Immigration and Nationality Act, the vote did not occur along party lines, primarily because of the opposition of Southern Democrats. Overall, Southern members were about 30 percent less likely to support the bill than non-Southern members (Table 4.2). Constituencies played an important role, as those with a high proportion of minority and foreign-born residents favored passage. There was also a component of rural conservatism that divided yes from no voters. Those in the most highly agricultural districts were about 26 percent less likely to favor passage of the bill than those in the least agricultural districts. Apparently, agriculture's demand for cheap farm labor is narrowly focused only in certain specialty sectors of the rural economy and not sufficient to counteract the conservative ideology of members representing rural districts.

When the conference report was passed by the House later in the fall of 1965 on a 320–69 vote, the results were similar to original House passage (318–95), with more members not voting. Southern members remained opposed, as did those in agricultural districts and with predominantly native-born populations. This time, however, the legislation lost the support of many minority members of Congress—the blacks, Hispanics, and Asians—as roughly half of them voted against the legislation. By this time, the Senate had successfully incorporated into its draft of the legislation a version of the MacGregor Amendment placing a cap of 120,000 (5,000 more than MacGregor had proposed) on immigration from Western Hemisphere nations. That was enough to lose the support of many members.

Senate Action on the 1965 Act

On the same day that the House was killing the MacGregor Amendment on the floor, Senators Sam Ervin (D-NC) and Everett Dirksen (R-IL), the key members of the Senate subcommittee on immigration, insisted on adding a ceiling of 120,000 to Western Hemisphere immigration over the objections of the Johnson administration. The administration realized that Senator Ervin's support was crucial to passage of the bill and came to agreement. Ervin's subcommittee voted in favor of the Western Hemisphere cap by a 5–3 vote that displayed considerable sectional cleavage, with Senators Eastland (D-MS), Ervin (D-NC), and McClellan (D-AR) among the yeas and Senators Kennedy (D-MA), Hart (D-MI), and Javits (R-NY) casting the no votes. The full committee reported out the bill on September 15 on a 14–2 vote with minor amendments, and, again, two Southerners voted in opposition— Eastland (D-MS) and McClellan (D-AR) (*CQ Almanac* 1965, 478). On the Senate floor, only a single amendment was offered, to set an overall annual ceiling of 290,000 on immigration, but it was rejected on a voice vote. With no amendments adopted, the legislation passed by a 76–18 roll-call vote after four days of debate. It was opposed, predictably, by a majority of 13 of the 22 Southern Democrats.

Viewed from the perspective of the more contentious immigration battles yet to come in the 1980s and 1990s, the consensus prevailing on the 1965 Act is remarkable, if not amazing. But it is not hard to explain this consensus. Reform was noncontroversial in the mid-1960s because the United States was at the end of a long period of very low immigration. In addition, unemployment was low, the economy was strong, and there seemed to be few reasons to oppose an opening of the door. Objections reflected concerns about what could happen to the racial composition of the country should the old quota system be abandoned. But these concerns were easy to dismiss as either racist or as exaggerated fears of something that would not happen. Others worried about the loyalties of the potential pool of Asian newcomers— expressing concerns about their capacity to assimilate politically. But once again, this was a fear about what might happen in the future. There was no clear evidence that Asian immigrants would be Communist subversives. Most Communists during the postwar era, including, for example, the Rosenberg spies, had clearly been of European descent. So the objections and concerns of the mid-60s restrictionists were easy to ignore, and with that the door to the world was opened to permit the largest immigrant influx in the nation's history.

Immigration Policy 1966–1972

In the 1960s and 1970s, immigration policy generally originated in the U.S. House of Representatives; later, the U.S. Senate followed by reporting its own legislation. As in other areas of policymaking, though, the Senate was the slower and more reluctant partner, often never acting even as the House had stormed ahead. Institutional reasons may account for this. With only one hundred members, the Senate has a heavier workload. Still, institutional differences in workload will not account for why some policy areas received the Senate's attention but others did not. Immigration legislation was bottled up in the Senate for one main reason: Senator James Eastland, a conservative Democrat from Mississippi, chaired both the Judiciary Committee and that body's immigration subcommittee. Aside from the 1965 Act, he opposed virtually all serious efforts to overhaul the immigration system. He remained in control of the Judiciary Committee until his retirement in 1978 (see Table 4.3). The result is that the House set the pace for immigration reform, and, indeed, most proposals for reform in the 1970s came out of the House subcommittee on immigration, chaired initially by Michael Feighan (D-OH), and then taken over in 1971 by Peter Rodino (D-NJ) who, in turn, was followed by Joshua Eilberg (D-PA) and Elizabeth Holtzman (D-NY) (see Table 4.3).

Table 4.3   House and Senate Judiciary Committee and Immigration
Subcommittee Chairs 1965–1997

Year	Congress	House Judiciary	House Immigration Subcommittee	Senate Judiciary	Senate Immigration Subcommittee
1965	89th	Emanuel Celler (D-NY)	Michael Feighan (D-OH)	James Eastland (D-MS)	James Eastland (D-MS)
1967	90th	Emanuel Celler (D-NY)	Michael Feighan (D-OH)	James Eastland (D-MS)	James Eastland (D-MS)
1969	91st	Emanuel Celler (D-NY)	Michael Feighan (D-OH)	James Eastland (D-MS)	James Eastland (D-MS)
1971	92nd	Emanuel Celler (D-NY)	Peter Rodino (D-NJ)	James Eastland (D-MS)	James Eastland (D-MS)
1973	93rd	Peter Rodino (D-NJ)	Joshua Eilberg (D-PA)	James Eastland (D-MS)	James Eastland (D-MS)
1975	94th	Peter Rodino (D-NJ)	Joshua Eilberg (D-PA)	James Eastland (D-MS)	James Eastland (D-MS)
1977	95th	Peter Rodino (D-NJ)	Joshua Eilberg (D-PA)	James Eastland (D-MS)	James Eastland (D-MS)
1979	96th	Peter Rodino (D-NJ)	Elizabeth Holtzman (D-NY)	Edward Kennedy (D-MA)	Edward Kennedy (D-MA)
1981	97th	Peter Rodino (D-NJ)	Romano Mazzoli (D-KY)	Strom Thurmond (D-SC)	Alan Simpson (R-WY)
1983	98th	Peter Rodino (D-NJ)	Romano Mazzoli (D-KY)	Strom Thurmond (D-SC)	Alan Simpson (R-WY)
1985	99th	Peter Rodino (D-NJ)	Romano Mazzoli (D-KY)	Strom Thurmond (D-SC)	Alan Simpson (R-WY)
1987	100th	Peter Rodino (D-NJ)	Romano Mazzoli (D-KY)	Joseph Biden (D-DE)	Edward Kennedy (D-MA)
1989	101st	Jack Brooks (D-TX)	Bruce Morrison (D-CT)	Joseph Biden (D-DE)	Edward Kennedy (D-MA)
1991	102nd	Jack Brooks (D-TX)	Romano Mazzoli (D-KY)	Joseph Biden (D-DE)	Edward Kennedy (D-MA)
1993	103rd	Jack Brooks (D-TX)	Romano Mazzoli (D-KY)	Joseph Biden (D-DE)	Edward Kennedy (D-MA)
1995	104th	Henry Hyde (R-IL)	Lamar Smith (R-TX)	Orrin Hatch (R-UT)	Alan Simpson (R-WY)
1997	105th	Henry Hyde (R-IL)	Lamar Smith (R-TX)	Orrin Hatch (R-UT)	Spencer Abraham (R-MI)

Since the 1965 Act was designed to be phased in over three years, there was little action on immigration during the late 1960s. In the 90th Congress (1967–1968), several reform proposals were considered in hearings, and at least one major bill was introduced, but there was no floor action. Only one piece of legislation, permitting the expedited naturalization of aliens serving in the U.S. armed forces in Vietnam, reached the floor. The legislation directly affected about 4,800 legal aliens who had served in combat positions since 1961 (*CQ Almanac* 1968, 715). The measure passed on voice votes in both the House and Senate.

In the 91st Congress (1969–1970), immigration legislation remained noncontroversial, with only a few pieces of legislation coming to the floor. One of these removed a prohibition against being naturalized within 60 days preceding a general election. Originally, this prohibition was designed to prevent machine politicians from rushing aliens through the naturalization process at the last minute in order to influence the outcome of an election. Since subsequent legislation now required that aliens be residents for five years prior to naturalization, their votes were judged to be less easily manipulable than in times when there was no substantial residency requirement. Hence, the 60-day prohibition prior to elections could be safely eliminated. The measure was approved by both the House and Senate on voice votes.

A more serious reform authorized the entry of aliens with special skills to fill permanent positions in the U.S. labor force. Under existing law, such aliens were only allowed to fill temporary positions (*CQ Almanac* 1970, 236). Some new categories of admission were newly labeled nonimmigrant—including those engaged to U.S. citizens who were to be admitted for the purpose of marriage, providing the marriage took place within 90 days. Employees of international companies were granted nonimmigrant status permitting them to remain in the United States temporarily while they were working for a U.S. firm. Again, these reforms had the effect of liberalizing U.S. immigration policy, opening the door wider, creating more ways of getting around annual numerical limits. Nevertheless, the legislation passed on voice votes in both the House and Senate and was signed into law by President Nixon.

In the 92nd Congress (1971–1972), there were new stirrings as three measures came up on the floor that proposed to open the doors just a little wider. The first measure raised to 18 from 16 the age at which children could become automatic citizens based on the naturalization of their parents (*CQ Almanac* 1971, 416). The second bill expedited the naturalization process for elderly aliens who have lived in the United States for at least twenty years even if they had not become English-proficient during that time. This legislation passed 192–84 in the House. The third measure proposed to give European countries additional immigrant visas for a four-year period in order to reduce backlogged applications from these areas where emigration had been historically high prior to the passage of the 1965 Act. The Senate failed to act on any of this legislation.

In 1972, though, the House made its first attempt to penalize employers for hiring illegal aliens, imposing mild civil and criminal penalties for knowingly hiring undocumented workers. The debate on this measure was remarkably prescient of later debates about the issue. Members from border states argued that, given persistent labor shortages, hiring illegal aliens was necessary for the harvesting of crops. Hispanic members were also concerned about discrimination in employment. In opposing the sanctions legislation, Representative Herman Badillo (D-NY) made the point often voiced in later debates that employer sanctions would introduce employment discrimination, especially against Mexican-Americans. Anyone with a foreign accent would be suspect and employers under fear of penalty simply would not bother to hire such applicants. Nevertheless, a motion to recommit (kill) the bill was rejected soundly on a 53–297 recorded vote, and the legislation was then approved by a voice vote. The Senate, however, again failed to take action.

While the two roll-call votes in the 92nd Congress did not result in any change in U.S. immigration law, it is worthwhile to pause and analyze the floor division on these measures (see Table 4.4). Following the model used earlier to assess House action on the 1965 law, our task is to explain these votes in terms of the partisanship and race of the members, whether members represent Southern or border states, whether they are members of the Judiciary Committee, and by virtue of constituency characteristics such as the proportion of the district population that is black, foreign-born, Asian, and unemployed. Table 4.4 shows the probabilities of voting for each measure associated with various values of the independent variables. Are these bills partisan measures? The evidence suggests that some partisanship is present—particularly on the bill to expedite citizenship for elderly immigrants. An estimated 92 percent of Democrats voted for the legislation, compared with 77 percent of Republicans. That a modest partisan cleavage would emerge on a bill to allow elderly immigrants to naturalize without having to display English proficiency is also suggestive of the constituency factors at work, as those with the largest proportion of foreign-born voters were about 31 percent more likely to vote in favor of the legislation than were those from districts with the fewest. Members representing large black populations, however, were against the legislation, while those representing significant Asian, Hispanic, and other populations favored it.

The vote to kill the most ambitious employer sanctions bill yet to surface in Congress was not especially partisan, since most Southern Democrats objected to the legislation. Republicans were actually slightly less likely to favor killing the bill than were Democrats. For the first time in the history of immigration policymaking, a strong cleavage emerged on the floor vote between border states and nonborder states, with members from areas along

Table 4.4   Estimated Probability of Voting Yes on Two Immigration Measures, 92nd Congress, U.S. House of Representatives

Variable	Expedite Elderly Immigrant Citizenship	Motion to Kill Employer Sanctions Bill
Democrat	.92	.13
Republican	.77	.06
White member	.87	.10
Nonwhite member	.99	.52
Non-South	.92	.07
South	.74	.25
Nonborder state	.88	.08
Border state	.90	.29
Not Judiciary	.88	.11
Judiciary Committee	.95	.03
Foreign born = .12	.68	.09
Foreign born = 28.9	.99	.15
Agriculture = .05	.92	.09
Agriculture = 36.01	.64	.17
Black = 0.0	.91	.10
Black = 87.1	.43	.09
Asian/other = .02	.83	.10
Asian/other = 67.3	.99	.28
Unemployment = 1.6	.72	.09
Unemployment = 13.2	.99	.13

Values represent the estimated probability of a Yes vote at the lowest and highest value of the independent variables, with all other variables held constant at their sample means.

the U.S. southern border about 22 percent more likely to favor killing employer sanctions than those from other states. Similarly, those with significant Asian and Hispanic populations in their districts were more hostile to employer sanctions than those lacking these groups. Finally, the nonwhite members of Congress may have bought into Representative Badillo's (D-NY) argument about the discrimination that would follow from employer sanctions, as nearly all of them voted against it.

Immigration Policy in the 93rd Congress

Under the leadership of Peter Rodino (D-NJ), the House Judiciary Committee found new energy to take up immigration legislation. Rodino represented a working-class ethnic district that included the increasingly black city of Newark as well as a substantial stock of older immigrants from Italy, Poland, and Germany. European immigrants and their children comprised roughly 39 percent of his constituents in 1970, with native blacks making up another 31 percent. Rodino had served in Congress since 1948 and had chaired the immigration subcommittee in the previous Congress (see Table 4.3). As subcommittee chair, he had initiated a series of ambitious field hearings on the illegal alien population. Rodino had strong ties to organized labor, and labor leaders complained that undocumented workers were being used as strike-breakers (Corwin 1984, 225). He used the field hearings to advance the call for penalties on employers who hire illegal aliens.

In his early years as chairman, Rodino generally favored a more restrictive immigration policy, aimed particularly at limiting Mexican immigration. Accordingly, in the 93rd Congress (1973–1974), Rodino marshaled several new policy initiatives through the immigration subcommittee, the full Judiciary Committee, and onto the floor. The gist of the most sweeping bill was to impose the per-country ceiling of 20,000 visas per year upon the Western Hemisphere nations. The 1965 Act had imposed that limit on other nations, but had subjected Canada and Latin America only to an overall limit of 120,000 visas to be allocated on a first-come, first-served basis. The proposed revision would apply the 20,000 limit to all nations, including Mexico, even though the annual demand for visas from Mexico was running more than twice that. Cuban refugees were to be excluded from the 20,000 per-country limit and automatically granted status as resident aliens (*CQ Almanac* 1973, 853). The bill maintained separate overall hemispheric ceilings established in the 1965 Act—120,000 for the Western Hemisphere and 170,000 for the Eastern Hemisphere. A provision of major significance was that of codifying a separate refugee status for aliens from all countries, not just those fleeing communism or from certain Middle Eastern nations, as that had been the practice under existing U.S. law. Supporters of this notion argued that existing refugee policy discriminated against those fleeing other types of oppression.

The Nixon administration supported legislation to give Canada and Mexico special treatment, an allocation of 35,000 visas each. Rodino's limit of 20,000 for Canada and Mexico, so it was argued, would damage relations with our neighbors and aggravate the problem of undocumented workers. In deference to the administration, Rodino offered a floor amendment to his own bill that would raise the allocation of visas to 35,000 annually for Canada and Mexico. Several amendments were then offered to the Rodino Amendment, but all were soundly defeated, including one by San Antonio Representative Henry Gonzalez (D-TX) to exempt Mexico from any annual visa ceiling. When the vote on the Rodino Amendment was called, the measure failed on a relatively narrow 174–203 vote. The consensus that had prevailed on so many previous rounds of immigration policymaking seemed to be

Box 4.3

Peter W. Rodino (D-NJ) chaired the House Judiciary Committee in the 1970s and 1980s. Rodino counts as one of the most influential immigration policymakers in the history of Congress. Courtesy of Peter W. Rodino.

Peter Rodino (D-NJ)

Representative Peter Rodino served as chairman of the Immigration Subcommittee in the 92nd Congress (1971–72), then was House Judiciary Committee chairman from 1973 through 1988. With close ties to organized labor, Rodino opposed guest-worker programs and employment-based immigration; but, with a large foreign-born constituency, he favored family-based immigration. Rodino was among the first to advance the idea of penalizing employers for hiring undocumented workers in the 1970s. In 1986, he was instrumental in shepherding immigration reform through the legislative process after the legislation had stalled in two previous congresses.

Rodino was born June 7, 1909, in Newark, N.J. He taught public speaking and citizenship classes at the YMCA and Federation of Clubs in Newark from 1930 until 1932. In 1935 and 1936, Rodino was managing editor of the *Jersey Review*. He graduated from the University of Newark (now Rutgers) and the New Jersey Law School with his LL.B. in 1937. He then practiced law in Newark.

On March 10, 1941, Rodino enlisted in the U.S. Army. In World War II, he served in North Africa and Italy in the First Armored Division. He was awarded the Bronze Star, the War Cross, and Italy's Knight of Order of Crown. He left the military in 1946 as a captain.

He lost his first campaign for Congress in 1946. However, Rodino won his second attempt in 1948. On most issues, he took liberal positions. Rodino managed the 1965 immigration bill in the House.

But Rodino's most prominent role came a year after he became chairman of the full committee. He presided over the impeachment hearings against President Richard Nixon. Rodino earned respect through his handling of those proceedings. The *Almanac of American Politics* reported, "His chairing of the hearings was even-handed and fair; he was careful to give the minority every opportunity to advance its views." *Politics in America* wrote that Rodino "work[ed] with Republicans to avoid the appearance of partisanship and [went] the extra mile to cooperate with the White House."

In 1989, Rodino retired to Newark. He had served a full forty years in Congress and undoubtedly counts as one of the most influential legislators in the twentieth century.

(Sources: *Almanac of American Politics*, 1984; *Biographical Directory of the U.S. Congress 1774–1989; Politics in America*, 1986)

evaporating. A second amendment offered by El Paso area Representative Richard White (D-TX) was designed to limit to five years the number of one-year extensions that could be granted to migrant workers. This amendment was also defeated on a 70–310 vote. Consensus prevailed, however, on the House passage of the bill as the measure was approved 336–30.

In later action in the 93rd Congress that was also ignored by the Senate, Rodino and the new immigration subcommittee chair Joshua Eilberg (D-PA) made yet another run at employer sanctions legislation. This bill, H.R. 982, took as its concern the illegal aliens who, in the eyes of the Judiciary Committee majority, had an adverse impact on the U.S. labor market and were beginning to burden federal and state public assistance programs (Corwin 1978). According to the Judiciary Committee's report, employers who hired undocumented workers not only exploited those workers at low wages but also denied U.S. citizens job opportunities (*CQ Almanac* 1973, 854). Given the difficulty of detecting undocumented workers, many of whom were no longer confined to the rural Southwest, sponsors of the legislation reasoned that imposing sanctions on employers who hired illegals was superior to tracking them down one-by-one. By threatening employers with sanctions, the demand for undocumented workers would dry up and they would stop coming across the border in search of employment. Among the groups pushing for the legislation were the NAACP and the AFL-CIO. Union support for employer sanctions was understandable given organized labor's history of favoring both limits on immigration and the regulation of employment practices of business and industry. Employer sanctions seemed to be the perfect option for controlling both the size of the labor market at the macro level and the inclination of businesses to subvert unionization efforts at the micro level by hiring workers who were averse to organizing. Many of the undocumented workers were perfect substitutes for the kind of low-skilled wage labor that comprised the labor union rank and file. For unions, the threat posed by the entry of a half million illegal immigrants per year was obvious. For the NAACP, on the other hand, the interest in controlling the flow of illegal aliens across the border is less obvious. But there was mounting evidence in the mid-1970s that blacks were losing out in urban labor markets to competition from illegal aliens. Long before Roger Waldinger (Waldinger 1996) and others (Bailey 1987; Mollenkopf and Castells 1991) documented the effects of immigration on the position of blacks in urban labor markets, the U.S. Commission on Civil Rights heard repeated testimony from black leaders in Los Angeles and elsewhere that black youth were being pushed out of jobs by immigrants, and especially low-skilled undocumented workers (Horn interview 3/3/97).

The analysis of the House votes on these measures in the 93rd Congress shows that partisanship divided the chamber only on the issue of increasing visas for Mexico and Canada, and on the passage of the 20,000 visa limit for nations of the Western Hemisphere (see Table 4.5). That Republicans would favor limiting visas for Western Hemisphere nations is certainly consistent with arguments they had made in the 1965 debate about how an unlimited supply of visas for these nearby nations effectively discriminated against the others. This time, they could use the discrimination argument to apply not to overall caps on hemispheric migration, but to numerical limits on individual nations. The floor division also shows that Republicans were taking a more consistently restrictionist stand on immigration questions by the mid-70s.

As for the votes on the employer sanctions legislation, regional cleavages supplant partisan ones. Those in border states, in particular, were far more likely to vote in favor of striking the employer sanctions provisions than those in nonborder states. Not only did members in border states have business constituents who employed undocumented workers and were therefore threatened by sanctions, many also represented large Hispanic constituencies that may have been threatened with discrimination if sanctions were employed. The vote to strike the employer sanctions provisions also shows that the minority members of Congress bought the discrimination argument made by Edward Roybal (D-CA), Henry Gonzalez (D-TX), and other members of the Hispanic caucus that the threat of sanctions would encourage employers to avoid hiring employees of color, and those with Hispanic or Caribbean accents, altogether. Table 4.5 suggests that House passage of the employer sanctions legislation also appeared to depend on Judiciary Committee membership. Peter Rodino was, for the first time in many recorded votes on immigration matters, able to maintain cohesion among the members of the Judiciary Committee on passage of employer sanctions legislation.

Members from districts with high proportions of black residents were ambivalent on these immigration matters. They were supportive of the general attempt to place a per-country quota on Western Hemisphere nations, but they were also hostile to employer sanctions, voting with the effort to strike them from the legislation. Minority members of Congress were not inclined to follow the NAACP's recommendations on employer sanctions. They were sharply divided. An estimated 51 percent of the nonwhite members voted to strike employer sanctions language, and support for passage of employer sanctions was lower among the minority members than the white members.

Several prominent floor cleavages that appeared in previous Congresses do not appear particularly influential here, especially the division between Southern and non-Southern members. Southern Republicans were still a rather small number by the mid-1970s, so the change cannot yet be the result of the long-term partisan shift of Southern seats. Clearly Southern attitudes on immigration had not grown less restrictionist in the eight years since the 1965 Act had passed. Southerners had opposed the employer sanctions bill of the previous Congress along with their border state companions (Table 4.5),

Table 4.5   Estimated Probability of Voting Yes on Five Immigration
Measures, 93rd Congress, U.S. House of Representatives

Variables	Increase Visas for Mexico/ Canada	Limit Extensions of Migrant Worker Visas	Passage of 20,000 Visa Limit for W. Hemisphere Nations	Delete Employer Sanctions Provisions	Passage of Employer Sanctions Bill
Democrat	.70	.08	.93	.20	.89
Republican	.24	.13	.97	.25	.86
White member	.45	.10	.96	.21	.88
Nonwhite member	.96	.05	.76	.51	.72
Non-South	.52	.06	.96	.22	.88
South	.41	.32	.90	.23	.86
Nonborder state	.37	.07	.97	.16	.91
Border state	.87	.32	.81	.62	.59
Not Judiciary	.49	.11	.95	.24	.85
Judiciary Committee	.47	.05	.98	.11	.98
Foreign born = .15	.48	.20	.95	.20	.89
Foreign born = 39.6	.58	.01	.98	.43	.78
Agriculture = .14	.46	.08	.95	.19	.89
Agriculture = 65.43	.86	.82	.96	.90	.37
Black = .05	.50	.12	.92	.19	.90
Black = 88.9	.43	.02	.99	.58	.60
Asian/other = .04	.51	.09	.95	.22	.88
Asian/other = 61.4	.05	.69	.97	.46	.39
Unemployment = 0.3	.44	.05	.96	.22	.91
Unemployment = 10.6	.61	.33	.92	.23	.78

Values represent the estimated probability of a Yes vote at the lowest and highest value of the independent variables, with all other variables held constant at their sample means.

but in the 93rd, the results show that being from a Southern state has no significant impact on the vote once other variables are taken into account. The variable for agricultural employment may be picking up the influence of some of these Southern seats. On the Roybal Amendment to delete employer sanctions, members in the most agricultural districts were about 71 percent more likely to vote in favor of this option than those in the least agricultural districts. Although the Senate took no action on these measures, the debates and votes in the 93rd Congress served the important function of putting many members on record and building momentum for future action.

The 94th and 95th Congresses:
Legislating the Admission of Refugees

The 94th Congress (1975–1976) brought in a huge new freshman class of liberal Democrats, "Watergate babies" as they came to be called. One might well have expected a dramatic legislative assault in a number of broad policy areas, including immigration, but action in this arena was mostly modest and noncontroversial. The reason for this may well be that immigration was still not an issue that brought unity to either party. The dominant theme in the previous two congresses was that illegal immigration should be controlled through the imposition of employer sanctions. This split rather than unified the Democratic party. In addition, the weakness of the national economy in the mid-70s did not encourage many members to think about lifting existing ceilings on legal immigration. Arguably one could contend that the restrictionists achieved a temporary victory in the 93rd Congress. The attempt to limit Western Hemisphere migration by imposing the same per-country cap that limited Eastern Hemisphere nations to 20,000 visas annually had gone nowhere in the U.S. Senate in the 93rd Congress, but it sailed through easily in the 94th and was signed into law by President Ford, just before he was voted out of office.

The Northern and liberal Judiciary Committee leadership in the House remained untouched by the sweeping internal reforms instigated by the younger Democrats. Peter Rodino (D-NJ) remained firmly in control of the chairmanship of the full committee and Joshua Eilberg (D-PA) in command of the subcommittee on immigration. First elected in 1966, Eilberg, a liberal from Philadelphia's northeast side, had compiled a strong antiwar record in his ten years in Congress. His district contained a large proportion of European immigrants, particularly Russians, Germans, Italians, and Poles, and his thinking matched that of other liberal Northern urban members: generally in favor of a generous legal immigration policy, but favoring employer sanctions as a means of attacking the problem of illegal immigration.

Refugee admissions were a dominant theme in the 94th and 95th Congresses. Refugees differ from immigrants in that immigrants leave their countries voluntarily, whereas refugees are considered to have been forced to leave by religious or political persecution. Because of their difficult circumstances, there was some question as to whether refugees should be considered immigrants and therefore counted toward the worldwide visa ceilings put in place by the 1965 Act. This question would be decided in several congressional battles of the late 1970s. Early in 1975 the United States had withdrawn all troops from Vietnam, and it was only a matter of time before the South Vietnamese regime would completely collapse. South Vietnamese government officials and soldiers who had fought the Viet Cong alongside U.S. troops were more than anxious to exit with their families in the face of the imminent Communist takeover. Having a longstanding precedent (dating to the early 1950s) of accepting refugees from Communist countries, from Hungary and Czechoslovakia to Cuba, few could oppose the admission of these latest victims of cold war politics. The U.S. military was put into action to aid the evacuation effort, but the state of panic in Saigon rendered the entire operation chaotic and unmanageable. In hearings held early in 1975, Eilberg criticized the Ford administration's handling of the evacuation of Vietnamese refugees as clumsy and poorly planned (*CQ Almanac* 1975, 316). In a speech before a joint session of Congress, the president requested the authorization and appropriation of emergency evacuation assistance and humanitarian aid.[3] The administration used its discretionary power to authorize the admission of 130,000 refugees, and Congress began action on legislation to provide aid and assistance; but events in Vietnam were moving far faster than the legislative process. As the floor action was about to conclude with a conference report, Saigon fell on May 1. Events had rendered the aid bill obsolete. Saigon had already been evacuated (*CQ Almanac* 1975, 316). New legislation moved through Congress quickly and was passed by mid-May. The authorization legislation included generous amounts for resettlement assistance, language and vocational training, and medical care for the newly arrived refugees.

In the House Judiciary Committee markup, several prominent Democrats greeted the legislation with hostility, including Jack Brooks (D-TX), John Conyers (D-MI), and Barbara Jordan (D-TX). Jordan and Conyers, both influential black members, apparently feared the threat posed to black constituents by the generously assisted entry of large numbers of Asian refugees, many of whom could potentially undercut the wages and working conditions of many in the black working class. More generally, both were concerned that not enough was being done to assist needy Americans. The House legislation was particularly controversial because its authorization of funds was open-ended—not designating a set funding level. Estimates by the administration suggested that initial resettlement costs could well run a half billion dollars. The authorization would be approved for fiscal years 1976 and 1977, and the refugee program would be reassessed at that point. While all of the committee's Republicans voted for the legislation, four Democrats voted against it, including Conyers, Jordan, and Brooks. In the Senate, the refugee authorization bill was reported out on May 12, with a set funding level of $405 million through 1977 (*CQ Almanac* 1975, 319). In almost all other respects it was similar to the House bill.

House floor action saw the consideration of several amendments, including one by Congresswoman Elizabeth Holtzman (D-NY) to set a ceiling of $507 million on the authorization. The House rejected on a standing vote an

---

[3]While action on the legislation moved through several committees, we will deal only with the Judiciary Committee here.

attempt to set the ceiling at $407 million, close to what the Senate Foreign Relations Committee had suggested in its action just two days before. Holtzman's amendment prevailed, however, on a 158–261 vote. Three amendments were flatly rejected on roll-call votes. The first was an amendment to require the president to report to the House and Senate authorizing committees every 30 days on progress in the resettlement effort. The second reflected the concerns of a significant bloc of members, including John Conyers (D-MI), who resented the assistance given to foreigners and would bar aid to refugees unless similar assistance was also available to other Americans facing similar hardship. This was defeated on a 71–346 vote. A third amendment, offered by ultra-liberal Congresswoman Patsy Mink (D-HI), would have provided an open-ended authorization for education assistance to refugees beyond fiscal year 1977. This measure was also resoundingly defeated on an 80–327 vote. Following the defeat of the Mink Amendment, the legislation was approved by a 328–47 vote.

The Senate followed the House in approving the authorization legislation a few days later, with a lower cap on funding, authorizing $405 million through fiscal year 1977. Three minor amendments were accepted on voice votes, and the legislation then passed by a 77–2 vote, with two Southern Republicans, Jesse Helms (R-NC) and William Scott (R-VA), opposing it. In the House-Senate conference committee, conferees agreed on a compromise funding level of $455 million—about midway between House and Senate proposals. Both Houses accepted the compromise legislation by voice votes. A corresponding appropriations bill was passed by both the House and Senate at about the same time (late May 1975). The House bill was adopted by voice vote. The Senate concurred on a recorded 79–2 vote, with Helms and Scott again in opposition.

In the following year, one of the most significant reforms since passage of the 1965 Act cleared on a voice vote late in 1976. Peter Rodino succeeded in passing legislation from the previous session bringing Western Hemispheric immigration into line with that of the Eastern Hemisphere. From then on, Canada and Latin America would be governed by the same 20,000 annual visa limit that applied to other nations under the 1965 Act. Rodino's legislation set an overall annual quota of 120,000 for the Western Hemisphere. In addition, a seven-point preference system would now govern immigration from both hemispheres. Previously, immigrants from Canada and Latin America were dealt with on a first-come, first-served basis. This generated a long waiting period for close relatives who would have gained easier entry had a preference system been in place. With no preference system, those with skills were also forced to stand in line (*CQ Almanac* 1976, 414). Reflecting pressure from labor interests, the legislation put into place the same certification requirements that had governed the Eastern Hemisphere since 1965, namely, that the Secretary of Labor could deny labor certification for immigrants if equally qualified Americans were available to fill those positions. The legislation also provided that Cuban refugees in the country prior to enactment of the bill who seek to become legal residents would not be charged to the overall annual total of 120,000. Both the House and Senate approved similar versions of the legislation with virtually no debate, House leaders from both parties arguing that the measure had easily passed the House in the previous Congress, and it became law on October 20, 1976, just days before Jimmy Carter won the presidential election.

The floor divisions on the immigration legislation in the 94th Congress are presented in Table 4.6 (also see Appendix Table A4.4).[4] In reviewing these votes, one must keep in mind that they are all on the refugee assistance legislation relating to the collapse of Saigon, and as such, are unique from other immigration measures considered since 1965. Reflecting the wishes of the Ford administration, Republicans resisted all amendments. On final passage, however, the vote was similar to many others on immigration issues of the time, largely consensual, with no partisan cleavages evident. Ninety-two percent of those voting favored the bill.

The vote of the minority members is worth special mention. They voted strongly in favor of barring the use of funds for refugee assistance if such aid was not also made available to natives facing economic hardship. In the end, the nonwhite members were less likely to vote for the refugee assistance package than the white members, with John Conyers (D-MI) being among the dissenters. Peter Rodino was able to keep many of his Judiciary Committee members in line to vote as a bloc against amendments to the legislation. Consistent with their austerity, Southern members were more likely than non-Southerners to vote against the liberal amendments offered to extend the authorization of education assistance to refugees and to bar the use of funds unless similar aid programs were also made available to natives. These same members voted with the effort to limit the amount authorized. None of the variables describing demographic features of members' constituencies appear to be relevant to any of these votes, except that those with high proportions of immigrants were about 20 percent more likely to vote in favor of final passage than those in districts with the fewest immigrants.

The 95th Congress (1977–1978) saw little action on immigration, but at least one major reform passed easily. Two measures came to the House floor. One bill, introduced early in 1977, sought to expedite citizenship to Vietnamese, Laotian, and Cambodian refugees. This legislation also extended public services to refugees, including income supplements, vocational training, and job placement programs and medical assistance. Just as in the 94th Congress, the measure had little opposition, passing on an overwhelming

---

[4] Appendix Table A4.6 presents the complete logistic regression result that are summarized in Table 4.6.

Table 4.6   Estimated Probability of Voting Yes on Five Refugee Assistance Measures, 94th Congress, U.S. House of Representatives

Variables	Requiring President to Report	Barring Use of Funds	Extend Authorization of Education Assistance	Limit Authorization to $507 Million	Passage of Refugee Assistance
Democrat	.52	.21	.18	.92	.95
Republican	.10	.03	.02	.83	.97
White member	.33	.11	.08	.90	.96
Nonwhite member	.52	.59	.60	.94	.72
Non-South	.39	.14	.19	.88	.96
South	.21	.07	.01	.95	.97
Nonborder state	.33	.12	.06	.91	.97
Border state	.35	.09	.34	.84	.93
Not Judiciary	.35	.13	.09	.91	.96
Judiciary Committee	.21	.04	.06	.77	.95
Foreign born = .15	.36	.10	.08	.91	.81
Foreign born = 39.6	.20	.27	.22	.76	.99
Agriculture = .14	.33	.14	.10	.89	.96
Agriculture = 65.43	.38	.01	.03	.99	.99
Black = .05	.33	.12	.08	.91	.96
Black = 88.9	.34	.10	.18	.83	.93
Asian/other = .04	.33	.13	.09	.88	.96
Asian/other = 61.4	.48	.01	.05	.99	.80
Unemployment = 0.3	.29	.10	.10	.83	.96
Unemployment = 10.6	.44	.16	.07	.97	.95

Values represent the estimated probability of a Yes vote at the lowest and highest value of the independent variables with all other variables held constant at their sample means.

390–22 vote. Opponents of the legislation were from Southern and border states, particularly Florida, Texas, and Arizona. The Senate approved the legislation on a voice vote, and President Carter then signed it into law.

The second, more consequential bill came up in 1978 and it sought to establish a single worldwide ceiling on immigration, combining the separate quotas for both Eastern and Western Hemispheres into an annual limit of 290,000. An identical seven-category preference system would remain in effect for all immigrants, independent of their nationality. The House passed this legislation with little debate on a 396–20 vote. Southern members from Florida, Georgia, Alabama, Mississippi, and Texas numbered among the small number of opponents, including Trent Lott (R-MS), the future Senate

majority leader. The Senate concurred with the judgment of the House, passing this legislation on a voice vote without debate, and it was signed into law
by President Carter (*CQ Almanac* 1978, 198).

The 96th Congress: More Refugee Admissions

Legislative action on immigration in the 96th Congress (1979–1980) again
centered on the growing number of refugees seeking asylum. In the 1979 session, the focus was on increasing the number of refugees allowed to enter the
country. For the first time in memory, action on immigration began in the
U.S. Senate where an activist liberal, Senator Edward M. Kennedy (D-MA),
had just taken over the reins of the Judiciary Committee upon the retirement
of James Eastland (D-MS). Kennedy introduced a bill (S. 643) to increase the
total annual ceiling of immigrants and refugees combined to 320,000, up 10
percent from the old ceiling of 290,000. The annual refugee limit from any
given country was increased from 17,400 to 50,000. In fact, the president had
been given the power to exceed the 17,400 annual limit under extraordinary
circumstances and had been regularly exceeding it in the late '70s to allow
entry of Indochinese refugees (Zucker and Zucker 1987, 54–55). Attacking
the piecemeal refugee policy that had heretofore been Congress's dominant
approach, Kennedy insisted that higher ceilings were required so that admissions could proceed without long delays and prolonged human suffering.
The legislation gave the president discretionary power to raise the annual
ceiling above 50,000 prior to each fiscal year if justified by "urgent humanitarian concerns" or the national interest (*CQ Almanac* 1979, 392). The bill
also broadened the definition of "refugee" to include those who were
uprooted for reasons other than communism, such as racial, religious, or
political persecution. Proponents argued that the old definition of refugee,
which emphasized victims of communist oppression or those fleeing from
certain Middle Eastern countries, placed an ideological constraint on who
could be considered a refugee. Of course this served to expand the potential
pool of refugees considerably.

Refugees were to be given lawful permanent residency upon their arrival
rather than having to wait for two years under probationary status as current
law required. More ambitious still, the legislation proposed to make many
temporary refugee assistance programs permanent, including cash assistance,
medical care, vocational and English language training, social services, and
family planning. States were to be completely reimbursed by the federal government for the costs of providing medical and employment programs for
two years following a refugee's arrival. About $40 million in new authoriza-
tions was to be approved for new programs to administer English language
and job training.

Looking back on the vote from the perspective of the contentious nature of immigration admissions in the 1990s, it seems almost astonishing that the Senate went along with these sweeping changes on an 85–0 floor vote. Several amendments were accepted on voice votes, the most significant of which was one offered by Walter Huddleston (D-KY) to sunset the 50,000 limit provision after three years (at the end of fiscal year 1982), at which time the annual refugee ceiling would be reevaluated. Huddleston also successfully pushed an amendment that would require the House and Senate to hold hearings on any request from the executive branch to increase admissions of refugees above the 50,000 limit.

A Bumpy Ride in the House

The House proceedings were not as smooth on similar legislation introduced by the new immigration subcommittee chair Elizabeth Holtzman (D-NY). Holtzman had won a seat in Congress just six years before by defeating the most senior member of the House, Judiciary Committee Chair Emanuel Celler, in a primary (Box 4.4). She had taken issue with Celler's support for the Vietnam war and claimed he had lost touch with his Brooklyn constituency. Because Holtzman was a thoroughgoing liberal on immigration and refugee issues, the transition to her leadership of the subcommittee from that of Eilberg was hardly noticeable. By 1978, however, the Republican minority had began to take a more aggressive and combative stance toward the Democratic leadership. Jimmy Carter's presidency was foundering in a bad and worsening economy. A number of conservative Republicans were elected to the House in 1978, including Newt Gingrich (R-GA). The conservatives brought with them new ideas and a stronger ideological commitment than that of the old guard. While Republican moderates such as John B. Anderson (R-IL) and Robert Michel (R-IL) maintained control of the party's leadership positions, Republicans found themselves challenging administration policies for the first time since 1968, the last time a Democrat had occupied the White House. These conditions set the stage for a number of challenges to the majority's initiatives. Democrats maintained a solid membership edge on the committees, however, and this helped Holtzman defeat any amendments that would have substantially altered the bill, including an attempt to impose a three-year sunset provision such as the Senate had adopted. The Judiciary Committee approved the legislation 20–6, with several leading Republicans voting against the legislation on the grounds that it gave the president too much authority to adjust the ceilings on refugee admissions so as to exceed the annual 50,000 limit.

On the floor, the bill came up on December 20, 1979, just as the first session of the 96th Congress was about to expire. Many of the amendments that had been defeated by the liberal membership of the Judiciary Committee had

Box 4.4

Elizabeth Holtzman (D-NY) chaired the House immigration subcommittee in the late 1970s and was especially active on refugee policy. Holtzman is shown here at a Judiciary Committee hearing on President Nixon's impeachment. Credit: AP/Wide World Photos

Elizabeth Holtzman (D-NY)

Representative Elizabeth Holtzman chaired the House Immigration, Refugees and International Law Subcommittee during the 96th Congress in 1979 and 1980.

Holtzman was born August 11, 1941, in Brroklyn, New York. She earned her bachelor's degree at Radcliffe College in 1962. Her law degree was awarded by Harvard in 1965.

Holtzman practiced law in New York City beginning in 1966. She became involved in politics, serving as an adviser to New York City Mayor John Lindsay in 1969 and 1970. She was Democratic state congresswoman and district leader from 1970 until 1972. She founded the Brooklyn's Women's Political Caucus and served as a delegate to the 1972 Democratic National Convention.

In 1972, Holtzman was easily elected to the U.S. House of Representatives after defeating House Judiciary Chair Emmanuel Celler in the Democratic primary. On the Judiciary Committee, Holtzman was particularly active on refugee matters and convened a series of high-profile hearing and investigations on Nazi war criminals still thought to be at-large. Deciding against a reelection bid for her House seat in 1980, she ran for U.S. Senate that year but was defeated by Alfonse D'Amato.

Holtzman returned to Brooklyn, where she became district attorney for Kings County. She served in that capacity from 1981 till 1989. She was then comptroller of New York City. Holtzman once again practiced law in New York and served on the advisory board of the National Women's Political Caucus.

(Sources: *Who's Who in American Politics, 1995–1996; Biographical Directory of the U.S. Congress 1774–1989*).

more support on the floor. The sunset provision, for example, was adopted on a voice vote. So, too, was an amendment by Carlos Moorhead (R-CA) to permit a legislative veto of presidential action to admit more than 50,000 refugees per year. A legislative veto would provide either House of Congress the power to disapprove a presidential effort to raise the ceiling on refugee admissions except in special emergency situations. Holtzman and Rodino spoke against the legislation on the floor, but they knew Moorhead had the votes to pass it easily (*CR*12/20/79, 37205–37206). A stiffer requirement demanding that the House and Senate Judiciary Committees give their approval before the president could admit more than 50,000 refugees was defeated on a voice vote. An amendment requiring congressional hearings following the president's decision to admit more than 50,000 refugees was adopted.

One of the most interesting and controversial proposals offered by James Sensenbrenner (R-WI), to reduce immigrant admissions in a given year by one for every two refugees admitted over the 50,000 limit, was defeated on a standing vote after vigorous opposition from floor managers Holtzman and Rodino. The debate on these amendments is particularly interesting because it clearly demarcated, for the first time, the Republicans on the Judiciary Committee as the proponents of immigration restriction. In few previous discussions of immigration and refugee policy were the Republicans so vigorous in their intention to weaken the legislation. With James Eastland no longer present in the Senate to bottle up any action on immigration and refugee policy, and with the most liberal Democrats firmly in charge of the House Judiciary Committee, the Republicans in the House who were opposed to liberal immigration and refugee policy had to assume new responsibility. A few Republicans, including Hamilton Fish (R-NY), the ranking member on the immigration subcommittee, spoke out against the efforts to restrain refugee admissions by conservatives in his own party. Early in his career, Fish, of Irish extraction himself, had worked in Ireland as a vice consul in the U.S. consulate in Cork. In that role, he processed visa applications and came to sympathize with people facing economic, political, and religious hardship in their homeland. His own ancestors had emigrated from Ireland for religious reasons. When he ran for Congress in 1966 in a heavily Irish New York district, he made a trip to Vietnam and had visited refugee resettlement sites. As one of his personal aides explained, Fish's interest in the plight of refugees was the product of these influences:

> As the war dragged on during the Nixon years, Fish came to realize that we had created an untenable situation for the South Vietnamese and the Hmong who had been our strong allies. We had to do something about this. Fish could see that the s___ was going to hit the fan for them when the North [Vietnamese] took over. Of course, many people in Congress were exhausted and wanted to wash their hands of the whole refugee mess. They had faced constituency pressure to

get out of the war, and they didn't want to deal with refugees. The intelligence we were getting out of that area was awful with the rise of Pol Pot. Our friends in Thailand were reporting that they were receiving thousands of people per day.

"Fish's support for immigration and refugee policy meant that he and Rodino had a lot of common ground. In those days there just wasn't much division along party lines," recalled a Judiciary Committee lawyer who had worked with Fish in the early 1980s. In spite of, or perhaps because of, Fish's moderate leadership, the boldness with which the conservatives took to the floor was clearly unprecedented. Those supporting the Sensenbrenner Amendment made the emphatic point that immigration and refugee policy should not be considered separately. Much of the nation was suffering from double-digit unemployment and rampant inflation, and the government was spending close to $1 billion annually on resettlement assistance. There was increasing evidence that many of the refugees were going on public assistance programs and remaining on them for long periods of time. Refugee-receiving states and localities were requesting that their members of Congress fight for federal aid to defray the costs of paying for these services. For the first time, immigration and refugee admissions could clearly be considered a redistributive policy, much like welfare and other public assistance programs designed to aid the native poor.

New Voting Patterns on Immigration Policy

The refugee tide had begun to produce a new set of cleavages in the committee and floor voting of Congress on immigration policy. Immigration and refugee policy began to take on the rhetorical color of many classic liberal–conservative issues fundamentally related to government spending and the government's role in the economy. In the end, however, enough changes were made to temper the opposition of the conservative opponents, including several California members on the Judiciary Committee who had pressed for changes. By the time the floor vote was called, Fish had brought many Republicans on board with persuasive arguments about how we owed these refugees something, given that they had been on our side in Vietnam. "The conservatives were not heartless when there was a group of people getting the s___ beat out of them. We owed something to the Hmong for the help they gave us in Vietnam," Fish's former chief of staff recalled. The legislation passed comfortably on a 328–47 vote, with dissent coming primarily from a handful of conservative Republicans and members in border and Southern states.

The legislative session expired before the House and Senate conferees could finish work on a compromise bill. In the new session, however, several major provisions were dropped. The legislative veto provision that the

Box 4.5

Hamilton Fish (R-NY) served as the Republican leader of the House immigration subcommittee and later the House Judiciary Committee opposite Peter Rodino in the 1970s and 1980s. Fish is shown here with a Nicaraguan refugee in a Central American refugee camp in 1986. Credit: Nicholas Hayes.

Hamilton Fish, Jr. (R-NY)

Congressman Hamilton Fish, Jr., was ranking Republican member of the House Judiciary Committee from 1981 until he retired from Congress in 1995. He served on the Subcommittee on Immigration, taking particular interest in refugee issues. Fish was particularly instrumental in working for passage of the 1980 Refugee Act.

Fish, who came from a prominent Republican family from the Hudson Valley, was born June 3, 1926, in Washington, D.C., while his father was serving in Congress. He earned his A.B. at Harvard in 1949 and his LL.B. at New York University in 1957.

Fish served in the U.S. Naval Reserve during World War II. He practiced law, then joined the U.S. Foreign Service, becoming vice consul in Ireland from 1951 till 1953. He worked at the New York Assembly as counsel to the Judiciary Committee in 1961. Fish served as Dutchess County Civil Defense Director in 1967 and 1968.

In 1968, Fish won election to the U.S. House of Representatives (he beat the future Watergate conspirator G. Gordon Liddy, then a local prosecutor, in the GOP primary). He established a record as being generally conservative on economic issues and liberal on social issues—though he was pro-life.

On the Judiciary Committee, Fish worked closely with Chair Peter Rodino. Throughout the 1980s, Fish played a moderating and conciliatory role between the liberal Democrats on the committee and his increasingly conservative Republican colleagues.

Fish died July 24, 1996.

(Sources: *Almanac of American Politics*, various years; *Biographical Directory of the U.S. Congress 1774–1989*; *Who's Who in American Politics 1995–96*)

House Democrats had opposed was eliminated. The sunset provision on the authority to admit 50,000 refugees that House Republicans had pushed for was also eliminated. Republicans looked with considerable consternation on the creation of a new agency within the Department of Health, Education, and Welfare (HEW) called the Office of Refugee Resettlement. The original House legislation had proposed moving responsibility for resettlement from the State Department to the White House, but that was far from creating an entirely new bureaucracy within HEW. The conferees also agreed to give refugees permanent residence status after one year. This was a compromise between the Senate version, which would have granted immediate legal residency, and the House version, which required a two-year wait (*CQ Almanac* 1980, 379). The conference report had eliminated some major provisions the inclusion of which had guaranteed easy passage in December, particularly the legislative veto. When the conference report came up for a vote in March 1980, it won approval by a narrow 207–192 vote. Even the docile and gentlemanly Robert McClory (R-IL), the ranking Republican on the Judiciary Committee, spoke out against it on the floor. He was joined by nearly all of the Republicans on the committee except for Fish in voting against the conference product.

The most far-reaching change adopted in the passage of the 1980 Refugee Act was the alteration of the 1965 preference system. As described earlier in this chapter, the seventh preference reserved 6 percent of all annual visas for refugee admissions. This preference category was abolished, and refugees would no longer count toward the overall annual immigration limit. They would now be admitted separately and independently of traditional family-based and business-oriented visa quotas. The 6 percent of visas that had formerly been reserved for refugees was awarded to the second preference, spouses and unmarried sons and daughters of permanent resident aliens.

In other controversial action in the 96th Congress, members of the House were sharply divided on emergency supplemental appropriations for refugee resettlement assistance. Congress passed a $100 million appropriation over the objections of Republicans and about half the Southern Democrats on a narrow 210–188 vote. The Senate passed the legislation as part of a larger spending package that became a "Christmas tree" of favorite projects and proposals that would have failed had they been advanced alone.

The only other legislation in the 96th Congress addressing immigrants and refugees was the reauthorization of public assistance programs and education services for refugees in the wake of the rapid influx of Cubans, Haitians, and Indochinese boat people, which appeared to be reaching its high-water mark in 1979. Just as it was looking like the refugee tide was subsiding, Fidel Castro suddenly opened his borders in April of 1980 and allowed Cubans to flee. Over 125,000 did so, many of whom were school-age children (*CQ Almanac* 1980, 430). Some estimates put the Asian refugee school-age population at 40 percent of the total incoming flow. The House legislation would authorize additional federal education assistance to affected school districts. Termed "impact aid," the bill would provide an additional $350–$750 per refugee child through 1983. Aid would be allocated according to the number of refugee children in the school district. The original bill also authorized the president to reimburse states and localities for other social services, such as Medicaid and AFDC, but these provisions were stripped out in the Education and Labor Committee markup, leaving only the educational assistance in the bill. The House passed the legislation on a voice vote. The Senate added the reimbursement provision the House had stripped out and passed the legislation by voice vote. The House then went along with the Senate version on a 303–94 vote.

Floor divisions in the recorded votes on immigration legislation in the 96th Congress are shown in Table 4.7 (also see Table A4.5 in the Appendix). Partisan divisions are more consistently prominent in the floor votes here than in many of the previous legislative sessions. In the 93rd Congress, for example, party divisions were present on two of the five roll-call votes. In the 1980 vote on the Refugee Act, an estimated 74 percent of Democrats voted for the legislation, while 76 percent of Republicans voted against it. Again, on the resettlement appropriations vote, the cleavage was about as wide, with 75 percent of the Democrats favoring the bill while only 28 percent of Republicans voted yes. There were far fewer voice votes in the 96th Congress than in those congresses earlier in the decade. The consensus that used to hold on immigration policy was beginning to evaporate over the issue of refugees and the cost of resettlement.

Black members who may have had problems with refugee aid in the 94th Congress apparently had overcome their reservations by the 96th. Leading black legislators, such as John Conyers (D-MI), Augustus Hawkins (D-CA), Shirley Chisholm (D-NY), and Charles Rangel (D-NY), voted for both the Refugee Act and for education assistance. Those with sizable black constituencies were neither no more nor no less likely to vote for refugee assistance. Those representing Southern blacks often voted against the legislation, while those from racially diverse Northern districts generally voted in favor. One exception was Illinois, where one Chicago-area Democrat voted no while several others avoided voting altogether. Southern members continued to oppose refugee assistance more than Northern members, and were especially hostile to the Refugee Act. Exceptions to this generalization include the Southern Democrats in leadership positions, those from more urban, liberal districts, and those with small but growing refugee populations in their districts (such as the delegation from South Florida). Those with high proportions of foreign-born residents were predictably supportive of all four refugee measures.

Table 4.7　Estimated Probability of Voting Yes on Four Refugee Assistance Measures, 96th Congress, U.S. House of Representatives

Variables	Raise Admission Limit on Refugees	Refugee Act of 1980 Conference Report	Resettlement Assistance Appropriations	Authorize Refugee Education Assistance
Democrat	.98	.74	.75	.88
Republican	.89	.24	.28	.73
White member	.96	.54	.57	.83
Nonwhite member	.97	.80	.77	.89
Non-South	.96	.65	.60	.87
South	.93	.28	.52	.70
Nonborder state	.97	.56	.60	.83
Border state	.89	.57	.51	.86
Not Judiciary	.96	.55	.59	.83
Judiciary Committee	.97	.65	.45	.87
Foreign born = .15	.79	.31	.33	.69
Foreign born = 39.6	.99	.99	.99	.99
Agriculture = .14	.96	.56	.62	.85
Agriculture = 65.43	.66	.53	.11	.30
Black = .05	.95	.55	.59	.83
Black = 88.9	.98	.63	.48	.89
Asian/other = .04	.96	.56	.58	.84
Asian/other = 61.4	.16	.50	.45	.67
Unemployment = 0.3	.94	.47	.48	.73
Unemployment = 10.6	.98	.74	.77	.95

Values represent the estimated probability of a Yes vote at the lowest and highest value of the independent variables, with all other variables held constant at their sample means.

Refugee Policy Transforms the Debate

Refugee admissions in the late 1970s introduced a new and controversial element into immigration policy, that of redistribution. For the first time, immigration policy had become redistributive policy at the national level.

Certainly immigrants in previous times required public assistance, but that assistance was rarely provided by the federal government. When the federal government did step in to provide aid, the refugee flows were sufficiently small that fiscal conservatives were unconcerned about the small amounts of aid that were distributed mostly through the annual appropriations process via existing state and federal agencies. The late 1970s changed all that. The refugee flows from 1975 to 1981 were unprecedented in both their size and the neediness of their populations (Stein 1979). These new peoples also looked different and would be much easier targets of discrimination than their European predecessors in the 1940s and 1950s. Add to this the problem that the American economy was in the middle of a long-term industrial decline and restructuring process characterized by a diminishing supply of good-paying, low-skill jobs. With double-digit unemployment rates and high inflation, liberal Democrats sized up the problem and responded with a host of aggressive spending programs and an entire new agency within the nation's largest welfare bureaucracy, HEW. Conservative Republicans reacted by opposing both refugee admissions and the expansion of refugee assistance programs. Opposition to the Cubans from the Mariel boatlift only heightened the tension on Capitol Hill. "The reaction to this was panic!" recalled a congressional aide who worked on immigration issues at the time. "It was like, holy s___! These people have invaded our shores! Castro has opened the asylums and let the lunatics out!"

For many, the tension was one between a humane refugee policy, on the one hand, and the future of the U.S. economy on the other. The last thing the national economy and native workers needed at the time was an influx of low-skilled, impoverished refugees, many of whom would come to rely on public assistance. Competition for jobs and housing induced by the settlement of these new arrivals in urban settings would only fuel interracial tension later. As for the Mariel Cubans, they were stereotyped as criminals, homosexuals, and the mentally ill. Much of the panic on the East Coast involved worries about the costs of incarcerating and providing medical treatment for this troubled population. Yet it did not seem right to slam the door in the face of these pathetic cases from abroad when we had established a long precedent of coming to the aid of the politically oppressed. These were people, after all, not numbers, and legislation is moved far more by anecdote than by cold facts and projections.

The 97th Congress: Warming Up for a Major Round

The 96th Congress taught many members to view immigrants in a new and not so attractive light: as unskilled and impoverished consumers of costly federal benefit programs. Members who believed in a generous immigration policy, including moderate New York Republican Fish, had often worried that the problem of illegal immigration would turn the public and Congress away from legal immigration, but now refugees were beginning to have this effect. Conservatives from districts both North and South began to identify immigrants with redistributive policymaking and all of its negative connotations: endless welfare payments, bloated bureaucracies, and old decaying cities. For some members and their constituencies, race was also stirred into the mix. European refugees were one thing; at least they were white. Now the public was being asked to tolerate refugees of color, from radically different cultures. Language was just one of the barriers to assimilation. The disparate levels of development between Southeast Asia and the United States put the Asian refugees at an additional disadvantage (Stein 1979, 36–37). Opponents of our open-door policy had vigorously supported the Vietnam War to keep these people where they were. Their arrival in nearby cities and neighborhoods was a reminder that the war had been lost.

The 97th Congress (1981–1982) ushered in a new era of conservatism. Ronald Reagan had won 489 out of 538 electoral votes (91 percent) in the November 1980 election, and he brought with him a Republican majority to the U.S. Senate. The GOP had picked up 35 seats in the House, now holding 192 to the Democrats' 243, the most the Republicans had held since 1968. House and Senate incumbents had taken the worst beating in years.

Elizabeth Holtzman (D-NY), who had been the prime mover of immigration policy in the 96th Congress, ran for a U.S. Senate seat and lost to Alfonse D'Amato (R-NY). She would subsequently go on to run for several other statewide offices, as well as the New York mayoralty and lose one race after another. While Peter Rodino remained in control of the Judiciary Committee, a new, more conservative voice moved into the immigration subcommittee chair—Romano Mazzoli (D-KY), from Louisville. While the Louisville population is as racially diverse as many other cities, Kentucky has virtually no recent immigrants. Those who have settled in Kentucky do not reside in any sizable concentrations. Perhaps for this reason Mazzoli considered himself free to push for major immigration reform, focusing particularly on illegal immigration, upon assuming power over the subcommittee.

In the Senate, the Republican takeover meant that Edward Kennedy (D-MA) lost the chair of the Judiciary Committee to Strom Thurmond (R-SC). This meant, of course, that he lost the immigration subcommittee chair also, to Alan Simpson (R-WY). Wyoming has even fewer immigrants than Kentucky; Simpson's hometown of Cody is 99 percent white. Simpson was even more free than Mazzoli to pursue new restrictions on legal and illegal immigration. Mazzoli, at least, had to contend with opposition within his own party that would undoubtedly temper the restrictionism of proposals reaching the House floor. Simpson's party was in control of the Senate. It was easy to imagine coalitions of Northern Republicans and Southern Democrats providing comfortable victory margins on the floor. That gave Simpson considerable confidence to pursue his legislative goals.

The Select Commission on Immigration and Refugee Policy

The story of the Simpson-Mazzoli legislation begins with the charter of the 1981 Select Commission on Immigration and Refugee Policy. This commission had been legislated into existence back in 1978 by Joshua Eilberg (D-PA), then chair of the House immigration subcommittee. The commission was chaired by Father Theodore Hesburgh, president of Notre Dame University, and its work was directed by Brandeis political scientist Lawrence Fuchs. With an impressive budget and a prestigious membership including members of Congress and of President Carter's cabinet, the commission held seven public meetings and twelve regional hearings and sponsored a major study, *U.S. Immigration Policy and the National Interest,* which was submitted to Congress and President Reagan in March 1981 (Donohue 1982; Reimers 1992, 88–89). The Commission's recommendations centered around four themes: employer sanctions, enhanced border enforcement, dealing humanely with illegal aliens already in the country, and stopping illegal immigration as a means to opening the door wider to legal immigration. The Commission's members, including Hamilton Fish (R-NY), the ranking Republican on the immigration subcommittee, remained concerned that negative attitudes toward illegal immigrants would eventually poison attitudes toward legal immigrants. Congruent with this reasoning, the Commission recommended taking a very hard line against illegal immigration. When commission members voted on policy resolutions to stop illegal immigration through increased border enforcement and deportation, the votes were mostly unanimous. Employer sanctions, however, proved to be an area of controversy. While most commissioners agreed that some type of employer sanction was in order, there was no consensus on what form of identification should be used to check workers' employment eligibility.

Granting amnesty to illegal aliens who have lived in the country for long periods was surprisingly noncontroversial, too. Commissioners recognized that there were few reasonable alternatives. What were the alternatives? The illegal population could remain illegal and in a permanent "second-class status." That seemed undesirable because undocumented workers are often afraid to confront authorities when they experience or witness crimes or have health problems. In this sense, their illegal status posed a threat to public safety and health. Another alternative was to pursue illegals and institute massive deportation efforts. That was judged to be too threatening to U.S.

liberties, subject to court challenge and costly (U.S. Select Commission 1981). In short, legalization was judged to be in the national interest because those qualifying for legal papers would no longer have to hide, they would no longer be subject to exploitation in the workplace, it would allow the INS to target its enforcement resources on newer immigrant flows, and it would permit information gathering about illegal immigration and the characteristics of undocumented aliens (U.S. Select Commission 1981, 74).

Aside from employer sanctions, the Commission was most divided on the issue of refugees and resettlement assistance. On divided votes, the commissioners recommended that programs set in place by the 1980 Refugee Act remain in place, that reimbursement of states and localities by the federal government be extended, that cash assistance programs be modified so that there is no overuse of the welfare system, and that medical benefits be made available independent of cash assistance so that refugees could leave welfare for work but not lose their health insurance.

Action on Simpson-Mazzoli in the 97th Congress

Initial action on immigration policy in the 97th Congress was modest and noncontroversial. Mazzoli and Simpson both managed to pass legislation streamlining the INS bureaucracy by eliminating certain rules that appeared to be cramping the agency without contributing to its enforcement efforts. The House and Senate approved the legislation on voice votes and President Reagan then signed it into law. Later, in 1982, the House reauthorized the Refugee Act of 1980 on a solid 357–58 vote, now amended to require refugees to participate in a job or language training program as a condition of receiving public aid. The Senate followed on a voice vote.

Early in 1982, based largely on the recommendations of the Select Commission's report, Simpson and Mazzoli introduced major reform bills in their respective chambers. Both subcommittees held extensive hearings in 1981, inviting input from the Reagan administration and major interest groups. Drawing on suggestions made by the Hesburgh Commission, Simpson argued that an acceptable immigration reform package should be analogous to a "three-legged stool," including improved border enforcement, penalties for employers who hire undocumented workers, and the creation of a national identification card verifying eligibility to work (*CQ Almanac* 1981, 423). In spite of the fact that the House had twice passed employer-sanctions legislation in hopes of cutting off the incentive to emigrate here, this portion of the legislation drew immediate opposition from both liberal Democrats— such as Senator Kennedy (D-MA), who expressed reservations about the discriminatory impact of sanctions—and business groups fearful that business was being asked to enforce immigration laws. Hispanic and minority-rights groups registered opposition. Organized labor was divided. Some unions favored employer sanctions as a means of purging the workforce of immigrant competition. Many union leaders were less than thrilled, however, with the prospect of amnesty for several million illegal aliens, and certainly the rank and file were prone to blaming immigrants for their declining wages. Nevertheless, the AFL-CIO ultimately supported Simpson-Mazzoli after the Senate Judiciary Committee included a provision that barred the hiring of foreign workers during a labor dispute.

Senate Action on Simpson-Mazzoli

In the Senate markup of the Simpson bill, Kennedy did manage to pass an amendment providing amnesty to all illegal aliens arriving in the United States before January 1, 1982. The original bill granted amnesty only for those arriving before January 1, 1978, awarding a temporary residence status to those arriving between 1978 and 1982, after which they would become eligible for permanent status (*CQ Almanac* 1982, 406). Kennedy's amendment passed on an 8–6 vote. In line with his pro-labor sympathies, Kennedy had long opposed measures easing the admission of temporary workers and preferred that temporary-worker status be the responsibility of the Department of Labor rather than INS. The Department of Labor had a closer working relationship with labor interests than did the INS and would be more likely to keep temporary-worker admissions to a minimum. Nevertheless, an amendment to give the Secretary of Labor more authority to regulate temporary-worker programs failed to pass the Republican-controlled Judiciary Committee.

The Reagan administration, for its part, expressed serious reservations about the amnesty program. Refugees were already placing an enormous burden on federal, state, and local social service agencies. The prospect of this suddenly new pool of mostly impoverished legal immigrants flooding to states and localities in search of public aid was understandably frightening to officials in border areas. Attorney General William French Smith argued that costs to states and the federal government would run in the billions of dollars. Smith and administration officials urged Congress to adopt an amnesty proposal but grant permanent resident status only after ten years of continuous residence in the U.S. (*CQ Almanac* 1982, 406). Under this proposal, only those aliens here before 1976 would be given amnesty. Those entering between 1976 and 1981 would be given temporary resident status, and would therefore be ineligible for public assistance. Simpson and Mazzoli argued that the administration's cost estimates were exaggerated because illegal immigrants were not as prone as refugees to using public services.

The employer sanctions provisions were reasonably serious, setting civil penalties of $1,000 per illegal alien hired for the first violation and $2,000 per alien for the second violation. Criminal penalties could be imposed if employers engaged in the habitual hiring of undocumented workers. Regarding employment eligibility checks, the Senate exempted small employers—those with less than three employees—from the requirement to examine employee's documents. Another employment-related measure designed to please agricultural interests expanded the existing "H-2" (the area of the U.S. Code where the program is described) program providing the seasonal entry of temporary agricultural workers.

Other major provisions included an elevated ceiling for legal immigration. The new ceiling would be 425,000 per year worldwide, a considerable increase from the previous limit of 320,000. Of these visas, 350,000 were to be awarded to preference categories for purposes of family reunification and 75,000 were to be awarded to preference categories covering special labor needs. But there were also some important new restrictions proposed in the legislation. Simpson included a provision to eliminate an entire preference category—the brothers and sisters of adult U.S. citizens—on the ground that this category created a backlog in other, more immediate family reunification preference categories. In other words, those waiting for a visa for a more immediate relative, such as a married or unmarried child, would be forced to wait longer because of the demand placed on the total annual visa quota from the adult brothers and sisters category. Eliminating that preference category would speed up the reunification of more immediate relatives of citizens and legal residents. As an additional restriction, the Simpson bill proposed that visas for immediate relatives of U.S. citizens be subtracted from the total number of visas allowed for family reunification. In existing law, those entering as immediate relatives of U.S. citizens were not charged to an annual quota. Finally, the bill streamlined the process by which aliens were determined eligible for asylum, creating a more informal, simplified process of exclusion and deportation.

Senate floor action went smoothly, and only two amendments were adopted, the first declaring English the official U.S. language, and the second by Charles Grassley (R-IA) to restrict the bill's amnesty provisions, moving the date of illegal alien entry from January 1, 1978, to January 1, 1977—a compromise with the administration proposal. More importantly, Grassley's amendment also prohibited aliens who were granted amnesty from using federal benefits for three years. Grassley's amendment moved the date of entry required for temporary residence status from January 1, 1982, to January 1, 1980, maintaining the illegal status for all those entering after January 1, 1980. The fundamental thrust of Grassley's amendment was to shrink the pool of undocumented workers eligible for amnesty. In addition, it created a block grant program to reimburse states for certain public services utilized by aliens who would be granted amnesty under the bill. The Grassley Amendment changed the bill's character considerably, but was accepted easily on an 84–16 vote (*CQ Almanac* 1982, 407). Two proposals by John Tower (R-TX) and Kennedy (D-MA) to weaken the employer sanctions provisions in the bill were defeated resoundingly.

House Action on Simpson-Mazzoli

In the House, the bill was embroiled in controversy from the beginning. Key players on the Judiciary Committee, including Chair Peter Rodino (D-NJ), were opposed to much of what had been passed in the subcommittee markup. Mazzoli had tried to follow the Senate's example by adopting a 450,000 ceiling on legal immigration while restricting the number of visas to be used for family reunification. Taking Rodino's lead, the full committee deleted these additions on a 15–12 vote (*CQ Almanac* 1982, 408). The issue of federal reimbursement to states and localities for the costs of amnesty was hotly contested. Don Edwards (D-CA), realizing that his state would bear the brunt of the fiscal burden, moved to require the federal government to pay 100 percent of the costs of the amnesty for a full three years after enactment of the legislation. This amendment passed on a narrow 16–12 vote. Rodino realized that this would not be a popular provision on the floor and could kill the entire bill. With the help of Reagan administration officials, Rodino succeeded in persuading three Republicans to switch their votes, thus eliminating the provision (*CQ Almanac* 1982, 408). Californians were especially active in this debate. Dan Lungren (R-CA), who would later become California's attorney general and run for governor in 1998, urged the committee to require a longer residency requirement of those receiving amnesty. He followed Grassley in proposing January 1, 1977, rather than 1978 and also restricting access to public benefits for three years. These proposals were adopted. On two occasions, Floridian Bill McCollum (R-FL) made the audacious move of trying to delete the amnesty provisions altogether. He lost by narrow margins both times on votes that split the committee by both party and region, with Southern Democrats joining Southern and Western Republicans against Northern Democrats and Republicans. A last-minute attempt to kill the bill by Sam B. Hall (D-TX) was just barely defeated on a 13–15 vote.

House leadership was not eager to have this bill reach the floor in an election year. The measure was controversial, particularly to groups within the Democratic caucus. Hispanic members argued that employers who faced sanctions for hiring illegals would avoid hiring anyone who looked or sounded Hispanic. Other Democrats were opposed because they represented urban constituencies with deep immigrant roots. For these members there were questions about whether legal immigration should be addressed at all. Peter Rodino (D-NJ), for example, opposed the effort to limit legal immigration until the issue of illegal immigration was handled first. Rodino even considered striking the legal immigration provisions altogether. Civil libertarians, black legislators, and the hyperactive American Immigration Lawyers Association (AILA) worried about the otherwise noncontroversial provisions in the bill that would streamline exclusion and deportation proceedings. These proceedings would be used disproportionately to exclude Haitians and those fleeing right-wing oppression, while those fleeing left-wing political regimes would nearly always be given asylum, no questions asked (Stepick 1984). Moreover, the streamlined procedures, so it was argued, were contrary to due process and would violate the civil rights of asylum-seekers.

Business groups, including the National Association of Manufacturers and the Chamber of Commerce, opposed employer sanctions on the grounds that it would turn businesses into enforcement agents of the INS. The AFL-CIO supported the sanctions provisions but remained concerned about temporary-worker programs that would undercut the wages and working conditions of natives.

Simpson-Mazzoli Dies on the Floor

Late in a lame-duck session called after the 1982 election, Mazzoli succeeded in bringing the bill to the floor. House leadership, however, had saddled it with an open rule inviting virtually unlimited amendments. By December 16, as debate was to begin, 300 amendments had been filed. Nearly 70 of these were filed by Congressman Edward Roybal (D-CA), a Hispanic member and fierce opponent of employer sanctions. He represented East Los Angeles, an area of Mexican-American concentration from which he managed to be easily reelected from 1962 until his retirement in 1992. On the initial motion by Peter Rodino (D-NJ) to bring the legislation up for consideration, Roybal and his allies managed to muster 65 no votes, indicating that a considerable number of members were opposed to even debating the bill. However, debate proceeded, with members of the Judiciary Committee controlling the time. The discussion was not especially partisan. Moderate Republican committee members such as Hamilton Fish (R-NY) and Robert McClory (R-IL), both of whom had served as members of the Select Commission, were behind the legislation. The strongest opposition came from Hispanic members and from conservative Republicans opposed to employer sanctions. As debate proceeded, more members became convinced that such a complicated bill should not be brought up in haste so late in the session. In spite of the open rule, only five hours of debate had been scheduled. The next day, on another procedural motion to bring the bill to the floor, there were 113 no votes. It was becoming clear to Mazzoli (D-KY) and Rodino (D-NJ) that this legislation would not pass in the 97th Congress. One amendment was offered by Congressman Augustus Hawkins (D-CA), requiring employers to compile and retain job applicant data. This measure was defeated on a 110–213 vote. Sensing that time was running out for the members to deal with the legislation before the holidays, Mazzoli (D-KY) made the decision to pull the bill from the floor and reintroduce it in the 98th Congress.

The floor divisions on the votes in the 97th House of Representatives are shown in Table 4.8 (also see Table A4.6 in Appendix). Racial divisions are quite pronounced in this Congress. Minority members are far more likely to vote in favor of the reauthorization of refugee assistance than whites. The major cleavages on this issue also divide the chamber by region and party, with Southern members about 13 percent less likely than Northerners to vote in favor of the bill and Republicans about 6 percent less likely to vote in favor of reauthorization than Democrats. On the motions to consider the Mazzoli legislation on the floor, the results in Table 4.8 show that Republicans were hostile to the idea, as were the nonwhite members and those in border states. So it was a coalition of Hispanic members and Republicans, who were hostile to employer sanctions for different reasons, that ultimately defeated the attempt to pass this bill. Those with high proportions of foreign-born constituents, on the other hand, were far more supportive of considering the legislation than members from homogeneous, white, nonethnic districts. The members with large foreign-born constituencies were those closest to Rodino (D-NJ) and Mazzoli (D-KY) and whose urban districts were substantially similar in composition to those of the bill's sponsors.

Lessons from the 97th Congress

The 97th Congress marked an interesting departure in the recent history of immigration policy. First, the Senate had seized the initiative, pushing through a sweeping set of reforms that the House simply lacked the will to address. During the 1970s, it was the Senate, and particularly Judiciary Committee Chair James Eastland (D-MS), that had done the foot-dragging. Eastland was alleged to employ cheap alien labor on his own Mississippi plantation (Corwin 1984, 225). With the change in membership in 1978, followed by the change in party control in 1980, the stage was set for renewed action on many controversial immigration matters that Peter Rodino (D-NJ) and his colleagues had urged the House to consider earlier. Now that the Senate no longer stood in the way of these proposals, House opposition had to be more organized and more intense. In the early and mid-1970s, House opposition to employer-sanctions legislation had been halfhearted.

Table 4.8 Estimated Probability of Voting Yes on Refugee Assistance and Immigration Reform Measures, 97th Congress, U.S. House of Representatives

Variables	Reauthorization of Refugee Assistance	First Motion to Consider Immigration Reform Bill	Second Motion to Consider Immigration Reform Bill	Require Employers to Keep Job Applicant Data
Democrat	.92	.93	.72	.53
Republican	.86	.67	.48	.02
White member	.91	.88	.67	.18
Nonwhite member	.31	.55	.06	.73
Non-South	.92	.87	.66	.32
South	.79	.89	.55	.04
Non-border state	.90	.91	.69	.20
Border state	.89	.62	.38	.20
Not Judiciary	.90	.87	.60	.20
Judiciary Committee	.44	.92	.90	.20
Foreign born = .15	.89	.77	.54	.11
Foreign born = 39.6	.96	.99	.97	.98
Agriculture = .14	.91	.88	.69	.24
Agriculture = 65.43	.73	.52	.02	.01
Black = .05	.92	.88	.61	.17
Black = 88.9	.66	.81	.79	.52
Asian/other = .04	.89	.88	.62	.21
Asian/other = 61.4	.99	.53	.97	.04
Unemployment = 0.3	.89	.85	.68	.13
Unemployment = 10.6	.93	.91	.53	.47

Values represent the estimated probability of a Yes vote at the lowest and highest value of the independent variables, with all other variables held constant at their sample means.

Opponents knew it had little chance. The 97th Congress drastically altered the strategic calculations of those opponents. The Hispanic caucus, led by the likes of Edward Roybal (D-CA) and Robert Garcia (D-NY), had to launch a full-scale war against a bill thought to be so inimical to the civil rights of their constituencies.

The Republicans, for their part, were highly skeptical of this legislation on the grounds that it forced employers to do the work of INS agents, raising the cost of doing business by forcing them to scrutinize documents and imposing penalties if they made a mistake. But the House GOP was also internally cleaved. Roughly one-third of Republicans voted no on the first motion to consider the bill, and about half refused to go along with the second motion. Partly the split reflected the growing liberal–conservative division within the House GOP (Connelly and Pitney 1994). Younger, more recently elected members were taking a hard line of noncooperation with the Democratic majority. They knew that, with the assistance of the dissenting Democrats, they could put this debate off for another year or two. Aggressive conservatives like Robert Walker (R-PA), Newt Gingrich (R-GA), and Vin Weber (R-MN) stalked the floor demanding roll calls on nearly every procedural and substantive move. Older, more liberal members in senior committee slots—people like Hamilton Fish (R-NY)—had an accommodating attitude toward the Democratic leadership. Rather than rejecting Democratic ideas out of hand, their legislative proposals were cut-rate compromises with Democratic ideas (Connelly and Pitney 1994, 23).

Every new election year heralded the growing seniority and power of the ideologically conservative Republicans elected increasingly from the South and West. In the 1960s, immigration remained mostly nonpartisan because so many Southern Democrats voted against open immigration policies. The new partisanship on immigration policy emerging in the 1980s was part of the broader polarization of Congress that was occurring as Southern Democrats were replaced by Republicans. But membership replacement and party realignment in the South does not tell the entire story. The needs of the new immigrant and refugee populations were met by Democratic policy proposals modeled after New Deal and Great Society human service programming. In some cases, immigrants were on the receiving end of spending programs more generous than what was being offered to natives in similar circumstances. With immigration and refugee policy taking on this redistributive dimension, it is no surprise that partisanship becomes a more important predictor of the yeas and nays.

Finally, regional divisions separating border from nonborder states seem to supplant the older Southern-versus-Northern cleavage in previous rounds of immigration reform. Members from Florida, Texas, California, New Mexico, and Arizona were about 30 percent less likely to support consideration of the Mazzoli bill than those from nonborder states. The emergence of employer sanctions as a threat to both business and minority constituencies was enough to create a strange liberal–conservative coalition among members in border regions that would appear again and again in the coming rounds of immigration reform.

Keith Poole and Howard Rosenthal (1997; 1991; 1985) have made the argument that much of congressional roll-call voting can be explained with reference to a single continuum, a unique underlying partisan dimension that defines members primarily in terms of their attitudes toward redistribution (Poole and Rosenthal 1997; 1991). One implication of this theory is that when once noncontroversial matters such as immigration policy become controversial enough that recorded votes are demanded, we might look for a substantive change in the nature of the policy. Issues that were once noncontroversial enough to warrant easy voice votes may have become controversial because they have taken on a redistributive character. In this chapter, we have suggested that in the area of immigration policy the number of recorded votes has steadily risen with the shift of immigration policy toward redistribution in the late 1970s.

We have indicated that the debates over refugee admissions in 1978, 1979, and 1980 turned immigration policy into a redistributive issue. Some might object that refugee policy is not really immigration policy—that we have muddled together two policy areas that should be kept separate. Admittedly, refugees and immigrants are different in one critical respect: Refugees are not fleeing their homelands voluntarily and may seek to return home some day. But once they arrive in the United States, they usually do not want to go home even if they can, eroding much of the distinction that is often made between refugees and immigrants. Furthermore, after a short period, refugees receive a work permit—that is, they become lawful permanent residents.

Most members of Congress saw no real distinction between refugees and immigrants in the period from 1978 to 1980 and certainly the public failed to see much of one. Perhaps this is the reason why the consensus on immigration policy disappeared as a result of the refugee crisis. In confronting the refugee influx from Southeast Asia, Cuba, Iran, Haiti, and elsewhere, members of Congress correctly perceived that they were opening the doors to a permanent immigrant population, not a temporary one. Most of these refugees were unskilled, illiterate, penniless, and unsuited to a rapid assimilation into the U.S. mainstream. They would need some kind of aid and assistance. What kind of aid, how much to give, and for how long then became the major questions for debate. Since the New Deal, the answer to these common questions about government assistance has been a major source of disagreement between the two major political parties.

The Democratic majority's solutions to pressing problems posed by legal and illegal immigration followed a familiar pattern. The answer to the poverty of refugees and other legal immigrants was to declare them eligible for generous government benefit programs that were redistributive in nature. In response to the illegal immigration problem, the solution was also familiar and just as easy to imagine in liberal/conservative terms: Impose additional regulatory burdens on employers in the form of work-verification requirements. Republicans instinctively reacted against such policies and in so doing forced even this aspect of immigration policy into Poole and Rosenthal's familiar mold. Democrats and Republicans have come to represent a stable set of interests that return again and again to old policy prescriptions in response to new problems. Once these interests involved themselves fully in the immigration policy debate, it was only a matter of time before bipartisan consensus would break down and Congress would begin to bicker about immigration in these conventional and totally predictable terms.

APPENDIX TO CHAPTER 4

Table A4.1   Logistic Regression Estimates of a Yes Vote on the 1965
Immigration and Nationality Act Amendments in the U.S.
House of Representatives

Variables	MacGregor Amendment	House Passage	Conference Report
Party (0 = D, 1 = R)	4.59**	−.42	.67
	(.45)	(.38)	(.47)
Minority member	−6.15	.65	−2.85**
	(15.56)	(1.36)	(1.42)
Judiciary Committee	−.26	.85	.58
	(.62)	(.66)	(.70)
Southern state	1.27**	−2.17**	−2.82**
	(.52)	(.47)	(.54)
Border state	−.35	−.31	−.11
	(.43)	(.51)	(.52)
Percent foreign born	−.24**	.26**	.17**
	(.06)	(.08)	(.08)
Percent black	.02	−.03*	−.01
	(.02)	(.02)	(.02)
Percent Asian/other	−.06	−.02	.01
	(.11)	(.05)	(.04)
Percent agriculture	.04*	−.05**	−.07**
	(.02)	(.02)	(.02)
Percent unemployment	−.18*	.18	.07
	(.11)	(.11)	(.14)
Constant	−4.91	1.59	2.02
% Correctly classified	85.5	87.4	82.3
Null model	53.6	77.0	87.9
χ^2 =	295.9	191.3	168.5
Significance	p < .0001	p < .0001	p < .0001
N =	407	413	389

Source: Congressional Quarterly Almanac and *Congressional District Databook*, various years.
Dependent variable: 0 = No vote; 1 = Yes vote.
MLE Coefficients; standard errors in parentheses;
*p < .10; **p < .05 two-tailed tests.

Table A4.2   Logistic Regression Estimates of a Yes Vote on Two
Immigration Measures, 92nd Congress, U.S. House of
Representatives

Variables	Expedite Elderly Immigrant Citizenship	Motion to Kill Employer Sanctions Bill
Party (0 = D, 1 = R)	−1.17**	−.84*
	(.41)	(.43)
Minority member	4.92	2.34**
	(14.05)	(.84)
Judiciary Committee	.92	−1.43
	(.66)	(1.09)
Southern state	−1.33**	1.47**
	(.58)	(.51)
Border state	.25	1.60**
	(.62)	(.41)
Percent foreign born	.24**	.02
	(.08)	(.04)
Percent black	−.03*	−.001
	(.02)	(.02)
Percent Asian/other	.45	.02
	(.33)	(.03)
Percent agriculture	−.05**	.02
	(.03)	(.03)
Percent unemployment	.30**	.03
	(.12)	(.12)
Constant	.95	−2.11
% Correctly classified	83.0	86.9
Null model	69.6	84.8
χ^2 =	137.3	75.4
Significance	p < .0001	p < .0001
N =	276	350

Source: Congressional Quarterly Almanac and *Congressional District Databook*, various years.
Dependent variable: 0 = No vote; 1 = Yes vote.
MLE Coefficients; standard errors in parentheses;
*p < .10; **p < .05 two-tailed tests.

Table A4.3   Logistic Regression Estimates of a Yes Vote on Five Immigration Measures, 93rd Congress, U. S. House of Representatives

Variables	Increase Visas for Mexico/ Canada	Limit Extensions of Migrant Worker Visas	Passage of 20,000 Visa Limit for W. Hemisphere Nations	Delete Employer Sanctions Provisions	Passage of Employer Sanctions Bill
Party (0 = D, 1 = R)	−2.03*	.45	.86*	.28	−.25
	(.28)	(.34)	(.49)	(.31)	(.36)
Minority member	3.45*	−.88	−1.93	1.37**	−1.04
	(1.90)	(1.44)	(1.23)	(.84)	(.82)
Judiciary	−.08	−.93	.91	−.90	2.34*
Committee	(.48)	(.80)	(1.14)	(.58)	(1.09)
Southern state	−.42	1.90**	−1.08	.01	−.17
	(.43)	(.50)	(.70)	(.52)	(.46)
Border state	2.43**	1.78**	−1.93**	2.14**	−2.01**
	(.42)	(.42)	(.53)	(.36)	(.39)
Percent foreign	.01	−.17**	.03	.03	−.02
born	(.03)	(.07)	(.06)	(.04)	(.03)
Percent black	−.003	−.02	.05*	.02*	−.02
	(.01)	(.02)	(.03)	(.01)	(.01)
Percent Asian/other	−.05	.05	.01	.02	.04
	(.04)	(.04)	(.04)	(.03)	(.03)
Percent agriculture	.03	.06**	.0008	.06**	−.04
	(.02)	(.03)	(.06)	(.03)	(.03)
Percent	.08	.24**	−.10	.001	−.10
unemployment	(.10)	(.11)	(.16)	(.11)	(.12)
Constant	1.92	−3.89	2.20	−2.67	3.62
% Correctly classified	73.2	83.7	93.2	79.5	83.3
Null model	53.8	81.6	91.8	73.6	82.5
χ^2 =	142.1	94.9	45.6	82.8	73.5
Significance	p < .0001	p < .0001	p < .0001	p < .0001	p < .0001
N =	377	380	366	361	360

Source: Congressional Quarterly Almanac and *Congressional District Databook*, various years.
Dependent variable: 0 = No vote; 1 = Yes vote.
MLE Coefficients; standard errors in parentheses;
*p < .10; **p < .05 two-tailed tests.

Table A4.4   Logistic Regression Estimates of a Yes Vote on Five Refugee Assistance Measures, 94th Congress, U. S. House of Representatives

Variables	Requiring President to Report	Barring Use of Funds	Extend Authorization of Education Assistance	Limit Authorization to $507 Million	Passage of Refugee Assistance
Party (0 = D, 1 = R)	−2.28**	−2.21**	−2.44**	−.92**	.49
	(.31)	(.54)	(.52)	(.33)	(.47)
Minority member	.79	2.50**	2.84**	.64	−2.34**
	(.65)	(.74)	(.91)	(1.26)	(1.00)
Judiciary committee	−.72*	−1.13*	−.53	−1.10**	−.15
	(.44)	(.69)	(.57)	(.43)	(.70)
Southern state	−.89**	−.84*	−3.30**	.99*	.39
	(.37)	(.49)	(.72)	(.58)	(.60)
Border state	.10	−.32	2.04**	−.65	−.82
	(.34)	(.46)	(.48)	(.54)	(.59)
Percent foreign born	−.02	.03	.03	−.03	.38**
	(.02)	(.03)	(.03)	(.03)	(.12)
Percent black	.0003	−.002	.01	−.008	−.008
	(.01)	(.01)	(.02)	(.02)	(.02)
Percent Asian/other	.01	−.07	−.01	.17	−.03
	(.03)	(.06)	(.03)	(.15)	(.04)
Percent agriculture	.003	−.05	−.02	.04	.02
	(.03)	(.05)	(.05)	(.04)	(.05)
Percent unemployment	.07	.06	−.05	.21	−.04
	(.09)	(.12)	(.12)	(.14)	(.15)
Constant	2.32	1.07	1.35	2.28	1.14
% Correctly classified	69.7	84.9	86.2	87.2	92.7
Null model	62.3	82.9	80.3	86.7	92.5
χ^2 =	91.7	70.9	125.5	29.6	30.1
Significance	p < .0001	p < .0001	p < .0001	p < .001	p < .0008
N =	419	417	407	407	412

Source: Congressional Quarterly Almanac and *Congressional District Databook*, various years.
Dependent variable: 0 = No vote; 1 = Yes vote.
MLE Coefficients; standard errors in parentheses;
*p < .10; **p < .05 two-tailed tests.

Table A4.5   Logistic Regression Estimates of a Yes Vote on Four Refugee
Assistance Measures, 96th Congress, U. S. House of
Representatives

Variables	Raise Admission Limit on Refugees	Refugee Act of 1980 Conference Report	Resettlement Assistance Appropriations	Authorize Refugee Education Assistance
Party (0 = D, 1 = R)	−1.56**	−2.24**	−2.02**	−.98**
	(.39)	(.29)	(.27)	(.28)
Minority member	.57	1.21	.92	.54
	(1.84)	(.94)	(.93)	(1.15)
Judiciary Committee	.36	.43	−.59	.31
	(.81)	(.48)	(.47)	(.55)
Southern state	−.76	−1.56**	−.32	−1.03**
	(.58)	(.47)	(.41)	(.44)
Border state	−1.30**	.04	−.36	.21
	(.53)	(.40)	(.36)	(.42)
Percent foreign born	.39**	.22**	.23**	.18**
	(.12)	(.05)	(.05)	(.06)
Percent black	.01	.004	−.005	.006
	(.02)	(.02)	(.01)	(.02)
Percent Asian/other	−.08**	−.004	−.009	−.02
	(.03)	(.03)	(.03)	(.03)
Percent agriculture	−.04	−.002	−.04	−.03
	(.03)	(.03)	(.03)	(.03)
Percent unemployment	.11	.13	.14	.23**
	(.14)	(.10)	(.10)	(.11)
Constant	3.47	1.95	1.76	1.37
% Correctly classified	89.8	79.0	77.9	79.1
Null model	87.0	52.0	53.0	76.0
χ^2 =	67.3	184.1	151.2	77.1
Significance	p < .0001	p < .0001	p < .0001	p < .0001
N =	375	399	398	397

Source: Congressional Quarterly Almanac and *Congressional District Databook*, various years.
Dependent variable: 0 = No vote; 1 = Yes vote.
MLE Coefficients; standard errors in parentheses;
*p < .10; **p < .05 two-tailed tests.

Table A4.6   Logistic Regression Estimates of a Yes Vote on Refugee
Assistance and on Immigration Reform Measures, 97th
Congress, U. S. House of Representatives

Variables	Reauthorization of Refugee Assistance	Motion to Consider Immigration Reform Bill	Motion to Consider Immigration Reform Bill	Require Employers to Keep Job Applicant Data
Party (0 = D, 1 = R)	−.66*	−1.92**	−1.02**	−4.06**
	(.35)	(.39)	(.30)	(.58)
Minority member	−3.15**	−1.80	−3.39**	2.49**
	(.72)	(.77)	(1.03)	(1.18)
Judiciary Committee	.57	.63	1.77**	.003
	(.76)	(.71)	(.70)	(.66)
Southern state	−1.17**	.24	−.47	−2.45**
	(.46)	(.49)	(.44)	(.70)
Border state	−1.30**	−1.77**	−1.28**	−.03
	(.53)	(.48)	(.43)	(.55)
Percent foreign born	.03	.16**	.09	.15**
	(.05)	(.07)	(.05)	(.05)
Percent black	−.02	−.006	.01	.02
	(.04)	(.02)	(.02)	(.02)
Percent Asian/other	.07	−.03	.05	−.03
	(.06)	(.05)	(.04)	(.05)
Percent agriculture	−.02	−.03	−.07*	−.05
	(.04)	(.04)	(.04)	(.05)
Percent unemployment	.05	.06	−.07	.20
	(.13)	(.12)	(.11)	(.14)
Constant	3.40	4.09	2.35	3.13
% Correctly classified	88.0	76.1	68.2	88.0
Null model	86.0	76.0	57.0	77.0
χ^2 =	61.5	56.9	58.6	200.5
Significance	p < .0001	p < .0001	p < .0001	p < .0001
N =	415	272	255	316

Source: Congressional Quarterly Almanac and *Congressional District Databook*, various years.
Dependent variable: 0 = No vote; 1 = Yes vote.
MLE Coefficients; standard errors in parentheses;
*p < .10; **p < .05 two-tailed tests.

CHAPTER 5

THE CONGRESSIONAL POLITICS OF IMMIGRATION POLICY, 1982–1994

In the last chapter we described how immigration policy was gradually converted from a consensus issue to a highly divisive one. The divisions within Congress have increasingly reflected traditional partisan and ideological cleavages. Keith Poole and Howard Rosenthal (1997) have suggested that policies that are controversial enough to come to a recorded vote can often be explained in terms of a single liberal–conservative political dimension defined by the attitudes of members toward redistribution and the role of government in the economy. While Poole and Rosenthal modestly refrain from suggesting that their single-dimension theory operates to predict specific issues and votes, we have argued that immigration policy votes have been increasingly easy to predict in these liberal–conservative terms. Another trend worth noting is that the number of recorded votes as a percentage of all votes has risen steadily since 1965, as Figure 5.1 indicates. In the mid-1960s, recorded votes on immigration policy were demanded, at most, only one-third of the time. By 1996, however, 75 percent of the votes occurring on the floor were recorded roll calls. The increase in the number of recorded votes is only partly explained by the move to electronic voting in the House with the convening of the 93rd Congress in January 1973. The surge in the demand for recorded votes occurs in the 97th and 98th Congresses during the time the House and Senate were considering controversial measures to impose employer sanctions and to legalize large numbers of undocumented workers (see Figure 5.1).

As the number of recorded votes has risen, the floor division has reflected ever-narrower majorities (Figure 5.2). Figure 5.2 shows the drop in the difference between the majority and minority percentages of the vote from the 89th to the 104th Congresses. With each new Congress, the difference in the size of the majority and minority blocs has diminished an average of 1.4 percent. This is a clear sign that immigration matters have become increasingly controversial. Action in the 98th and 99th Congresses was the most divisive, while action in earlier times saw majorities 20 percentage

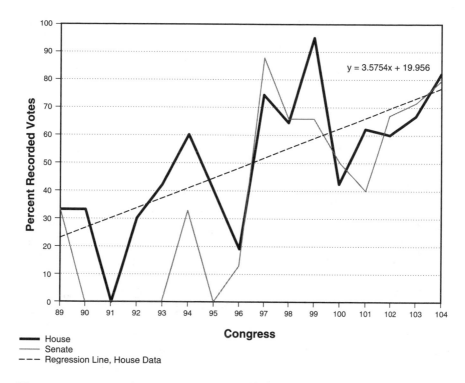

$y = 3.5754x + 19.956$

House
Senate
Regression Line, House Data

Figure 5.1   Recorded Floor Votes as a Percentage of All Floor Votes on Immigration Legislation, 89th–104th Congresses

points larger than in the more recent rounds of policymaking. The absence of consensus reflects the changing nature of immigration policy. Since the passage of Proposition 187 in California in 1994, most observers have realized that immigration has become a redistributive issue. But redistribution interposed itself as early as 1977 and 1978 in debates about refugee entry and resettlement assistance, and with redistribution has come party division. In the 1960s and early 1970s, partisanship was not an especially good predictor of floor divisions on most votes. A legislator's behavior could be better predicted by looking at constituency characteristics and by determining whether the member was from a Northern or Southern state. By the late 1970s, however, decisions about the fate of the foreign born were decided mostly along party lines, with other constituency influences figuring in only occasionally.

In this chapter, we will detail the congressional action on immigration policy from the 98th through the 103rd Congresses. This period, spanning the years from 1982 to 1994, involved two major rounds of reform, one in 1986, the other in 1990, and both rounds expanded the number of legal

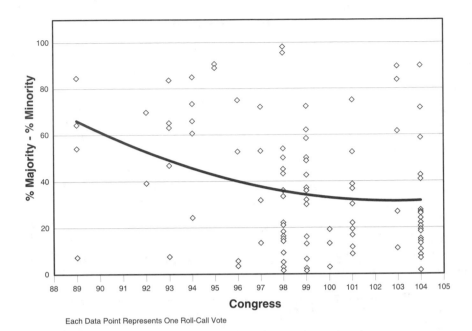

Each Data Point Represents One Roll-Call Vote

Figure 5.2   The Narrowing Floor Division on Immigration Votes in the
U.S. House of Representatives (curve fit using regression with
2nd-degree polynomial)

immigrants admitted into the country. In 1986, the primary tool of this
expansion was a blanket amnesty program for undocumented residents. In
1990, the worldwide cap on admissions was increased considerably and annual
immigration reached its historical high-water mark. Interspersed between and
after these reform efforts were numerous smaller measures that we will discuss briefly in the order in which they came to the floor.

The 98th Congress: Simpson and Mazzoli Thwarted Again

In Chapter 4, we described how the 97th Congress expired just as Romano
Mazzoli (D-KY) was bringing his major reform legislation to the floor. House
leaders, and particularly Speaker Thomas P. O'Neill (D-MA), were not
enthusiastic about immigration reform and had postponed it until literally the
last minutes of the session. In the 98th Congress (1983–1984), the leadership
corps in the House remained much the same as in the 97th, with O'Neill easily reelected Speaker. In the Senate, Republicans remained in control, which
meant immigration subcommittee chair Alan Simpson (R-WY) would again
have a relatively easy time passing his version of the legislation (S. 529).

Senate Action in the 98th Congress

The legislation remained substantially the same as in the 97th Congress (see Chapter 4 for details). Simpson's subcommittee met for only thirty minutes in markup on April 7 with only three members present—Simpson, Edward Kennedy (D-MA), and Strom Thurmond (R-SC), the full committee chairman (*CQ Almanac* 1983, 287). The major change in legal immigration Simpson had pushed was the elimination of the fifth preference—the one for brothers and sisters of U.S. immigrants. This was later deleted by the full committee in its markup on April 21. The Senate Judiciary Committee approved the legislation on a 13–4 vote on April 21. Several amendments were rejected, including one by Senator Dennis DeConcini (D-AZ) that would have ended employer sanctions after eight years unless Congress explicitly reauthorized them.

The amnesty provisions of the legislation were not questioned, which was surprising given that it was bound to have a dramatic impact on the subsequent number of immigrants that would be allowed to enter the country. There were several million illegal immigrants who qualified under the Senate proposal for permanent residence: Any illegal who had lived in the United States since before January 1, 1977, would be granted legal status. Those who had arrived before January 1, 1980, but after January 1, 1977, would be given temporary status that could become permanent after three years upon further review. But once granted amnesty, these new residents could petition to bring in their relatives under the preference system, and for those who took the additional step of becoming citizens, their relatives could be admitted not subject to the numerical cap on annual admissions. Amnesty, in other words, would result in a tremendous demand to emigrate and cause the immigrant population to soar to annual heights never before reached. A few members expressed concerns that amnesty would swell the welfare rolls. Once legal, these formerly undocumented workers could take advantage of public benefit programs. The addition of several million welfare beneficiaries could have a devastating impact on local, state, and federal budgets for entitlement programs. In response, Senator Alan Simpson (R-WY) did add a provision to the bill that would restrict the use of welfare benefits by those granted amnesty for a period of three years. This was loosely consistent with precedent on immigration policy dictating that immigrants should not be admitted if they were likely to become public charges.

There was only one amendment addressing amnesty at the full committee markup, and that was offered by Kennedy to liberalize the program by moving forward the cutoff date for eligibility for temporary resident status to December 31, 1981, rather than 1980, adding many more undocumented aliens to the number of eligibles. This amendment was defeated on a 3–12 vote, but there were no amendments offered to reduce the number of eligibles by pushing the dates back, as Senator Grassley (R-IA) had done in the previous Congress (see Chapter 4). Few questioned the costs of legalization, either, and Senate legislators calmly approved a billion-dollar block grant program for states to cover government services such as education and health care for the newly legal immigrants.

The bill came to the Senate floor in mid-May and was approved on a 76–18 vote. Only a few conservative Senators, including Jesse Helms (R-NC), raised objections to the amnesty program on the grounds that it would encourage more illegal aliens to stream across the borders. Helms proposed an amendment that would strike the legalization provisions from the bill altogether. His amendment lost on a 21–76 vote and in response, Simpson (R-WY) took the opportunity to spell out the central rationale for the amnesty program:

> ...legalization is not a reward for violation of our immigration laws. It is a very practical solution to a very serious national problem. We have a fearful subculture of human beings in the United States, who, according to the information received at hearings in the subcommittee, for fear of being discovered, fail to report crimes against their property, their person, or their family, do not seek medical help unless it is to give birth to a U.S. citizen, and who will not complain about exploitation in the workplace. That cannot be good for this country and somehow, indeed, it diminishes us in known and unknown ways. (*CR* 5/17/83, S6813)

In other words, Simpson and the bill's supporters cast their argument in support of amnesty as a crime control and public health matter, while acknowledging that the INS lacked the capacity to pursue and deport the estimated six million undocumented aliens who now called the United States home.

No sooner had Helms's amendment been defeated, when he introduced another amendment to allow states to deny public schooling and other benefits to illegal aliens. This proposal foreshadowed the fight that would occur both in California in 1994 over Proposition 187 and in the 104th Congress in 1996 over the so-called "Gallegly Amendment," which would permit the states to deny public schooling to the children of illegal aliens. Helms made the simple appeal that states should be permitted to decide whether they wanted to preserve their already scarce resources for their own taxpayers and legal residents (*CR* 5/17/83, S6814). The purpose of the amendment was to circumvent a Supreme Court ruling in the case of *Plyler v. Doe* in 1982 (457 U.S. 202) stating that the states did not have the right to deny illegal aliens the benefit of a free public education since Congress had not passed a law granting them this power. The ever-vigilant Helms had made a career out of challenging Supreme Court decisions he found to his disliking. He was now trying to provide the states with what the Court had insisted was presently lacking under existing law: Congress's permission to deny benefits for those who were in the country unlawfully. Senators Simpson and Kennedy vigorously opposed this measure, arguing that it would impose a lifetime of hardship on children who were not accountable for their illegal status. Helms's effort to protect states' rights was defeated on a 34–60 vote, but had strong Southern support, including Democrats Sam Nunn (D-GA) and Lloyd Bentsen (D-TX).

On the following day, another measure that would foreshadow things to come was brought to the floor by Senator Gordon Humphrey (R-NH). This amendment would have denied the undocumented workers who had been granted amnesty the right to take advantage of public benefits, including welfare, until they had become citizens. Simpson had included a provision that denied benefits for a period of three years, but Humphrey wanted a stronger restriction. He insisted that lawbreakers were not entitled to public aid and that the costs of providing benefits to such a large population would be astronomical (*CR* 5/18/83, S6908). Simpson and Kennedy vigorously opposed this measure also, and both made the point that legal residents were contributing, taxpaying members of society, and did not deserve to be excluded from benefits and protections the country provides. Simpson prevailed, and the Humphrey Amendment was defeated on a 31–63 vote.

Another amendment worth noting for its anticipation of future debates was one offered by Senator Bill Bradley (D-NJ) that opened up the controversial issue of reimbursement to states for the costs of providing education and other services to aliens granted amnesty. The federal government, Bradley reasoned, was making a *federal* decision to change the status of certain people, and the federal government should therefore pay for that decision (*CR* 5/18/83, S6931). Senator Lawton Chiles (D-FL), who would later become governor of Florida, cosponsored Bradley's amendment and reminded the chamber that Florida was still bailing out from the expenses incurred by the Mariel Boatlift and the Haitian influx of just two years before. Federal immigration decisions of this scope amount to little more than high-priced, unfunded mandates that shift the costs of decisions made by the national government down to the local level. As logical and rational as these arguments sounded, they did not prevail. Bradley's amendment was defeated by a 37–57 vote.

Senator Pete Wilson (R-CA), who would come to take such a hard line against illegal aliens in his California gubernatorial reelection bid of 1994 and in his unreserved support of Proposition 187 that same year, introduced an amendment that would extend the employment eligibility of illegal alien farm workers for an additional two years beyond the three-year eligibility that was written into the legislation. This measure was soundly defeated on a 20–72 vote.

In the end, most of the amendments offered in the Senate floor debate were either noncontroversial and therefore adopted on a voice vote, or they were easily defeated in lopsided roll calls. The most divisive vote that spring was on an amendment offered by Dale Bumpers (D-AR) to strip from the bill a provision that would provide a special "investor visa" allotment for wealthy immigrants making more than $250,000, who promise to employ at least four nonfamily members. Bumpers persuasively argued that it was equivalent to selling off bits and pieces of America to those who are rich while others have been waiting patiently in line (*CR* 5/17/83, S6811). By including this provision in the bill, Simpson had hoped to reemphasize skilled immigration, something that had taken a backseat to family-based immigration in the 1965 legislation. Since 1965, the vast bulk of immigrant visas were granted to the family preference categories of admission (see Table 5.5). The family emphasis left relatively few visas for "independent" immigrants—those without family members already in the country. Given that family members were permitted into the country without any estimation of their education, skill level, or potential to contribute to the economic well-being of the nation, Simpson had hoped to carve out a very small percentage of visas for immigrants who had a strong potential, by virtue of their wealth, to stimulate economic growth. Senator Kennedy had always been skeptical of nonfamily immigration, figuring that businesses used these preference categories to hire cheap foreign labor. He opposed Simpson on this measure and spoke in favor of the Bumpers Amendment. Bumpers prevailed on a mostly party-line 51–46 vote, with several liberal Republicans joining the Democratic side. Perhaps because the Senate had been through many of these issues in the preceding Congress, the Bumpers vote proved to be an exception and the Senate seemed mostly satisfied with Simpson's work.

The Ususal Controversy in the House

While the Senate managed to maintain a strong element of consensus on Simpson's version of the bill, in the House, Romano Mazzoli (D-KY) faced considerable controversy. Early in April 1983, the subcommittee plodded through 36 amendments in two days of markup. Like the Senate bill, the House version incorporated a two-tiered amnesty program, but in the subcommittee markup, Mazzoli simplified the program by doing away with temporary resident status. Instead, all immigrants arriving before January 1, 1981, would be given permanent resident status (*CQ Almanac* 1983, 288). This amendment did specify that those granted amnesty would be ineligible for public benefits for four years, rather than three as specified in Simpson's bill. Led by Dan Lungren (R-CA), the Republican members opposed the idea of changing the dates governing amnesty because doing so smacked of a full amnesty program for illegals. Lungren was a staunch conservative from Southern California and represented the Los Angeles suburbs of Huntington Beach—part of Long Beach—and the Palos Verdes Peninsula. He had every reason to be concerned about immigration, as the district was predominantly white when he was elected, with only 6 percent Asians and 6 percent Hispanics. Throughout the 1980s, however, parts of the district had experienced a rapid influx of Asians and Hispanics, putting native white Californians ill at ease. Lungren left the House to become California state treasurer in 1988, and later attorney general. He would run for governor in 1998. Following the defeat of Lungren's amendment to limit amnesty, Bill McCollum (R-FL) responded by offering an amendment to strike the amnesty provisions, but the measure again failed as it had in the previous Congress. Lungren then took up Senator Pete Wilson's mantle and talked his colleagues into an amendment that would phase out the use of illegal aliens in agricultural jobs and replace them instead with temporary but legal workers. After three years, all growers would have to seek permission from the Secretary of Labor to hire workers under the H-2 guest-worker program.

At the House Judiciary Committee markup in May, members faced a full schedule of amendments and met for three contentious days. The committee was highly cleaved ideologically, and these divisions surfaced frequently in the debates over amnesty and employer sanctions. The amnesty provisions were the most controversial. On a narrow 15–14 vote, the committee adopted an amendment offered by Barney Frank (D-MA) to move the date of eligibility for amnesty back to January 1, 1982, in the hopes that it would encourage more illegal aliens to come forward (*CQ Almanac* 1983, 290). More restrictive alternatives offered by Republicans Dan Lungren (R-CA) and E. Clay Shaw (R-FL) failed on party-line votes.

Employer sanctions was the second major thrust of the legislation, and the debate generated the same coalitions it had in previous years. The penalties mandated by the legislation set the fines to be assessed at $1,000 per undocumented worker for the first violation and $2,000 per worker for the second. Hispanic members remained opposed because of the potential for discrimination. Business interests that heretofore had been opposed to sanctions decided instead to weaken the provisions by backing an amendment that would make employers subject to penalties only if they were caught with an undocumented worker on their payroll a second time. This amendment was adopted on an 18–10 vote. Republican efforts by F. James Sensenbrenner (R-WI) to lower the worldwide immigration ceiling and restrict the fifth visa preference only to the unmarried brothers and sisters of U.S. citizens failed by large margins.

The bill was also considered by three other committees: Agriculture, Education and Labor, and Energy and Commerce, each with its own limited jurisdiction. The Agriculture Committee adopted a more generous guest-worker program in its version of the bill while weakening the employer sanctions provisions by capping the fines and giving judges the option to impose lesser amounts (*CQ Almanac* 1983, 291). The three committees finished their modifications in late June, and the legislation moved to the Rules Committee. Before assigning the rule for floor debate, Rules Chairman Claude Pepper (D-FL) asked the four committees to work out a compromise bill. Pepper knew that a completely open rule would not be sensible given the level of controversy surrounding the legislation. In 1982, an open rule had been

Box 5.1

Romano Mazzoli (D-KY) chaired the House immigration sub-committee during the 1980s. Working with Senator Alan Simpson (R-WY), Mazzoli was responsible for authoring the 1986 immigration legislation. Credit: Commonwealth of Kentucky.

Romano Mazzoli (D-KY)

Representative Romano Mazzoli served as chairman of the House immigration sub-committee from 1981 until he retired from Congress in 1995, except for the two years of the 101st Congress (1989 and 1990). He attributed his interests in immigration to his exposure to Notre Dame's president, Theodore Hesburgh, who chaired the Select Commission on Immigration and Refugee Policy.

Mazzoli worked closely with his Senate counterpart, Senator Alan Simpson (R-WY), a coalition that Mazzoli termed the Mutt and Jeff Sideshow. Together, they fashioned an immigration reform package that bore their names and would eventually become the 1986 Immigration Reform and Control Act on the third legislative try in as many Congresses.

Mazzoli took moderate positions on immigration policy, often opposing employment-based immigration and agricultural guest-worker programs while favoring family reunification. He worked so well with Republicans that liberal party leaders removed him from the chairmanship of the immigration subcommittee in 1989 and 1990.

Mazzoli was born in Louisville, Kentucky, November 2, 1932. He received his bachelor's degree from Notre Dame in 1954. He joined the U.S. Army in 1954 and served for two years. He earned his J. D. degree at the University of Louisville in 1960.

From 1960 till 1962, Mazzoli worked in the law department of the L&N Railroad Co. He practiced law in Louisville from 1962 until 1970. As well, Mazzoli was a business law lecturer at Ballarmine College from 1963 till 1967. He was elected to the Kentucky Senate, where he served from 1968 through 1970. He won a seat in Congress in 1970, representing Louisville. He was subsequently reelected 11 times. In 1995, Mazzoli retired from Congress and returned to Louisville.

(Sources: *Almanac of American Politics*, various years; *Biographical Directory of the U.S. Congress 1774–1989; Who's Who in American Politics 1995–96;* Tolchin 1982)

assigned and Hispanic members and other opponents of the legislation had prepared a full-scale assault that resulted in Mazzoli's decision to pull the bill from the floor (see Chapter 4). Committee leaders were unable to come to an agreement on even the basic provisions of the bill, let alone the number of amendments to be permitted. It was clear that Democrats were highly divided among themselves, and a competitive presidential primary season began in January 1984. Reacting to these events, Speaker Tip O'Neill (D-MA) again blocked consideration of the legislation so candidates could avoid taking positions on the issue until the primaries had ended.

Déjà Vu on the House Floor, Again

House floor action didn't begin until June of 1984, following the California primary, and a full year after the legislation had been reported out of the committee. After hearing testimony from more than 30 members, Pepper's Rules Committee decided to use the Judiciary Committee version of the bill as the base document and allow the other committees to offer their versions as substitutes for sections of the bill. In total, 69 amendments were declared in order under a modified open rule specifying five hours and thirty minutes of general debate with no overall time limit governing the consideration of amendments (*CQ Almanac* 1984, 230). On the floor, Pepper warned the members that if the bill became bogged down by dilatory tactics, the Rules Committee would reconvene and set more restrictive guidelines for debate. The leading Hispanic members, including Roybal (D-CA) and Robert Garcia (D-NY), stirred up as much opposition to the rule as they could muster among liberals who opposed employer sanctions because of their potentially discriminatory impact, conservatives opposed to employer sanctions because they would force business into the role of immigration police, and those in both parties opposed to amnesty. Despite determined opposition, the rule was adopted on the floor on June 11, 1984, by a vote of 291–111.

Because a detailed rehash of every amendment is beyond the scope of this analysis, we will instead focus on the debate and amendments offered on the major sections of the bill: employer-sanctions and amnesty. The 5½ hours of general debate opened up with both bipartisan support and opposition. Objections surfaced almost immediately on the employer-sanctions provisions. Some complained that, without secure identification, employer sanctions would be pointless. While employer sanctions were designed to ensure that employers undertake some means of identifying whether a person is authorized to work, the ease with which official documents could be forged and duplicated would undermine these attempts at verification. While the bill included a special section that would provide penalties for using forged documents, opponents of employer sanctions pointed out that the threat of criminal prosecution had never dissuaded people from entering the country illegally. Other opponents emphasized the issue of discrimination voiced in earlier debates on the issue (see Chapter 4). The employer who thinks there is a possibility of a jail term or a fine for hiring an undocumented worker would be very reluctant to hire anyone resembling someone of Hispanic or Asian ancestry.

Several attempts to amend the employer sanctions provisions are worth special note. First, there was the attempt to set up a more thorough process for verifying the employment eligibility of workers through a toll-free telephone number. This amendment was sponsored by Sam B. Hall (D-TX), a strong opponent of employer sanctions and a member of the immigration subcommittee. His argument was that it made no sense to subject employers to the threat of employer sanctions if there were no reliable means by which employers could determine employment eligibility. Few employers would be trained to detect counterfeit documents. A call-in phone system would permit an employer to verify the validity of a Social Security number in much the same way that credit card purchases are verified. If the number was inaccurate, defunct, or otherwise invalid, the employer would be informed at that time (*CR* 6/12/84, H15947). This would also protect the employer from possible penalties since the source of employment authorization information would be the government itself.

The Hall Amendment was opposed by the other subcommittee members, including Dan Lungren (R-CA) and Romano Mazzoli (D-KY), primarily on the basis of its estimated cost. Fish (R-NY) pointed out the difficulties of implementation. No master index of valid card numbers existed in a single computer database. Furthermore, Social Security numbers had often been issued without reference to work eligibility. It would take an estimated 10 years and as much as $1 billion to issue a tamper-proof Social Security card that could be used for purposes of work eligibility verification. Others raised the specter of civil liberties violations, suggesting that this was a step toward a national identification card that everyone would be required to carry. In spite of these concerns, Hall's amendment passed by a comfortable margin of 242–155.

No sooner had the amendment passed than Edward Roybal (D-CA) took to the floor again complaining that the bill's language strongly implied the establishment of a national identification card, anathema to a free country. Roybal offered an amendment to delete the employer sanctions language in the House version of the bill. His hope was that, with no employer sanctions language in the House version, there would be an opportunity to compromise with the Senate's version of the bill in a conference committee, and thereby drastically weaken the sanctions and verification provisions, including the Hall Amendment that had passed just minutes before. In opposing the Roybal Amendment, the bill's authors called attention to a statement explicitly written into the legislation to counter this fear, "Nothing in this section shall be construed to authorize, directly or indirectly, the issuance or use of national identification cards." Apparently, this was enough reassurance to persuade a majority of the legislators to vote against Roybal's amendment. It was defeated on a 120–304 vote. A slightly weaker amendment sponsored by Patricia Schroeder (D-CO), designed to weaken the employer sanctions provisions by providing for their expiration after three years, garnered greater support but was also defeated on a 137–274 vote.

The debate over amnesty centered around several alternative proposals for its implementation. Dan Lungren (R-CA) offered an amendment to bring the House provisions into line with those passed by the Senate: a two-tier system allowing those who have permanently resided in the country since January 1, 1977, to obtain permanent resident status, while those who entered after January 1, 1977, but before January 1, 1980, would be given temporary resident status. Those falling in the temporary resident category could apply for permanent resident status after three years. Lungren also added language requiring those wishing to alter their status from temporary to permanent residents to have some minimal facility with English or be pursuing English language training. Opponents charged that the additional complexity of temporary resident status would bog down the INS in bureaucracy and limit the number of illegals who would come forward and apply for amnesty, sustaining the desperate underclass status of many undocumented workers. Lungren's amendment was defeated on a 181–245 vote that fell largely along party lines.

A second amendment to limit the number of undocumented workers eligible for amnesty was offered by E. Clay Shaw (R-FL). His amendment had no temporary-residence provision, but would have moved the bill's amnesty eligibility date to January 1, 1980, compared with January 1, 1982, in the House bill. In opposing this alteration, Peter Rodino (D-NJ) reminded the chamber that the very essence of the legalization program was to reach as many people as possible. If one of these weaker alternatives were to be adopted, representatives would be "condemning unknown millions of hard-working, law-abiding people—and their children—to an inhumane existence, with the constant dread of discovery and the protection of our laws denied them" (*CR* 6/19/84, H17026). The Shaw effort failed on a 177–246 vote.

A subsequent "middle-ground" amendment by Majority Leader Jim Wright (D-TX) would provide temporary resident status to illegal aliens who had arrived before 1982 and would make them eligible for permanent residence status two years later, providing they had a minimal understanding of English and of American Government. Roybal (D-CA) and the other members of the Hispanic Caucus again warned that these provisions would discourage illegal residents from coming forward to apply for legal status. Nevertheless, the chamber seemed happiest with this compromise, and it passed on a 247–170 vote.

Controversy over Amnesty

Finally, the most sweeping of the amnesty amendments came to the floor. Bill McCollum (R-FL) had earlier in the debate successfully offered an amendment to streamline the deportation and asylum procedures on a narrow 208–192 vote. McCollum represented a conservative, white, central-Florida constituency in and around the city of Orlando. A firm believer in limiting criminal rights and fierce opponent of gun control, he would certainly not be first in line for an award from the ACLU. One of the busiest and most hardworking legislators in Congress, he seemed to draw great energy from being the isolated conservative voice on a Judiciary Committee packed with liberals. Since first winning election in 1980, he had been a consistent opponent of amnesty and had offered amendments to strike this provision as often as he could. Recalling the fight over amnesty 11 years after its passage in 1986, McCollum reiterated his central concerns:

> The biggest problem is that you've got a large number of people who get amnesty and they bring others in. Plus it encourages people to come over illegally in hopes that they too will get amnesty someday. But the major problem is that there is a multitude of them who are coming in because of the original ones granted amnesty. The critics are justified in being concerned about this. Anytime you grant an amnesty, you have to deal with major demand under our generous family reunification provisions. (McCollum interview, 5/16/97)

McCollum also objected to amnesty on the grounds that it was a slap in the face to those who had been waiting to enter the country legally. Millions who had entered illegally would suddenly be granted permanent residence, essentially cutting to the head of the line. At the time, few other than McCollum accurately forecast the enormous demand that would be stimulated by the legalization program. The legalization provisions were not accompanied by any quota or ceiling for immediate family members or relatives. This would inevitably expand the size of the labor market and put pressure on an economy that could not generate new jobs fast enough to meet the much larger demand. Amnesty ultimately drove annual legal immigration levels to their peak in the late 1980s, dramatically distorted historical immigration patterns, and contributed to the groundswell of opposition to legal and illegal immigration in the 1990s. But in 1984 (and in 1986), McCollum was in the minority. Those favoring the amnesty insisted that the country would be better off if undocumented workers and their families were granted legal status. McCollum's amendment to eliminate amnesty failed on a 195–233 vote.

With the last of the amendments to legalization defeated, the vote was called on final passage. Nearly everyone in the House could find some reason to dislike the legislation. The sanctions language was either too hard or too soft. Similarly, with legalization, the bill did not go far enough, or it went too far. The vote on final passage proved to be the narrowest of any in the

Box 5.2

Bill McCollum (R-FL) served on the House immigration subcommittee in the 1980s where he vigorously opposed legislation granting amnesty to undocumented workers. He is shown here in the mid-1980s visiting a Hong Kong refugee camp. Credit: Nicholas Hayes.

Bill McCollum (R-FL)

Congressman Bill McCollum played an influential role in the 1996 immigration debate. A member of the immigration subcommittee and formerly the ranking Republican on the subcommittee, McCollum had also actively worked against the liberalization of immigration policy in the 1990 legislation and had fought to strike the amnesty provisions in the 1986 Act. Among the Republicans who have served on the Judiciary Committee in the twentieth century, few members have been as influential as McCollum.

McCollum was born July 12, 1944, in Brooksville, Florida. He earned a B.A. in 1965 at the University of Florida, then his law degree in 1968. He served in the U.S. Navy JAG Corps as commander from 1969 to 1972. McCollum practiced law from 1973 until 1981 in the Orlando area.

McCollum became active in Republican politics, serving as chairman of the Seminole County Republican Committee in 1976. He ran for Congress in 1980, winning the seat in the largely Republican district and succeeding an Abscam defendant. His conservative record matches his constituency—McCollum won reelection in 1992 with nearly 70 percent of the vote and stood unopposed in 1994.

Referred to as "one of the most active and articulate Republicans in the House" by the *Almanac of American Politics*, McCollum has legislated on a range of issues. He served as a member of the Iran Contra committee in the mid-1980s.

McCollum served as vice chairman of the House GOP Conference beginning in 1988. He ran for Republican whip in 1994, but lost to Texas Congressman Tom DeLay, running third in a three-way race.

When the GOP took control of Congress following the 1994 elections, McCollum became chair of the crime subcommittee. He also was a senior member of the immigration subcommittee, where he was an ally of Lamar Smith.

(Sources: *Almanac of American Politics*, various years; *Biographical Directory of the U.S. Congress 1774–1989*)

debate, with Mazzoli and Lungren barely prevailing in a 216–211 floor division. The liberal legalization provisions proved to be a major stumbling block for many members.

As approved, the House version did a number of other things, including providing full reimbursement to states for the costs of the legalization program, the same provision that had failed in the Senate when offered by Bill Bradley (D-NJ). It also expanded the H-2 temporary foreign worker program that was championed by California growers as a means for obtaining low-cost labor.

The conference committee was faced with the chore of ironing out major differences between the House and Senate versions of the bill. Conference meetings began in mid-September 1984. In the meantime, presidential election-year politics caught up with the bill. As a bow to Hispanic interests, Walter Mondale came out against it. The Reagan administration preferred the Senate version to the House version (*CQ Almanac* 1984, 236). Conferees managed to come to terms with many of the differences between the chambers by making compromises in the areas of employer sanctions, legalization, and the guest-worker program but these negotiations used up valuable time. By the second week in October, a potential last-minute deal breaker remained—how to fund the costs of the legalization program, costs such as education and health care that would fall heavily on Florida, Texas, California, and other immigrant-receiving states. Conferees from the affected states insisted upon the House provision of full reimbursement of costs. Simpson's Senate bill had instead proposed a block grant to be distributed according to the number of legalized aliens in each state. A last-minute effort to cap the reimbursement costs at $1 billion failed to overcome the reservations of border state representatives, and the result was stalemate. With Election Day just three weeks away, Congress adjourned and action on immigration died.

Voting in the 98th House

The floor divisions on selected immigration votes in the 98th House of Representatives are shown in Table 5.1 (for full model see Appendix Table A5.1).[1] Partisanship is clearly decisive in the voting for most amendments. Generally, Republicans had stronger support on the amnesty amendments they offered (Lungren, Shaw, McCollum), than Democrats did on their amendments modifying employer sanctions. The Democrats were more divided on employer sanctions than the Republicans. An estimated 43 percent of Democrats voted for the Roybal Amendment to delete the sanctions language, compared with only 18 percent of Republicans. Clearly, if the Democrats were to pass an immigration reform bill, they would have to bring more of their own members on board.

[1]The complete logistic regression results are presented in Appendix Table A5.1 at the end of this chapter.

Table 5.1 Estimated Probability of Voting Yes on Immigration Amendments and Final Passage of House Bill, 98th Congress, U.S. House of Representatives

Variables	Hall Amendment 1–800 Employer Verification	Schroeder Amendment Three-Year Expiration on Employer Sanctions	Roybal Amendment to Delete Employer Sanctions	Lungren Amendment for 2-Tier System	Shaw Amendment Changing Dates	Wright Amnesty Amendment	McCollum Amendment to Strike Amnesty Language	Final Passage of House Bill
Democrat	.67	.43	.43	.13	.12	.51	.24	.47
Republican	.45	.18	.18	.80	.77	.71	.64	.47
White member	.70	.28	.20	.37	.33	.62	.42	.51
Nonwhite member	.02	.85	.99	.09	.18	.18	.08	.10
Non-South	.50	.38	.43	.27	.30	.53	.29	.45
South	.87	.19	.12	.55	.38	.73	.67	.53
Nonborder state	.67	.25	.26	.34	.29	.61	.36	.51
Border state	.45	.63	.55	.32	.41	.54	.46	.33
Not Judiciary	.64	.33	.33	.34	.33	.59	.39	.45
Judiciary Committee	.43	.27	.21	.26	.22	.60	.29	.67
Foreign born .37	.76	.39	.37	.49	.40	.67	.60	.36
Foreign born 52.2	.01	.05	.07	.01	.03	.08	.01	.97
Agriculture .13	.62	.38	.32	.32	.27	.56	.38	.43
Agriculture 18.05	.62	.11	.31	.44	.65	.75	.39	.89
Black .05	.63	.32	.31	.32	.50	.64	.40	.48
Black 92.05	.57	.35	.39	.47	.50	.26	.29	.36
Asian/other .53	.51	.27	.23	.34	.48	.60	.40	.60
Asian/other 71.9	.99	.95	.96	.34	.01	.50	.26	.01
Unemployment 1.9	.59	.24	.24	.39	.44	.58	.46	.59
Unemployment 28.1	.74	.73	.69	.18	.05	.63	.15	.12

Values represent the estimated probability of a Yes vote at the lowest and highest value of the independent variables, with all other variables held constant at their sample means.

Other variables related to member and constituency characteristics were influential in dividing the floor. The minority members were more hostile than the white members to employer sanctions. Southerners also remained a solid voting bloc on many amendments. An estimated 87 percent of the Southern delegation voted for Hall's amendment for establishment of a toll-free employment verification system. Members from border states were uncomfortable with employer sanctions and were much more likely to vote for the measures that would weaken them than those from nonborder states. Unemployment rates in home districts appear to have almost no statistically significant impact on voting on the amendments. Members rarely stopped to consider the economic conditions of their districts when voting on either employer sanctions or amnesty for illegal entrants. Economics was instead overridden by considerations of race and ethnicity. Moreover, districts with the highest unemployment rates were in urban areas where there was a high proportion of black and foreign-born residents. There are differences, however, in the voting of those with white and nonwhite foreign-born populations. Those in areas with high proportions of Asians and Hispanics were far more likely than those without such populations to vote to weaken employer sanctions. Members with foreign-born constituencies comprised of mostly white ethnics (Italians, Irish, Jews), such as Peter Rodino (D-NJ) and John Dingell (D-MI), voted against nearly all amendments, attempting to preserve the bill as it was voted out of the Judiciary Committee. This group of legislators also voted overwhelmingly in favor of final passage.

The model for final passage of the legislation (see Tables 5.1 and A5.1) indicates that the decision on Simpson-Mazzoli in 1984 was not a partisan one, as both parties were about equally split on the vote. Instead, the floor cleavage divided the chamber by race, with only 10 percent of the nonwhite members voting in favor of final passage, while 51 percent of white members voted for it. The floor was also divided between border and nonborder states. About half of the nonborder state representatives voted for the legislation, compared with only one-third for the border states. While economic conditions played no apparent role in voting on the amendments, the vote on final passage does show that those representing districts with the highest unemployment rates were far less likely to vote for the bill than were those in more prosperous districts. Among these no voters from high unemployment districts were Judiciary Committee member John Conyers (D-MI) from Detroit, Dale Kildee (D-MI) from Flint, and Philadelphia representatives Tom Foglietta (D-PA) and William Gray (D-PA). As other analysts have noted, the opposition coalition boiled down to minority interests in areas of high unemployment coupled with legislators from border states (Lowell, Bean, and de la Garza 1986).

This series of votes shows what an agonizing problem Simpson-Mazzoli posed for the Democratic leadership. A large bloc of their core membership was dead-set against passage of any legislation imposing employer sanctions. The sharp floor divisions in the House also forecast the difficulty that would plague the bill in the conference committee with the Republican-controlled

Senate. With Democrats so divided among themselves, how could they possibly come to terms with Alan Simpson and the Senate Republicans? Nevertheless, it is likely that an agreement would have been forthcoming had the House leadership not stalled until June 1984 in permitting floor action. Speaker O'Neill had delayed consideration of the bill for fear that the Reagan administration would veto the legislation to win the support of Hispanic constituents (Hoefer 1991; *CQ Almanac* 1984). The delay proved fatal, as Congress recessed for much of the summer for the two national conventions. As it turned out, President Reagan had no intention of vetoing the legislation even though it contained the amnesty provisions most conservatives detested. By fall, a Reagan victory in November was a virtual certainty, and a veto would have made little difference to the election's outcome anyway.

The 99th Congress: Simpson-Mazzoli Becomes Law

For four years from 1981 to 1985, the U.S. Congress—and particularly the House—grappled unsuccessfully with the issue of immigration reform. But it is common for controversial issues to run into the legislative roadblocks that immigration reform did in the mid-1980s. Many bills require repeated introduction just to develop enough momentum for a committee hearing. At least immigration reform had been brought to the floor and members had gone on record with their votes. It would be difficult for those who had voted in favor of the legislation the first time to vote against it when it came up again.

Senate Action in the 99th Congress

In the Senate, Simpson introduced the legislation in May 1985, and it raced through the legislative process, passing the full committee in July on a 12–5 vote and passing on the floor in September of that year on a solid 69–30 vote. In committee, the major controversy surrounded changes Simpson had proposed in the legalization program. Correctly sensing widespread public opposition to amnesty, he wrote into the new legislation a provision that would allow amnesty to proceed only if a special commission concluded that the country had finally gained control of its borders (*CQ Almanac* 1985, 223). Simpson justified this new qualification on the basis of the Select Commission's report, which stated that no legalization program should go into effect until new enforcement measures had been instituted to curtail new flows of undocumented aliens. Hispanic and minority rights groups greeted this stipulation with considerable hostility. Responding to these interests, Senator Edward Kennedy (D-MA) sponsored an amendment in the full committee markup to restore the amnesty provisions that had been settled in the previous year's conference committee. Kennedy's amendment was voted down by the Republicans and the one Southern Democrat on the committee, Howell Heflin (D-AL). Later Simpson agreed to an amendment sponsored by Howard Metzenbaum (D-OH) that would guarantee that an amnesty program would go into effect no later than three years following the enactment of the legislation (*CQ Almanac* 1985, 224). Kennedy also tried to add a sunset provision to the employer sanctions section if the General Accounting Office discovered that the implementation of sanctions resulted in widespread discrimination. This measure also failed in committee and on the floor in September.

On the Senate floor, the major controversy surrounded the attempt by Pete Wilson (R-CA) to add a new foreign guest-worker provision to the bill to accommodate growers who were in the habit of hiring undocumented workers. While foreign farm workers are a rather small part of the total farm workforce, farmers who hire them have long insisted that without them they would go out of business (Martin 1990, 71). Wilson's amendment would authorize the admission of up to 350,000 workers for purposes of harvesting perishable agricultural products for a three-year period, after which the attorney general could set a new cap based on a needs assessment. The first attempt to pass this amendment failed, as it lacked any numerical cap and opponents objected to the open-ended nature of the authorization. This proposal was fiercely opposed by labor interests, and Howard Metzenbaum (D-OH) succinctly summarized labor's objections:

> ...but this amendment is sort of in tandem with some of the trade legislation we have pending around the Senate, only in the trade legislation we are trying to keep foreign workers from stealing American jobs in foreign countries. This amendment makes it possible for foreign workers to come in and take jobs that Americans could otherwise hold.
>
> The argument is made that American workers do not want those jobs, will not take those jobs. I reject that argument. I question how hard an effort has been made to obtain workers to do those jobs. I think it is a bad amendment. The purpose is simply to legalize the current system by enacting a massive migrant foreign worker program.
>
> ...Massive employment of illegal aliens only keeps working conditions bad and wages low. (*CR* 9/17/85, S11601)

Wilson had carefully crafted his revised amendment with several swing voters in mind. The addition of the numerical cap brought five Senators on board who had voted against the same proposal just days before. Wilson's amendment passed on a 51–44 vote. The next day, Wilson's guest-worker program was weakened slightly by the successful passage of an amendment by Paul Simon (D-IL) terminating the program after three years unless Congress explicitly voted to continue it.

The 99th House More Determined than Ever

In the House, the guest-worker program proved to be the primary obstacle to speedy action. To build early support in the new Congress, Peter Rodino

(D-NJ) cosponsored the House bill with Mazzoli, effectively throwing the weight of the Judiciary Committee chairmanship behind the legislation well before the full committee markup. The Rodino-Mazzoli bill did not contain any provision for farm workers and Rodino, who had strong labor ties, adamantly opposed such a provision (*CQWR* 6/21/86, 1411). The House immigration subcommittee met in November of 1985. The subcommittee bypassed a discussion of the guest-worker program while key Democrats tried to reach a compromise on the matter. To try to neutralize the opposition to employer sanctions, subcommittee members agreed to an amendment to set up a new office of special counsel in the Justice Department charged with investigating and prosecuting cases of discrimination resulting from implementation of the new law (*CQ Almanac* 1985, 228). Bill McCollum (R-FL) once again tried unsuccessfully to strike the legalization provisions from the bill. The subcommittee agreed overwhelmingly to provide states with a 100 percent reimbursement for the cost of services provided to legalized aliens.

In the full committee, the sticking point proved to be the farm worker program. Labor-connected Democrats insisted that foreign guest-workers would have an adverse impact on the wages and working conditions of domestic workers. But influential Democrats on the House Agriculture Committee, including Leon Panetta (D-CA), had insisted on a farm worker program as a condition for supporting the bill. Arguments about the farm worker program had stalled the legislation in 1984. Fearing that the bill could die without an agricultural provision, Judiciary Committee Democrats Howard Berman (D-CA) and Charles Schumer (D-NY) drafted an amendment to grant permanent resident status to agricultural workers who had been employed at least 60 days between May 1985 and May 1986. Schumer contended that these workers had to be granted permanent residence to ensure that they would have the freedom of movement and bargaining power enjoyed by every other worker in the nation (*CQWR* 6/28/86, 1480). The amendment would allow for the admission and granting of permanent residence of additional workers as needed so long as they worked at least 60 days in agriculture each year they were here. These workers could immediately petition to bring their immediate family members into the country. After five years, they could apply for citizenship. To encourage agriculture to use domestic workers, the guest-worker program was to be phased out gradually. In the meantime, however, these newly legalized workers would be eligible for public assistance, including food stamps and welfare, even though aliens granted permanent residence under the bill's other legalization provisions would be denied such benefits for five years. The amendment was narrowly accepted on a 19–16 vote. Mazzoli himself objected to it, as did nearly all of the Republicans, including Dan Lungren (R-CA) and Bill McCollum (R-FL).

For some, like Mazzoli and other white urban Democrats, the issue was one of labor versus agribusiness. The continued hiring of illegal immigrants undermined the wages and working conditions of American workers, as

Box 5.3

Dan Lungren (R-CA) served on the House immigration subcommittee in the 1980s and mustered bipartisan support to force significant compromises in the 1986 legislation. Lungren would later become California Attorney General and run for governor.
Courtesy of Daniel Lungren.

Daniel E. Lungren (R-CA)

Representative Dan Lungren was ranking Republican on the House immigration subcommittee in the mid-1980s as the 1986 bill was being crafted. In that debate, he fought to limit the extension of amnesty to illegal immigrants and led a successful floor fight to defeat the rule governing consideration of the 1986 legislation on the grounds that it did not permit consideration of several key amendments. By this action, Lungren forced House Democrats to compromise on a number of provisions, and he ultimately supported passage of the legislation.

Lungren was born September 22, 1946, in Long Beach, California. In 1968, he graduated from Notre Dame with his A.B. degree. He began law school at the University of Southern California, which he attended his first year in 1968–69, then transferred to Georgetown University in Washington, where he received his J.D. in 1971.

While at Georgetown, Lungren served on the staff of U.S. Senator George Murphy of California in 1969 and 1970, then joined the staff of Tennessee's U.S. Senator Bill Brock in 1971. He became a special assistant at the Republican National Committee in 1971.

Lungren returned to California in 1973 to practice law with a prominent Long Beach firm. He became active in GOP politics, as well. From 1974 till 1979, he was a delegate to the state Republican conventions. He also cochaired the National Congressional Council in 1977 and 1978.

In 1976, Lungren challenged an incumbent Democratic congressman, but lost by less than 3,000 votes. Lungren launched a second challenge in 1978 and won handily. His solidly conservative record fit well with the conservatism of his suburban constituency. *Politics in America* characterized Lungren as "a legislator of considerable substance."

Lungren served on the Judiciary Committee. In 1983, he switched to the ranking minority slot on the Immigration, Refugees, and International Law Subcommittee. His close association with subcommittee Chairman Romano Mazzoli gave Lungren the opportunity to help shape and advance the Simpson-Mazzoli bill, which would become the 1986 Immigration Reform and Control Act.

Lungren continued to serve in Congress until 1989, when he returned to California. He became a partner with a Sacramento law firm, then sought election as California's attorney general in 1990. He won that election, as well as reelection in 1994.

(Sources: *Almanac of American Politics*, 1984; *Biographical Directory of the U.S. Congress 1774–1989; Politics in America*, 1986; Lungren's biography on State of California Internet homepage)

Howard Metzenbaum (D-OH) had so plainly pointed out in the Senate floor debate. For the Republicans, however, the issue was primarily a redistributive one. The immigrants who would be entering under any guest-worker program would be poor, uneducated, and easy targets of discrimination. These characteristics would enhance the likelihood that they would one day come to depend on public aid. In reaction to these fears, Lungren attempted to have much of the guest-worker language eliminated, but failed on a 16–19 vote. Opponents of the guest-worker provision insisted that it undermined other aspects of the legislation, including employer sanctions. The entire point of the bill was to dissuade illegal aliens from coming across the border to find work. This provision only provided an enticement for them to come. Lungren labeled it a "super super amnesty" program that granted citizenship rights on the basis of a mere 60-day presence in the country. Aside from the guest-worker program, the bill remained substantially similar to the version passed the previous year.

On the House floor, once again the bill arrived late in the session on September 26, and immediately ran into trouble. To limit debate and preserve some delicate compromises, Rodino and Mazzoli had pushed for a rule that sharply curtailed the number of amendments offered. Thirty-two amendments were allowed under the rule, and 53 were disallowed. The rule would provide for amendments on legalization and on employer sanctions, but amendments germane to the agricultural section of the bill were expressly prohibited. This officially fenced out Lungren's amendment to strip the bill of the farm worker provisions, as well as more modest proposals to change these provisions. Republicans vehemently protested that the rule was undemocratic for sheltering many controversial provisions from motions to strike. When a recorded vote on the rule was demanded, it was defeated on a 180–202 vote. Lungren was elated and could barely contain himself. He had been denied the chance to offer his amendment because the House leadership knew he would have succeeded, because it would have been the majority position. Now in the fashion of David conquering Goliath, he could rub this defeat in their faces. Stunned by their defeat, Rodino, Mazzoli, Schumer, and House leaders slunk away to reconsider their options for salvaging immigration reform. Rodino was particularly pessimistic in a postmortem news conference, expressing doubts about whether the measure could be resurrected (*CQWR* 9/27/86, 2267).

Salvaging Immigration Reform

Time was once again running out, but Schumer, to his credit, would not give up. With input from Berman, Lungren, Mazzoli, Rodino, and Fish, Schumer crafted a more limited agricultural worker provision. It provided temporary (not permanent) resident status for up to 350,000 foreign workers who had resided here for three years and who could prove that they had worked at least 90 days in each of those years. The original proposal had required only

60 days of agricultural work. Those who had worked 90 days in agriculture between May 1985 and May 1986 would be granted temporary resident status. They could become permanent residents in two years. Workers would be allowed in on a "replenishment" basis in subsequent years until 1993 when the program was to end (*CQ Almanac* 1986, 66). Most importantly for the Republicans, these special agricultural workers (or SAWs) were disqualified from receiving welfare benefits for a period of five years. These compromises brought the House version much closer to the Senate version as drafted by Pete Wilson (R-CA). It would ultimately smooth the way for successful conference action.

The bill was brought up for House consideration again on October 9, two weeks after the first rule for debate had been defeated. Two members, F. James Sensenbrenner (R-WI) and Henry Gonzalez (D-TX), a conservative and a liberal, respectively, immediately tried to stall proceedings by postponing the debate. This effort failed, and consideration of the rule went forward. The rule allotted only two hours of general debate and only 14 amendments, including one major substitute amendment. Edward Roybal (D-CA) immediately objected to the rule for the obvious reason that it gagged debate but he was in the minority. Most members wanted to get on with consideration knowing that a defeat of the rule would almost certainly kill immigration reform in yet another Congress. The new rule was approved on a 299–103 vote.

Peter Rodino (D-NJ) opened debate by reminding the House that members had approved a very similar proposal in the previous Congress. The core of the legislation remained employer sanctions coupled with legalization. Rodino and the Republican leadership of the House and Senate Judiciary Committees met with President Reagan earlier in the year, and the president lent his strong support to the legislation. Opponents raised the usual objections to employer sanctions and amnesty, but there were no arguments that had not been voiced before. Gonzalez (D-TX), Roybal (D-CA), and the other members of the Hispanic Caucus had a weary tone in their voices. They knew that momentum was not on their side. Republican leaders on the Judiciary Committee, including Lungren (R-CA) and Shaw (R-FL), spoke in favor of the bill.

Few amendments were offered and here we will focus on only the most divisive ones. The first was the effort by McCollum (R-FL) to strike the amnesty provisions in the bill. McCollum made the now-familiar arguments against amnesty but lost by the narrowest of margins on a 192–199 vote. The second was an amendment offered by Hamilton Fish (R-NY) to strike so-called EVD provisions that had been added at the last minute. EVD stood for "extended voluntary departure," and it would delay the deportation of Salvadoran and Nicaraguan illegals until a GAO report had been completed determining the safety of living conditions in Central America. In essence, EVD constituted a temporary grant of asylum on a wholesale basis. Church groups that were part of the "sanctuary movement" had been sheltering many illegal entrants from El Salvador and Nicaragua. Members of these churches, as well as clergy, were facing arrest and prosecution by government authorities for harboring the illegal entrants, and the illegals themselves faced deportation proceedings. In the past, EVD had been granted to refugees of other countries, realizing that conditions were not safe for them at home, but in the hope that they would one day be able to return. Fish and Lungren argued that more information was unnecessary and that the United States was not the only safe haven for those fleeing the two war-torn Central American countries (*CR* 10/9/86, H30071–H30074). Objecting to EVD was justified in the minds of Fish and Lungren because they believed that the U.S. was bearing too much of the world refugee burden. Japan, for instance, would take advantage of the U.S.'s refusal to trade with Vietnam by selling to the Vietnamese, but at the same time Japan refused to admit any Vietnamese refugees. The Reagan administration was on record opposing the perpetuation of extended voluntary departure, claiming that most of those fleeing Central America were doing so for economic reasons, not political ones. It had become no more dangerous to live in these countries than in many other areas around the world, or even in the United States. Lungren summarized these objections and warned that this provision could kill the bill altogether via a presidential veto:

> …If you establish the idea that we should grant extended voluntary departure to this group, where do you stop?
> …If you take general conditions, my God, we should give extended voluntary departure to the people who live in downtown District of Columbia. People who live in Chicago, who live in Los Angeles. It is more dangerous, statistically, in those areas than in El Salvador.
> This throws the whole immigration bill out the window…(*CR* 10/9/86, H30074)

Following these remarks, the vote was called and the amendment to strike the EVD language was defeated by a scant two-vote margin, 197–199. Speaker Tip O'Neill (D-MA) then took over the Committee of the Whole and called for the vote on final passage. The Simpson-Mazzoli bill finally passed the House on a 230–166 vote.

Conference action went more smoothly than in 1984 because more deals had already been made. The agriculture worker program had been agreed upon in advance by Schumer and Simpson. After three days of meetings, including a four-hour meeting on a Saturday morning, the committee came to agreement. With the weight of the administration on its side, the Republican-led Senate gave up less than the House. The House conferees agreed to give up on extended voluntary departure for Salvadorans and Nicaraguans. The House also agreed to give up on a 6½-year sunset provision on employer sanctions that had bought some support for the bill among minority members. The Senate agreed to the House's date for legalization: To be eligible for amnesty, undocumented workers would have to have entered the country by January 1, 1982. The federal role in funding the costs of legalization had been a major sticking point in the 1984 negotiations. The House provision demanded 100 percent reimbursement of states. The Senate version provided $3 billion over six years. The compromise reached was to authorize $1 billion per year for the next four years (*CQWR* 10/18/86, 2596). Both chambers approved the conference report; the Senate on an easy 63–24 vote, the House by a margin of 238–173.

The House floor votes on immigration reform in the 99th Congress are instructive because they reveal the nature of both the support and opposition to the legislation. An analysis of selected floor votes shows that the voting sharply divided Republicans and Democrats (see Table 5.2 and Appendix

Table 5.2 Estimated Probability of Voting Yes on Immigration Amendments and Final Passage of House Bill, 99th Congress, U.S. House of Representatives

Variables	Vote on 1st Rule	Vote on 2nd Rule	McCollum Amendment to Strike Amnesty	Fish Amendment to Strike EVD	Passage of House Bill	Passage of Conference Report
Democrat	.77	.84	.19	.15	.79	.70
Republican	.07	.50	.71	.87	.32	.38
White member	.43	.74	.41	.45	.65	.60
Nonwhite member	.54	.43	.03	.11	.44	.43
Non-South	.52	.74	.25	.28	.70	.65
South	.24	.73	.69	.78	.44	.38
Nonborder state	.44	.74	.34	.39	.61	.56
Border state	.45	.72	.42	.52	.70	.65
Not Judiciary	.43	.74	.37	.41	.63	.58
Judiciary Committee	.60	.65	.30	.53	.68	.63
Foreign born = .37	.27	.66	.74	.56	.46	.47
Foreign born = 52.2	.99	.98	.01	.01	.99	98
Agriculture = .13	.35	.73	.42	.38	.58	.52
Agriculture = 18.05	.85	.76	.13	.64	.83	.85
Black = .05	.43	.76	.38	.45	.66	.60
Black = 92.05	.52	.57	.24	.24	.43	.46
Asian/other = .53	.48	.78	.31	.44	.71	.67
Asian/other = 71.9	.18	.29	.79	.27	.07	.05
Unemployment = 1.9	.31	.71	.50	.44	.64	.62
Unemployment = 28.1	.89	.81	.05	.32	.60	.43

Values represent the estimated probability of a Yes vote at the lowest and highest value of the independent variables, with all other variables held constant at their sample means.

Table A5.2). Only 7 percent of Republicans went along with the first rule, compared with three-fourths of the Democrats. Republican support was critical for the passage of the second rule and about half the Republicans went along with it. McCollum's motion to eliminate amnesty gained more support among Republicans in the 99th Congress than it had in 1984, but he also lost the votes of some Democrats.

Lessons from the 99th Congress

The biggest difference in the floor voting between 1984 and 1986 was that in the former round there were many party-line votes, but the vote on final passage cut across party lines. In the 99th Congress, though, the votes on both House passage and the conference report were divided along party lines. The differences can be accounted for by the fact that the new version of the legislation won over many Democrats who had dissented previously. The figures in Table 5.2 show that an estimated 70 percent of Democrats voted for the 1986 legislation compared with only 47 percent who voted for the 1984 bill (for comparison see Table 5.1). Hispanic members Bill Richardson (D-NM), Solomon Ortiz (D-TX), and Esteban Torres (D-CA), for example, voted in favor of the bill because they wanted legalization and were willing to give up other demands to get it. Many black members went along this time, as did members from areas of high unemployment, such as Thomas Foglietta (D-PA) and Dale Kildee (D-MI). Interestingly, the inclusion of the modified farm worker program did little to boost support for the bill in the most agricultural districts. About 90 percent of the members from areas with large agricultural sectors voted for the legislation. But nearly the same proportion (85 percent) had favored the bill in 1984. This strongly suggests that the agony that Schumer (D-NY) and the other committee members went through on the guest-worker program did little, in the end, to build support for the legislation on the floor. At most, it swayed only three or four votes.

Given that many interests had reasons to oppose passage of the legislation upon its initial introduction, it is no surprise that it took such a long time to work out the deals that would guarantee smooth sailing. We are led to wonder, in retrospect, if the legislation would not have had an easier time moving through the legislative process if it had been divided into separate vehicles. The bill, as it was originally constructed, created a kind of preference intransitivity problem often discussed by public-choice theorists (Hinich and Munger 1997). A unique majority could be found on employer sanctions; a unique majority could be found on legalization; a unique majority could be found for various other provisions of the bill once they were isolated. But none of these majorities added up to a clear majority in favor of the entire package. The bill was so complex and so controversial that it may have made better sense to split the various provisions into separate bills and take advantage of the distinct majorities that would prevail on each proposal in isolation from the others.

Box 5.4

Edward R. Roybal (D-CA) was a strong opponent of employer sanctions legislation, believing it would have a discriminatory impact on Hispanics. Working with the Hispanic caucus members and other allies, he successfully delayed passage of the Simpson-Mazzoli legislation until 1986. Courtesy of Edward R. Roybal.

Edward R. Roybal (D-CA)

Though not a member of the House Judiciary Committee, Representative Edward Roybal played a key part in immigration policymaking. He led the opposition to the Simpson-Mazzoli immigration legislation in 1982 and 1984, almost single-handedly defeating attempts to pass it. He was a die-hard opponent of employer sanctions, fearing that the threat of sanctions would lead employers to discriminate against anyone who looked or sounded foreign.

Roybal was born in Albuquerque, New Mexico, on February 10, 1916. He moved to Los Angeles in 1922. He participated in the Depression-era Civilian Conservation Corps until 1935. He attended UCLA and Los Angeles's Southwestern University.

From 1942 to 1944, Roybal worked for the California Tuberculosis Association as a public health educator. He served from April 1944 until December 1945 in the U.S. Army. He returned to Los Angeles after military service to become director of health education with the L.A. County Tuberculosis and Health Association.

Roybal entered politics in 1949, gaining election as a Los Angeles city councilman. He was the Democratic candidate for lieutenant governor of California in 1954. In July 1961, he became the council's president pro tempore. He served as councilman until 1962.

In 1958, Roybal became president of the Eastland Savings & Loan Association, a position he held until 1968, when he was named chairman of the board.

Meanwhile, Roybal sought a congressional seat. He won election to Congress in 1962, where he established a liberal record. He reliably spoke out on behalf of Hispanic interests, as he represented a district that was about 60 percent Hispanic. The House reprimanded Roybal in 1978 for lying about the personal use of a campaign contribution. But in 1981, he became chairman of the Congressional Hispanic Caucus. This positioned him to take charge of the opposition effort against the Simpson-Mazzoli bill.

In 1983, Roybal succeeded Representative Claude Pepper at the helm of the Select Committee on Aging. He also was a senior member of the powerful Appropriations Committee, where he chaired a subcommittee. Of his seat on Appropriations, *Politics in America* reported, "He has used his place there to push for more spending on programs benefiting Hispanics, migrant workers and the elderly."

Roybal served in Congress until 1992, when he retired.

(Sources: *Almanac of American Politics*, 1990; *Biographical Directory of the U.S. Congress 1774–1989*; *Politics in America*, 1986)

Our analysis only strengthens our argument that, by the mid-1980s, immigration reform had been translated into an issue that was highly partisan. Amnesty and employer sanctions were controversial proposals. Amnesty was viewed by many as just wrong, as a reward for those who had broken the law. For conservatives, amnesty alone was sufficient grounds to vote against the bill. To be sure, employer sanctions did not divide the chamber totally along party lines, because the civil rights community and the business community were both hostile to the idea. For Hispanic members, such as Edward Roybal (D-CA), the threat of discrimination was sufficient to justify a no vote, while those close to the business community, including many GOP legislators, voted no because employer sanctions meant additional regulation. But far more Republicans voted against the bill because of employer sanctions than did Democrats, indicating that the reaction to this proposal was still tinged by partisanship.

Much of the partisanship emerged because Republicans could foresee the redistributive implications of legalization. Thousands of newly legalized residents and their families could soon become dependent upon public aid. These were not highly skilled workers with many choices in the labor market. Those granted amnesty would be particularly vulnerable to unemployment and economic downturn, and the legalization provisions would declare that millions of such workers would eventually be eligible for entitlement programs. Providing education and health care to a population of truly unknown size suddenly declared eligible for welfare would be very costly. Indeed, the 1984 conference foundered on the redistributive issue of federal reimbursement for states. No one could accurately estimate how much such services would cost because no one knew how many illegals would come forward to apply for amnesty. Bill McCollum (R-FL) moved to strike amnesty primarily because of its high cost. In the Senate, Phil Gramm (R-TX) led an unsuccessful eleventh-hour effort to kill the bill also because of its high cost, particularly in the entitlement area.

The 1986 Immigration Reform and Control Act (IRCA) had the most sweeping impact on immigration policy since the repeal of national origins quotas in 1965. In the next several years, immigrant admissions would soar to new heights as the new permanent residents brought in their family members. This created unanticipated problems, including long backlogs in the queue for immigrant visas, skyrocketing costs for the provision of government services in the areas where the immigrants and their families settled, and sustained border control problems. It was clear that the implementation of employer sanctions would be no quick fix. The magnet had not been demagnetized. An exodus of emigrants from Central America continued through the late 1980s, and this influx raised questions about the asylum system. Applicants needed only to make a minimal showing that they faced a "well-founded fear of persecution" in their homeland in order to be granted an asylum review. By late in 1988, the INS office in Harlingen, Texas, was receiving 1,700 applications for asylum each week (*CQ Almanac* 1989, 273).

Business interests, particularly those in high-tech fields, were putting pressure on Congress to grant more employment-oriented visas in response to alleged shortages of skilled labor. It soon became evident that the 1986 IRCA had not only failed to stem the flow of illegal immigrants and generated some unintended consequences, but that it totally ignored some areas of immigration law that major interests badly wanted to address.

The 100th Congress: The Pressure Builds

Worn out from the immigration battles of 1981 through 1986, the House Judiciary Committee stayed away from major immigration policy in the 100th Congress (1987–1988). Members were concerned about implementation of the 1986 Act and held regular oversight hearings, but very little new legislation was proposed. Advocates for the humane treatment of Salvadoran and Nicaraguan refugees continued to push for the "extended voluntary departure" (EVD) measure that Democrats had written into the 1986 bill only to have it stripped out in the conference committee by Alan Simpson (R-WY) and the Republicans. With the 1986 elections, however, Republicans had lost control of the U.S. Senate, and Edward M. Kennedy (D-MA) once again assumed control of that chamber's immigration subcommittee. Kennedy used his new position to push a major bill reforming legal immigration by reordering the preference system to emphasize skilled immigration. The bill was designed to stimulate more immigration from Western Europe. With Simpson's help, Kennedy managed to pass the bill in the Senate, but Peter Rodino (D-NJ) and Romano Mazzoli (D-KY), neither of whom had ever been backers of employer-oriented immigration, refused to take it up in the House.

The prospects for refugee policy did not seem so grim. Kennedy had long been concerned about refugees and had been the primary sponsor of the 1980 Refugee Act. His feelings on the matter stemmed from his roots as a strong supporter of civil rights and equal opportunity. Kennedy's philosophy of immigration was anchored in the belief that everyone has something to contribute regardless of where he or she comes from. Legislation to grant temporary residency to these victims of political strife was the least the United States could do.

In addition, many liberal Democrats were hostile to the Reagan administration's aggressive foreign policy in Central America. They were upset about alleged human rights violations perpetrated by Reagan administration allies in Nicaragua and El Salvador. Bad foreign policy choices had created the situation whereby an estimated 500,000 Salvadorans and 200,000 Nicaraguans were now residing illegally in the United States, liberals said. This became a popular defense of a more open and generous immigration and refugee policy.

Box 5.5

Edward M. Kennedy (D-MA) served as Chair of the Senate Judiciary Committee in the late-1970s following James Eastland's retirement, and as an influential member of the Senate immigration subcommittee since the late 1960s. He fiercely opposed efforts to restrict immigrant eligibility for welfare benefits in the 1996 legislation. Courtesy of Edward M. Kennedy.

Edward M. Kennedy (D-MA)

Senator Edward M. Kennedy served as ranking member of the Senate immigration subcommittee during the 104th Congress. He had served as that body's chair in several previous congresses. Conscious of his own Irish immigrant roots, Kennedy generally favored open and generous immigration policies, although he remained skeptical of the need for employment-based immigrants. In 1996, he fiercely opposed welfare provisions restricting immigrants' eligibility for public benefits. He has been one of the most influential members in the history of immigration policymaking.

Kennedy was born in Boston on February 22, 1932, the youngest of nine children in one of America's most notable families. He served in the U.S. Army from 1951 until 1953 as an infantryman stationed in Europe. He then attended Harvard, graduating with his bachelor's degree in 1956. He went on to law school at The Hague and then the University of Virginia, from which he earned his LL.B. in 1959.

In 1960, Kennedy helped his older brother, John, campaign for the presidency. The youngest Kennedy was the campaign's western states coordinator. He next became assistant district attorney in Suffolk County, Mass., from 1961 till 1962.

With his older brothers as president and U.S. attorney general, Kennedy pursued a U.S. Senate seat from Massachusetts in 1962, which he won at age 30. His Senate career coincided with that of his brother, Robert, from 1965 till 1968.

From the beginning of his career, Kennedy developed a reputation as an outspoken advocate for liberal causes. On immigration issues, Kennedy regularly has taken the side of ethnic groups and labor unions. He was floor manager of the 1965 immigration bill, and played central roles on subsequent immigration bills, particularly after Senator James Eastland's retirement in 1979, when he succeeded Eastland as chair of the Judiciary Committee.

Kennedy ran for the Democratic presidential nomination in 1980, losing out to incumbent Jimmy Carter. Kennedy held senior positions—often either as chair or ranking member—on his committee and subcommittee assignments throughout the 1980s and 1990s.

(Sources: *Almanac of American Politics*, various years; *Politics in America*, 1986; Senator Kennedy's biography on Internet homepage)

Congressman Esteban Torres (D-CA) clearly expressed the connection many members saw between U.S. foreign policy and refugee policy:

> People will say that wars we waged, or our foreign policy, has generated an out-pouring of people displaced by conflict. In a way, we are participating in this and causing these people to come here. This is true of Haitians, Cubans, Iranians, Cambodians, Vietnamese, El Salvadorans and many others. The desire to emi-grate by these people is a consequence of our foreign policy. We have to pay the cost of that foreign policy. It has often been an ill-founded foreign policy attitude that has created the demand in the first place. (Torres interview 5/17/97)

Since our foreign policy had created the problem, it was our responsibility to remedy it with policies granting temporary asylum. The bill passed the Senate subcommittee in early July 1987, and the House subcommittee passed it on July 28. The bill denied the temporary residents most forms of public assistance, and states were authorized to deny aid if they so chose (*CQ Almanac* 1987, 284). As in 1986, the Reagan administration opposed EVD, arguing that it would undercut the 1986 IRCA law designed to discourage the entry of illegal aliens. The administration repeated the argument that these were not political refugees, but economic refugees. They were not fleeing political oppression, they were fleeing poverty. Poverty had never been considered a ground for refugee admission.

On the floor, on July 28, the measure was debated for three hours and passed on a 237–181 vote. Forty-one Democrats voted against the measure, while only a handful of liberal Republicans supported it. Republicans were in a difficult position. The government that the administration was supporting in El Salvador favored the legislation, arguing that the return of refugees to El Salvador would destabilize the country. Dan Lungren (R-CA) attacked the bill on the floor, calling it "special-interest legislation" because it was designed only to please liberal constituency groups (*CR* 7/28/87, H21327). The new Republican leader of the immigration subcommittee, Pat Swindall (R-GA), opposed the legislation on predictable grounds: cost. Swindall, Lungren, and other Republicans figured correctly that very few of these Salvadorans and Nicaraguans would seek to return once they entered. Other arguments were voiced against the legislation, but the GOP members' basic premise was that this new class of residents, and others like them, would prove to be more of a burden than a benefit. Granting EVD would open the floodgates encouraging others to come, adding to the burden. The measure died in the Senate, and in any case, would not have survived a presidential veto.

In the second session of the 100th Congress (1988), House Democrats pushed for an extension of the 1986 legalization provisions. Administered by INS officials, the amnesty program was scheduled to run from May 1987 to May 1988. The proposed six-month extension was designed to maximize the number of amnesty seekers. All aliens who had arrived in the country prior to January 1, 1982, were eligible for temporary resident status providing they met certain other minor requirements. After 18 months of temporary resident status, they could convert to permanent resident status and eventually apply for citizenship. While there were arguments about the numbers, the INS estimated that, through May 1987, about 1.8 million undocumented aliens had come forward, with another 1.2 million who had come in under the 1986 law's foreign farm worker provisions (*CQ Almanac* 1988, 83). Proponents insisted that the legalization program had worked slowly and that more time was needed. The INS took most of the one-year application period to get its processing apparatus in place. The House Judiciary Committee approved the legislation on a 22–12 vote over the objections of conservative Republicans and the Reagan administration. Dan Lungren (R-CA) and Hamilton Fish (R-NY) supported the bill.

The costs associated with extending amnesty were very much on the minds of the GOP members. On the floor, George Gekas (R-PA), a kindly member and son of Greek immigrants, opposed the amnesty extension and contrasted taxpayers with illegal immigrants, arguing that "taxpayers are not accorded any extension of the deadline past April 15 every single year except with severe penalties, except with certain good cause shown, and here we are in the business of extending the right of amnesty to illegal aliens" (*CR* 4/20/88, H7986). As a compromise, Gekas offered an amendment that would allow applications after the May 1988 deadline had passed so long as applicants could show "good cause" for not having met the original deadline. The amendment was defeated on a 167–246 vote. The measure then passed on a narrow 213–201 vote on April 20. The idea of an amnesty extension was not warmly received on the Senate floor. The opposition was led by Alan Simpson, and after a short debate the measure was defeated on a 40–56 vote just eight days later.

The analysis of the floor votes on these measures indicates that the earlier patterns of behavior continued to hold in the 100th Congress (see Table 5.3). The votes on amnesty and extended voluntary departure were highly partisan. An estimated 91 percent of Democrats voted to extend the amnesty deadline, compared with only one-third of Republicans. The vote for EVD was even more partisan, with only 19 percent of House Republicans favoring the legislation, compared with 89 percent of Democrats. Predictably, Republicans were joined by many Southern Democrats in voting against both the amnesty extension and extended voluntary departure. Reflecting the fear of high costs resulting from the legalization program, members from border states were far less likely to support the extension of amnesty than those from nonborder states.

As in previous Congresses, economic conditions prevailing in congressional districts seem to encourage liberal voting on immigration policy rather

Table 5.3 Estimated Probability of Voting Yes on Amnesty Extension and Extended Voluntary Departure (EVD), 100th Congress, U.S. House of Representatives

Variables	Gekas Amendment to Modify Amnesty	Vote on Extension of Amnesty Deadline	Vote on Extended Voluntary Departure
Democrat	.11	.91	.89
Republican	.65	.34	.19
White member	.30	.63	.62
Nonwhite member	.09	.99	.93
Non-South	.23	.80	.76
South	.44	.57	.35
Nonborder state	.24	.80	.69
Border state	.43	.54	.57
Not Judiciary	.28	.74	.67
Judiciary Committee	.23	.81	.63
Foreign born = .37	.65	.34	.52
Foreign born = 52.2	.01	.99	.99
Agriculture = .13	.25	.75	.71
Agriculture = 18.05	.45	.72	.41
Black = .05	.30	.73	.67
Black = 92.05	.17	.84	.61
Asian/other = .53	.25	.67	.69
Asian/other = 71.9	.45	.99	.35
Unemployment = 1.9	.43	.56	.50
Unemployment = 28.1	.02	.99	.97

Values represent the estimated probability of a Yes vote at the lowest and highest value of the independent variables, with all other variables held constant at their sample means.

than restrictions, even after controlling for variables such as the racial composition of the population. Apparently members do not draw much of a connection between immigration levels and labor market conditions. Members from impoverished areas instead vote ideologically, seeing generous immigration policy as a matter of social justice and civil rights. The 100th Congress ended with the frustration of the Democrats and the election of another Republican president, George Bush, whose commitment to open immigration policy would be severely tested by world events.

The 101st Congress: Throwing Open the Doors

With the collapse of communism in Eastern Europe and the Soviet Union, the 101st Congress (1989–1990) was confronted with another world refugee crisis. These Eastern bloc nations had traditionally allowed only a few emigres to trickle out, usually Jews, Evangelicals, well-known dissidents, and other persecuted minorities. Their newly liberalized policies threw open the borders for the first time, allowing Soviet Jews and other minorities to exit at will. On a smaller scale, the student uprising in China forced Congress to rethink asylum policy. Democrats who had supported extended voluntary departure for Salvadorans and Nicaraguans in the previous two Congresses saw these major world events as opportunities to once again press for the establishment of the United States as a safe haven. The third attempt to pass EVD would succeed.

New Faces in the House

In the House, some new faces emerged to do battle over these issues. On the Democratic side, Peter Rodino (D-NJ) finally retired after a long and distinguished career. The chairmanship of the Judiciary Committee was taken over by Jack Brooks (D-TX), presumably a more conservative member, but one who had taken very little interest in immigration legislation. Unlike Rodino, he would prove to be a hands-off chairman, delegating the negotiations to the subcommittee Democrats. The immigration subcommittee chairmanship was given to Bruce Morrison (D-CT). The Democrats on the Judiciary Committee voted to strip Romano Mazzoli (D-KY) of the chair because of his disloyalty to important Democratic causes. In the previous Congress, Mazzoli had voted with Republicans against extended voluntary departure and on a number of economic and foreign policy issues. Morrison, who represented New Haven, Connecticut, was a far more reliable and liberal Democrat. He was trusted by the pro-immigration interest groups to fight their battles with an energy and conviction that Mazzoli had recently been unable to muster.

On the GOP side, the leadership of the immigration subcommittee went to Lamar Smith (R-TX), a soft-spoken but firm conservative first elected in 1986. Smith represented a predominantly rural Texas district that covered a vast swath of southcentral and southwest Texas extending from the border to the outskirts of San Antonio. Having been born and raised near San Antonio, Smith had grown up with an acute awareness of immigrants, both legal and illegal. Immigration was clearly a source of concern for many of his constituents from the start but, unlike the city of San Antonio, where there was a majority Hispanic population, Smith's district was predominantly white and offended by the people trafficking, the drug trafficking, the school overcrowding, and the other problems associated with the failure to control the borders. Over the course of a few years of studying the issue, Smith had developed a detailed philosophy of immigration, and he would lay it out in clear and certain terms. Priority in immigration admissions should go to immediate family members and skilled and educated immigrants. Lower priority should be given to extended family and unskilled and uneducated immigrants. Unskilled immigrants were not equipped to produce in or contribute to the American economy. The unskilled were also high risks for going on public assistance. The American people did not want immigrants coming here to live off the taxpayer. Smith finally expressed coherently what a large number of Republican legislators had thought for several years. Immigration policies lately had done little more than import poverty. This had to stop.

Smith would see little success in his first years in the minority on one of the most liberal committees in Congress. He strenuously objected to the extended voluntary departure bill in both the subcommittee and full committee markups. The bill was voted out of the full committee on a 20–14 vote and was then combined with legislation to extend the visas of Chinese students currently in the country. On October 25, 1989, the measure came to the House floor and was approved on a 258–162 vote. The Senate stalled on the measure, however, and the first session of the 101st Congress expired with the matter unresolved.

Senate Action on the 1990 Bill

The Senate, meanwhile, had been working on a separate immigration agenda through most of 1989. Unlike 1986, where the bulk of the provisions were aimed at addressing illegal immigration, the focus this time was on legal immigration. Edward M. Kennedy (D-MA) had grown increasingly dissatisfied with what he had wrought with the repeal of national-origins based admissions in 1965. This system had all but shut out European immigrants, including Irish immigrants, with whom Kennedy was particularly concerned. Together with Simpson, Kennedy had drafted legislation in the 100th Congress to revise visa allocations to reemphasize skilled immigration. The current system heavily emphasized family reunification as the pathway to legal resident status. While there was no annual cap on the number of immediate relatives (parents, spouses, minor children) of U.S. citizens who could enter the country, there was an annual ceiling of 270,000 set on other immigrants. Nearly all of these visas went to other relatives of U.S citizens and relatives of permanent residents (*CQ Almanac* 1989, 266). These visas were utilized primarily by Asian and Latin American immigrants. Very few Europeans were admitted. The House had been reluctant to consider these proposals in 1987 and 1988, but the 101st Congress presented a new opportunity to advance these ideas into law.

Kennedy and Simpson proposed a plan to cap total annual immigration at 590,000, including the immediate relatives of U.S. citizens. Their proposal also sought to cut the fifth preference: that allotted for the adult brothers and sisters of U.S. citizens and their children. Their revised proposal granted visas only to adult *unmarried* brothers and sisters and sharply reduced the number of visas allocated to this category. Simpson insisted that priority be given to more immediate relatives. To emphasize skilled immigration, the bill established a new preference category designed to admit people based not on family ties but on their skills, their command of English, their education, and their work experience deemed of value to the U.S. economy. The legislation incorporated sections to permit the extended stay of Chinese students, and language that would stall the deportation of spouses and unmarried children of illegal entrants granted amnesty under the 1986 law.

In the full committee markup, several of these provisions were changed. The total annual visa limit was set at 600,000—480,000 for those with family ties and 120,000 for those with special skills. The preference system was restructured and new visa allotments were adopted. The English language stipulation associated with skilled immigration was stripped from the bill as a result of pressure from Hispanic and Asian interest groups. Only Simpson and Strom Thurmond (R-SC) voted to keep the English language provision in the bill (*CQ Almanac* 1989, 268).

In Senate floor action, several of the bill's provisions were again altered. In final form, the bill was amended to authorize 630,000 visas—480,000 for family reunification and 150,000 for skilled immigrants, a 30,000 visa increase from the committee version (*CQ Almanac* 1989, 270). Most amendments were adopted on lopsided votes. Simpson tried to replace the English language provision that had been stripped out in committee, but he failed on a 43–56 vote. Jesse Helms (R-NC) tried to further limit the number of visas available for adult brothers and sisters of U.S. citizens and provide more business-oriented visas. This was rejected on a 27–71 vote. The bill passed the Senate on July 13 on an 81–17 vote.

House Action on the 1990 Bill

In the House, Bruce Morrison (D-CT) began working on his own version of the legislation in September 1989. Morrison's bill set higher visa allotments than the Kennedy-Simpson proposal, possibly allowing as many as 100,000 more annual visas (*CQ Almanac* 1990, 475). Several members of the immigration subcommittee believed that the preference system required modification in order to reduce the waiting period for family reunification visas. In 1990, the wait was averaging about three years, and for some countries it was much longer. Asian and Hispanic interest groups insisted that it was antifamily to allow such long separations and that the long backlogs for legal visas only encouraged illegal immigration. In response, Howard Berman (D-CA) proposed legislation that would treat the immediate relatives of permanent residents the same as immediate relatives of U.S. citizens—permitting their unlimited and immediate entry. This constituted a sweeping change in the preference system, but was adopted easily in the subcommittee markup in

April 1990. Charles Schumer (D-NY) added a provision for "diversity visas" ensuring that areas of the world that had been sending relatively few immigrants in recent years would receive a special allotment of visas. Under this allotment system, Europeans would be heavily favored relative to Asians and Latin Americans. Lamar Smith (R-TX) offered numerous amendments to temper the generosity of Morrison, Berman, and the other subcommittee Democrats, but all of these measures were defeated in the subcommittee markup.

In the full committee markup that began July 31, 1990, Smith continued to argue with committee Democrats Morrison (D-CT) and Berman (D-CA) about whether immigrants contribute more than they consume in public benefits. Smith also insisted that the higher immigration levels proposed in Morrison's bill would increase crime, lower wages, and lead to higher unemployment (*CQWR* 8/4/90, 2519). He was joined in his opposition to the legislation by fellow Texan John Bryant (D-TX), who would later become Smith's ally in supporting immigration restrictions in the 1996 round of reforms (see Chapter 6). What divided the two sides was the fundamental question of how open America's borders should be. Morrison and the Democrats insisted that it was in the national interest to increase immigration.

Even so, some provisions in the original bill were scaled back. Reflecting the interests of their labor constituency, Democrats had always been uneasy with employment-based immigration, figuring that it was often used by business not to fill legitimate needs but to hire cheaper workers than could be found in the domestic labor market. Employment-based immigration was originally allotted 95,000 visas in Morrison's bill. This was reduced to 65,000. Under current law, 54,000 visas were allowed for permanent workers. Again at the behest of organized labor, leading Democrats wanted to protect domestic workers from competition from immigrant workers and thus incorporated several worker-protection provisions. Employers were to be taxed for every foreign worker hired: $1,000 for companies with 200 employers or more; $500 for companies with 50–199 workers, and no tax for those with fewer than 50 workers (*CQ Almanac* 1990, 478). The proceeds from these taxes were to go for training and retraining of U.S. workers. Companies that desired to hire foreign workers had to petition the Secretary of Labor, saying that they had made a good-faith effort to hire domestic workers, and then wait 30 days to see if U.S. workers lodged protests.

Howard Berman (D-CA) also won approval of a proposal to suspend the deportation of spouses and minor children of persons legalized under the 1986 Act. Republicans objected that this was tantamount to a second amnesty, but Berman prevailed over attempts to delete the proposal. Charles Schumer's provision for "diversity" visas for Europeans remained intact. In the end, the House bill proposed letting in 800,000 immigrants a year, 27 percent more than the 630,000 proposed in the Senate bill. The committee divided on the bill on a 23–12 vote. Four Republicans, including Hamilton

Fish (R-NY), voted with the majority. Three Democrats, including John Bryant (D-TX), voted in the minority, joining nine Republicans in dissent.

Floor Debate in the House

The bill came to the floor late in the 1990 session, on October 3. The rule specified 90 minutes of debate, with the consideration of 23 amendments, 11 of those to be offered by Republicans. In response to objections raised by the Ways and Means Committee, the Rules Committee had eliminated the "head-tax" provision that would have charged businesses a fee for every foreign worker they hired. Under longstanding House rules, revenue measures are the sole jurisdiction of the Ways and Means Committee.

Republicans on the Rules Committee spoke out against what they considered an unfairly restrictive rule, but Hamilton Fish (R-NY) defended it on the floor on the grounds that members had sufficient time to be familiar with the legislation, it was late in the session, and unlimited amendments would kill the chance for passage in the 101st Congress. Lamar Smith (R-TX) pointed out that some of the most important amendments had been ruled out of order, including a number of amendments important to Texas and other border states that would require the federal reimbursement of state and local governments for the costs of providing services to new immigrants. Democrats had only ruled in order those Republican amendments that could be most easily defeated. The rule passed on a 245–165 vote that fell largely along party lines. Fish was joined by fellow New York Republicans Susan Molinari (Staten Island) and Ray McGrath (Nassau County) in supporting adoption of the rule.

The Bush administration had gone on record in opposition to the bill. In committee hearings, witnesses from several cabinet agencies predicted problems in implementing it and testified that it would do more harm to the U.S. economy than good. The administration welcomed the focus on skilled immigrants, but worried about the increases in the family reunification categories. Lamar Smith (R-TX) repeated these same concerns on the floor, emphasizing that the United States had to be more selective about who it admitted than in times past when the economy was growing more rapidly. Reflecting his desire to eliminate the fifth preference for adult brothers and sisters of immigrants, Smith insisted that admissions priorities should be on *immediate* family members and on skilled workers, not more distant relatives. Smith pointed to academic studies indicating that the United States was becoming a welfare magnet because of the generous transfer payments that recent legal immigrants were receiving and concluded by citing public opinion studies that showed considerable opposition to increasing legal immigration (*CQWR* 10/2/90, 8636). Bruce Morrison (D-CT) replied that legal immigration had been a great strength to the nation. He argued that the bill was pro-family because it allowed the families of permanent residents to immediately reunite rather than wait in a visa queue, and it reduced the backlogged queues for less immediate family members. Charles Schumer (D-NY) insisted that immigrants solve problems rather than create them by bringing in new vigor and ideas.

Of the major changes considered in the floor debate, four amendments are worth special mention. The first was an amendment by Lamar Smith to limit the number of legal immigrants admitted to 630,000 per year, similar to the Senate version of the legislation. Smith's amendment would allocate 430,000 visas to family-based immigrants, 150,000 to employment-based immigrants, and 50,000 visas under the diversity category. The change was opposed by Berman and Morrison as a killer amendment, and when the vote was called for, the amendment failed 143–266.

Several amendments were accepted on voice votes and often Lamar Smith (R-TX) was the lonely voice speaking out on the floor against them. Smith had done his homework, knew the issues, and was well prepared to force his opponents to justify and defend their legislation. In addition, the other members realized that passage of these measures was a foregone conclusion, given the way the Rules Committee had structured the debate. The smell of defeat was in the air. Opposing Democratic amendments that were sure to pass was wasting one's energy. On the subject of reimbursement of costs for states, Smith offered an amendment to extend funding granted to states and localities for the costs of legalization under the 1986 Act for an additional three years. Morrison and Berman immediately objected that this amendment would cost too much, to which Smith replied, tongue-in-cheek:

> Mr. Chairman, let me say first of all that I am absolutely delighted to hear the concern about spending that has been expressed by the gentleman from Connecticut and the gentleman from California. I can only assume that that represents a change in their political thinking and I welcome it. (CR 10/2/90; H8682).

Smith saw great irony in the Democratic objections to increased spending. Liberal Democrats, in particular, rarely evaluated the programs that they favored in terms of their cost. Cost was something a member only raised when objecting to a program. Democratic proponents of increased immigration were reluctant to admit that immigration placed a heavy fiscal burden on state and local government. But Berman and Morrison also had more immediate concerns in mind in objecting to Smith's amnesty reimbursement scheme. At that very moment, President Bush was locked in budget negotiations with Democratic House leaders in the now infamous "budget summit" of 1990. It was this summit where Bush reneged on his "no-new-taxes" pledge of 1988, a move that would cost him a second term. While House Democrats won some major compromises from the president at that summit, Berman and Morrison knew that talking about a major new spending initiative at the very time this budget deal was being reached would surely kill the entire bill. When the vote was called, Smith's amendment was decisively defeated on a 53–368 vote that was split mostly along regional lines. Members from California, Texas, and Florida were especially supportive.

Bill McCollum (R-FL), ever ready to strike entire sections of generous immigration initiatives, marched to the floor to eliminate the provision for extended voluntary departure for refugees from a number of foreign countries. Originally, EVD had been designed to protect Salvadoran and Nicaraguan illegals from deportation. The provision evolved, however, to cover refugees from a number of different states, including Kuwait, Liberia, and Lebanon—countries that were currently experiencing civil strife. Morrison had not included this language in the Judiciary Committee bill. Instead it had been added in the Rules Committee by its sponsor, Joe Moakley (D-MA), who was the chairman of that committee. McCollum insisted that existing asylum laws would protect these people if their lives were threatened at home. This provision would indiscriminately protect those who had entered the country illegally. If there is no well-founded fear of persecution, those here illegally should go back to their country, McCollum said. The amendment garnered 131 votes in its favor, mostly from Republicans and particularly from those in affected border states.

In a rather bold stroke, on the second day of debate, immigration subcommittee member John Bryant (D-TX) moved to strike the entire bill and to substitute instead a provision that would only permit the legalization of the spouses and children of those illegals who had been granted amnesty under the 1986 Act. Gone would be everything but a rather limited extension of the 1986 amnesty provisions. Bryant had repeatedly made the point that the United States was straining to take care of its current population. There was clearly no justification for bringing in another 800,000 immigrants each year. Because it was offered by a Democrat, this was clearly the most threatening of the amendments offered during the debate. Nevertheless, Bryant's amendment mustered only 165 votes in its favor, mostly from Republicans.

On October 3, the bill was brought up for final passage in the House, and the vote was surprisingly narrow, given how easily most of the amendments had been defeated. Members in favor numbered 231, with 192 against.

The House and Senate bills looked very different from one another. A conference agreement on immigration legislation was never easy to reach, and this one would be at least as difficult as 1986. The chief obstacle to agreement was the difference between the House measure, which granted 800,000 immigrant visas annually, and the Senate measure, which granted only 630,000. While both bills were more generous than existing law, the House version was much more so. Alan Simpson emerged as a major conference player, in spite of his minority status. Kennedy respected Simpson's expertise in the area and knew Simpson could be an obstacle to the bill's final approval in the Senate. Simpson opposed the House provision that allowed the children and spouses of permanent residents to be permitted unrestricted entry. He also opposed any extension of amnesty or stay of deportation.

Box 5.6

Alan K. Simpson (R-WY) served as Chair of the Senate immigration subcommittee from 1981 to 1987 and again from 1995 to 1997. During his service, Simpson was clearly the Senate's leading expert on the subject of immigration policy. Credit: Library of Congress.

Alan K. Simpson (R-WY)

Senator Alan Simpson chaired the Senate Judiciary Subcommittee on Immigration in the 104th Congress. He wrote both legal and illegal immigration reform bills that he moved through the Senate in 1995 and 1996 in record time, compared with the earlier struggles to pass Simpson-Mazzoli. In 1979, Simpson was appointed to serve on the Select Commission on Immigration (the Hesburgh Commission), where he became a student of immigration law. He advanced many of the commission's recommendations into law with passage of the 1986 Immigration Reform and Control Act. Eventually, Simpson became known as the Senate's leading GOP expert on the subject, and he played an influential role in shaping the 1990 law. Generally, Simpson favored stronger enforcement efforts against illegal immigration and reductions in legal immigration in both the employment- and family-based categories. He also opposed immigrant use of welfare benefits.

Simpson was born in Denver on September 2, 1931. As a teenager in Cody, Wyoming, during World War II, Simpson played with Japanese-American children living in a nearby internment camp. He later said that this early brush with immigrants shaped his approach to immigration legislation in the Senate.

Simpson graduated from the University of Wyoming in 1954—the same year his father was elected governor—with his bachelor's degree and in 1958 with his law degree. From 1954 until 1956, Simpson took an interlude from school, serving in the U.S. Army.

Simpson's legal career began in 1959, when he started practicing as a trial lawyer. He served as Wyoming's assistant attorney general in 1959 and as Cody's city attorney from 1959 until 1969.

In 1964, Simpson won election to the statehouse, in which he served till 1977. He captured a leadership position in 1975, when he became majority floor leader. Simpson held that position for two years, then served as Speaker Pro Tem in 1977.

He was elected to the U.S. Senate in 1978. When the 1980 elections put a Republican majority in the Senate, Simpson became the chair of the Senate immigration subcommittee. Simpson played active roles on the 1986 and 1990 immigration bills. He continually pushed the illegal immigration legislation, known as Simpson-Mazzoli, for three straight Congresses; the bill finally passed in 1986. He worked closely with subcommittee chairman Edward Kennedy to draft and pass the 1990 bill.

Simpson also aspired to join the leadership structure of the Senate. He became GOP whip in 1984. He held that position until after the 1994 election, when he lost in a challenge from Mississippi Senator Trent Lott on a 27–26 vote of the Senate Republican Conference.

At 6'7", along with a blunt, witty sense of humor, Simpson combined cowboy courage with tenacity and a willingness to study the details of legislative issues. He never shrank from the thorny issue of immigration. He retired from the U.S. Senate in 1997.

(Sources: *Almanac of American Politics*, various years; *Politics in America*, 1986; Tolchin 1982)

A compromise emerged late in October. Legal immigration visas were set at 700,000 annually for each of the three years following enactment, whereupon the figure would be reduced to 675,000. Of that number, 520,000 were dedicated to the family reunification categories of admission, to be reduced to 480,000 after three years. The balance would fall into the employment visa and diversity visa preference categories. Consistent with earlier law, refugees were not counted toward this limit. Simpson gave up on EVD and allowed the House provision to stay the deportation of those from war-torn countries to remain in the bill. He also gave up the demand to strike the language granting amnesty to the spouses and children of those legalized under the 1986 law. In return, Simpson won concessions such as a provision that would provide special visas for those who were willing to invest at least $1 million in a new enterprise and hire at least ten U.S. workers (*CQWR* 10/27/90, 3609). This investor visa provision was consistent with his belief that U.S. immigration policy should welcome those who were clearly poised to contribute. He also won approval for a pilot program to be carried out in three states to produce a fraud-proof driver's license that could be used to help verify employment eligibility. This was not in the original Senate bill, but a GAO report released earlier in the year found that the fear of employer sanctions enacted in 1986 was causing employers to discriminate against foreign-looking workers (GAO 1990; Kendall 1996). In response, Simpson insisted that employers needed a more certain means for determining whether a worker was legal. Judging the legislation in historical perspective, Simpson won only small concessions. Backed by a fully flowered pro-immigration lobby consisting of ethnic and religious groups and immigration lawyers, House conferees came away with most of what they wanted. The House succeeded in moving the Senate in its direction more than the other way around.

The battle was not won, however, at the conclusion of the conference. Hispanic legislators, led by the ever-present Edward Roybal (D-CA), were hostile to Simpson's driver's license program. Roybal correctly pointed out that since this provision had not been included in either the House or Senate versions of the legislation when they were passed, it was outside the scope of the conference committee to insert the pilot program this late in the process (*CR* 10/26/90, H12981–H12982). The Hispanic members were joined by liberals who feared that this was the first step toward a national identification card that would infringe upon civil rights (*CQWR* 11/3/90, 3753). Bruce Morrison (D-CT) defended the bill as the best possible compromise and one that contained many provisions that the Hispanic Caucus did want. Lamar Smith was silent during the debate but voted in favor of the rule, pleased that the Senate had managed to win even a few concessions from the House conferees. Nevertheless, an opposition that included Hispanics, civil libertarians, and the vast majority of Republicans managed to defeat the rule for the conference report's consideration on a 186–235 vote. The 1990 midterm elections were less than two weeks away. Once again, it looked like another major immigration bill would die before action could be completed.

One day remained in the House's legislative session—October 27, a Saturday. Morrison and Berman conferred with Simpson on how to save the bill. Simpson quietly agreed to drop the pilot driver's license program. On Saturday morning, Lamar Smith (R-TX), Bill McCollum (R-FL), and Hamilton Fish (R-NY), the leading immigration experts on the Republican side, spoke approvingly of the conference report. John Bryant (D-TX) complained about the addition of investor visas, the provision Simpson had inserted encouraging the immigration of those who intended to invest at least $1 million and hire at least ten native workers. He argued that this was tantamount to putting American citizenship up for sale (*CR* 10/17/90, H12361). Bryant found a few members willing to speak out against passage, but the Hispanic members had come on board with the supporters. Coupled with significant Republican support, a victory for the bill was assured. The final vote was 264–118. The president signed the legislation into law one month later.

An analysis of the House floor voting on the 1990 immigration bill illustrates that the conference report was far more acceptable to Republicans than the House version of the bill (see Table 5.4). An estimated 69 percent of Republicans voted for the conference version, compared with just 25 percent who had voted for the House bill. Differences between Southern and Northern members also persist in the votes in the 101st Congress and are actually slightly stronger than partisan differences on the passage of the conference report. The most significant division on the floor on final passage of the conference report, however, was the split between members from border states and those from nonborder states. An estimated 81 percent of members from interior states voted for the conference report, compared with only half of those from Florida, California, Texas, New Mexico, and Arizona. This bill stood for an increase in the number of legal residents who would be migrating to settle in these states. Or, in the cases of the illegals granted amnesty under the 1986 law, they were already clustered in these areas. The 1990 Census indicated that 40 percent of the legal-resident population resided in California alone. For members from the affected areas, the costs associated with this influx were worrisome indeed.

The vote on the Smith Amendment to cap legal immigration at 630,000 is indicative of how the Senate version of the bill as originally authored by Alan Simpson (R-WY) and Edward Kennedy (D-MA) would have fared in the House (see Table 5.4 and Table A5.4). Although the vote occurred along party lines, the measure lost partly because it drew the support of only half of the Republicans and only 7 percent of the Democrats. The interest groups supporting the legislation had convinced many GOP legislators that legal immigration was a different animal from illegal immigration. Even the most rural and nonethnic members of Congress could point to at least one legal

Table 5.4 Estimated Probability of Voting Yes on Immigration Amendments and Final Passage of House Bill, 101st Congress, U.S. House of Representatives

Variables	Vote on Rule	Smith Amendment to Cap Immigration	Smith Amendment to Reimburse Costs	McCollum Amendment to Strike EVD	Bryant Amendment Family Reunification	House Passage	Vote on Rule Conference Report	House Passage of Conference Report
Democrat	.93	.07	.02	.02	.11	.82	.50	.80
Republican	.09	.50	.11	.67	.63	.25	.25	.69
White member	.61	.29	.04	.09	.31	.56	.42	.73
Nonwhite member	.91	.01	.01	.29	.04	.96	.14	.94
Non-South	.64	.17	.02	.06	.19	.71	.42	.80
South	.64	.21	.17	.36	.57	.33	.31	.62
Nonborder state	.68	.16	.02	.06	.22	.66	.42	.81
Border state	.50	.25	.32	.43	.45	.45	.30	.52
Not Judiciary	.65	.18	.03	.10	.26	.61	.38	.76
Judiciary Committee	.62	.21	.11	.11	.32	.66	.54	.77
Foreign born = .37	.44	.41	.03	.22	.50	.28	.20	.62
Foreign born = 52.2	.99	.01	.17	.01	.01	.99	.99	.99
Agriculture = .13	.64	.16	.04	.09	.25	.59	.38	.78
Agriculture = 18.05	.65	.35	.03	.20	.40	.71	.43	.63
Black = .05	.67	.12	.08	.17	.23	.70	.44	.75
Black = 92.05	.45	.85	.01	.01	.65	.10	.11	.82
Asian/other = .53	.72	.17	.05	.14	.31	.65	.57	.71
Asian/other = 71.9	.07	.34	.01	.01	.05	.31	.01	.96
Unemployment = 1.9	.54	.31	.01	.28	.25	.52	.44	.77
Unemployment = 28.1	.91	.01	.74	.01	.33	.87	.22	.72

Values represent the estimated probability of a Yes vote at the lowest and highest value of the independent variables, with all other variables held constant at their sample means.

immigrant among their ancestors. The notion that the United States is a nation of *legal* immigrants was highly persuasive in drawing over GOP support for the bill. Many GOP members were persuaded to vote for increases in legal immigration, believing that it was *illegal* immigrants who cost Americans jobs and taxpayers money, not those who played by the rules. The pro-immigration interest groups would follow this same strategy of drawing a sharp distinction between legal and illegal immigration in 1996 with even greater success (see Chapter 6). Finally, Republican support for the bill can be explained by the fact that business groups were supportive of expanding the allocation of employment-oriented visas. If that meant also expanding the number of slots in the family reunification categories, it was worth the trade.

Among Democrats, the Hispanic Caucus, led by Edward Roybal (D-CA), undoubtedly played an important role in defeating the Simpson-Kennedy version of the legislation in favor of the House's stronger version. Black and Hispanic members joined with white members from districts with large foreign-born populations to vote unanimously against Smith's attempt to pass the Senate version of the bill. These same members were sufficiently powerful that they managed to defeat a watered-down version of the Simpson-Kennedy legislation in the vote on the rule for its consideration. Only when Simpson agreed to drop his provision for a fraud-proof identification program did the minority caucuses come aboard.

Scope of the 1990 Reforms

The modifications written into the 1990 Act thought to have the most lasting implications were the changes in the immigrant preference system. These changes can be more clearly understood if one compares Tables 5.5 and 5.6. These tables detail the preference system enacted in 1965, compared with the changes made by the 1980 Refugee Act and the 1990 Act. The major change made by the Refugee Act was to eliminate refugees as an immigration preference category, subject to the limitations of the overall ceiling as established in the 1965 law. The 6 percent of visas once allocated to refugees were then transferred to the second preference: spouses and unmarried sons and daughters of permanent residents. The 1990 Act implemented a new preference scheme divided into three categories of immigrants: family-based immigrants (approximately 74 percent of total), employment or business-related immigrants (20 percent of total), and the diversity category (6 percent of total). As the percentages indicate, the new preference system did little to alter the *proportion* of visas granted to business-related immigrants. Under the 1965 and 1980 laws, 20 percent of the annual visas were allocated to skilled immigrants and their families under the third and sixth preferences. There was a slight reduction in the proportion of family-related visas under the 1990 law, from 80 percent down to 74 percent, and after 1995 a further reduction was scheduled. This loss in the proportion of family visas can be

Table 5.5   Preference System Created in 1965 and as Amended by the 1980 Refugee Act

Preference	Provision	Percent of Visas	
		1965	1980
First	Unmarried adult sons and daughters of U.S. citizens	20%	20%
Second	Spouses and unmarried sons and daughters of permanent resident aliens	20%	26%
Third	Members of the professions of exceptional ability in sciences and arts and their spouses and children	10%	10%
Fourth	Married sons and daughters of U.S. citizens and their spouses and children	10%	10%
Fifth	Brothers and sisters of U.S. citizens aged 21 and over and their spouses and children	24%	24%
Sixth	Skilled or unskilled workers in occupations in which labor is in short supply and their spouses and children	10%	10%
Seventh	Refugees	6%	Admitted separately
Nonpreference	Other qualified applicants	Any remaining	Any remaining
Worldwide Ceiling		290,000	270,000
Per Country Ceiling		20,000	20,000

Source: Immigration and Naturalization Service

attributed to the creation of the diversity category, a preference that did not exist until the 1990 law. The point to emphasize here is that, whatever changes the 1990 law wrought, it was the increase in the overall cap to 700,000 (675,000 after 1995) that mattered most. The proportion of visas going to each visa category changed only slightly.

Table 5.6   Immigration Preference System as Amended by the 1990
Immigration Law

Category of Admission	1992–1994	Percent*	1995 and After	Percent*
Family-Sponsored Immigrants	**520,000**	**74%**	**480,000**	**71%**
Immediate family members of U.S. citizens or permanent residents	239,000	34%	254,000	38%
1st Preference: Unmarried adult children of U.S. citizens	23,400	3%	23,400	4%
2nd Preference: Spouses and unmarried children of permanent residents	114,200	16%	114,200	17%
3rd Preference: Married adult children of U.S. citizens	23,400	3%	23,400	4%
4th Preference: Brothers and sisters of adult U.S. citizens	65,000	9%	65,000	10%
Nonpreference: Spouses and children of 1986 amnesty recipients	55,000	8%	0	0%
Business-Related Immigrants	**140,000**	**20%**	**140,000**	**21%**
1st Preference: Workers with extraordinary skills	40,000	6%	40,000	6%
2nd Preference: Advanced degree holders and workers with special skills	40,000	6%	40,000	6%
3rd Preference: Skilled workers, professionals, and other workers	40,000	6%	40,000	6%
4th Preference: Special immigrants and religious workers	10,000	1%	10,000	1.5%
5th Preference: Investor Immigrants	10,000	1%	10,000	1.5%
Diversity Immigrants	**40,000**	**6%**	**55,000**	**8%**
Total Immigration	**700,000**	**100%**	**675,000**	**100%**

Source: Immigration and Naturalization Service
*Percentages reflect the number of annual visas in each row category over total immigration, including diversity, family, and business. Percentages are rounded.

A final provision of the 1990 Act would prove to have important implications for subsequent rounds of reform, and particularly 1996: the charter of a commission on immigration reform modeled after the select commission that was created in 1978. The commission was to be comprised of nine members, with the chairman to be appointed by the president and the remaining members appointed by Democratic and Republican leaders in Congress. Former Congresswoman Barbara Jordan (D-TX) would come to chair the commission, and its bold policy recommendations would serve as the foundation for heated debates in the years to come.

The 102nd and 103rd Congresses

The 102nd Congress (1991–1992) was uneventful as far as immigration policy was concerned. Discussion of immigration issues was confined to the Appropriations Committees, where funding decisions were being made about the cost of refugee and other immigrant-related assistance programs, including bilingual education. Several noncontroversial measures passed, including one that would allow Chinese nationals living in the country at the time of the Tiananmen Square uprising to apply for permanent residence (*CQ Almanac* 1992, 335).

President Clinton took no particular interest in immigration policy upon assuming office in January 1993. His only major immigration policy stand in the opening months of his presidency was to oppose the ban on the entry of HIV-infected immigrants. He eventually backed down on this when the 103rd Congress (1993–1994) enacted a ban against the permanent immigration of HIV-positive foreigners in the authorization bill for the National Institutes of Health (NIH). Like the NIH issue, nearly all of the controversial action on immigration policy in the 103rd Congress was related to larger, nonimmigration bills. Congress increased the authorization and appropriation for the Border Patrol, and passed legislation to expedite the deportation of aliens convicted of felonies and to speed the processing of asylum claims.

The Restrictionist Movement in California

Several measures reflected the groundswell of opposition to immigration that was building in California. All three occurred in 1994, and all were offered by California members. The first was an amendment to an education bill by Orange County Congressman Dana Rohrabacher (R-CA) to require schools receiving federal funding to report on the number of enrolled students who are illegal aliens or who do not have at least one parent who is a legal resident. This amendment triggered a firestorm of protest from Hispanic members. Rohrabacher insisted that his proposal did nothing to deny education benefits to these students, as California's pending Proposition 187 intended to do, but was designed to gather data on the number of illegals in the school system for purposes of cost estimates. Opponents charged that it was the equivalent of compiling a "Schindler's list" of those to be deported and that it would turn children into spies sneaking about inquiring into the legal status of parents (*CR* 3/3/94, H1021–H1025). Supporting the amendment, Elton Gallegly (R-CA), from Simi Valley, a white middle-class suburb of Los Angeles, pointed out that these students burdened the California school system: "We are not talking about a few hundred or a few thousand. We are talking about several hundred thousand individuals that [sic] are in our public schools that [sic] have no legal right to be in the United States" (*CR* 3/3/94, H1027). The issue was dismissed by other members as a California problem. Rohrabacher's amendment was defeated on a lopsided 78–329 vote, drawing most of its support from border states, and particularly from Republicans.

The second measure came up as an amendment to the annual appropriations bill that funds the Department of Justice and other agencies. Gary Condit (D-CA) proposed a 2.5 percent across-the-board cut in appropriations for purposes of transferring $600 million to states and localities for costs related to the incarceration of illegal immigrants. California estimated that its prisons held 18,000 undocumented felons at a cost of over $300 million (Starkey 1993b). Florida, New York, and Texas were in similar straits as a result of the federal government's failure to curb illegal immigration. Opponents jealously argued that the funding would go only to a few high-immigration states while cutting back law enforcement efforts in the remaining states. Condit's amendment failed on a 148–256 vote that reflected regional lines of cleavage (*CR* 6/27/94, H5141–H5151).

A third measure once again expressed the frustration that Californians felt about the inundation of legal and illegal immigrants in their state. This was an amendment by Jay Kim (R-CA), himself a Korean immigrant, to a housing program reauthorization bill. Kim's amendment would prohibit illegal immigrants from receiving disaster assistance from the Federal Emergency Management Agency. More precisely, the amendment authorized temporary emergency assistance for seven days, after which the case would be turned over to the INS. Kim elaborated:

> …This amendment gives the members of this chamber the opportunity for an up or down vote on the subject of taxpayer funded handouts for illegal immigrants.
> We are dealing with people who have no legal right to be here. We should not feel guilty and uncompassionate because we want to put Americans first.
> …We cannot have indefinite assistance to illegal aliens, knowing that they are illegals, while we are having budget problems here. We are cutting back all kinds of programs for our own citizens. (CR 7/22/94, H6119–H6122)

Kim was pointing out that money that went to illegal immigrants would not be available to legal immigrants and to poorer U.S. citizens, whether they be Hispanic, Asian, or black. Richard Durbin (D-IL) responded that the Kim Amendment lacked compassion. Others objected that the Federal Emergency Management Agency lacked the capacity to determine who was legal and who was illegal. Kim's amendment was amended slightly to apply only in crisis situations where the president had not declared a national disaster—in other words, only in very limited, minor disasters. The amendment in its weakened form passed on a 220–176 vote.

These three floor votes show the same consistent patterns evidenced in the 101st Congress. Partisanship was the major dividing line, with Republicans favoring the amendments to a far greater extent than Democrats (see Table A5.5 and Table 5.7). Understandably, members from border states were about 56 percent more likely to favor the Condit Amendment on reimbursement than those from nonborder states. Black members, and minority members more generally, continued to see the issue of government treatment of the illegal population in terms of redistribution and civil rights. Minority members were about 70 percent less likely than white members to support Kim's proposal. Similarly, members from districts with large foreign-born populations were hostile to the idea of limiting disaster assistance to illegal residents. The issue divided Congress along regional lines reflecting the ideological cohesion of Southern members. An estimated 93 percent of Southerners voted for the Kim Amendment, compared with only 61 percent of Northerners (see Table 5.7).

While two of these three amendments did not pass, they signaled the growing pressure the California representatives were feeling from their home state. Governor Pete Wilson's (R-CA) 1993–94 state budget calculated that the state government spent $4.8 billion the previous year on services to legal and illegal immigrants, including health, welfare, education, and criminal justice costs. The state was in the midst of a serious economic slump, which fueled anxieties about job competition with immigrants. During his 1994 reelection campaign, Governor Pete Wilson (R-CA) remained in regular contact with the California congressional delegation, pressing for federal action on illegal and legal immigration that would relieve the fiscal pressure. At the same time, the furious campaign to pass Proposition 187 was being waged in the streets of California cities and towns. Proposition 187 sought to deny public education, nonemergency health care, and government-provided welfare benefits to undocumented immigrants and their children (Margolis 1995). Fifty-nine percent of the state's electorate voted in favor of Proposition 187 in November 1994. Support for the measure was strongest in those California counties with the highest percentage of Hispanic immigrants (see Map A5.1), including agricultural areas in central and northern California. This pattern of support indicates that Proposition 187 was not a reaction against immigrants in general so much as it was a reaction against the group of immigrants who comprised the vast majority of illegal residents in the

Table 5.7   Estimated Probability of Voting Yes on California-Sponsored Immigration Measures, 103rd Congress, U.S. House of Representatives

Variables	Rohrabacher Amendment on Illegals in School	Condit Amendment to Pay for Incarceration	Kim Amendment to Restrict Illegals from Disaster Aid
Democrat	.01	.15	.16
Republican	.36	.59	.99
White member	.02	.34	.82
Nonwhite member	.02	.11	.13
Non-South	.02	.26	.61
South	.05	.42	.93
Nonborder state	.02	.18	.74
Border state	.03	.74	.74
Not Judiciary	.02	.31	.75
Judiciary Committee	.01	.16	.61
Foreign born = .22	.03	.22	.90
Foreign born = 58.5	.01	.84	.01
Agriculture = .17	.02	.27	.69
Agriculture = 24.74	.01	.62	.96
Black = .13	.04	.32	.80
Black = 73.95	.01	.19	.31
Asian/other = .34	.01	.36	.71
Asian/other = 68.5	.61	.04	.91
Unemployment = 2.5	.03	.32	.68
Unemployment = 41.3	.01	.24	.91

Values represent the estimated probability of a Yes vote at the lowest and highest value of the independent variables, with all other variables held constant at their sample means.

state—those of Mexican ancestry. Election day polls indicated that even 22 percent of Latinos voted for the initiative. Voters favoring passage of Prop. 187 indicated that they voted yes in order to send a message and to force the federal government to face the problem of illegal immigration (see Table A5.6). Voters opposing 187 justified their no votes mainly on grounds that the measure really didn't solve the problem of illegal immigration, that it was cruel to throw children out of school and that it was racist (Table A5.6). The popularity of 187, coupled with the Republican takeover of Congress in November 1994, would ensure that the issues raised in the 103rd Congress would not disappear.

Box 5.7

Pete Wilson (R-CA). As governor of the state with the most legal and illegal immigrants, he became known in the 1990s as one of the nation's most influential proponents of immigration restrictions. He is shown here at the Statue of Liberty launching his unsuccessful bid to become the 1996 Republican presidential nominee. Credit: AP/Wide World Photos.

Pete Wilson (R-CA)

Senator Pete Wilson actively worked on the Simpson-Mazzoli bill as a senator defending the interests of California growers. Then as governor he helped lead the efforts to pass California's Proposition 187, a ballot initiative to deny most public benefits to illegal immigrants. Wilson's interest in limiting benefits to illegal immigrants was sparked by a severe economic recession in California in the early 1990s, which called attention to the cost of the state's generous welfare, health care, and social insurance programs. In response, Wilson became a forceful advocate for federal reimbursement of state and local costs arising from immigration. Throughout the 104th Congress, Wilson repeatedly urged the California delegation to pass the Gallegly Amendment giving states the option to deny education benefits to the children of illegal immigrants.

Wilson was born in Lake Forest, Illinois, on August 23, 1933. He grew up in St. Louis, then graduated from Yale in 1956. From 1955 through 1958, Wilson served in the U.S. Marine Corps as an infantry officer. In 1962, he earned his law degree at the University of California at Berkeley.

Wilson began his law practice in 1963 in San Diego. In 1966, he won election to the California Assembly. Wilson left the state legislature in 1971, when he was elected mayor of San Diego, a position he held until 1983.

In 1982, Wilson was elected to the U.S. Senate. He won reelection in 1988, then embarked on a campaign two years later for California governor. He was reelected governor in 1994, the same year Proposition 187 passed. Wilson led California through a severe economic recession in the early 1990s and had presidential aspirations for 1996. His 1996 presidential bid was short-lived, however, and his primary campaign ended less than a month after his well-publicized announcement speech under the Statue of Liberty.

(Sources: *Biographical Directory of the U.S. Congress 1774–1989*; Governor Wilson's biography on State of California Internet homepage)

The End of Democratic Control

Most of the members had no clue that 34 Democratic incumbents would lose their bids for reelection to the House on November 8, 1994, and that the Republicans would control Congress for the first time since 1952 (Gimpel 1996). While the change in control of Congress would give the Republicans a crucial upper hand in the debate, the substance of immigration policy would not change. With the GOP takeover, immigration policy would become more partisan, not less (see Chapter 6).

Our thesis all along has been that the battle over immigration policy became particularly partisan when the issues at stake came to reflect long-standing redistributive cleavages involving the prospect of increased transfer payments to the immigrant population and higher taxes to pay for those benefits and services. Once an issue is converted into the familiar terms that have served as the foundation for party allegiance since the New Deal, congressional voting on that issue is easy to predict. Our analysis of the House votes on the 1990 bill mostly supports this thesis, but also shows that legal immigration did not pose quite as clear-cut an issue as amnesty did. Amnesty was by far the most controversial issue during these debates, when judged in purely partisan terms. Some may argue that amnesty was an issue of law and order, not redistribution. To be sure, many members did argue that law-breakers should not be rewarded. But this aspect of the issue was the source of regional and ideological cleavages, not partisan ones. Conservative Southern and border state Democrats opposed amnesty on law-and-order rather than on redistributive grounds. The partisanship on amnesty resulted from the prospect that the legalized population could take advantage of programs and services for which they would then be eligible. For liberal Democrats, they were a hardworking but exploited underclass population that should be made eligible for these programs. Republicans, however, saw them as a population that, once legalized, would be able to claim legitimate title to government aid while petitioning to bring in even more of their relatives. A resolution to the debate about whether immigrants were a net contribution or a net cost was elusive owing to the lack of data about the contributions the new arrivals made to the economy. Government agencies could and did record who consumed public benefits, but less was known about who was paying in. For reasons identified in Chapter 2, linking the immigration issue to welfare and public benefits also made for a good political campaign, particularly in California (Starkey 1993a). Some Democrats saw Pete Wilson's exploitation of this issue in the 1994 gubernatorial contest as pure opportunism, but others jumped aboard the anti-immigrant bandwagon themselves (Starkey 1993a). In the months and years following the 1994 election, the issue of immigration would be ever more closely identified with redistribution and would become central to the debate over entitlements as Congress and the president grappled to get control over government spending.

APPENDIX TO CHAPTER 5

Table A5.1 Logistic Regression Estimates of a Yes Vote on Amendments and Final Passage of House Immigration Bill, 98th Congress, U. S. House of Representatives

Variables	Hall Amendment 1–800 Employer Verification	Schroeder Amendment Three-Year Expiration on Employer Sanctions	Roybal Amendment to Delete Employer Sanctions	Lungren Amendment for 2-Tier System	Shaw Amendment Changing Dates	Wright Amendment Amnesty	McCollum Amendment to Strike Amnesty Language	Final Passage of House Bill
Party (0 D, 1 R)	1.55**	-1.24**	-1.26**	3.34**	3.13**	.83**	1.72**	.02
	(.29)	(.30)	(.33)	(.32)	(.31)	(.25)	(.27)	(.23)
Minority member	-4.90**	2.63**	8.85	-1.78	-.78	-1.99**	-2.05**	-2.24**
	(1.41)	(1.23)	(16.31)	(1.27)	(1.23)	(.87)	(1.19)	(1.17)
Judiciary Committee	-.85*	-.25	-.59	-.37	-.54	.05	-.43	.89*
	(.46)	(.49)	(.58)	(.58)	(.59)	(.44)	(.51)	(.46)
Southern state	1.89**	-1.00**	-1.70**	1.20**	.39	.85**	1.61**	.34
	(.45)	(.42)	(.49)	(.45)	(.45)	(.37)	(.42)	(.33)
Border state	-.92**	1.67**	1.22**	-.13	.50	-.28	.43	-.78**
	(.41)	(.40)	(.43)	(.44)	(.50)	(.35)	(.43)	(.36)
Percent foreign born	-.11**	-.05*	-.04	-.11**	-.06	-.06**	-.15**	.08**
	(.03)	(.03)	(.03)	(.05)	(.05)	(.03)	(.05)	(.03)
Percent black	-.003	.002	.004	.007	.009	-.02	-.005	-.006
	(.01)	(.01)	(.02)	(.01)	(.12)	(.01)	(.01)	(.01)
Percent Asian/other	.06**	.06**	.06**	.0004	-.09**	-.006	-.008	-.07**
	(.02)	(.02)	(.02)	(.03)	(.04)	(.02)	(.02)	(.02)
Percent agriculture	.0001	-.09*	-.004	.03	.09*	.05	.001	.06
	(.04)	(.05)	(.05)	(.05)	(.05)	(.04)	(.04)	(.04)
Percent Unemployment	.03	.08	.08	-.04	-.10	.01	-.06	-.09**
	(.05)	(.06)	(.06)	(.06)	(.07)	(.05)	(.05)	(.05)
Constant	-1.48	.19	-.22	-4.63	-3.78	-.40	-1.71	.61
% Correctly Classified	76.6	78.1	82.6	81.5	81.6	72.2	76.4	65.3
Null model	61.0	67.0	72.0	58.0	58.0	59.0	54.0	51.0
χ²	142.6	138.6	158.8	233.2	227.9	92.6	172.9	71.3
Significance	p <.0001	p <.0001	p <.0001	p <.0001	p <.0001	p <.0001	p <.0001	p <.0001
N	397	411	424	426	426	417	428	427

Source: Congressional Quarterly Almanac and *Congressional District Databook*, various years. Dependent variable: 0 = No vote; 1 = Yes vote. MLE Coefficients; standard errors in parentheses; *p < .10; **p < .05 two-tailed tests.

Table A5.2   Logistic Regression Estimates of a Yes Vote on Amendments and Final Passage of House Immigration Bill, 99th Congress, U. S. House of Representatives

Variables	Vote on 1st Rule	Vote on 2nd Rule	McCollum Amendment to Strike Amnesty	Fish Amendment to Strike EVD	Passage of House Bill	Passage of Conference Report
Party (0 = D, 1 = R)	−3.86**	−1.66**	2.37**	3.60**	−2.05**	1.32**
	(.39)	(.27)	(.32)	(.37)	(.27)	(.25)
Minority member	.45	−1.40**	−3.03**	−1.87	−.83	−.66
	(.86)	(.63)	(1.38)	(1.36)	(.67)	(.62)
Judiciary Committee	.71	−.45	−.31	.49	.21	.19
	(.59)	(.42)	(.52)	(.60)	(.47)	(.43)
Southern state	−1.26**	−.02	1.87**	2.21**	−1.09**	−1.11**
	(.48)	(.36)	(.49)	(.51)	(.37)	(.33)
Border state	.04	−.12	.34	.52	.37	.39
	(.47)	(.35)	(.49)	(.50)	(.36)	(.34)
Percent foreign born	.13**	.06**	−.28**	−.10**	.12**	.08**
	(.05)	(.03)	(.06)	(.05)	(.04)	(.03)
Percent black	.003	−.009	−.01	−.001	−.01	−.006
	(.01)	(.01)	(.02)	(.02)	(.01)	(.01)
Percent Asian/other	−.02	−.03	.03	−.01	−.05**	−.05**
	(.02)	(.02)	(.03)	(.03)	(.02)	(.02)
Percent agriculture	.13**	.01	−.09*	.06	.07	.09**
	(.06)	(.04)	(.05)	(.05)	(.04)	(.04)
Percent Unemployment	.11*	.02	−.11*	−.01	−.007	−.02
	(.06)	(.05)	(.07)	(.07)	(.05)	(.05)
Constant	3.46	3.27	−1.55	−5.14	3.22	2.32
% Correctly classified	84.8	72.2	79.0	85.6	74.6	66.7
Null model	53.0	68.0	51.0	51.0	67.0	58.0
χ^2	234.0	65.5	210.4	256.7	131.3	69.5
Significance	p < .0001	p < .0001	p < .0001	p < .0001	p < .0001	p < .0001
N	382	407	391	396	406	411

Source: Congressional Quarterly Almanac and *Congressional District Databook*, various years.
Dependent variable: 0 = No vote; 1 = Yes vote.
MLE Coefficients; standard errors in parentheses; *p < .10; **p < .05 two-tailed tests.

Table A5.3   Logistic Regression Estimates of a Yes Vote on Amnesty Extension and Extended Voluntary Departure (EVD), 100th Congress, U. S. House of Representatives

Variables	Gekas Amendment to Modify Amnesty	Vote on Extension of Amnesty Deadline	Vote on Extended Voluntary Departure
Party (0 = D, 1 = R)	2.70**	–2.98**	–3.56**
	(.31)	(.35)	(.36)
Minority member	–1.51	6.77	2.10**
	(1.39)	(13.84)	(1.38)
Judiciary Committee	–.24	.40	–.17
	(.52)	(.53)	(.57)
Southern state	.99**	–1.10**	–1.78**
	(.46)	(.52)	(.49)
Border state	.89**	–1.22**	–.50
	(.46)	(.60)	(.46)
Percent foreign born	–.27**	.30**	.10**
	(.06)	(.07)	(.05)
Percent black	–.008	.007	–.003
	(.06)	(.02)	(.02)
Percent Asian/other	.03	.05	–.02
	(.03)	(.04)	(.02)
Percent agriculture	.05	–.01	–.07
	(.05)	(.05)	(.05)
Percent Unemployment	–.13**	.16**	.13**
	(.07)	(.07)	(.06)
Constant	–2.78	1.82	4.98
% Correctly classified	80.4	82.4	81.3
Null model	60.0	51.0	57.0
χ^2	214.1	267.0	254.2
Significance	$p < .0001$	$p < .0001$	$p < .0001$
N	413	414	418

Source: Congressional Quarterly Almanac and *Congressional District Databook*, various years.
Dependent variable: 0 = No vote; 1 = Yes vote.
MLE Coefficients; standard errors in parentheses; *$p < .10$; **$p < .05$ two-tailed tests.

Table A5.4 Logistic Regression Estimates of a Yes Vote on Amendments and Final Passage of House Immigration Bill, 101st Congress, U. S. House of Representatives

Variables	Vote on Rule	Smith Amendment to Cap Immigration	Smith Amendment to Reimburse Costs	McCollum Amendment to Strike EVD	Bryant Amendment Family Reunification	House Passage	Vote on Rule Conference Report	House Passage of Conference Report
Party (0 = D, 1 = R)	-4.94**	-3.21**	2.02**	4.81**	2.61**	-2.61**	-1.10**	-.60**
	(.43)	(.80)	(.46)	(.58)	(.32)	(.32)	(.24)	(.27)
Minority member	1.82	-7.77	-1.39	1.36	-2.42*	2.83**	-1.44*	1.72
	(1.25)	(16.02)	(1.54)	(1.46)	(1.31)	(1.04)	(.85)	(1.16)
Judiciary Committee	-.13	.19	1.24**	.03	.28	.21	-.66*	.10
	(.67)	(.48)	(.59)	(.63)	(.49)	(.49)	(.40)	(.45)
Southern state	-.03	.26	2.30**	2.13**	1.74**	-1.49**	-.46	-.86**
	(.57)	(.46)	(.58)	(.72)	(.46)	(.45)	(.35)	(.41)
Border state	-.74	.56	3.20**	2.45	1.07**	-.89**	-.50	-1.39**
	(.55)	(.46)	(.54)	(.61)	(.50)	(.46)	(.38)	(.45)
Percent foreign born	.14**	-.20**	.04	-.15**	-.17**	.24**	.16**	.11**
	(.05)	(.06)	(.04)	(.06)	(.06)	(.05)	(.03)	(.05)
Percent black	-.01	.04**	-.07**	-.05	.02	-.03**	.01	.005
	(.02)	(.02)	(.03)	(.03)	(.01)	(.01)	(.04)	(.02)
Percent Asian/other	-.05*	.01	-.04	-.04	-.03	-.02	-.10**	.03
	(.02)	(.03)	(.03)	(.03)	(.03)	(.02)	(.03)	(.03)
Percent agriculture	.002	.06	-.03	.05	.04	.03	.01	-.04
	(.07)	(.05)	(.07)	(.06)	(.05)	(.05)	(.04)	(.04)
Percent unemployment	.08	-.14**	.20*	-.23**	.02	.07	-.04	-.01
	(.08)	(.06)	(.10)	(.09)	(.06)	(.06)	(.05)	(.06)
Constant	6.65	-3.21	-7.91	-6.85	-4.41	2.98	1.67	1.60
% Correctly classified	91.8	78.1	91.5	87.8	80.0	82.1	68.6	69.0
Null model	58.0	65.0	87.0	67.0	61.0	53.0	56.0	69.0
χ^2	340.8	177.8	132.8	289.1	209.6	233.4	97.0	75.8
Significance	p < .0001	p < .0001	p < .0001	p < .0001	p < .0001	p < .0001	p < .0001	p < .0001
N	413	411	423	418	424	425	424	377

Source: Congressional Quarterly Almanac and *Congressional District Databook*, various years. Dependent variable: 0 = No vote; 1 = Yes vote.
MLE Coefficients; standard errors in parentheses; *p < .10; **p < .05 two-tailed tests.

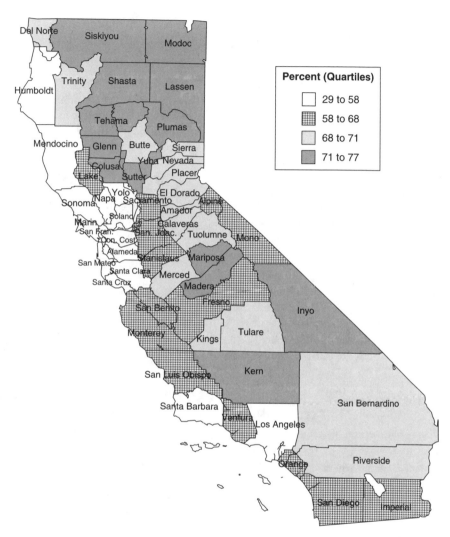

Map A5.1   Percent Favoring Passage of Proposition 187, by County

Table A5.5 Logistic Regression Estimates of a Yes Vote on California-Sponsored Immigration Measures, 103rd Congress, U. S. House of Representatives

Variables	Rohrabacher Amendment on Illegals in School	Condit Amendment to Pay for Incarceration	Kim Amendment to Restrict Illegals from Disaster Aid
Party (0 = D, 1 = R)	5.48**	2.08**	6.62**
	(1.12)	(.31)	(.98)
Minority member	−.39	−1.47**	−3.40**
	(1.15)	(.68)	(1.09)
Judiciary committee	−.47	−.86	−.64
	(.63)	(.55)	(.92)
Southern state	1.26**	.74**	2.12**
	(.53)	(.36)	(.54)
Border state	.57	2.58**	−.01
	(.54)	(.44)	(.63)
Percent foreign born	−.06*	.05*	−.15**
	(.03)	(.03)	(.05)
Percent black	−.06	−.01	−.03
	(.04)	(.02)	(.02)
Percent Asian/other	.07*	−.04	.02
	(.03)	(.03)	(.03)
Percent agriculture	−.02	.06	.10*
	(.08)	(.06)	(.07)
Percent Unemployment	−.12	−.02	.08
	(.11)	(.08)	(.10)
Constant	−10.50	−4.41	−7.78
% Correctly classified	84.3	57.0	88.6
Null model	81.0	63.0	56.0
χ^2	177.2	163.1	341.2
Significance	p < .0001	p < .0001	p < .0001
N	402	400	395

Source: Congressional Quarterly Almanac and *Congressional District Databook*, various years.
Dependent variable: 0 = No vote; 1 = Yes vote.
MLE Coefficients; standard errors in parentheses; *p < .10; **p < .05 two-tailed tests.

Table A5.6   Reasons Given by California Voters for Supporting
or Opposing Proposition 187

Which of these statements do you agree with most regarding the illegal immigration initiative?*	% of All Voters	% of those Favoring 187	% of those Against 187
It sends a message that needs to be sent	49%	78%	12%
It would throw children out of school	19%	2%	40%
It would save the state millions of dollars	19%	32%	3%
It is racist/anti-Latino	18%	1%	39%
It would force cops to I.D. illegal immigrant criminals	8%	7%	9%
It could create a health crisis	13%	2%	25%
It will force the federal government to face the issue	32%	51%	8%
It is poorly written/doesn't solve the problem	29%	4%	60%
It will stop immigrants from using state services	20%	34%	3%
It would cost the state billions in federal funds	8%	3%	15%
None of the above	3%	3%	5%

*Indicates multiple responses accepted
Source: Los Angeles Times Exit Poll of California Voters
Los Angeles Times 11/9/94, p. A22.

IMMIGRATION REFORM
IN THE 104TH CONGRESS

The Republican majority swept into Congress in November 1994, driven by a widespread public backlash against the Clinton administration and on the strength of a pledge articulated in the Contract with America. The Contract contained ten items Republican House candidates had pledged to take up in the first 100 days of the next session of Congress, should the electorate give Republicans a majority of House seats (Gimpel 1996). The Contract included items such as ending unfunded federal mandates on the states, shortening the death penalty appeals process, passing a balanced budget constitutional amendment, and imposing congressional term limits. Immigration reform was not among the issues considered in framing the Contract. While immigration concerns unified congressional constituencies in some parts of the country, such as Southern California, in other areas of the country it was divisive, and in still others it was not salient at all. The Contract had been framed around issues that were popular throughout the nation, and immigration was still considered a regional matter. It was difficult to excite members of Congress from interior states about campaigning on reforming the nation's immigration laws.

By the time the 1994 election cycle began in earnest, the off-year elections—which normally break in favor of the party out of the White House—appeared to portend a significant Republican gain. By the end of September, the GOP was surging ahead in House and Senate races. By late October, Republicans seemed on automatic pilot—or perhaps riding a runaway snowball. Nevertheless, the magnitude of the victory was surprising. On the morning of November 9, Republicans awoke to find themselves holding majorities in both houses of Congress.

Importantly, California voters overwhelmingly passed Proposition 187 that same day. Proposition 187 would cut off most public services to illegal residents. Of course, the measure faced an immediate court challenge from its opponents. A federal judge enjoined the popular initiative, thus enraging many Californians and maintaining the high salience of the immigration issue in that state for the next several years. Throughout the 104th Congress, the California delegation pressured the GOP leadership to move ahead with immigration legislation (*CQWR* 4/15/95, 1065–1071).

The change in party control of Congress brought new leadership to the House and Senate Judiciary Committees. In the House, the Judiciary Committee chairmanship was awarded to Henry Hyde (R-IL), a conservative member known for his pro-life views, but, like the previous chairman, Jack Brooks (D-TX), one who had never taken much interest in immigration. Opposite Hyde, John Conyers (D-MI) took over as the ranking Democrat. Brooks had been defeated in his reelection bid, leaving Conyers as the most senior Democrat on the committee. The immigration subcommittee was turned over to Lamar Smith (R-TX). Owing to Hyde's ambivalence on immigration issues, Smith would have free rein to pursue his own legislative agenda.

In general, Smith's philosophy on immigration required one to weigh the good of immigration with the bad. Immigration should further the national policy aims of the United States. We should always ask how immigration is contributing to America's national interest:

> I believe in legal immigration. I think it has been good for the country and has contributed. But you can't lump all immigrants together and say they all contribute equally to the American economy.
>
> I believe we should give priority to immediate family members and to skilled and educated immigrants. Less priority should be given to extended family and unskilled and uneducated immigrants. As far as actual numbers, 40 percent of the immigrants arriving, that's about 400,000, are unskilled and not equipped to produce and contribute. The American people don't want immigrants coming here to live off the taxpayer.
>
> Now on high-tech jobs, these are increasing, so we can absorb immigrants who do this kind of work. But unskilled jobs are stagnant. There is no growth. It makes no sense to admit unskilled immigrants to compete with immigrants and unskilled natives that are already here. (Smith interview 2/26/97)

Smith's focus was on the numbers. While critics wondered aloud if his views were an expression of racist nativism, he had no intention of turning the clock back to 1965 so as to change the country of origin of the immigrants. "It's not where they're from that matters, it's where they're going," Smith insisted. In a phrase, Smith wanted fewer immigrants, more skilled and more self-sufficient immigrants. Smith admitted that immigration was a serious concern to his constituents in south central Texas where he had also been born and raised. "People back home are aware of the people trafficking, the drug trafficking, the overcrowding, and the other problems associated with immigration. My constituents want to talk about immigration more than any other issue." But the constituency connection was only the source of

Box 6.1

Lamar Smith (R-TX) chaired the House immigration subcommittee in 1995 and 1996 and launched the most ambitious effort since the 1920s to reduce the level of legal immigration to the U.S. Courtesy of Lamar Smith.

Lamar Smith (R-TX)

Representative Lamar Smith served as the chair of the House Subcommittee on Immigration and Claims beginning in the 104th Congress. In the 101st Congress, he worked against the Democratic majority to maintain low limits on legal immigration and refugee admissions. His efforts proved largely unsuccessful. Smith became the ranking Republican on the immigration subcommittee in 1991.

When Republicans won a congressional majority in 1994, Smith ascended to chair the Judiciary Subcommittee on Immigration and Claims. He led the immigration reform effort in the House during the 1995–1996 term, managing to navigate a major bill through stormy seas of opposition. In addition to favoring stronger enforcement efforts against illegal immigration, Smith argued for new restrictions on legal immigration in both the employment and family-based visa categories. With Senator Alan Simpson (R-WY), he opposed the extension of welfare benefits to legal immigrants. Smith repeatedly insisted that immigration issues be thought of in terms of the "national interest" rather than the special interests that seemed so intent on shaping immigration law.

Born November 19, 1947, in San Antonio, Texas, Smith earned his bachelor's degree at Yale in 1969. Smith got his first taste of government working at the U.S. Small Business Administration after college graduation. He then worked two years as a business writer for the *Christian Science Monitor*. Smith attended the Southern Methodist University law school from 1972 until 1975, where he earned his J.D.

Smith practiced law, served in the Texas state legislature, and then won election as Bexar County Commissioner. In 1986, he was elected to the U.S. Congress.

He has also served on the Budget Committee since 1993, and he headed the Republican "theme team" that same year.

(Sources: *Almanac of American Politics*, 1996; Rep. Smith's biography on Internet homepage)

his initial interest. He could easily please his constituents simply by expressing restrictive views on immigration and focusing elsewhere in Congress. Instead, he had jumped into a complicated area of the law and was now highly regarded by party leaders and other members as a source of valuable expertise.

On the Senate side, Orrin Hatch (R-UT) assumed the chairmanship of the Judiciary Committee. A conservative ally of business interests, Hatch had never been fond of employer sanctions or verification. His preferences on these issues would come to play a critical role in defining the output of the committee in the months to come. Alan Simpson (R-WY), by this time the Senate's leading immigration expert, took over from Kennedy as the chair of the Senate subcommittee.

While Simpson was better known than Smith, both were viewed as holding conservative views on the subject of immigration. Figuring that Smith and Simpson might press for new restrictions on legal immigration, interest groups with a stake in the issue wasted no time in contacting them. The minority rights groups, traditionally allied with the Democrats, had few inroads with the GOP membership, but businesses that relied on immigrant labor did. Between the elections and the start of the 104th Congress, groups such as the U.S. Chamber of Commerce, the National Association of Manufacturers, the Farm Bureau, and a coalition of high-tech companies expressed concerns about the potential impact of immigration restrictions on their constituencies (Kirschten 1995).

During his years combating expansionist immigration policies, Smith had acquired a clear vision for reform. No sooner had the new Congress convened than he immediately launched hearings on the subject, notwithstanding the tight Contract with America deadlines during the first 100 days. The members of Smith's subcommittee were run ragged by the pace of those initial months. Several of the members of the subcommittee, Ed Bryant (R-TN), Sonny Bono (R-CA), and Fred Heineman (R-NC), were freshmen, unfamiliar with how Congress works, and could barely keep up with the frenetic pace. The Judiciary Committee held jurisdiction over a large portion of the Contract items. To add comprehensive immigration reform to the agenda at that time created an incredible workload for these new House members. But Smith was well aware of the history of immigration reform in Congress. If you did not begin early, the clock would run out. He pressed on.

The new House Speaker, Newt Gingrich (R-GA), developed an unusual approach to congressional leadership in the 104th Congress. Almost parallel to the traditional committee system, Gingrich established a number of task forces constituted by leading members to address a number of lower-tier issues. These ad hoc groups made recommendations to House leaders, and some task forces even drafted legislative language. Among those task forces was the Congressional Task Force on Immigration Reform, chaired by Elton Gallegly (R-CA). Gallegly had been elected in 1986 and was beginning his fifth term in 1995. He ranked second to Smith on the immigration subcommittee and hailed from a suburban Los Angeles district that had overwhelmingly supported Proposition 187. "Gallegly's views are very close to those of his constituents on the issue of illegal immigration," said one of his staff aides. "His district is made up of people who, like him, fled Los Angeles to escape big-city problems. Now they want to protect their quality of life from crime, traffic congestion, school overcrowding, crime, crime, and crime." Los Angeles was a drastically different place in the early and mid-1960s when Elton Gallegly was growing up there than it was in the mid-1990s. Gallegly and his constituents had watched the city become more crowded and more violent, and illegal immigration was associated, in their minds, with both the overcrowding and the crime. Controlling illegal immigration in Southern California boils down to a quality-of-life issue. Accordingly, Gallegly's immigration task force focused on curbing illegal immigration. Its 54 members served on six working groups, essentially the equivalent of subcommittees. The working groups examined border enforcement, workplace enforcement, public benefits, political asylum, deportation, and visa overstays. Its June 30, 1995, report included recommendations pertaining to each of these areas, as well as dissenting views. Many of the recommendations mirrored those of the U.S. Commission on Immigration Reform's (also known as the Jordan Commission) 1994 report and those Smith's subcommittee was considering. Several task force proposals eventually found their way into Smith's bill.

The new House leadership was ambivalent on immigration reform. Majority Leader Richard K. Armey (R-TX) sided with libertarians, viewing immigrants as a net plus for the country and preferring a more generous policy than Lamar Smith. Armey argued that immigrants helped to fill U.S. labor needs by doing jobs natives refused to do and that they brought with them the impetus to work hard and succeed. Armey is an economist by training, and this position flowed from his strong and consistent convictions on free-market economics. Speaker Newt Gingrich (R-GA) was more supportive of Smith because he could read the polls. The public was overwhelmingly against increased immigration and a considerable proportion favored cuts. He also recognized the importance of California on the electoral map and took careful note of the 59 percent support behind Proposition 187. Figuring that there were political gains to be made in supporting Smith's legislation, Gingrich spoke out in favor of it on several occasions and was instrumental in clearing the way for its consideration.

The Jordan Commission

The U.S. Commission on Immigration Reform had been created by the 1990 immigration law (see Chapter 5) and was originally chartered to study illegal immigration. Technical amendments pushed by Alan Simpson (R-WY) passed in 1991, striking the term "illegal" and substituting the term "comprehensive." The 1981 report by the previous Select Commission on Immigration Reform (also known as the Hesburgh Commission) had been a tremendous success. Members of Congress had taken its recommendations seriously. It had influenced ten years of immigration policymaking and led to major changes in immigration law. Leaving major policy recommendations to a bipartisan commission surely made sense, given the highly controversial nature of immigration policy.

Simpson's vision for the new Commission was initially even more ambitious. He originally had in mind a sort of Federal Reserve Board of immigration policymakers, prominent appointees serving limited terms, who would be insulated from political pressures in making all admissions decisions. In the House-Senate conference committee over the 1990 bill, Bruce Morrison (D-CT), the House immigration subcommittee chairman, had opposed this idea, arguing that the government should not make immigration decisions; Americans should, through their representatives. Morrison won the argument and Simpson agreed to a more limited mandate for the Commission following the tradition of the earlier one. The new Commission would study and report recommendations on both illegal and legal immigration by 1994. Chaired by former Congresswoman Barbara Jordan (D-TX), the Commission's first report on illegal immigration was issued in September 1994, and the second report was issued nine months later in the summer of 1995.

The Commission's most notable recommendation on illegal immigration drew fire from both conservatives and civil libertarians, while garnering support from various positions along the political spectrum. That recommendation called for the creation of a computerized registry of Social Security numbers for verification of work eligibility. The Commission argued that such a verification system would help eliminate the "job magnet" that draws many undocumented workers to the country. Commissioners reasoned that if an unauthorized would-be worker couldn't find work, even with fraudulent documents in hand, the illegal border crossings would drop off. The Commission determined that a Social Security–based computer system would allow employers and authorities to work together to verify the validity of a Social Security number and establish that the number tendered had been issued to the person being hired.

Commission Chairwoman Barbara Jordan testified at several of the House subcommittee hearings during the spring of 1995. She shared the Commission's ideas at hearings on visa overstays, and employment and benefits eligibility verification. Other Commission members testified at House hearings, including Lawrence Fuchs, the Brandeis political science professor who had directed the work of the earlier Select Commission, and Bruce Morrison (D-CT), now retired from Congress. Jordan had been appointed to

Box 6.2

Barbara Jordan (D-TX) served on the House Judiciary Committee in the 1970s and later as the chair of U.S. Commission on Immigration Reform. She is shown here giving the keynote address at the 1976 Democratic National Convention. Credit: Library of Congress

Barbara Jordan (D-TX)

Representative Barbara Jordan served on the House Judiciary Committee from 1973 through 1978. She was appointed by President Clinton to chair the U.S. Commission on Immigration Reform in 1993 and served in that capacity until her death. Jordan believed that legal immigration was a good thing for the United States but that the current system was too easily subverted by unauthorized entries. Accordingly, she took a hard line against illegal immigration but opposed efforts to cut welfare benefits to legal immigrants.

Jordan was born February 21, 1936, in Houston. She graduated from Texas Southern University in 1956 with a B.A. degree, and from law school at Boston University in 1959 with an LL.B. She returned to Houston, where she practiced law beginning in 1960.

She became active in politics, organizing precincts for the Kennedy-Johnson ticket in 1960. Jordan ran and lost a 1962 bid for a state House seat. She repeated the attempt in 1964 and again failed. On her third electoral try in 1966, Jordan won a reapportioned state Senate seat, which she held until 1972. She also served as an administrative assistant to a Harris County judge in 1966.

Jordan served as delegate to state Democratic conventions in 1967 and 1969, and to the Democratic National Convention in 1968.

In 1972, Jordan ran for Congress and won. From her post on the Judiciary Committee, she played a key role in the committee's impeachment proceedings against President Richard Nixon in connection with the Watergate scandal. Jordan gained national attention through her oratorical and lawyering skills, which came to bear in the impeachment process. She delivered the keynote address at the 1976 Democratic National Convention.

Jordan did not seek reelection in 1978, but took a faculty position as professor at the Lyndon B. Johnson School of Public Affairs, University of Texas.

The 1990 Immigration Act called for the establishment of a commission to study U.S. immigration policy and make recommendations for reform. Former Congresswoman Jordan was named chairman of that commission.

In 1994, Jordan was awarded the Presidential Medal of Freedom. She died in Austin, Texas, January 17, 1996.

(Sources: *Biographical Directory of the U.S. Congress 1774–1989; Notable Black American Women*, 1992; *Who's Who in American Politics 1995–96*)

chair the commission by President Clinton in 1993. She brought credibility to the Commission's work because of her reputation for fairness. Also, her Democratic party affiliation helped curb potential charges that the Commission amounted to another adjunct of the newly Republican-controlled Congress. And the charges perennially leveled by ethnic advocacy groups that immigration reform was motivated by nativism and racism just could not stick to the civil rights–minded, black woman. Jordan herself never made much of her ethnicity. Reporters would frequently call the Commission staff asking if she would prefer to be known as "black" or "African-American." Jordan's response was always that she was an American first and a Texan second. She often boasted that one of the proudest accomplishments of her congressional service was extending the Voting Rights Act to Hispanics. She brought a Texan's outlook to the Commission's work, recognizing that the relationship between Texas and Mexico was different from the one between California and Mexico. Texas and Mexico had good relations along the border. She approached the issues posed by legal and illegal immigration as problems to be resolved through compromise rather than confrontation.

The Jordan Commission released its report on legal immigration in June 1995. This report, while generally supporting the current three-part framework of family-based, employment-based, and refugee immigration, asserted that "the Commission is convinced that our current immigration system must undergo major reform to ensure that admissions continue to serve our national interests" (CIR Report, 1995, cover letter). The report called for cutting yearly immigration levels and setting new priorities for admissions. The Commission said the national interest would best be served by prioritizing the admission of nuclear family members—spouses, minor children, and parents—and skilled workers. Under the current system (see Table 5.6), there were extended backlogs of visa applicants who had been waiting, in some cases, for years to obtain a visa to reunify with their immediate family member(s) already in the country. These backlogs had been created, in part, by the 1986 law that had granted amnesty to so many undocumented workers. These newly legalized residents were now petitioning for admission of their spouses and children. Not surprisingly, this created long waiting lists for visas. To eliminate these long waiting periods, the Commission settled on a proposal to eliminate all of the nonnuclear preference categories, including the one for brothers and sisters and for *adult* sons and daughters, and transfer those visa allotments to the more immediate family members. This would speed up the reunification of immediate families. Under the Commission's plan, the visa backlog would be reduced to zero by the year 2002. Susan Martin, the Commission's executive director, explained the rationale behind this policy:

> We felt that it was in the U.S. interest that the nuclear family take precedence over the extended family. We arrived at this by examining the U.S. legal system.

In the U.S. legal system, who has responsibility for whom? First, spouses have responsibility for each other. Second, parents have responsibility for minor children. Parents are not responsible for an adult child. A person is not responsible for an adult brother or sister, either. We also felt that children should be able to bring in their parents because the parent-child relationship is so fundamental. We backed from there into a rank ordering of the preferences along the following continuum:

> 1st preference: U.S. citizens and their spouses and minor children,
> 2nd preference: U.S. citizens and their parents,
> 3rd preference: Permanent residents and their spouses and minor children.
>   (Martin interview 6/17/97)

Recommending the elimination of the nonnuclear preference categories was bound to generate controversy (CIR Report 1995, 70–72). Not even Smith and Simpson were confident they could go this far. But the Commission went further in recommending that the admission of parents should be contingent upon a legally enforceable affidavit of support. This idea was a direct response to reports cited by the Commission showing that elderly immigrants were using SSI disability benefits, Medicaid, and similar state and local benefits, rather than rely upon the income of their sponsors for support. Under current law, affidavits of support were not legally enforceable and meant nothing. The Commission also recommended renewed emphasis on Americanization—the enculturation and naturalization of immigrants.

Many of the Commission's recommendations sounded similar to the legislation Smith and Simpson had been moving toward. The pro-immigration ethnic groups, such as the National Council of La Raza and various Asian-Pacific American organizations, wondered if Simpson and Smith had influenced the Commission's findings and recommendations. There were rumors that the staff of the Commission had not arrived at their decisions independently, but had been subject to political pressures from Capitol Hill. Others opposed to the Commission's recommendations charged that it had become an advocacy organization, lobbying against a more generous immigration policy. The CATO Institute's Stuart Anderson, who was instrumental in shaping the coalition against the legal reform effort, was highly critical of the Commission:

> The Jordan Commission wasn't influential. Everything they recommended was defeated. They were lobbying and had their people up on the Hill. Here was a taxpayer-funded commission that was in the business of lobbying. They had a press guy who was a real jerk. He would attack anyone who came out for open admissions. (Anderson interview 1/16/97)

The "jerk" was Paul Donnelly, the communications director for the Commission. He had worked as Bruce Morrison's (D-CT) press secretary when Morrison had served in Congress. Donnelly had lived through the battles surrounding the 1990 round of reform and was no novice when it came to immigration policy. Press spokesmen in Washington are not known for having substantive expertise, but Donnelly had it and he came across as a policy wonk rather than an empty-headed public relations man. He could (and often did) go toe-to-toe on the details with anyone. Those opposed to the Commission's recommendations deeply resented his aggressive style of defending its findings. In fact, it is difficult to determine how much influence Simpson and Smith had on the Commission's work and its recommendations. They had no more access to the Commission than did the executive branch. Many of the Commission staff members were detailed from executive branch agencies. Political operatives from the executive branch and from Capitol Hill were invited to join the Commission on site visits and did so on several occasions. There were many routine and informal information exchanges between Commission staff and congressional staff. After the Commission released its reports, it conducted numerous detailed briefings for congressional staff. It is true that the Commission wanted to be relevant to the policy debate. Commissioners and staff aimed to provide information that would serve as the basis for legislative action. To the opponents of legislative action, however, this was tantamount to lobbying for reform.

It is also true that Simpson and Smith were generally pleased with the Commission's work and eventually came to cite its reports in supporting many of their proposals. But there were areas of disagreement, too. Barbara Jordan and the commissioners in general opposed banning welfare benefits for legal immigrants, an idea that became popular with Republicans in the House. Several commissioners argued that such policies amounted to letting immigrants in, but not permitting their equal treatment once they were here. Upon arrival, immigrants should not have to live by a code of conduct distinct from natives. Arguably, there were also a number of politically unrealistic recommendations, such as the elimination of all nonnuclear preference categories, that one doubts would have seen the light of day had the report been drafted with congressional politics in mind. A commission could make such recommendations and get them on the table, though, realizing that it may take several attempts to pass reform legislation.

The Clinton Administration

Initially, President Clinton's most significant action on immigration policy was to appoint Barbara Jordan to head the U.S. Commission on Immigration Reform. Following the release of the Commission's reports, the president endorsed each set of recommendations. By the summer of 1995, there seemed to be strong consensus between Smith, Simpson, and the administration that the Jordan Commission's recommendations should be adopted. The president never made immigration reform a key talking point. Rather, he awaited the Commission's work and recommendations. As it became increasingly evident that the Republican-led Congress would squarely take on the immigration issue, the administration had Howard Berman (D-CA) introduce its immigration bill, H.R. 1929. Titled the Immigration Enforcement Improvements Act, Berman's legislation focused primarily on illegal immigration. On this subject, it generally mirrored the Jordan Commission's recommendations, as well as overlapping with the illegal immigration provisions in H.R. 1915, Lamar Smith's bill.

Politically, President Clinton could not ignore the salience of the immigration issue in California, a state top-heavy with immigrants legal and illegal, and with 52 electoral votes. He had won California in 1992 with 46 percent of the popular vote, and the margin was not sizable enough for him to take the state for granted in his 1996 reelection bid. On the other hand, ethnic interest groups opposed to the Simpson and Smith legislation began to put pressure on the administration to speak out against it. Immigration issues put Clinton on a tightrope politically. In addition to facing cross pressures from California and from minority rights groups, he had a strong sense of political obligation to Barbara Jordan, whom he had appointed.

By early 1995, the Clinton administration had become notorious for its obsession with polls. Polls showed that many of the Commission's recommendations were popular. Not much controversy arose among average Americans on the matter of illegal immigration. To a majority of citizens, regardless of race, cracking down on illegal entry and streamlining procedures for deportation seemed perfectly reasonable. Restricting the access of noncitizens and illegal residents to public benefits was slightly more controversial, but even this proposal failed to provoke a popular outcry because the public largely supported it. The matter of restricting legal immigration generated more controversy, but even this was confined mostly to the pro-immigration lobby in Washington, which consisted of business groups concerned about employment-related visas, immigrant rights groups that claimed to represent the interests of immigrants and their families, and immigration lawyers whose clients were immigrants. Since the president could find very little guidance for policy action simply from reading the polls, these interest groups would become increasingly influential as the debate continued.

House Subcommittee Action

Between February 8, 1995, and the June 22 introduction of Smith's comprehensive bill, H.R. 1915—The Immigration in the National Interest Act—Smith held eight hearings with more than 100 witnesses appearing to probe the key issues relating to immigration (Judiciary Committee Activities Report 1997). These inquiries ranged broadly to cover everything from INS management practices to border security to employment verification. Smith's subcommittee examined the major immigration-related issues, including visa overstays, employer sanctions, criminal alien removal, verification of alien eligibility to work and obtain public benefits, the impact of illegal aliens, and legal immigration reforms.

On February 24, 1995, the House subcommittee held a hearing on the matter of those who overstay the term of their visas. Barbara Jordan testified, using the opportunity to lay out the Commission's seven-point strategy for curbing illegal immigration, essentially describing the highlights of the previous fall's interim report. Jordan said the Commission advocated the following changes: better border management; improved worksite enforcement, primarily through a computerized worker validation system; making illegal aliens ineligible for most public benefits as a further disincentive to illegal entry; federal financial reimbursement of state and local costs, especially criminal justice costs; deportation of public charges; stronger immigrant sponsor requirements; detention and removal of criminal aliens; preparation for managing emergency refugee situations; improvements in data collection concerning the impact of immigration; and efforts to enhance international cooperation to combat illegal migration.

Among the recommendations, Jordan discussed a proposed border crossing user fee. Legal crossers would pay a user fee to help fund improvements in traffic flow across the border. However, subcommittee ranking member John Bryant (D-TX) panned the idea outright. "There ain't going to be a border crossing fee, and [the Clinton administration] ought to quit talking about it," Bryant said. Bryant drew bipartisan support for his remarks against the border crossing fee proposal. Elton Gallegly (R-CA) added: "The cost, the fact that we are charging people that [sic] are legally going through the hoops rather than penalizing those that [sic] are not, I have a basic problem with that." The border crossing user fee proposal wasn't included in Smith's bill.

Lamar Smith (R-TX) endorsed Jordan's electronic worker verification proposal. "In my judgment, and I think we agree here, the only way you can end discrimination in the workplace, the only way you can ensure that jobs and benefits go to those who are entitled to them is through some form of a verification system," Smith remarked. Not surprisingly, the electronic verification system found its way into H.R. 1915 in the form of a new telephone verification system. Pilot projects in five of the states with the most illegal immigrants present would be established. Employers in those states with four or more employees would be required to call a toll-free number for each new hire and to verify the employee's employment eligibility by Social Security number or alien registration number.

Commissioner Jordan returned to testify at a March 30 subcommittee hearing devoted to verification of eligibility for U.S. employment and public benefits. Ranking Democrat John Bryant (D-TX) lent his support to improving the verification system: "I'm a supporter of establishing a very up-to-date and workable verification system." Likewise, Howard Berman (D-CA) said, "You can talk about Proposition 187s and we can fight about benefits and we

Box 6.3

Howard Berman (D-CA) served on the House immigration sub-comittee in the 1980s and 1990s. Berman successfully fought attempts to restrict legal immigration in the 1995–1996 round of reform. Courtesy of Howard Berman.

Howard Berman (D-CA)

Representative Howard Berman played an active role in the 104th Congress's immigration legislation as a senior Democrat on the House Judiciary Committee. He advanced the Clinton administration's proposals on illegal immigration, finding common ground with Lamar Smith on this subject, but he opposed Smith's efforts to place new restrictions on legal immigration. Together with two freshman Republicans, Berman sponsored a successful floor amendment to the Smith bill striking the restrictions on legal immigration.

He was also influential in several previous rounds of immigration reform during the 1980s. Elected in 1982, Berman was called by *The Almanac of American Politics* "a major force on immigration." As a freshman member, Berman was named a conferee on Simpson-Mazzoli in 1984 and 1986, where he worked out an amendment to grant permanent resident status to farm workers who had been working illegally. He sponsored a family reunification visa program in 1988, fought for increased immigration in the 1990 bill, and has advocated federal reimbursement of state expenses connected with illegal immigration. Berman has left a lasting imprint on immigration law and policy.

Berman was born April 15, 1941, in Los Angeles. He attended U.C.L.A., where he earned his bachelor's degree in 1962 and his LL.B. in 1965. He volunteered in the Vista program, serving from 1966 to 1967.

Berman became active in the Federation of Young Democrats while at U.C.L.A., teaming up with Henry Waxman (who would later be his congressional colleague). They led the federation to middle ground between liberal and traditional factions of the state Democratic party throughout the 1960s.

He practiced law from 1967 until 1972, specializing in labor law. In 1972, he won election to the California Assembly. From 1974 until 1979, Berman served as majority leader in the state legislature. As a state assemblyman, Berman became an ally of farm workers, pushing legislation that advanced California farm workers' unionization.

He lost an attempt to capture the Assembly Speaker spot in 1980, but won his congressional seat representing California's 26th District two years later. Berman's district, which is 52 percent Hispanic, displayed its liberal inclinations when it threw 56 percent of its presidential vote to Dukakis in 1988. Berman has reflected that liberalism, earning a 90 rating from Americans for Democratic Action and a zero from the American Conservative Union. His close labor union ties are demonstrated in his 88 rating by the AFL-CIO's COPE.

(Sources: *Almanac of American Politics*, various years; *Politics in America*, 1986; *Biographical Directory of the U.S. Congress 1774–1989*)

can talk about them, but unless you've dealt with the issue of verification, all those initiatives and all those propositions and all those proposals are really pretty meaningless."

Step by step, Smith was cobbling together a comprehensive bill, in principle at this stage, that would garner bipartisan support. His hearings laid the groundwork and contributed to both the education and the consensus building necessary to advance legislation. Smith's staff was new on the job, and these hearings gave them the chance to learn about members' preferences— what they would accept and what they would not accept. Once the concepts were committed to legislative language and introduced as a bill, they could be picked apart by various special interest groups, each with its own axe to grind and turf to protect. In spite of never having chaired a committee before, Smith demonstrated skill and patience, first establishing that certain changes were needed in immigration policy, and waiting nearly six months before revealing actual legislation. From the outside, however, the pro-immigration lobby was growing increasingly uneasy. They saw that Smith had momentum on his side. Lobbyist Frank Sharry, a major strategist for the immigration groups, recalled the feeling of being outgunned:

> In the spring of 1995, we didn't think we could turn the restrictionist tide, couldn't stop the reform juggernaut, and it looked like something close to zero immigration was on the verge of being enacted. The current system would be gutted, the safety net for legal immigrants would be shredded, and a national work verification system would be imposed...
>
> Lamar Smith has a capable staff and they came roaring out of the blocks. Smith wrapped himself in the Jordan Commission's cloak and wanted to get the bill to the floor by the end of the year. (Sharry interview 2/13/97)

In June, the Jordan Commission's report calling for restrictions in legal immigration levels and new priorities within the preference system added momentum to the "reform juggernaut." Furthermore, President Clinton endorsed the report's findings immediately, increasing the likelihood that something would eventually be done on a bipartisan basis (*CQ Almanac* 1995).

Smith's Original Proposals

The recommendations of the Jordan Commission served as the basis of Smith's H.R. 1915 (Judiciary Committee Activities Report 1997). The comprehensive bill contained eight titles: border security, alien smuggling, removal of illegal and criminal aliens, employer sanctions and verification, legal immigration reforms, eligibility for benefits and sponsorship, facilitation of legal entry, and miscellaneous provisions, including H-1B skilled nonimmigrant visas. Smith introduced this legislation on June 22, 1995, with 38 original cosponsors from both political parties, including John Bryant (D-TX), the ranking Democrat on the subcommittee.

To improve border security, H.R. 1915 sought to add 1,000 Border Patrol agents each year for five years. It funded additional fences along the border near San Diego. It called for new Border Crosser ID cards, including some permanent identifier such as an alien's fingerprint that would be harder to counterfeit. These cards would be issued to aliens who live across a land border and have reason to cross frequently. This section also would establish several pilot projects, such as use of closed military bases for detaining illegals facing deportation.

With regard to alien smuggling and document fraud, Smith's legislation included wiretapping authority and subpoena of bank records for investigations, and it subjected smuggling and fraud activities to possible racketeering charges. It allowed for asset forfeiture in connection with alien smuggling and document fraud. The bill also set forth new civil and criminal penalties for immigration-related fraud.

The third section of Smith's bill sought to streamline the process for removing inadmissible or deportable aliens. One process, known as expedited exclusion, had been advanced by Bill McCollum (R-FL) in previous rounds of reform. It would apply to aliens arriving at a U.S. port of entry with either no documents or fraudulent documents. The other process, known as removal, would combine the old deportation and the exclusion processes. Both processes, as proposed, significantly limited what many members considered the overly generous due process rights that had previously been accorded these noncitizens. As part of the streamlining, the right to appeal deportation judgments to federal court would be curtailed. Other provisions of this section would impose fines on those who fled while waiting for removal, require detention of criminal and terrorist aliens under removal proceedings, and set up new procedures for removing alien terrorists.

The employment section of the bill would add 500 new employer sanctions investigators to the Immigration and Naturalization Service. It would reduce the number of employment authorization documents from 29 to six. It would create an employment eligibility confirmation system, similar to that proposed by the Jordan Commission. The system would involve the use of a toll-free telephone number that employers would call in order to compare information a new employee submitted with information on government databases. A further provision of this section would require the Social Security Administration to report the number of Social Security numbers that had been issued to aliens who had not been authorized to work, and for which wages had been reported.

The fifth title of H.R. 1915 would reform the legal immigration system. Any alien seeking to immigrate permanently would have to be admitted under one of three categories: family-sponsored, employment-based, or humanitarian. Under the family-sponsored category, the preferences would be reduced to spouses and minor children of U.S. citizens and lawful permanent residents and the parents of U.S. citizens. Adult brothers and sisters, along with adult children preferences, would be eliminated, as the Jordan Commission recommended. This change was intended to cut chain migration—the phenomenon whereby immigrant visa backlogs continued to swell as the result of the demand to bring in extended family members. The proposed family category had a yearly ceiling of 330,000, with provisions for reducing existing backlogs.

The employment-based category would have a 135,000 annual limit, with requirements for immigrants to have superior skills or abilities, or educational attainments. Immigrants who would invest at least $1 million in a U.S. company could also seek employment-based admission. The humanitarian categories would include refugees, those adjusting to asylum status, and other humanitarian immigrants, with an annual cap of 70,000.

The next section sought to limit public benefits. Illegal aliens would be ineligible for public benefits, and federal agencies would have to check an applicant's documents to verify citizenship or lawful residence. It would strengthen the public-charge grounds for inadmissibility, and allow an alien's removal as a public charge if he or she received federal welfare assistance for a total of 12 months during the first seven years of admission to the country. The bill also sought to tighten the "deeming" rules and make a sponsor's affidavit of support legally binding. Deeming is simply the notion that in the determination of the eligibility of a legal resident for public assistance programs, the income of that legal resident's sponsor should count as the legal resident's income. Under current law, a sponsor could bring in an elderly family member, and that family member could apply for public assistance declaring that he had no income. Smith proposed to count or "deem" the sponsor's income as the new arrival's income—the idea being that sponsors should be responsible for their family members. Further, the bill set forth sponsorship requirements, primarily that a sponsor be the person petitioning for the immigrant's admission and earn annual income equal to at least 200 percent of the poverty level.

The seventh title sought to facilitate legal entry by increasing the number of INS and Customs inspectors and by expanding pilot programs for commuter lanes for frequent crossers. It set up preinspection stations at the ten foreign airports with the largest numbers of departures for the United States. It also would increase training for airline personnel in the detection of fraudulent documents.

The final title contained miscellaneous provisions. Among them were sections to exempt employers with ten percent or less of their workforce holding temporary nonimmigrant visas from many of the associated regulatory requirements. For employers dependent upon temporary foreign hires (or H-1B workers as they were called, based on the section of the U.S. Code where the program is delineated), they could not have laid off or fired an American worker within six months of seeking a temporary foreign worker, unless the employer paid the nonimmigrant 110 percent of the American worker's wage. Other miscellaneous provisions included allowing the attorney general to disclose confidential information from INS files for terrorist or criminal investigations, and a pilot program to match birth and death records in three of the states with the heaviest illegal alien populations.

Ranking member John Bryant (D-TX) began the 104th Congress disposed to support Smith's immigration reform efforts. Besides listing his name as an original cosponsor of H.R. 1915, Bryant joined Smith at a press conference touting the bipartisan legislation. The Texans would ride a long trail together to advance the Immigration in the National Interest Act. Only later would Bryant's support turn sour.

On June 29, 1995, Smith convened a subcommittee hearing on the Immigration in the National Interest Act itself. Eighteen witnesses on four panels testified, representing a wide range of viewpoints on the legislation. In his opening statement, Smith named five goals that H.R. 1915 was designed to achieve. Smith said he sought to make America more competitive, to secure the border, to protect American lives, to unite nuclear families, and to make immigrants self-sufficient.

Anticipating objections and sniping from pressure groups, including some of the organizations represented by that day's witnesses, Smith drew his line in the sand and issued a challenge to those who would testify: "That gets me back to the final point, which is that we have every right to put the interests of the American worker and the American taxpayer and the American family first. I would like the panelists on each panel, if they would during their comments, to point out what they feel is the American interest that should be served by an immigration policy" (House Subcommittee hearing June 29, 1995, 2).

Howard Berman (D-CA) introduced his own legislation on behalf of the Clinton administration. Like other Southern California constituencies, his had long complained about immigration. Berman represented part of Los Angeles County. The county nearly went bankrupt in 1996, partly as a result of the cost of providing health care benefits to illegal immigrants. Berman frequently faced complaints about both legal and illegal immigrants from constituents in town meetings. Berman's response to these complaints was to draw a sharp distinction between legal and illegal immigration. He supported efforts to impose employer sanctions and implement a work verification system. But he viewed Smith's cuts in legal immigration as entirely too severe. Like so many others, Berman called up his family history in defending America's legal immigration tradition: "I am a son of an immigrant. My sense of history is that a generous immigration policy has been good for this country. It is in our national interest to keep people coming in through legal channels" (Berman interview 3/25/97). Over the course of the 104th Congress, Berman would serve as the administration's chief negotiator on the subcommittee.

Among those testifying at the June 29 hearing, the Immigration and Naturalization Service, the Department of Justice, the Department of Labor, and the Social Security Administration each had a representative as a witness. In essence, these witnesses endorsed the ideas in Smith's legislation on behalf of the administration. Each noted some differences between the Smith bill and the Berman bill. Yet the thrust of the testimony suggested that the administration had few problems with the Smith version.

Modest Changes to the Smith Bill

The subcommittee spent a week marking up H.R. 1915, beginning July 13 and passing the bill July 20, 1995, by a voice vote that reflected more the resignation of the Democrats than their consent. Berman raised objections to the restrictions on legal immigration, but he realized that Smith had the votes to pass the bill and saved his most aggressive amendments for later action. The subcommittee considered more than 40 amendments during that week (*CQWR* 7/15/95, 2074–2076; *CQWR* 7/22/95, 2187). Perhaps the most substantial change to the bill came from Bill McCollum (R-FL), who sought to require that asylum applications in most situations be filed within 30 days of the applicant's arrival in the country. The amendment also contained the requirement that the asylum-seeker be removed to a third country and his asylum application rejected if the third-country option were available. Asylum applications would also have to be adjudicated within six months of filing. Reports from Justice Department officials suggested that the asylum process was subject to rampant abuse. Aliens would enter the United States and file asylum claims when faced with the prospect of being deported or otherwise returned to their home country. The time involved during the adjudication process ensured that these claimants would spend considerable time in the United States, during which they would often find work and settle down. Despite thousands of asylum claims, perhaps only a small proportion met the criterion of fleeing persecution (*CQ Almanac* 1995). McCollum's amendment was adopted on a voice vote.

The subcommittee also adopted, by voice vote, amendments offered by Elton Gallegly (R-CA). One amendment dealt with detention. It authorized an increase in the INS's detention bed space from 3,000 to 9,000. It also required detention and prosecution of aliens who had illegally entered the country three or more times. Gallegly also addressed alien smuggling and document fraud by moving to increase the penalties for these crimes (*CQ Almanac* 1995).

On the subject of reimbursement of costs to states, Gallegly (R-CA) successfully offered an amendment to allow the federal government to reimburse public hospitals for the costs of emergency care provided to illegal aliens. The hospitals would have to verify the person's immigration status in order to receive the payment. The argument made was that the federal government had failed in its responsibility to secure the borders, and the state and local governments were bearing the economic burden and would continue to do so for emergency medical services (*CQWR* 7/22/95; 2188).

Xavier Becerra (D-CA) successfully amended the bill to call for an appeals process for workers to challenge erroneous determinations that they were ineligible to work in the United States. Becerra said the phone employment verification system, which would rely on existing government databases, would contain inaccuracies and incomplete information, and that misinformation would lead to denials of workers who were in fact eligible to work here. The subcommittee indicated its agreement by adopting the amendment by voice vote (*CQ Almanac* 1995).

When the subcommittee favorably reported H.R. 1915 on July 20, it instructed that the bill be reintroduced as a clean bill, which was subsequently awarded a new number, H.R. 2202. The reported bill was arguably stronger than when it was originally introduced. Smith's bill had survived any substantial weakening amendments. No major portions had been stripped. And the streamlined asylum process added by McCollum's amendment strengthened the reforms of the entire package. Smith had been fair, but firm. The Democrats planned to fight their major battles in the full committee markup.

House Judiciary Committee Action

On August 4, 1995, Chairman Smith reintroduced the Immigration in the National Interest Act as his subcommittee had amended and reported it. The new bill, H.R. 2202, had 119 original cosponsors. The Judiciary Committee spent nine days between September 19 and October 24, 1995, marking up H.R. 2202. The committee adopted 74 amendments, rejecting 28 more (Judiciary Committee Activities Report 1997). Nevertheless, at the end of that period, Smith's bill remained largely intact.

Sixty-four of the amendments adopted were approved by voice vote, which usually indicates a relative absence of controversy. That appearance would belie the case here. Rather, the fact that so many issues were resolved with as little bloodletting was a tribute to Smith's shepherding skills. "He surmounted the pockets of opposition during the markup with tireless negotiation and some strategic concessions," as *Congressional Quarterly's* observers put it (*CQ Almanac* 1995, 6–11). Even liberal Democrats on the committee such as Barney Frank (D-MA) admitted that the markup had been inclusive and "reasonable" (Frank interview 2/7/97). Yet, core partisan differences were in evidence with increasing frequency over the course of the markup.

Addressing Illegal Immigration

On illegal immigration, Smith's legislation wound up splitting the difference between amendments that toughened and weakened law enforcement provisions in the bill. A number of amendments to these provisions could be viewed as noncontroversial. The committee was able to reach consensus on most illegal immigration issues. A Berman amendment adopted by voice vote made an exception to the ten-year bar on admission for those who had lived illegally in the U.S. for more that a year. These illegal aliens could seek readmission if they had work authorization or could gain family unity protection. This weakened H.R. 2202's provisions somewhat. However, Smith received voice vote approval for amendments to make clear that stowaways interdicted at sea are to be placed in the expedited removal procedures, as well as face detention, thus strengthening the bill. And a McCollum amendment defining immigration judges and setting their compensation could be regarded as neutral, not generating any protest.

Mel Watt (D-NC) joined with Becerra of California and Jerrold Nadler (D-NY) to seek roll-call votes on contentious weakening amendments that would have affected the illegal immigration sections. Watt would have removed the requirement of additional fence construction along the San Diego border, eliminated the allowance of electronic surveillance information in special removal proceedings against alien terrorists, and required judicial review of exclusion orders under expedited removal proceedings. Watt's views were heavily informed by the immigrants' rights community. As one of the four black members on the committee, his overriding concern had always been on procedural justice and civil rights. Watt believed that the American court system was the final check against arbitrary lawmaking by the masses. McCollum's language on expedited removal rankled Watt. Deportation should be a judicial determination, and not left to an ordinary INS bureaucrat at the airport. Becerra (D-CA) tried to strike the provision barring aliens from readmission to the country if they have illegally resided in the U.S. for over a year. Nadler sought to limit the use of classified information in the special removal proceedings against alien terrorists (*Immigration in the National Interest Act* committee report, part 1 1996). All of these amendments were defeated on largely party-line votes.

Elton Gallegly (R-CA) offered a controversial amendment requiring that public assistance payments be made only to those personally eligible for the benefits. This addressed the troublesome situation in which illegal alien parents could receive government benefit checks on behalf of their U.S. citizen minor children, who actually qualified for the benefit, though the parents were ineligible. Of course, this posed a problem for assistance administrators: To whom do you give a check if you are legally prohibited from giving it to the beneficiary's parent because of his or her illegal status? Still, committee members voted 16–11 to adopt Gallegly's amendment. No Democrats voted in favor of the amendment, and California Republican Carlos Moorhead opposed it.

An amendment offered by Ed Bryant (R-TN) lost despite its tough stance against illegal immigration. Bryant's amendment would require that public hospitals, in seeking reimbursement for emergency treatment of an illegal alien, provide the INS with identifying information about the illegal resident. Bryant argued that the medical facilities already would have to verify the immigration status of these aliens. Thus, to require that they turn over basic information to immigration authorities posed a minimal requirement in exchange for federal funds. The Bryant Amendment was based on a recommendation of the House Immigration Task Force. Democrats argued that the threat of being caught would deter many aliens from seeking emergency medical care, and that adult illegals would not take their children for care, thus causing the children to suffer most. Some Republicans argued that such a requirement turned public hospitals into de facto immigration police. In a roll-call vote, four Republicans joined 11 Democrats against 11 Republicans to defeat the Bryant Amendment.

Making Legal Immigration Policy

On legal immigration, Smith succeeded at keeping the legal reforms in the bill free of weakening amendments. The principal threat was Berman (D-CA), who sought to strike the legal reform provisions altogether. Berman had realized in the subcommittee that he was outgunned but thought he would have a better chance in the full committee, where there were several Republicans who held rather libertarian views on immigration or who had large business enterprises in their congressional districts that were dependent upon foreign labor. Nevertheless, Berman was still not able to come up with enough votes to eliminate Smith's legal reforms. Only one Republican—Steve Chabot (R-OH)—voted with Berman, while two Democrats—Bryant of Texas and Rick Boucher of Virginia—voted in opposition (*Immigration in the National Interest Act* committee report, part 1 1996).

Pennsylvania Republican George Gekas tried to restore the unmarried adult children categories for children of both citizens and permanent resident aliens. Gekas is a son of Greek immigrants who had what he described as "serious, sensitive, emotional conflicts" with Smith's proposals (Gekas interview 2/27/97). He had prepared to fight fully the new restrictions on family-based immigration. Gekas received support from many of the Democrats on the committee. Smith, trying to minimize the damage to the underlying bill, proposed a substitute amendment to allow visas for unmarried adult children of U.S. citizens and lawful permanent residents, as long as the children were under 26 years old and dependent on their parents. Gekas accepted the substitute, and the committee approved it 17–12 (*CQWR* 9/30/95, 3010; *CQ Almanac* 1995; *Immigration in the National Interest Act* committee report, part 1 1996). Judiciary Committee Chairman Henry Hyde (R-IL) was the only Republican to oppose the substitute amendment. No Democrats voted for it.

Texas Democrat Sheila Jackson Lee nearly succeeded upon revisiting the issue of the parents category. Jackson Lee proposed an amendment to increase the number of family-based visas from 330,000 to 400,000 annually. This amendment would have made it easier for children to bring in their parents. Jackson-Lee's amendment attracted two GOP votes—Chabot (R-OH) and Michael Patrick Flanagan (R-IL)—while Bryant of Texas joined most Republicans in opposition. Jackson Lee's amendment was defeated on a 16–16 tie vote.

Both Republicans and Democrats attempted to undo Smith's refugee provisions. H.R. 2202 limited humanitarian admissions to 70,000 per year. Refugees would receive 50,000 slots, asylees 10,000, and other humanitarian visa holders 10,000. The late Steve Schiff (R-NM) led the charge from the GOP side. Schiff was Jewish and had been born and raised in Chicago before moving to New Mexico to attend law school in his early twenties. It is no accident that the Jewish members of Congress have often been known for supporting a generous refugee policy. The Jewish people have an ancient history of migration and more recently, of course, European and Soviet Jews used refugee status to emigrate to the United States following World War II and throughout the cold war. Accordingly, Schiff sought to preserve the current refugee system, whereby the executive branch consulted with Congress to set admissions levels each year with no fixed limits. Schiff supported the more flexible system. Religious groups had lobbied vigorously on this issue. Lisa Zachary of the Council of Jewish Federations, a group involved in refugee resettlement, summarized the case against Smith's cap:

> The cap on refugee admissions was very troubling. Our nation has always had a commitment to refugee admissions as a matter of foreign policy. Requiring refugee admissions go through Congress was entirely contrary to past procedure. It involved a 150 percent reduction in current refugee admissions. We were alarmed at such a hard cap. We need emergency flexibility to respond to crises around the world. We prefer no cap at all on refugee admissions. (Zachary interview 5/1/97)

Chairman Hyde proposed a substitute amendment that kept the caps Smith favored but eased the president's ability to admit more refugees in emergency situations. Schiff then tried to amend Hyde's substitute to further loosen the refugee admissions process. Schiff lost on a 15–16 vote, with the support of Republicans Martin Hoke of Ohio, Chabot (R-OH), and Flanagan (R-IL). However, Smith carried the day with the help of Boucher (D-VA) and Bryant (D-TX). Hyde's amendment then was approved by voice vote (*Immigration in the National Interest Act* committee report, part 1 1996; *CQ Almanac* 1995). Schiff tried again another day with a similar amendment, but lost 14–16.

Hyde offered an amendment that Ed Bryant (R-TN) was planning to offer, except that Bryant had been delayed returning to Washington from his weekly home visit. Hyde, with his strong pro-life credentials, was well-suited to present the amendment to make flight from persecution in countries implementing coercive population-control policies a ground for refugee admission. Smith opposed the amendment, saying it would open the door to numerous Chinese claiming refugee status. Hyde negotiated a deal between Bryant (R-TN) and Smith, getting both to agree to an annual cap of 1,000 admissions on these grounds. Barney Frank (D-MA) and Jerrold Nadler (D-NY) each spoke in favor of the Hyde-Bryant Amendment, and it passed on a voice vote.

Asylum reform also attracted amendments, many from Bill McCollum (R-FL), the sponsor of the bill's new limitations on the asylum adjudication process. McCollum responded to criticisms from the Clinton administration and refugee advocacy groups and loosened some of the provisions. But McCollum also amended the bill to make the asylum process tighter. McCollum's amendment required that, within 30 days from arrival, an alien must file an asylum petition. Further, it provided that asylum seekers would be rejected if they could go to a safe third country. The Democrats protested, but McCollum did gain one ally from across the aisle—Charles Schumer (D-NY), who noted the abuses of the asylum system (*CQ Almanac* 1995). McCollum's amendment passed on a voice vote.

Smith lost on the diversity visa issue. His bill would have eliminated the program that Charles Schumer (D-NY) had written into the 1990 law. The Jordan Commission had recommended that the diversity program be eliminated. Schumer offered a compromise amendment to shrink but save the program. Bob Goodlatte (R-VA) offered an amendment to gut Schumer's amendment, but lost 14–15. The Schumer Amendment then was adopted 18–11, thus setting back Smith's reform somewhat (*CQ Almanac* 1995; *Immigration in the National Interest Act* committee report, part 1 1996).

The Employment Provisions

Other tinkering loosened the work, education, and labor certification requirements for obtaining long-term employment visas and eased certain requirements for using temporary foreign workers (or H-1B workers)—another GOP bow to business. Smith's bill set up a two-track system concerning H-1B visa usage. Companies that used few H-1B workers received regulatory relief, while companies with 10 percent or more of their workforce comprised of H-1Bs faced tougher regulation, including a requirement that firms that fired American workers and hired H-1B replacements would have to pay the foreign workers 110 percent of the U.S. workers' salaries. Goodlatte offered an amendment to raise the H-1B workforce percentage to between 15 and 20 percent, depending on the size of the firm. The committee adopted this amendment 22–11, with Democrats Pat Schroeder of Colorado and Zoe Lofgren of California joining the Republicans in support. Also,

Goodlatte won voice vote approval of an en bloc amendment tightening potential areas of abuse of the H-1B program (*CQWR* 10/21/95, 3211–3212).

Another area that faced attack involved employer verification. H.R. 2202 called for the creation of a telephone verification system that would be mandatory and eventually deployed nationwide. Every employer would have to place a call regarding every new hire, in order to avoid discrimination charges. And, at least initially, the phone contact would duplicate existing paperwork requirements involving I-9 records and identification documents. Steve Chabot (R-OH) sided with a coalition of interests that usually find themselves on opposite sides, including the National Federation of Independent Business and the American Civil Liberties Union, in seeking to strike the employment eligibility verification system altogether. He characterized the system as "1-800-Big-Brother" and said it represented excessive regulation of business, while Democrats repeated arguments made in previous years about how employer verification requirements would lead to discrimination. The vote completely cut across party lines. Seven Republicans and eight Democrats voted in favor of Chabot's amendment, which was defeated 15–17. Four Democrats opposed the Chabot Amendment (*CQ Almanac* 1995; *Immigration in the National Interest Act* committee report, part 1 1996).

Although Smith's proposal survived the attack, the telephone system was weakened later when the committee vocally approved a Hoke (R-OH) amendment to implement the system as pilot projects in five of the seven states with the highest illegal populations. Both the Jordan Commission and the Clinton administration had supported pilot programs to test electronic employment verification (*CQWR* 4/15/95). Further, the pilot projects would expire in 1999. An additional amendment by Bob Barr (R-GA) to exempt employers of three or fewer employees from having to participate in the phone system passed on a 16–13 vote. Smith supported the Barr Amendment, as did six Democrats; seven Republicans, including Hoke, opposed it (*CQ Almanac* 1995; *Immigration in the National Interest Act* committee report, part 1 1996).

A number of amendments on verification passed on voice votes. For instance, Goodlatte (R-VA) offered an amendment granting employers immunity against civil or criminal liability for relying on information obtained through the phone verification system, another that granted three days after hiring for employers to make the phone inquiry, and a third to require regulatory movement toward electronic storage of I-9 forms (*Immigration in the National Interest Act* committee report, part 1 1996). Goodlatte received the National Restaurant Association's support for his verification-related amendments. The association sent Judiciary Committee members a letter to that effect. It paid off.

Democrats also moved to amend the verification system. Becerra (D-CA) proposed an amendment, which failed 12–18 along party lines, to create an appeals process and provide compensation for those mistakenly fired in connection with the telephone system (*CQ Almanac* 1995; *Immigration in the National Interest Act* committee report, part 1 1996). However, a Frank (D-MA) amendment was adopted by voice vote clarifying that such unfairly fired workers could seek remedy through the Federal Tort Claims Act.

Analysis of House Committee Action

When the committee finished its consideration of amendments, Smith's bill had suffered some hits, but retained its core provisions. It still reformed legal immigration and contained the telephone employment verification system. It still streamlined the exclusion, asylum, and removal processes. And it still required legal immigrants to rely on those who sponsored them instead of turning to government relief programs as a first resort.

The committee voted 23–10 to pass H.R. 2202 on largely a party-line vote. No Republicans opposed the bill, and Democrats Boucher (D-VA), Bryant (D-TX), and Reed (D-RI) supported it on final passage. To understand the nature of the divisions among committee members on both amendments and committee passage of Smith's bill, we used multidimensional scaling to analyze the relative positions of the members. Multidimensional scaling is a statistical technique used to construct a plot or "map" in two or three dimensions showing the relationships among the members based on the way in which they voted (Kruskal and Wish 1978; Young 1987). Members who voted alike are in close proximity on the plot, those who were most dissimilar are naturally far apart. The resulting plot of the Judiciary Committee members appears in Figure 6.1. Dimension one reflects primarily partisan differences between the members. The Republicans are all clustered together on the far left-hand side of the horizontal (x) axis. The Democrats are more scattered, reflecting their political heterogeneity, but they tend to be distributed to the right on the horizontal axis. On the far right of the plot are committee leaders John Conyers (D-MI) and Howard Berman (D-CA). The members grouped together on this side of the plot found themselves actively campaigning to defeat the majority of Smith's proposed reforms. The Democrats were not totally disciplined, however. John Bryant (D-TX), Rick Boucher (D-VA), and Charles Schumer (D-NY) are notable for not following their party leadership on many votes.

Whereas the horizontal axis represents partisan differences, the vertical axis reflects attitudes on immigration restriction or expansion (see Figure 6.1). Here the Judiciary Committee's Republicans are more spread out along the restriction-expansion continuum than along the partisan one, although they are clearly more restrictionist in their orientation than expansionist. The Democratic members are more scattered, with Bryant (D-TX) and Boucher (D-VA) standing closest to the Republicans in favor of some restrictionist measures.

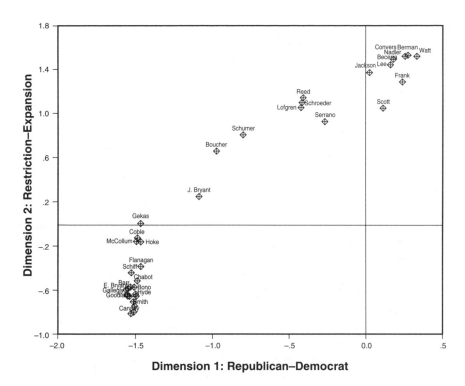

Figure 6.1   Two-Dimensional Placement of Judiciary Committee Members on Committee Immigration Votes, 104th Congress

The most consistent immigration expansionists are the Democrats plotted in the upper right corner: Howard Berman (D-CA), John Conyers (D-MI), Mel Watt (D-NC), Jerrold Nadler (D-NY), and Xavier Becerra (D-CA). These five members were the most opposed to Lamar Smith and the Republicans during the full committee markup.

The African American members—Watt (D-NC), Jackson-Lee (D-TX), Robert Scott (D-VA), and ranking Democrat John Conyers (D-MI)—voted as a bloc on nearly every amendment with Hispanic member Xavier Becerra (D-CA). Note that these members are similarly positioned in Figure 6.1. Their cooperation reflected the close working relationship of the Hispanic and Black Caucuses on the immigration issue. From the perspective of their constituencies, this cooperation was not easy to understand. There is evidence that immigrants have out-competed blacks for jobs in certain urban labor markets (Smith and Edmonston 1997, 5–24ff.; Levine 1995). The use of affirmative action programs by Hispanics and Asians has also undermined the position of blacks when these programs were originally designed to remedy the effects of segregation. The economic interests of Hispanics and the interests of blacks may seem at odds, but one would have never known this by looking at the Judiciary Committee's votes. Here black and Hispanic members cooperated independent of constituency interests to fight for the higher cause of civil rights for minorities.

The Aggies Get a Shot

The Judiciary Committee markup was not the end of committee action on H.R. 2202, however. Six additional House committees held some jurisdiction over the bill. The Agriculture Committee took the most active role of those other committees.

The Agriculture Committee amended H.R. 2202 to include a temporary guest-worker program. This, of course, would please growers who need field workers when their crops ripen. However, past guest-worker programs had been rife with abuse, particularly related to the use of undocumented laborers. Congressman Richard Pombo (R-CA) led the charge on behalf of agricultural interests, while Goodlatte (R-VA)—the same member who served on the Judiciary Committee—sought to revise the proposed program in terms of balancing the interests of those on the Judiciary Committee with those on the Agriculture Committee.

Pombo's amendment sought to create a new guest-worker program that made it easier for growers to hire help. Pombo's program would place a quarter of foreign workers' earnings in escrow, payable only after they had returned to their home country. Goodlatte (R-VA) gained approval for amendments to implement a more limited pilot program that would expire after three years instead of becoming permanent law, as well as imposing a cap of 250,000 agricultural guest workers the first year and decreasing by 25,000 each subsequent year. That action taken, the underlying Pombo Amendment was added to H.R. 2202.

The lines had been drawn. The next stop: the House floor.

Senate Subcommittee Action

Alan Simpson (R-WY) wasted no time upon reassuming the chair of the immigration subcommittee to produce a reform proposal. Before the end of the first month of the 104th Congress, Simpson had introduced S. 269, the Immigrant Control and Financial Responsibility Act. This legislation was a warmed-over version of a bill he had tried to advance in the previous Congress. He separately drafted legal-immigration reform legislation and stated his probable intention of joining the two bills later.

Simpson's first bill began as a fairly small legislative work, but grew by the time he acted upon it. In the end, S. 269 primarily addressed illegal immigration through many of the means proposed by the Jordan Commission and the Clinton administration, such as improved employment verification, tougher alien smuggling and document fraud penalties, and stronger border control. It also contained provisions to reduce welfare use by aliens. Simpson, too, included the border crossing user fee, which the Clinton administration favored.

Between the time of the introduction of S. 269 and subcommittee action, Simpson's staff was building an alliance behind the scenes. In May 1995, Simpson's subcommittee staff sat down with the staff of Senators Edward M. Kennedy (D-MA) and Dianne Feinstein (D-CA) in order to garner their support by inviting their input. At markup, Simpson would actually work from an amendment in the nature of a substitute bill, which constituted the staff's work. The Senate staffers essentially combined S. 269 as introduced with three other bills: S. 580, sponsored by Senator Feinstein, S. 754, the Clinton administration's bill introduced by Senator Kennedy, and S. 759, sponsored by Senator Bill Bradley (D-NJ). In the event more than one bill contained a similar provision, the staff members chose the toughest version.

In the past, Kennedy and Simpson had worked especially well together. They saw eye-to-eye on illegal immigration, worksite enforcement, verification of work eligibility, and employer sanctions. They both believed in strong border control. On legal immigration, they were both skeptical of employment-based immigration, believing that many employers do not really test the domestic labor market but instead have a foreign worker already in mind, often someone they have already hired. They parted ways on family-based immigration. Simpson, like Lamar Smith, believed that the system of chain migration was bad for the country. Simpson sympathized with the Jordan Commission's recommendations emphasizing the reunification of immediate family members and, in the early 1980s, had pressed for the elimination of the adult brothers and sisters preference. Kennedy held exactly the opposite view—that the last place preferences should be cut is in the family-based categories. In the end, this disagreement would lead Kennedy to vote against Simpson's proposals for legal reform. Despite bipartisan cooperation in crafting the bill, certain partisan splits would emerge as Senate action proceeded. In key instances, these would reflect the same differences seen in House committee action. Significantly, they would often relate to redistributive and cost questions, even though members might not always frame their positions in those terms.

In its first title, Simpson's legislation addressed immigration control. It would call for more Border Patrol agents and INS investigators, as well as establish a work and public assistance verification system, using a federal database. It also addressed alien smuggling and document fraud—in essentially the same manner as Smith's bill did. Simpson sought to establish new, streamlined deportation and exclusion procedures, with limitations on judicial review. His bill also called for pilot programs to combat multiple illegal entries into the country and to use closed military bases for detention. Interestingly, Simpson included provisions to count those who enter the United States under the attorney general's discretionary parole authority against the family category cap. Simpson's bill also dealt with asylum and refugees. It would restrict the asylum process and limit annual refugee admissions to 50,000.

The second title of S. 269 addressed the financial-responsibility issues related to immigration. The bill would limit many public benefits to aliens who were not permanent residents or under humanitarian categories. Illegal aliens faced restrictions from nearly all benefits, while legal immigrants would have to rely upon their sponsors for at least ten years. Following the recommendations of the Jordan Commission, Simpson's legislation also would strengthen public-charge deportation, as well as make the sponsor's responsibility legally enforceable.

Simpson included the border crossing fee in his bill. He also set forth pilot projects for improving border crossing by legally eligible crossers.

Unlike Lamar Smith in the House, Simpson didn't hold extensive hearings on immigration topics or on his bill. The full Senate Judiciary Committee convened hearings on S. 269 on March 14, 1995. That was the end of Senate committee action—aside from the behind-the-scenes staff work—until June 8, when the immigration subcommittee began marking up Simpson's legislation. In the subcommittee markup, Kennedy took on Simpson's limitation on legal immigrants' access to benefits. He offered an amendment to loosen the restrictions, which was rejected 2–4. Kennedy would have allowed immigrants access to public benefits once they became citizens or had worked for five years (*CQ Almanac* 1995).

Kennedy also took on the refugee cap of 50,000 through an amendment he and Charles Grassley (R-IA) offered. The subcommittee agreed with Kennedy and Grassley, who argued that the cap would be too rigid. The amendment passed on a 5–1 vote (*CQ Almanac* 1995).

The subcommittee reconvened on June 14 to complete its markup of the Simpson bill. At that meeting, Jon Kyl (R-AZ) proposed an amendment to eliminate the border crossing fee. Kyl held the same view as Texans Smith and Bryant in the House: The fee would harm border state economies with frequent legal border crossers. Simpson beat back Kyl's amendment, which suffered a 1–6 defeat, but offered his own substitute amendment. Simpson's amendment kept the fee, but called for a discounted rate for frequent crossers (*CQWR* 6/17/95, 1752).

The subcommittee finally voted to report the Immigrant Control and Financial Responsibility Act at the June 14 meeting. The four Republicans, along with California Democrat Dianne Feinstein, voted to report the bill. The remaining two Democrats, Kennedy and Paul Simon (D-IL), opposed S. 269.

Feinstein's support of the GOP legislation throughout the process is noteworthy. She had just run three bruising statewide campaigns, losing to Pete Wilson in the gubernatorial race in 1990, then winning Senate races in 1992 (Governor Wilson's unexpired term) and 1994. She was well aware of how upset Californians were about immigration. Feinstein considered Proposition 187 too extreme and had lost votes in the 1994 race because of her opposition. She remained politically ambitious, however, and wanted to use her seat on the Judiciary Committee to prove to Californians that she was as concerned about immigration as they were. In her committee statements, she took a very hard line against illegal immigration. "If you break the law, you're out," in the words of one Senate aide. On legal immigration, she seemed to equivocate, and her votes were hard to predict. Feinstein was sympathetic to the arguments by Simpson that the country needed a break from the large inflow of recent years. She was also a strong supporter of legally binding affidavits of support. But she was opposed to the elimination of welfare and other public services for immigrants. Pro-immigration interest groups were frustrated with Feinstein. Lisa Zachary, a lobbyist for the Council of Jewish Federations, described her as "fickle. She would commit one way, then vote another. It was hard to tell who she was in line with ideologically. She was a thorn in the wheel" (Zachary interview 5/1/97). "She's very smart politically," said a GOP committee staffer expressing a different viewpoint. "She put together a canvas of votes that would appeal to everyone in California."

Simpson's Legal Immigration Limits

The next Senate subcommittee action occurred late in 1995. Over the summer, Simpson's immigration staff fashioned a legal immigration reform bill. Simpson introduced it November 3 as S. 1394, the Immigration Reform Act, and the subcommittee marked up the legal immigration reform bill that month.

The bill's first section addressed immigrants, or those coming to the U.S. permanently. Simpson sought to restrict the number of visas granted to the parents of U.S. citizens, including making it a requirement that immigrating parents have health insurance coverage. This measure was directed at keeping elderly immigrants off expensive social insurance programs. Other provisions included labor certification changes, modifications within family-based and employment-based preference allocations, and regulation of judicial review of immigrant visa allocations or visa petition determinations.

Simpson also changed the numerical caps on family and employment immigration categories, as well as setting limits on immigrant numbers from any single foreign country. S. 1394 sought to lower legal immigration to 540,000 per year, 135,000 fewer arrivals than current law. The family category would retain the largest segment, with 450,000 admissions. The employment category would drop from 140,000 to 90,000 slots under Simpson's bill (*CQ Almanac* 1995; *CQWR* 12/2/95, 3657)

The second title dealt with nonimmigrants, or those who enter the country temporarily. The Immigration Reform Act changed the requirements for temporarily continuing to employ fashion models or specialty occupation nonimmigrants, including a fee imposed on employers. Simpson also wanted to tighten restrictions on student visas and make more information available electronically regarding aliens seeking or already here on nonimmigrant status, funded through a processing fee. S. 1394 halved the term of temporary work visas to three years (*CQ Almanac* 1995).

Business groups took issue with many of the provisions in Simpson's bill. Jennifer Eisen, now an Intel lobbyist, who was then working as a lobbyist at the American Immigration Lawyers Association (AILA), described her reaction upon studying the legislation for the first time:

> Simpson had introduced a bill that was far more onerous on business than anything the House had proposed. I did the section-by-section on it and stayed up until 4 A. M. Every section had radical changes. It was totally unrealistic from the perspective of the business community at every turn. At 3:45 A. M. I looked at my watch and said, I gotta get out of here. When I came in the next morning at 10 A. M., having slept in, my boss asked me, 'So what's wrong?' I said, 'This f—bill is terrible! I can't even lobby on this. There's no room to negotiate!' (Eisen interview 2/20/97)

Business found objectionable the fee on employers who hired permanent foreign employees. The fee, equal to the higher of $10,000 or 10 percent of the worker's first year's salary, would pay for education and training programs for American workers. Business objected to a fee for hiring temporary foreign employees, which hit the high-tech industries especially hard because of an alleged dearth of American engineers and computer programmers (*CQWR* 12/2/95, 3657–3658). Simpson weakened some of these provisions at the markup. He offered an amendment to address a number of their concerns, including deleting the fee for hiring temporary foreign workers. While this amendment didn't give business interests all they wanted, it won Simpson sufficient support from Republican members that the bill's passage seemed more likely.

The subcommittee also approved a Kyl amendment to require foreigners to secure child immunizations before becoming permanent residents. It adopted a Kennedy amendment to keep an employer from laying off an American worker and within six months hiring a foreign worker. Feinstein successfully offered an amendment to prohibit from attending public school those children who entered the U.S. with a visa to attend a private school (*CQ Almanac* 1995).

The Senate subcommittee November 29 voted 5–2 to approve the amended bill, with Kennedy (D-MA) and Simon (D-IL) opposing it. Simpson also led his panel to combine the legal and illegal immigration reform bills into S. 1394 as an omnibus proposal (*CQWR* 12/2/95, 3657–3658). This move would make the Senate legislation more like that of the House, as well as increase the chances of pushing through the controversial legal reforms on the back of the less controversial illegal immigration reforms.

The Special Interests Mobilize against Simpson

While Simpson had given ground on some of the immigrant employment provisions, business interests remained skeptical of Simpson's aims. They read him as an experienced but crafty legislator who had to be watched closely. In response, a new coalition of business interests formed to combat the bill. Jennifer Eisen was hired away from AILA by a consortium of high-tech companies, including Microsoft, Intel, Sun Microsystems, Motorola, and Texas Instruments, all of which relied upon foreign hires. Eisen's group took as its name, "American Business for Legal Immigration," or ABLI. Business had never been this involved in immigration legislation before because it had never felt so directly assaulted. Established groups such as the National Association of Manufacturers (NAM) and the U.S. Chamber of Commerce (COC) had always followed immigration legislation, but the business community had never spoken with one voice. Eisen brought businesses' representatives together in weekly meetings to cultivate an effective lobbying strategy.

Eisen and her coalition argued that there was a shortage of workers in high-tech fields. Computer software companies fight for technically skilled engineers and computer scientists on a worldwide basis, and among each other. Companies complained that restrictive immigration barriers would make them less competitive in the search for qualified workers. Even Microsoft founder and CEO Bill Gates, on tour promoting his book, joined the fight and was often heard saying, "This Simpson guy wants to tell us who we can hire and who we can't." The mandate of Eisen's coalition was to advance this message on Capitol Hill. The coalition drafted talking points, scheduled press conferences, briefed Capitol Hill staff, and brought in CEOs to lobby members directly. It was a determined, well-financed, and well-coordinated effort that would have considerable impact in 1996.

The immigrants' rights and ethnic minority groups had little in common with the business community. These groups were mostly fixated on the proposed elimination of the family preference categories for adult brothers and sisters. Employment immigration was, at most, a minor concern, and part of this coalition consisted of labor organizations, including the AFL-CIO, that had historically been opposed to immigration for employment purposes. Indeed, in previous rounds of reform, labor unions had opposed immigration, period (Reimers 1992; Tichenor 1997). But labor's constituency had changed since the 1960s. In control of the AFL-CIO was John Sweeney, a veteran of the service employees union whose rank and file increasingly consisted of Hispanics who were themselves immigrants. Sweeney and his associates at the top of the union ranks could see that the future of the union movement was increasingly with immigrants. Accordingly, Sweeney realigned national union leaders behind the effort to defeat the Simpson and Smith proposals.

With the Republicans in control of Congress, groups such as the National Council of La Raza, the Mexican American Legal Defense and Education Fund (MALDEF), the labor unions, and several organizations representing the Asian-Pacific community had little access to the levers of power on Capitol Hill. If they were going to have any influence at all, it would have to be in coalition with groups that did have access. The immigrants' rights and business coalitions were brought together largely by immigration specialists at the CATO Institute, a libertarian think tank based in Washington. CATO's key economic policy advisers, Stephen Moore and Stuart Anderson, had been communicating regularly with both sides. They were particularly valuable resources for the groups that had few GOP ties because they had strong relationships with leaders on Capitol Hill and could therefore provide information that these groups could obtain nowhere else. In the fall of 1995, Moore and Anderson began facilitating meetings between the business and immigrants' rights interests, and the product of this linkage became the much larger left-right coalition.

Senate Judiciary Committee Action

The Senate Judiciary Committee began consideration of a combined legal and illegal immigration bill on February 29, 1996. The unnumbered legislation, which became S. 1664, the Immigration Control and Financial Responsibility Act, was constituted by the provisions of S. 269 and S. 1394, Simpson's separate bills on legal and illegal immigration.

By this time, three months after the subcommittee markup, Jennifer Eisen's business coalition was at full strength. The coalition realized that many of the Democrats would vote against Simpson's legal immigration restrictions. In anticipation of the full committee's actions, the coalition focused on driving a wedge between the Republican members and Simpson. Key to this effort was their alliance with Spencer Abraham (R-MI). Abraham had just been elected to the Senate in 1994. He had strong business ties from his years as an adviser to Vice President Dan Quayle and shared Quayle's strong free-market views. As the grandson of Lebanese immigrants, a distinction he wore proudly, Abraham believed that immigrants strengthen the culture, bring in traditional values, maintain strong families, and teach their children the importance of education and entrepreneurship. Abraham thought Simpson held truly misguided views that reflected a cramped, zero-sum outlook on the economy and the culture.

Box 6.4

Spencer Abraham (R-MI) served on the Senate immigration subcommittee in 1995 and 1996, and served as its chair thereafter. Abraham successfully frustrated Alan Simpson's efforts to restrict legal immigration in 1995–1996. Courtesy of Spencer Abraham.

Spencer Abraham (R-MI)

In spite of his status as the most junior member of the Senate Judiciary Committee, Senator Spencer Abraham played a key role in the fight against efforts to place new restrictions on legal immigration in the 104th Congress (1995–1996). Abraham was largely successful in this battle, winning the praise of allies such as Senator Edward Kennedy (D-MA) and the respect of opponents such as Senator Alan Simpson (R-WY).

Abraham was born June 12, 1952, in Lansing, Michigan. Both of his grandfathers were immigrants, one finding a job in Pennsylvania coal mines, and the other opening a store in Detroit. Growing up in a working-class family of Lebanese ancestry, Abraham earned his bachelor's degree at Michigan State University in 1974. At Michigan State, he ran a congressional campaign for a GOP candidate who nearly defeated an incumbent Democrat, Representative Bob Carr.

Abraham attended Harvard Law School, where he earned his J.D. degree in 1979. At Harvard, he cofounded the Federalist Society and the law review, the *Harvard Journal of Law and Public Policy*.

Abraham taught at the Thomas M. Cooley Law School from 1981 until 1983. In 1982, he became the youngest state Republican party chairman, a position he held until 1990. Under Abraham's leadership, the GOP gained a majority in the Michigan State Senate in 1985 and helped John Engler win election as governor in 1990.

That same year, Abraham became deputy chief of staff for Vice President Dan Quayle. In 1991, Abraham was recruited to serve as cochairman of the National Republican Congressional Committee. Abraham has noted that Republicans picked up 10 congressional seats in 1992, despite the defeat of President George Bush at the top of the ticket.

Abraham returned to Michigan to become Of Counsel to a Detroit law firm. He ran for the U.S. Senate in 1994 against the same Democratic Representative Bob Carr. The *Almanac of American Politics* said of Abraham, "this is a small-business, not big-business, Republican," because the executives of the Big Three automobile makers supported Abraham's opponent.

In 1997, at the beginning of the 105th Congress, Senator Abraham assumed the leadership of the Senate's immigration subcommittee. He has begun to hold hearings emphasizing the contributions of immigrants to American society. Abraham also has the ear of Senate Majority Leader Trent Lott, serving as one of six Senators known as "The Council of Trent."

(Sources: *Almanac of American Politics*, 1996; Sen. Abraham's biography on Internet homepage; Freedberg 1997)

Having been appointed to the Judiciary Committee, he was in a position to challenge Simpson's leadership on immigration policy.

Another newly elected Republican who proved to be a key ally of pro-immigration interests was Mike DeWine (R-OH). He had previously served in the House on the Judiciary Committee where he had not always voted with the Republicans on immigration policy. He then served as lieutenant governor of Ohio from 1990 to 1994. Of Irish Catholic extraction, DeWine was both devout and one of the strongest pro-life members in the Senate. He was proud to point out that his grandfather had immigrated to the United States during the Irish potato famine. He took a law-and-order stand against illegal immigration, but greeted Simpson's legal immigration cuts with an open hostility that no other member could match. Restrictions on legal immigration alienated some pro-life members because part of the coalition favoring restrictions had consisted of population-control groups such as Zero Population Growth (ZPG) and Negative Population Growth (NPG) that had long advocated controversial family planning programs both in the United States and abroad. As a staffer for one pro-life senator put it, "The attitude of the population-control groups is that if these other countries didn't have so many kids, we wouldn't have so much immigration." During the winter of 1996, DeWine and Abraham began meeting regularly with the coalition of business and immigrants' rights groups, which had proposed splitting the Simpson bill into two separate vehicles—legal and illegal.

Splitting the Bill

The goal of the "split-the-bill" strategy was to take advantage of the controversy surrounding legal immigration to kill both House and Senate legal reform proposals altogether. On February 26, 1996, just a few days before the scheduled markup, Eisen and the business coalition had brought in a hundred high-tech business executives to lobby the Senate. They began the day with a breakfast with Senator Abraham and then fanned out to meet personally with individual senators. At the end of the day, at 5 P.M., they met with Simpson in a large room in the Russell Building. Simpson strode in and asked them what they wanted. A senior vice president at Texas Instruments, a large man with a booming voice and a pronounced Texas accent, stood up and said, "Every single thing in your bill hurts my company. We are trying to survive in the semiconductor market. We are currently ahead of Japan, but who knows how long that will last." Others chimed in. Finally Simpson said, "If I take all employment-based immigration provisions out of my bill, will you support it then?" There was a deafening silence. Everyone, especially the lobbyists, was speechless. They couldn't say yes, but how could they say no? The government relations officer from the National Association of Manufacturers (NAM) finally spoke up and said that the lobbyists would have to go

Box 6.5

Mike DeWine (R-OH) served on the House Judiciary Committee in the late 1980s and on the Senate Judiciary Committee in 1995–1996, where he joined with Spencer Abraham in opposing Alan Simpson's efforts to restrict legal immigration. Courtesy of Mike DeWine.

Mike DeWine (R-OH)

Senator Mike DeWine served on the House Judiciary Committee at the time both the 1986 Immigration Reform and Control Act and the 1990 Immigration Act passed, and on the Senate Judiciary Committee during the 104th Congress. As a practicing Catholic of Irish descent and a self-described traditionalist, DeWine fiercely opposed Senator Alan Simpson's reductions in family-based immigration. He played a pivotal role, with Senator Spencer Abraham, in the successful effort to split the 1996 bill's legal immigration reforms from the legislative package. Senator Simpson once described DeWine as a "dog on your pants who won't let go."

DeWine was born January 5, 1947, in Springfield, Ohio. He earned his bachelor's of science degree at Ohio's Miami University in 1969 and his law degree at the Ohio Northern University in 1972.

From 1973 through 1975, DeWine served as assistant prosecutor in Greene County, Ohio. In 1976, he ran against his boss and won the elected office of Greene County prosecuting attorney. He served in that position until 1980, when he was elected to the Ohio Senate. There he sponsored Ohio's mandatory sentencing and drunk driving laws.

After only two years, DeWine pursued a seat in Congress. He made a strong election showing, then won easy successive reelections.

In the House, DeWine held seats not only on the Judiciary Committee, but also on the Foreign Affairs and the Iran Contra special committees. He established a record as a conservative. His ardent pro-life position on the abortion issue derived from his devout Roman Catholicism. His tough-on-crime and pro-business, antiregulatory views were reflected in his low ratings from the Americans for Democratic Action (10 in 1989, 17 in 1990) and high ratings from the American Conservative Union (96 in 1989, 83 in 1990).

DeWine left the House after 1990 to return to Ohio and become its lieutenant governor. He challenged incumbent Senator John Glenn in 1992, but lost the election. He tried again for the Senate in 1994, beating the son-in-law of Senator Howard Metzenbaum, who was retiring. DeWine's opponent, plaintiffs' lawyer Joel Hyatt, garnered only 39 percent of the vote on Election Day 1994, a poor showing in a top-priority race of the national Democratic party.

Besides the Senate Judiciary Committee, DeWine serves on the Labor and Human Resources Committee and the Select Intelligence Committee.

(Sources: *Biographical Directory of the U.S. Congress 1774–1989*; *Politics in America*, 1996)

back to their full membership. To which Simpson replied, "That's cocka-mamie! I want to know right now what you think, right now, on the spot!" Some were supportive, others were noncommittal. The meeting broke up with no commitment given. Eisen and the business lobbyists were still intent on killing all legal reform efforts. By this time, they had become allied with the religious, minority and immigrants' rights groups that had also been working to defeat the legislation. They were working as part of the team, and legal reform had to die for the greater good.

In stripping out the business provisions, Simpson had secretly hoped to split the left-right coalition. He figured that business would have no objection to the cuts in family-based immigration and that once business had left the coalition, it would fall apart entirely. But Simpson had moved too late. Had he offered the deal to strip out the business provisions a month before, the coalition would have disintegrated. But by the time he finally agreed to the business demands, the coalition had crystallized around the goal of defeating the entire package of legal reforms.

Committee action three days later got off to a sluggish and controversial start. In his opening statement, DeWine fiercely attacked Simpson's approach to legal immigration, saying that none of it made any sense. To DeWine, Simpson's proposals for legal immigration were "death by a thousand cuts," as one of his aides put it. Individually, the cuts did not amount to very much, but collectively, they added up to major reductions. Simpson took DeWine's attacks quite personally, and relations between the two were poisoned throughout the rest of the legislative session. Ranking Democrat Kennedy argued that legal and illegal immigration should be addressed separately, and Spencer Abraham (R-MI) led the charge for splitting the bill (*CQWR* 3/2/96). Abraham relented temporarily only after the committee chair, Orrin Hatch (R-UT), implored him to give Simpson's bill a fair hearing.

Over nearly a month's time, the Judiciary Committee met six times to address the Simpson bill. The committee considered 73 amendments, adopting 39 by unanimous consent, four by voice vote, and 20 by roll-call vote. Simpson gave ground on the business visa front in order to reduce business lobby opposition (*CQWR* 3/9/96). While this tactic somewhat diminished the business opposition, it also angered Kennedy and other Democrats, who said Simpson was undermining the position of American workers. Simpson also agreed to convert the employment verification system into a more limited pilot program.

Similar to the debate months before in the House Judiciary Committee, the Senate committee battled over whether to eliminate the verification proposal altogether. Abraham offered such an amendment, which included new penalties against visa overstayers. Simon (D-IL) asked for a division of the amendment. The new penalties were adopted on voice vote, while the verification system survived on a 9–9 vote, with six Republicans and three Democrats voting to strike, and four Republicans and five Democrats voting to retain the system (*Immigration Control and Financial Responsibility Act* committee report 1996).

A substantial setback for Simpson occurred on March 14 when the Senate committee voted 12–6 to "split-the-bill," or separate the legal immigration reform provisions from the illegal reforms. By this time, Simpson was exceedingly angry at Abraham and DeWine for their conspiracy with the pro-immigration interest groups to defeat the legal reforms. "Simpson finally realized that he was going to lose and that Senator Abraham was not just a freshman with his head up his ass but had brought along DeWine and other senators," said Michael Hill, a lobbyist for the U.S. Catholic Bishops Conference (Hill interview 2/21/97). Simpson had treated both junior senators dismissively. "His attitude was sort of like who the f—are you? Go back to your sandbox," said one lobbyist who had been present at the markup. Simpson even went so far as to invoke a "point of personal privilege" on the basis of his seniority, to keep Abraham from offering the split-the-bill amendment. In his frustration, Simpson attacked Chairman Orrin Hatch (R-UT) for structuring the hearing so that Abraham could introduce his amendment, reeling to glare at Hatch at one juncture, pointing to Hatch's staff and demanding of the chairman, "Who is the senator here? You? Or them?!" Even Hatch voted for Abraham's motion. DeWine and Abraham had really gotten under Simpson's skin, but particularly DeWine. "Simpson respected Abraham because at least Abraham did his homework," said one committee aide. "Abraham had worked his tail off, lobbying and buttonholing Senators. Even if Simpson disagreed with him on the merits, he respected him. But there was something about DeWine 's attitude that made him different." "The Senator may have overstated his case against the Simpson bill," one of DeWine's aides admitted in retrospect. DeWine had called several of Simpson's proposals "stupid ideas." DeWine's style was more blunt and direct than Abraham's. "You do not leave a meeting with Mike DeWine unclear on anything," said a DeWine aide. As for Abraham, he had played Simpson's Brutus. This vote stimulated considerable momentum for those opposed to reforming legal immigration. The pro-immigration forces were elated.

The Amendments Keep on Coming

The committee also adopted other amendments favorable to business interests. Hatch (R-UT) and Kyl (R-AZ) succeeded in this effort, with Hatch weakening the penalties for hiring undocumented workers. The Hatch Amendment passed 10–8 on a largely party-line vote; two Democrats joined eight Republicans in favor of the amendment, while two Republicans (including Simpson) sided with six Democrats in opposition. Kyl won voice vote approval of two amendments, one striking provisions that would have allowed INS to retain most of the employer sanctions funds, the other limiting the liability of employers who relied in good faith on information from the employee verification system. Kyl argued that the former situation created too great an incentive for overzealous enforcement and that the money should instead go into the U.S. Treasury. The latter largely matched the efforts of Goodlatte (R-VA) in the House Judiciary Committee (*Immigration Control and Financial Responsibility Act* committee report 1996; *CQWR* 3/16/96, 697–701).

The Senate committee adopted a number of law enforcement amendments, including several by Abraham. And the committee adopted, 9–7, a Simpson amendment to set federal standards for birth certificates in order that they could no longer be as easily counterfeited.

On March 21, almost a month after starting, the Senate Judiciary Committee completed its markup of the immigration legislation. But not before more amendments were considered, and a few adopted. Most of the attention focused on the few provisions that remained regarding legal immigrants. The bill would apply sponsorship requirements, with respect to assessing an immigrant's income for public benefits eligibility, to all means-tested programs. The requirement would continue for five years for immigrants already in the country; it would last ten years for immigrants coming after the bill became law. Predictably, these redistributive provisions were a major source of interparty strife. Republicans had been pushing to exclude legal residents from welfare benefits as a matter of cost savings. Immigrant use of public benefits was seen as part of what was fueling runaway entitlement spending. Until the entitlement system was truly overhauled, exclusion of immigrants from its use was seen as a stopgap measure.

Senator Kennedy led the effort to liberalize the restrictions on welfare use. He largely lost. One Kennedy amendment would have granted so many exceptions to the income eligibility requirement as to render it useless. The committee rejected the amendment 7–8, with Arlen Specter (R-PA) and DeWine (R-OH) joining five Democrats, and Abraham (R-MI) opposing it along with Simpson.

Kennedy sought to exempt educational assistance—Pell grants and student aid—from sponsorship income requirements. This amendment lost 7–9. Again, Specter and DeWine joined five Democrats, but Dianne Feinstein (D-CA) this time sided with eight Republicans. Kennedy did win on another amendment, which expanded benefits for illegal aliens. Arguing that pregnant women here illegally were carrying unborn children who would be U.S. citizens, Kennedy persuaded a majority to make federal prenatal assistance available to such women who had lived in America at least three years. This amendment passed 8–7, with the support of Republicans Hatch, Specter, and DeWine. No Democrats opposed it.

Feinstein (D-CA) won support for an amendment to limit the term of sponsor income provisions. Adopted 11–5, Feinstein's amendment cut off the

Box 6.6

Dianne Feinstein (D-CA) served on the Senate immigration subcommittee in 1995–1996, where she joined with Alan Simpson and other Republicans to restrict legal immigration levels. Feinstein is shown here with Border Patrol officers near San Diego. Courtesy of Dianne Feinstein.

Dianne Feinstein (D-CA)

California Senator Dianne Feinstein was the only Democrat to sign the conference report on the 1996 immigration bill. As a Judiciary Committee member, and member of the immigration subcommittee, she frequently sided with Alan Simpson and the Republicans against her Democratic colleagues on matters relating to illegal immigration. On legal immigration, she held views more consonant with her Democratic colleagues, although she sponsored an unsuccessful floor amendment to reduce legal immigration.

Feinstein was born June 22, 1933, in San Francisco. She earned her bachelor's degree at Stanford in 1955.

Feinstein served on the San Francisco Board of Supervisors from 1970 until 1978. She was president of the board for three terms. In 1978, she was elected as San Francisco's mayor, a position she held until 1988. She was the first woman to hold that office. During her mayoral tenure, Feinstein served on the Executive Committee of the U.S. Conference of Mayors from 1983 till 1988.

Feinstein won the Democratic nomination for the 1990 California gubernatorial race. She lost that election to U.S. Senator Pete Wilson. However, in 1992, Feinstein pursued Wilson's unexpired Senate term. He had resigned from the Senate upon being elected governor. Feinstein won that race.

In 1994, Feinstein ran for a full Senate term and won reelection in spite of her opposition to California's popular Proposition 187. She considered running again for the California governorship in 1998.

(Sources: *Congressional Yellow Book*, 1996; Sen. Feinstein's biography on Internet homepage)

ten-year deeming requirements once the immigrant became a U.S. citizen. Five Republicans, including Hatch and Abraham, voted in favor of the amendment. The committee dropped the border crossing fee, which Jon Kyl (R-AZ) had vigorously opposed. Another amendment, passed on a 12–5 vote, struck language that would permit INS agents to conduct warrantless searches for undocumented workers in open farm fields.

Among other amendments, three more warrant mention. Kyl (R-AZ) won unanimous consent for a requirement that the federal government reimburse hospitals for treatment of illegal residents. He also won reimbursement of state and local government expenses for emergency ambulance service that was rendered to illegal aliens who were injured while illicitly crossing the border. A Grassley amendment allowed federal acceptance of local law enforcement assistance in carrying out immigration laws. A Brown amendment set a one-year time limit for filing an asylum application.

The committee approved the bill 13–4 on the same day H.R. 2202 passed the House. Democrats Heflin (D-AL), Kohl (D-WI), and Feinstein (D-CA) joined all of the Judiciary Republicans in favor of the legislation. Simpson's bill had undergone major surgery, if not complete dismemberment, with the most damaging cut being the elimination of restrictions on legal immigration.

A Last Look for Legal Reforms

A week after the House passed H.R. 2202 without most of the legal immigration reform provisions, the Senate Judiciary Committee met to sound the reprise. On March 28, the committee marked up and approved 13–4 a lightweight bill that addressed legal immigration policies. It was far less than Simpson had hoped for. Still, he held out hopes of achieving serious cuts in legal immigration once the legislation reached the Senate floor.

The legal reform legislation now being considered had been severed from the illegal immigration bill two weeks before. Kennedy (D-MA) and Abraham (R-MI) together offered an amendment to substitute a modestly restructured family reunification system for Simpson's cuts. Rather than reduce family-based visas from 480,000 annually to 300,000 and reformulate preferences to favor nuclear family members, Kennedy-Abraham proposed an *increase* in family visas, with 75,000 designated for those awaiting entry but caught in the lengthy backlogs. The amendment kept the diversity visa program Simpson had slated for elimination at half its current size. It also would change the rules in favor of the closest relatives; however, Kennedy and Abraham kept the extended family categories that promoted chain migration.

In turning to Abraham, Kennedy had given up on Simpson. Their close working relationship was over. In Senator Kennedy's office is a list of the more than 300 Senators with whom he has served in his long career. Kennedy arrived in the Senate in 1963, when Simpson's father was there. Simpson had declared his intention to retire, and Kennedy could now sense the changing of the guard. Abraham had informally taken control of immigration policy on the GOP side.

Simpson opposed the Kennedy-Abraham Amendment because it did nothing to address chain migration. Jon Kyl (R-AZ) added that the proposal did not take into account the size of the chain just down the pike. Many of the 1986 illegals who were amnestied, a million strong, will become naturalized citizens and petition for their relatives, further glutting the system, Kyl argued. But the Kennedy-Abraham Amendment was adopted 11–4 (*CQWR* 3/30/96, 882–884).

The amendment to remove limits on employment visas came from Simpson himself—not because Simpson had changed his mind, but because he was a man of his word. He had promised the CEOs that he would remove all employment-related provisions, and he intended to. Originally, the bill contained language to reduce the number of permanent employment-related visas from 140,000 to the amount actually used, 90,000. But certain business interests attacked the reductions as placing U.S. business and industry at a dire disadvantage. They claimed the Simpson cap would keep them from being able to bring in the world's best and brightest, on both permanent and temporary bases, and that the country would lose its competitiveness worldwide, especially in computer and high-tech industries. Simpson called the rhetoric "hype and hysteria." Still, he offered an amendment to eliminate all business-related restrictions, and it was adopted on an 11–4 vote (*CQWR* 3/30/96, 882–884).

Long skeptical of business-oriented immigration, Kennedy responded by attempting to reduce employment-based visas. He offered an amendment to cap that category of permanent visas at 100,000. But that amendment narrowly lost 7–9. Another Kennedy amendment to eliminate visas for unskilled workers passed 15–0.

The committee also addressed the H-1B temporary skilled worker program. This program was reportedly abused by unscrupulous employers who replaced American employees with foreigners. Abraham (R-MI) and Specter (R-PA) sought to crack down on this employment practice. They proposed an amendment to increase penalties for this abuse. However, Kyl offered a second-degree amendment to cut out a requirement that H-1B workers who are hired to replace American workers be paid 110 percent of the Americans' salary. The House bill had contained a similar requirement. But the Kyl Amendment passed 8–6, then the amended Abraham-Specter Amendment was adopted 11–5. The modest legal immigration bill advanced from committee to the full Senate. Simpson hoped to rejoin the legal and illegal immigration reform bills at the next stage, on the Senate floor.

Gearing Up for Floor Action in the House

Between the House Judiciary Committee's completed action on H.R. 2202 and floor consideration in the spring, House leadership had been wavering on the immigration issue. Jennifer Eisen's business coalition had also been lobbying House members and party leaders, and its efforts were beginning to pay off there as they had in the Senate. On November 2, 1995, 35 House members allied with Lamar Smith wrote Speaker Gingrich to express concern over leadership's increasing openness to strip the legal immigration reform provisions from the bill. The letter concluded, "…we simply cannot leave the job half done, and strongly urge the House Leadership to retain legal immigration reforms as the House considers H.R. 2202."

The next month, the House Republican Policy Committee adopted policy statements on both legal and illegal immigration. This move helped shore up support for keeping the legal immigration reforms in the House bill as it approached the floor. The policy statement on legal immigration, adopted December 19, 1995, included the following paragraph:

> House Republicans will reform our immigration laws to emphasize the education, skills, and accomplishments of potential immigrants, and to put the focus in family immigration where it belongs—on the nuclear family. *And we will thereby ensure swifter and fairer treatment for legal immigrants and their families* [Italics in original].

Lamar Smith could have written the policy statements, they were that reform-minded. And of course it didn't hurt that a Californian—Christopher Cox—chaired the Policy Committee.

As momentum built for bringing the immigration bill to the House floor, Smith could sense that the opposing side was gaining ground in the Senate. He pulled out all stops to build support for his bill. His staff coordinated a strategy to build a coalition of supportive House staffers. He tried to appear personally before every major ad hoc coalition group in Congress, and even recruited Jordan Commission members to help pitch the bill to groups of members, including the large class of House freshmen. Smith's office sent countless "Dear Colleague" letters in his effort. Many of those letters contained reprints of letters of support from outside groups or reprints of favorable news articles, columns, and editorials.

One "Dear Colleague" letter, cosigned by Smith and Cox, reprinted an endorsement of H.R. 2202 from the Hispanic Business Roundtable. Another, cosigned by Smith and Goodlatte, contained a letter from Ross Perot's populist United We Stand America group. Yet another letter reprinted statements from business groups supporting the employment-based immigration provisions of the bill. This "Dear Colleague" included a statement from the National Association of Manufacturers, which had earlier opposed sections of the bill. It also had statements from the American Council on International Personnel, the Information Technology Association of America, and the U.S. Business and Industrial Council. These tireless efforts helped sustain the level of support for Smith's legislation among House members. In spite of these letters, though, Smith was gradually losing ground. The advocacy groups on Smith's side were not well organized. The only active and credible group was the Federation for American Immigration Reform (FAIR). Other groups, such as Zero Population Growth (ZPG), were considered on the fringe. Some even doubted that FAIR was in the mainstream. Pro-immigration editors and reporters were fond of calling FAIR's founder, Dr. John Tanton, a whacko, racist xenophobe. Some of the restrictionist groups consisted mainly of a few angry people with little grassroots support. They did not know politics inside the Beltway.

Smith's opposition, coordinated largely by the American Immigration Lawyers Association (AILA), had not been standing still. While they had successfully derailed Simpson's legal reform effort in the Senate, they had also been assembling a coalition of Democratic and Republican supporters in the House. Following Senator Abraham's success at splitting the bill in the Judiciary Committee, efforts now turned to splitting the bill in the House. Those sympathetic with Abraham in the House included freshman Republicans Dick Chrysler (R-MI), Sam Brownback (R-KS), and Steve Chabot (R-OH). Getting these newcomers to cooperate with the legions of Democrats who were against legal reform was no easy task. The 104th Congress had been very polarized along party lines during the first 100 days and after. The veteran Democrats despised these freshman Republicans because they were the ones who had put them in the minority for the first time in 40 years. The freshman Republicans were contemptuous of the old Democrats because they were the source of everything that was wrong with society. Late in January of 1996, the pro-immigrant coalition assembled a staff meeting that brought the GOP freshmen and Democrats together for the first time. There was tension in the room. For the first half hour, Michael Hill, a lobbyist for the U.S. Catholic Conference, spoke about the voting trends and habits of different members on immigration policy. Hill compiled detailed voting histories on each member extending back several congresses. Other groups often turned to him for his analyses and advice. He would pause occasionally, inviting input from the staff members, but met only silence. Finally, a GOP staffer broke the silence, then a Democratic staffer responded. At the end of the meeting, every Republican staff member had joined with a Democratic staff member to pore over the list of members to see who might be supportive of an amendment to separate legal from illegal immigration. The group then sent out its own "Dear Colleague" letter, each one signed by a liberal Democrat and a freshman Republican.

Floor Action in the House

H.R. 2202 came up on the floor of the House on March 19, 1995. The rule provided for two hours of general debate followed by the consideration of 32 of the 130 amendments that had been submitted for review. The Rules Committee stripped out the Agriculture Committee's guest-worker provision, but permitted it to be offered as a floor amendment. Rules also prohibited several amendments relating to reimbursement of states for the costs of immigration. More significantly, the Rules Committee allowed consideration of an amendment to strike the legal immigration component from Smith's bill. "Naturally I preferred that it not be offered," Smith recalled. "But we had to have some amendments, we needed some openness and it was inevitable that we would have to deal with this. It was no surprise. We would have had to contend with this issue sooner or later" (Smith interview 2/26/97). Hispanic Democrat Xavier Becerra (D-CA) took up Edward Roybal's role of complaining about the restrictiveness of the rule (see Chapters 4 and 5). Few others spoke in opposition to it, however, and the rule passed on a 233–152 vote.

Smith led the floor consideration, controlling the time for the Republicans. The Democratic floor leader was John Conyers (D-MI), the ranking Democrat on the Judiciary Committee. Californians were particularly active in the debate. For those whose constituents had been enthusiastic supporters of Proposition 187, this day was long in coming. Finally they had their chance to go on record in support of cracking down on illegal immigrants and limiting legal immigration. Smith led off the consideration of amendments with an en bloc amendment of his own that, among other things, made participation in the employment verification pilot program voluntary. Becerra objected to the en bloc procedure, charging that the members had not had ample time to consider the various issues singly. No one else objected, however, and the amendments were agreed to on a voice vote.

By a narrow margin, the House rejected a McCollum amendment calling for a more secure, tamper-resistant Social Security card. The Floridian said a Social Security card that was more difficult to counterfeit was necessary to make a work-eligibility verification system work. McCollum (R-FL) acknowledged that the main reason for unauthorized entry was the search for jobs. The only way to eliminate that magnet was to eliminate document fraud. Social Security cards were too easily counterfeited. Opponents repeated their familiar argument that this would lead to a national identification card and infringe upon individual liberty. McCollum's amendment went down on a 191–221 vote.

The next floor amendment was a modified version of language that had been considered in the Judiciary Committee. Ed Bryant (R-TN) again offered his amendment linking hospital reimbursement for the costs of giving illegal immigrants emergency treatment to hospitals' providing immigration authorities with identifying information about the aliens. Bryant had sought to address a key concern that opponents had voiced in the committee markup. Bryant's new proposal created an exception from the proposed requirement if the patient was under 18 years old. He again appealed to the civic duty of medical facilities seeking federal reimbursement with taxpayers' dollars, saying they owed a minimal duty to the American public in exchange for public funds.

Opponents warned that illegal residents who needed emergency medical treatment would not seek it out if Bryant's amendment prevailed. The American Hospital Association whipped members against the Bryant Amendment, claiming it would turn hospitals into law enforcement agents and impose additional administrative burdens. Becerra (D-CA) and John Bryant (D-TX) led the opposition on the House floor, while the hospital trade group faxed its opposition to House members' offices. The Bryant Amendment was defeated 170–250.

The Gallegly Amendment

One of the most controversial amendments was offered by Elton Gallegly (R-CA), permitting states to deny illegal aliens admittance to public schools. Such a provision would overturn the Supreme Court's 1982 decision in *Plyler v. Doe*, which required states to educate all students regardless of their legal status. Gallegly noted that such a mandate cost California alone more than $2 billion per year. The amendment was modeled after California's Proposition 187. At Smith's request, Gallegly had reserved this amendment for the floor rather than offer it in the Judiciary Committee markup. Smith was very concerned that the controversy surrounding this issue would drag the bill under.

John Bryant (D-TX) and a number of other members stridently opposed Gallegly's amendment. "After I got over my initial reaction, I decided to be civil and not go out and commit any crimes of violence," replied Gary Ackerman (D-NY), when asked for his reaction to Gallegly's proposal (Ackerman interview 4/8/97). "I thought this was one of the most dangerous, damaging pieces of legislation we've considered in my 11 years here," responded Floyd Flake (D-NY) (Flake interview 4/17/97). "I thought this was a hideous idea," said Patsy Mink (D-HI) with a tone of disgust. "The denial of educational opportunity, to make schools become policemen. Prove your citizenship or we won't educate your children. Then the children float outside the system and make more problems for the state and the country" (Mink interview 5/23/97). And from San Jose area Congresswoman Zoe Lofgren (D-CA), a Judiciary Committee member, "Whatever you think about the behavior of adults, it is immoral to punish the minor children for the sins of their parents" (Lofgren interview 2/27/97). "It is stupid to say that we as a country are

Box 6.7

Elton Gallegly (R-CA) served on the House immigration subcommittee in the 1990s. He fought especially hard for tougher measures against illegal immigration, including efforts to deny free public education to the children of illegal immigrants. Courtesy of Elton Gallegly.

Elton Gallegly (R-CA)

Representative Elton Gallegly played an important role in the debate over the 1996 immigration legislation, serving on the House immigration subcommittee and chairing Speaker Gingrich's congressional immigration task force in the 104th Congress. Gallegly took hard-line positions against illegal immigration and generally supported Lamar Smith's efforts to place new restrictions on legal immigration. In 1996, he sponsored the contentious Gallegly Amendment to allow states to deny illegal aliens public education.

Gallegly was born March 7, 1944, in Huntington Park, California. Reared in a working-class Los Angeles suburb, he attended Los Angeles State College his freshman year 1962–63, then dropped out and entered the real estate field.

He won a seat on the Simi Valley City Council in 1979, then was elected mayor in 1980, a position he held until 1986. He was chairman of the Ventura County Association of Governments in 1983.

In 1986, Gallegly was elected to Congress. His record showed him to be generally conservative, reflecting his pro-Reagan district.

Gallegly has been a strong proponent of illegal immigration reform. He often carries a fraudulent "green card" to demonstrate how easy the Immigration and Naturalization Service document is to forge and how easy it is for illegal aliens to obtain false identification.

(Sources: *Almanac of American Politics*, various years; *Biographical Directory of the U.S. Congress 1774–1989*)

helped if kids aren't schooled," added Bob Filner (D-CA) from San Diego (Filner interview 2/27/97).

Others, however, were equally emotional in their support for Gallegly. "I was supportive of that," recalled Bob Barr (R-GA) with some intensity. "People in this country illegally have no right to anything!" (Barr interview 4/8/97). "Why should we be deciding who gets a public education?" asked Bill McCollum (R-FL). "States should have the right to decide that" (McCollum interview 5/16/97). Lamar Smith agreed with McCollum :

> All this does is give governors an option. I support this. Since states pay the bill for education, let them decide who they will educate.
>
> …George W. Bush said he wouldn't exercise this option, and I agreed with that. Those families should not be in the country in the first place. They should be deported. So it's moot because they shouldn't be here to begin with. I do believe that if they're here, they should be educated, and Governor Bush and I agreed on that point, too. But we also agreed that states should be given the option. (Smith interview 2/26/97)

"I voted yes," recalled Bob Ehrlich (R-MD), who added:

> This is tough and harsh, but I go back to the clear line I draw between legal and illegal immigrants. These people have done something against the law. Illegals bring a unique set of problems to Congress, the national debate, and to American society. It is a strong position to take, but I'm sorry, this is our line in the sand. We want to take away your motivation to come to this country pregnant and have your baby. (Ehrlich interview 4/29/97)

As these comments suggest, amendment opponents often couched their arguments in terms of children, who were present because of their parents' unlawful choices. They also argued that school attendance kept these young people off the streets. "Gallegly assumed that if their kids were kicked out of school, illegal immigrants would leave the country. But that's not going to happen. The kids will just cause trouble," said one California Democrat.

Proponents of the amendment argued in terms of states' rights and the financial burden placed on taxpayers: "You hear about this certain [illegal immigrant] child or this certain [illegal immigrant] mother who are [sic] having a hard time. But there are taxpayers, too, who are having a hard time. Should they be expected to support the illegals who are struggling when they are struggling, too?" asked Korean-American Congressman Jay Kim (R-CA) (Kim interview 2/27/97). Gallegly's supporters cited the inherent unfairness to legal residents who played by the rules to enter the country. Others argued that forcing states to provide education to illegal residents amounted to an unfunded mandate on states and localities. Education traditionally falls under state, not federal, jurisdiction. Even House Speaker Newt Gingrich (R-GA) engaged in the debate, speaking in favor of the amendment. Surprisingly, the proposal was adopted by a comfortable margin of 257–163.

Employment Verification

Smith's preemptive move to make electronic employment verification voluntary paid off. Steve Chabot (R-OH), who fought the program in the Judiciary Committee, again struck at the pilot program measures. Chabot offered an amendment March 20 to eliminate even the now-voluntary program, warning that it paved the way for national implementation and mandatory employer participation. He joined forces with the Judiciary Committee's ranking Democrat, John Conyers (D-MI). Chabot cited an array of program opponents in his remarks. These included the *Wall Street Journal*, former Senator Malcolm Wallop (R-WY), the Small Business Survival Committee, the U.S. Catholic Conference, the CATO Institute, the ACLU, the Christian Coalition, and the American Bar Association. He raised the specter of a coming national identification card.

Smith argued strenuously that "[a] vote for this amendment is a vote against protecting jobs for American citizens" (*CR* 3/20/96, H2497). He noted the job magnet and the holes in the present verification process, thanks to fake documentation and antidiscrimination provisions tying the hands of employers from questioning those documents' validity. Thus, only a central record to match names and Social Security numbers would provide an adequate remedy. Smith also cited groups behind his voluntary pilot project approach, including the National Federation of Independent Business, the National Rifle Association, the Traditional Values Coalition, and the Jordan Commission. When the vote was called, Smith prevailed. Chabot's amendment failed, 159–260.

Gallegly followed immediately with an amendment to make computerized employment verification mandatory rather than voluntary. But the House was unwilling to move in that direction, either. It rejected Gallegly's amendment 86–331.

The Blow to Legal Restrictions

The consideration of the amendment to strike provisions limiting legal immigration came up late on the second day of debate. The target of this amendment was the elimination of the provisions that reduced family visas from 480,000 a year to 330,000 and gave preference to immediate relatives, ending visas for siblings and adult children. Sam Brownback (R-KS) and Dick Chrysler (R-MI) offered the amendment to remove these provisions. Howard Berman (D-CA) joined their effort, and the amendment became known as "Chrysler-Berman-Brownback."

Whereas Berman had failed in a similar attempt at committee, the atmosphere had changed by the time of House floor consideration. Senator Abraham had successfully divided the Simpson bill just a week before, and the high-tech lobby had been in nearly every Hill office. President Clinton had shifted his position from favoring cuts in legal immigration levels to opposing reductions (Judiciary Committee Activities Report 1997; *CQWR* 3/23/96).

The president had endorsed the Jordan Commission's recommendations initially. He voiced support as late as February 11, 1996, for reducing legal immigration and eliminating the sibling categories—exactly what Smith and Simpson had been trying to do.

However, John Huang, a major Democratic Party fundraiser and former Clinton administration official, sent the president a memorandum in conjunction with a February 19 fundraising event with Asian-Americans. Huang, who had fought behind the scenes to keep the sibling preference in the 1990 immigration bill, informed the president that the potential political contributors' "top priority" was opposition to the pending legislation (Kranish 1/16/97).

An administration letter March 13 stated that the president favored "suspending" sibling immigration. "Suspension" slid to full reversal a week later. Clinton sent lawmakers word March 20 that he now supported the Chrysler-Berman-Brownback Amendment, which would effectively kill the prospects of legal reform (Kranish, 1/17/97).

The Chrysler-Berman-Brownback Amendment passed the House March 21 by 238–183. Seventy-five Republicans joined a majority of Democrats in supporting the amendment. Ranking subcommittee member John Bryant (D-TX) stayed with Smith and the majority of Republicans who favored legal reform. Observers on both sides were shocked by the margin of victory. That so many Republicans would vote to strike out the language on legal reform was particularly surprising. In both the House and the Senate, the bills' sponsors had given ground on many of the employment-related provisions in hopes that these concessions would bring pro-business GOP members back on board. But the high-tech groups were intent on killing legal reform altogether for fear that they might lose ground at some later stage of the legislative process. Following their success in the Senate, they had intensified their efforts in the House. Republicans in the Northeast were easy targets of these lobbying efforts because they were from districts with a rich and recent tradition of legal immigration. Twelve of the 14 New York Republicans voted for Chrysler-Berman-Brownback. To Peter King (R-NY), from Long Island, who voted in favor of the amendment, the joining of the issues was a way of scapegoating legal immigrants (King interview 4/8/97).

In the Midwest, there were many Republicans who simply did not have their minds made up on immigration issues. Immigration posed complications and complexities that made their eyes glaze over. For freshman members such as Mark Souder (R-IN), Jon Christensen (R-NE), and Todd Tiahrt (R-KS), immigration was not highly important to their constituencies, and they had been following the debate only from a distance. The pro-immigration interest groups had a plan in mind to reach these uncommitted members. The high-tech lobby hired Washington lobbyist and GOP insider Grover Norquist to persuade Ralph Reed, the executive director of the Christian Coalition, to support the Chrysler-Berman-Brownback Amendment. The Christian Coalition had previously refused to take a position. Its grassroots membership had expressed no strong opinions on an issue to which they had given little consideration. Norquist met with Reed at a dinner with Speaker Gingrich just days before the House floor debate and convinced him that the Smith bill would be harmful to families. The elimination of the preference categories for extended family members was surely contrary to traditional family values, Norquist insisted. Reed had also wanted to improve relationships with some of the other religious interest groups in Washington, including the Catholic Bishops. Siding with them on this issue would be instrumental to that end. Reed sprang into action and fired off a letter to GOP members stating the Christian Coalition's support for splitting the bill. It is impossible to determine how many members were persuaded by this action alone. Smith's forces were 29 votes short of victory, and it is hard to see how the Christian Coalition letter could have influenced this many votes, but it was clearly a factor that Smith and his staff came to resent. Adoption of the Chrysler-Berman-Brownback Amendment meant the preservation of the status quo.

No New Braceros

The agriculture lobby failed to win sufficient support for a new agricultural guest-worker program. First, farm supporters couldn't persuade the Rules Committee to include Agriculture Committee amendments as part of H.R. 2202. They did succeed, however, in having the committee provisions ruled in order as an amendment. Two agriculture-related amendments were made in order: the Pombo Amendment, which sought to replace a labor certification requirement with an easier attestation, and the Goodlatte Amendment. Pombo and farm-state representatives claimed that the current means of getting migrant workers approved was too onerous. Pombo sought to create an H-2B visa program as a three-year pilot program. Opponents, led by Goodlatte, Bryant of Texas, and Berman, argued that Pombo's program would make it easier for farmers to import undocumented workers.

"Take a lesson from the history books," Goodlatte said. "The *Bracero* program was the beginning of our illegal immigration problem we are attempting to curb in H.R. 2202. Hundreds of thousands of *braceros* became accustomed to the American standard of living and wages. Once the *Bracero* program ended, many *braceros* resorted to coming to this country illegally. That trend continues today" (*CR* 3/21/96, H2610).

Others argued the plight of unskilled American workers. They said Pombo's program would bring in 250,000 aliens a year to compete for work with sufficient numbers of Americans and legal resident aliens, and the foreigners would depress wages. They argued that a guest-worker program was a sop to agribusiness. Some said this program would undermine the illegal immigration efforts of H.R. 2202. When the vote was called, Pombo lost 180–242. "We got our asses kicked pretty soundly," said Bryan Little, a lobbyist for the American Farm Bureau. "This is an increasingly urban Congress that doesn't care about the 3 percent of the country that feeds the other 97 percent. It just wasn't a real political issue to a lot of members" (Little interview 1/17/97).

Next, Goodlatte offered his alternative agricultural guest-worker proposal. Under his amendment, 100,000 foreign agriculture workers could enter each year within the existing migrant worker visa program, H-2A, and employers would gain some relaxation of the requirements they found so onerous. While Goodlatte saw his proposal as a compromise, agricultural interests disparaged it as not sufficiently meeting their needs. They wanted all or nothing (see *CR* 3/21/96, H2626).

Lamar Smith (R-TX) endorsed Goodlatte's amendment as making needed adjustments to the existing program. Still, strong opposition came from advocates for indigenous farm workers, primarily from organized labor and Hispanic advocacy groups, as well as from agribusiness. The Goodlatte Amendment failed, 59–357.

Finishing Up House Business

Other significant amendments adopted on the House floor included extension of the deadline for asylum applications from 30 days, the limit adopted in committee, to 180 days. Also adopted was language authorizing state and local authorities to assist in immigration enforcement activities and a provision allowing federal reimbursement for local governments' costs of incarcerating criminal aliens (Judiciary Committee Activities Report 1997).

On March 21, the House voted 333–87 to pass H.R. 2202 as amended. Smith's bill had sustained heavy hits, most particularly the elimination of language to restrict and restructure legal immigration policies. Still, the Immigration in the National Interest Act remained afloat, indeed seaworthy—strengthened in some regards, changed modestly to moderately in other regards.

The strong, bipartisan vote on final passage—by a veto-proof margin—didn't include among its supporters John Bryant, who had originally cosponsored the bill with Smith. The ranking Democrat, in the end, could not bring himself to support the final draft because it had been recrafted to include the Gallegly Amendment, allowing states to deny education benefits to children of illegal residents.

Senate Floor Action

The Senate bill addressing illegal immigration, S. 1664, reached the floor April 15. However, it fell victim to class warfare as Democrats threatened to amend the bill with a minimum wage increase. That prompted Majority Leader Bob Dole to remove S.1664 from consideration on April 16 (*CQWR* 4/20/96).

In the spring of 1996, the immigration issue became entwined in presidential politics. GOP candidate Patrick Buchanan had raised the issue, and it struck a chord with his supporters. Buchanan's strong showing with rank-and-file Republicans, particularly in the South and West, forced other presidential hopefuls to address the issue. Voters in two key, delegate-rich states—Florida and California—paid close attention to the ongoing immigration debate. While Buchanan had made the most of the issue and enjoyed strong grassroots support, Dole had the support of the Republican party leadership. In an attempt to shore up his support among the rank and file, especially in California, Dole endorsed Gallegly's amendment that would allow states the option to refuse public education to illegal residents. But other GOP candidates, chief among them Lamar Alexander, opposed the measure, as did President Clinton.

A Last Run at Legal Restrictions

On April 24, the Senate again took up Simpson's illegal immigration bill. GOP leaders steered through the perilous shoals of Democratic gamesmanship on the minimum wage. Simpson proposed an amendment to cut family-based legal immigration, effectively attempting to rejoin legal and illegal immigration proposals after Abraham (R-MI) and DeWine (R-OH) had separated them in the Judiciary Committee. Simpson's new proposal sought to impose a temporary five-year restriction on certain family visas. He proposed a firm cap of 480,000 annual visas—current law contained that cap, but did not count the spouses and minor children of U.S. citizens against the quota—with priority placed on immediate family members of U.S. citizens, followed by the immediate family of permanent residents. He brought to the floor several charts to help illustrate the impact of chain migration whereby an immigrant enters and begins to petition for the entry of others, who upon entering petition for still others, until the original petitioner has been responsible for bringing in dozens and dozens of new arrivals. According to Simpson, the all-time record was a petitioner who brought in 83 people (*CR* 4/25/96, S4119).

Kennedy and Simon opposed the amendment and found many Republican Senators siding with them. Rather than arguing about the merits of immigration, Abraham and DeWine continued to insist that legal and illegal immigration were separate issues. Procedurally, it was wrong to lump them together. Simpson's amendment went down to a crushing defeat, 80–20.

Among the 20 in favor of the amendment were six Southern Senators, and eight Senators from the mountain states. Despite strong public opinion in favor of limiting legal immigration, even Simpson's temporary restriction on legal immigration had failed.

Senator Dianne Feinstein (D-CA) proposed an even more modest legal immigration compromise. While it contained the hard 480,000 annual limit on family visas, the amendment provided for the admission of the adult children of U.S. citizens. Feinstein had hoped that her amendment would split the difference between Simpson's amendment and the position of those hostile to any legal reforms. Feinstein was able to bring only another six Senators on board, including three more Southern Senators in addition to the six who had voted for Simpson's version, and presidential candidate and Senate Majority Leader Bob Dole. The 74–26 vote to table the Feinstein Amendment effectively squelched any further efforts to reattach legal immigration limits to the illegal immigration bill.

Warrantless Searches

Simpson proposed another amendment that would have granted INS agents the authority to search farm fields without a warrant. He argued that the other federal law enforcement agencies had authority to conduct warrantless searches under certain circumstances. But Senators on both sides of the aisle voiced opposition to the amendment. Senator Larry Craig (R-ID) cited past abuses of the privilege, which had prompted Congress to write the warrant requirement into the 1986 bill. And some Democrats said foreign-looking farm workers would be harassed as a result of warrantless searches. Simpson's amendment went down on another decisive 20–79 vote.

The Attack on Deeming

A Democratic tag team, consisting primarily of Bob Graham (D-FL), Kennedy (D-MA), and Paul Simon (D-IL), attempted to weaken Simpson's bill by attacking the sponsorship requirements. Partisanship became evident in this round of the debate, centering, as it did, on redistributive and welfare matters. One of the primary points of the original legislation was to reduce the number of immigrants using public assistance. Simpson and Smith proposed to limit immigrant access to welfare through so-called "deeming" requirements. Simpson proposed that, in determining the eligibility of a legal resident for federally funded public assistance programs, the income of that legal resident's sponsor should count as the legal resident's income. Under current law, a sponsor could bring in an elderly family member, and that family member could apply for public assistance declaring that he or she had no income. Simpson and Smith proposed to count or "deem" the sponsor's income as the new arrival's income—the idea being that sponsors, not the government, should be responsible for their family members (CIR Report 1995, 30, 54–63).

The ethnic, religious, and immigrants' rights groups despised the deeming proposal. Deeming directly threatened the economic well-being of their lower-income constituents who desired to reunite with their family members without having to support them financially. In response to their interests, Bob Graham (D-FL) offered an amendment to limit deeming requirements to 16 specific programs. Simpson's proposal had applied deeming to all means-tested public aid programs. Graham's amendment would have exempted certain programs, including Medicaid, job training, legal services, and other noncash programs. Graham's amendment was rejected 36–63. Abraham and DeWine voted against it, reflecting the consistency of their emphasis on "immigrants yes, welfare no." Similar amendments offered by Kennedy to exempt a host of public health benefits from sponsor deeming requirements were also rejected. Simon unsuccessfully tried to weaken language in the bill that provided for the deportation of immigrants who became public charges.

Graham (D-FL) offered another unsuccessful but cleverly designed amendment targeted at undermining deeming. This time, Graham proposed to suspend deeming requirements if their net costs imposed an unfunded mandate, as defined by law, on a state or local government. This approach sought to use Republican legislation enacted the previous year for purposes of weakening Simpson's bill. The unfunded mandate law, part of the Contract with America, ended the practice of mandating policy to states and localities without providing funds to support their compliance with the mandate. Graham reasoned that the deeming requirement would demand that states verify citizenship status, immigration status, and sponsorship status of welfare clients, thereby imposing the administrative burdens of data acquisition and record keeping.

The Graham Amendment would have exempted lower levels of government from implementing deeming in areas that attract impoverished immigrant populations. One reason immigrants flock to those areas is because of the generous welfare benefits they provide. By exempting such areas from deeming, the governments in those areas would be released from the paperwork the regulation required, but the exemption may also create a perverse incentive to expand the public assistance caseload in order to continue escaping the deeming requirement. Graham's confused emphasis on state and local administrative costs missed the point of deeming policy—to place principal responsibility for immigrants' financial welfare on the ones who pledged to provide for the immigrants: their family or other sponsor, not the public.

More Senate Amendments

Another Kennedy Amendment sought to strip the provision requiring that intentional discrimination be proved against employers who ask for additional employment verification documents. Instead, Kennedy wanted to give employers specific guidelines in order to verify work eligibility and not discriminate in the process. But the Senate rejected that amendment 32–67.

Besides Simon's attempts to weaken the bill's strong language on deportation of immigrants who become public charges, he went to bat to stop Abraham from eliminating the employment verification pilot programs. Reflecting his strong alliance with the business community, Abraham had proposed such an amendment during floor debate. His amendment would also strike Simpson's provisions calling for birth certificates and driver's licenses to meet national standards.

DeWine, who had called this a "stupid idea" when it had come up in committee, joined Abraham. Simpson had turned to him angrily in the committee hearing and asked him if he had been staffed on the issue and whether he had sent staff to a previous day's briefing when the issue had been discussed. To which DeWine abruptly replied, "Well, let's ask!" turning to look at his legislative aide and asking him if he had gone to Simpson's briefing. The terrified aide nodded that he had, in fact, been present at the briefing. DeWine reeled around and glared accusingly back at Simpson, demanding, "Well, what now?!"

On the floor, their arguments against setting national standards for state documents were familiar: employers would be burdened; after this would come a national identification card; why subject all workers to the verification system in order to keep out a small proportion of workers? and it would pose a heavy imposition on the states. Simpson and Feinstein argued that this pilot program and the more foolproof state documents were a key aspect of demagnetizing the "job magnet" drawing illegals into the country. Simon moved to table the Abraham Amendment. His motion was agreed to 54–46, thus killing the effort. This was one of Simpson's few victories.

Patrick Leahy (D-VT) took on the bill's summary exclusion provisions on behalf of asylum seekers. Simpson's bill would speed the process for turning back foreigners arriving with false documents and weak asylum claims. In fact, similar provisions had been part of a newly enacted antiterrorism law. Leahy had sought to change that part of the antiterrorism bill late in the process and failed. But Leahy lobbied hard in the intervening weeks. On the Senate floor during the immigration debate, Leahy proposed essentially to gut the streamlined process. With Republican support, he prevailed on a razor-thin 51–49 vote.

In addition, Graham (D-FL) offered a somewhat provincial amendment. The underlying bill contained language to repeal the Cuban Adjustment Act. Simpson argued that the law, which was enacted in 1966 to enable Cubans fleeing Fidel Castro's Communist regime to escape to America, effectively aided illegal means of immigrating. Under this law, any Cuban in the United States for a year could then adjust to permanent resident status.

Simpson's point was that visa overstayers, if Cuban, received forgiveness for their illegal status, while overstayers from all other countries could not. But Graham replied that as long as Castro remained in power, the law was valid. The Graham Amendment retained the Cuban Adjustment Act and added a provision that the law would remain in effect until Cuba put into place a certified, democratically elected government. The amendment was adopted 62–37.

Another amendment, this one offered by a liberal Republican, sought to weaken the provisions dealing with legal immigrants, but for a different reason. John Chafee (R-RI) sought to address somewhat different treatment of legal immigrants and illegal aliens under the Simpson bill regarding access to the same welfare benefits. Under the bill, lawmakers had carved out exceptions to the general ban on illegal aliens' eligibility for public assistance. Some exceptions were made for well-intentioned reasons. Senate advocates for illegal aliens granted them access to emergency medical care, prenatal and postpartum care, short-term disaster aid, and immunizations. Chafee made the perceptive point that because of these exceptions for illegal immigrants, *legal* immigrants would face a "disparity in access." Legal immigrants would be bound by sponsor-deeming requirements, which were being strengthened so that sponsors could not shirk their voluntarily agreed-to financial obligations. Of course, illegal aliens would not face sponsor-deeming requirements when they received aid. This was unfair, and Chafee proposed eliminating deeming for those programs for which illegal aliens were also eligible. Chafee's effort to weaken the deeming requirements failed on a 40–60 vote.

Passing The Simpson Bill, or What's Left of It

The Senate voted 100–0 on May 2 to invoke cloture, or limit further debate on S. 1664. The Senate then passed its illegal immigration bill, 97–3. This margin belied the partisan differences that had shown up, especially on cost and redistributive issues. Only Democrats Russ Feingold (WI), Graham, and Simon cast no votes. Kennedy, who had voted against the bill at the committee level because of its welfare stipulations, ultimately voted for final passage of the bill on the Senate floor once the summary exclusion provisions had been eliminated by Leahy's successful amendment.

Two monumental differences separated the House- and Senate-passed versions. The House bill included the Gallegly Amendment, relating to public education of illegal aliens, and the summary exclusion provisions stricken from the Senate bill by the Leahy Amendment. The next stop in the legislative process was a House-Senate conference committee to resolve the differences between the two bills. The conference report would then have to be passed by both Houses and finally go to the president's desk.

The House-Senate Conference Committee

Following Senate passage May 2, the sponsors of the legislation began to realize that much work remained if the 104th Congress were to enact an immigration bill. Each body had passed substantial packages, and reconciling the differences between the two would take time. The Republicans were divided among themselves, not to mention the disagreements between House and Senate members, Republicans and Democrats, and members from various regions of the country. Furthermore, a presidential election loomed, and the inevitable delays of election year politics had killed immigration reform in 1984 (see Chapter 5).

Different Chambers, Different Bills

Through the summer of 1996, Republican committee staffers met to take on the daunting task of sorting through the differences between the two bills. Smith and Simpson—and the majority leadership—needed a good idea of where Republicans in each chamber stood, which issues could be reconciled easily, and which ones would call for involved negotiations. Once House and Senate Republicans had reached agreement, Democrats could be brought into the process after conference committee members had been named.

The Clinton administration and the interest groups began to analyze both bills while fishing around for leads as to who the conferees would be. All interested parties were eager to pressure the people who would decide on the final legislative language.

Perhaps the greatest difference between House- and Senate-passed bills was the Gallegly Amendment. No similar provision appeared in the Senate version. Senator Jon Kyl (R-AZ) had considered offering the amendment but then decided not to for strategic reasons. A whip count showed little support for it in the Senate. Kyl and other Senate supporters knew that if it failed on the Senate floor it would be difficult to retain in the conference committee with the House. They opted to leave it out in hopes that it would weather the last stages of the legislative process.

Presidential politics entered the picture because the all-but-certain GOP nominee Bob Dole backed the Gallegly measure. President Clinton, the ethnic interest groups, and even some Republicans squared off against it. President Clinton named the Gallegly provision as sufficiently objectionable as to justify a veto of the entire bill (Gorelick letter May 31, 1996). *Congressional Quarterly* reported, "The issue has become the leading dispute holding up conference negotiations" (*CQWR* 7/6/96, 1924). The issue had exploded even before conferees had been named.

Another gulf between the House and Senate versions was the asylum language. The House bill contained provisions to expedite the asylum claims of petitioners arriving without documents or with fraudulent documents. The Leahy Amendment had knocked similar measures out of the Senate bill, instead providing the attorney general with discretionary power to invoke expedited procedures in emergencies. For aliens already present in the U.S., the House measure gave them 180 days from date of entering the country to complete an asylum application, with strict limitations placed on judicial review of the initial asylum determination. The Senate bill gave people placed in deportation proceedings the right to apply for asylum if they had been in the United States for no longer than one year; it also limited judicial review of the asylum ruling.

The 1996 antiterrorism law included measures to remove those who entered the country without inspection. EWIs (for "entry without inspection"), as they were called, were revisited in the immigration bills. The House legislation provided that these illegal residents would be permanently barred from reentering the U.S. if deported. Undocumented residents present for a year would be barred from reentry for ten years. The Senate bill barred EWIs from permanent residence or nonimmigrant visa petitioning for 10 years. Both measures softened the new antiterrorism law's procedure, which subjected EWIs to expedited exclusion, without the opportunity to seek suspension of their deportation because of extended presence in the country and extreme hardship to dependents.

Concerning worker verification, both bills established pilot projects to test electronic verification systems. The House bill made employer participation voluntary, while the Senate legislation required employer participation. The mandatory nature of the Senate language upset the business community because, for employers in the test areas, the telephone or computer verification would be required in addition to the current I-9 form and the associated checking of documents.

Similarly, each bill contained different provisions related to employment discrimination. The Senate bill granted employers broader protection against discrimination lawsuits. It allowed employers to request additional documents from those tendered and required the government to prove the employer's intent to discriminate. Current law prohibited additional document requests unless the ones shown were obviously invalid. The House legislation only allowed suspicious employers to check with the agency that supposedly issued the document in question.

The Senate bill also included language setting federal standards for state-issued driver's licenses and birth certificates that would have to be met. The House package contained no similar provision.

Another key difference involved the income requirements to be placed on those wanting to sponsor an immigrant. The House bill set the minimum sponsor income level at 200 percent of the poverty level. If the government-determined poverty level were, say, $15,000 per year, the House bill would require that sponsors earn $30,000 per year in order to petition for a family member to immigrate. The Senate legislation set the minimum considerably lower at, 125 percent—only $18,750, in this example.

The Senate bill contained a provision known as the Grassley Amendment. Charles Grassley, an Iowa Republican, added this measure by unanimous consent during the Judiciary Committee markup. The amendment exempted nonprofit, charitable organizations from the deeming requirements. It also stated that federal authorities were not precluded from performing the deeming activities. No comparable measure appeared in the House bill.

As GOP committee staff continued their work, they began to hold additional, broader discussions with the principal staffers of Senate Republican conferees and staffers of likely House GOP conferees. The idea was to gauge where Republican conferees stood on the issues and to try to arrive at staff recommendations.

The Executive Branch Weighs In

Those outside who sought to influence the course of the conference made their views known as the names of conferees and likely conferees surfaced. The Clinton administration sent INS Commissioner Doris Meissner and representatives from the Department of Health and Human Services to Capitol Hill to lobby. The INS commissioner voiced the administration's general opposition to the Gallegly Amendment and the deeming requirements. She then moved quickly to the agency's particular concerns. The antiterrorism law required detention of most criminal aliens. The House immigration bill restored some discretion and flexibility to the attorney general with respect to criminal alien detention, while the Senate bill continued the mandatory detention of most criminal aliens. The INS preferred the House version and even more flexibility, expressing concern about limited detention facilities and the agency's inability to abide by the law's requirements.

The INS favored the Senate version of expedited exclusion in emergencies only, as well as somewhat broader judicial and administrative review. The agency also preferred no time limits on filing asylum claims; however, the Senate's year was preferable to the House's six months. The INS favored the House's combining of deportation and exclusion proceedings into a single removal procedure. Yet INS wanted not only to retain a cancellation of removal provision, but to widen it from existing law.

On employment verification, the INS stated its preference for the Senate version, saying it included stronger privacy and discrimination protections. The INS also favored the Senate's flexibility on border barriers, while the House bill mandated construction of a triple fence near San Diego.

Interest groups intensively lobbied the pool of potential conferees, making their preferences known as to which version of the bill was best. Among those who addressed a range of concerns were the American Bar Association, the American Immigration Lawyers Association, the American Civil Liberties Union, and the Federation for American Immigration Reform. In addition, some religious entities such as the U.S. Catholic Conference's Migration and Refugee Services office expressed broad-ranging views. Other interest groups, such as Americans for Tax Reform, Catholic Charities USA, the National Conference of State Legislatures, the Law Enforcement Alliance of America, and the U.S. Chamber of Commerce, confined the subject of their communications to select provisions they either supported, opposed, or wanted changed. This unsolicited information deluge mounted up into piles, even boxes full of information in the offices of House and Senate committee members.

The Gallegly Amendment in Conference

The battle over the Gallegly Amendment dominated negotiations and strategizing. This was clearly an issue that could not be left to staff. The members would have to get involved themselves.

On May 20, 47 Senators, mostly Democrats, sent conferees a letter expressing their opposition to the Gallegly Amendment. The letter cited police unions' opposition to the provision, as well as the opposition of the education establishment and of certain Republicans.

In June, Senator Dole restated his support for the measure during campaign swings through California. But 46 Congressmen from both parties who had voted for H.R. 2202 on final passage wrote the House and Senate Judiciary Committee chairmen asking that the Gallegly language be removed from the final bill.

Smith, Simpson, Gallegly (R-CA), Hatch (R-UT), and Arlen Specter (R-PA) were the Republican conferees charged with negotiating the final language, in consultation with the majority leadership. Others made their voices heard. Texas Republican Senators Phil Gramm and Kay Bailey Hutchison declared their opposition to the Gallegly Amendment. The Law Enforcement Alliance of America, the Traditional Values Coalition, Eagle Forum, the Republican Governors Association, and the Hispanic Business Roundtable endorsed the Gallegly Amendment. In addition, the California and Arizona lodges of the Fraternal Order of Police broke with their national leadership and supported the provision.

Congress was short of time. In August, members took their traditional election-year break to campaign. Republican leaders wanted to adjourn the 104th Congress by the end of September, the end of the federal fiscal year. For those facing reelection, time at home with voters was of the essence.

Senator Specter's (R-PA) strong resistance to the original Gallegly language worked to the Democrats' and the White House's advantage. The original goal had been to have GOP agreement on all items by the end of June, meet with Democratic conferees following the Fourth of July break, and bring a conference report to the floor around mid-July. The key was to get Republican conferees to agree in order to present a unified front. Providing they were in agreement, the GOP could oppose Democratic efforts to weaken the bill.

Negotiations went back and forth among Republicans and, just before the August recess, Hatch and Specter finally agreed to compromise language. The compromise version "grandfathered" illegal alien students enrolled in public school by September 1996. In other words, the children of illegal immigrants who had enrolled by that date would be exempt from expulsion. Further, it called for studies by the General Accounting Office of state implementation of the option and its impact. It provided for an expedited process to consider legislation to repeal the amendment, as well as establishing a sunset provision should repeal legislation not be acted upon.

This compromise did not satisfy congressional Democrats, and it did not change President Clinton's mind. The president restated his veto intention should any version of the Gallegly Amendment remain in the bill upon its arrival at his desk (*CQWR* 9/7/96, 2531).

Dianne Feinstein (D-CA) wrote the Republican leadership September 9 urging that the Gallegly Amendment be removed from the conference report in order to pass the bill. Feinstein could recognize a killer amendment when she saw one. The GOP leadership sought the advice of the Dole campaign on the Gallegly question. Dole, having made the measure a California campaign issue, wanted the language included, thus placing Clinton in the position of vetoing the larger, popular illegal immigration reform bill. Dole thought that a Clinton veto over Gallegly would anger California voters and boost Dole's prospects in a state rich with electoral votes and overrun by illegal aliens.

Many vulnerable GOP Californians in Congress were urging the congressional leadership and conferees to scuttle the Gallegly Amendment if need be, and give them a strong immigration reform bill to campaign on in the weeks before the election. Gallegly himself fought to the end to retain his provision. He resented having to weaken the measure in order to mollify Republican opposition, and now he stuck by Dole in favor of keeping his amendment in the legislative package.

Gradually, though, the tide was turning against the amendment. In mid-September, a number of immigration-reform grassroots organizations voiced their opposition to the revised amendment on unusual grounds. Most of the amendment's opponents asserted the desirability of having all children attend school, regardless of their immigration status. But the reform groups opposed the compromise version as having watered down the measure too much so as to make circumstances actually worse, from their perspective. Looking back several months later, Lamar Smith could see that intraparty squabbling about the Gallegly provision had wasted valuable time. He regretted that this time had not been used to reach agreement on other issues (Smith interview 2/26/97).

On September 11, the House finally appointed conferees. The conference committee met formally September 24, even as the conference report was being readied for signature and filing. The conference report, stripped of the Gallegly Amendment, passed the House September 25 by a 305–123 vote. But even that wasn't the end of the matter. There still remained the end game.

Asylum and Summary Exclusion in Conference

The negotiations regarding asylum and summary exclusion provisions entailed different dynamics than those surrounding the Gallegly Amendment. The House had agreed that the asylum and deportation processes needed reform.[1] The Senate, on the other hand, had been divided on these issues.

Senate Judiciary Chairman Orrin Hatch (R-UT) found himself precariously perched, having himself voted for the Leahy Amendment on the Senate floor. At the same time, Simpson and Smith enjoyed virtually unanimous support for asylum and removal reform among Republican House conferees. Of course, liberal advocacy groups such as the ACLU, the American Bar Association, and the Lawyers Committee for Human Rights sought to weigh in, as they had done more effectively with Democratic Congresses. But these groups had few Republican allies, and the business community was ambivalent on these issues. The writing was on the wall that asylum and deportation proceedings would be streamlined. The question then became, by how much?

The 1996 antiterrorism law sharply restricted the rights of asylum claimants, so much so that Smith and Simpson felt compelled to agree to adjustments in the new law. The House immigration bill made minor adjustments concerning foreigners arriving without documentation, while the Senate bill, under the Leahy Amendment, returned to the unreformed, pre-antiterrorism law procedures unless the attorney general invoked an emergency process for expedited consideration. Asylum-seekers, under the new law, had to prove to an immigration officer at the port of entry that they had a "credible fear" of

---

[1]Some members had sought to offer related amendments during floor debate, but the House Rules Committee did not make those amendments in order. This kept the full House from considering asylum-related amendments.

persecution; that is, conditions in the home country would induce in those individuals a level of fear to justify flight to escape political persecution. Establishing that credible fear would gain the petitioner the right to an asylum hearing. If the person's claim was denied, another immigration officer would review the initial decision. If the alien failed to demonstrate a credible fear within the meaning of the law, he or she would immediately be sent home. There was no right to judicial review.

The antiterrorism law treated EWIs similarly if they sought asylum. Both immigration bills loosened this new measure. The House bill gave 180 days from date of entry to file an asylum application, with limited and expedited judicial review, while the Senate bill made asylum a defensive claim in case an alien were caught and placed in deportation proceedings.

Hatch accepted expedited exclusion, but with more checks in the system, including a larger role for the courts in order to check the power of the immigration agency and to guard against returning someone who actually faced persecution. On asylum, Hatch pressed for a one-year time limit with "exceptional" or "extraordinary" circumstances allowed to affect the deadline.

Staff negotiated at length over these provisions, involving the members and swapping draft proposals and counterproposals. At issue were the legal standard to be required, the degree of judicial review, and the process of administrative review. Republicans finally settled on an expedited exclusion procedure that set a "credible fear" standard for arriving asylum claimants. Those applicants could be detained while waiting for their application to be adjudicated. Judicial review was allowed in limited manner and put on a fast track—within 24 hours if possible, no more than a week, and could be held by telephone or video conference.

Republicans also agreed to an expedited removal process that repealed the so-called "entry doctrine," which had given illegal entrants expanded rights in deportation proceedings. The negotiators decided to set the parameters for removing aliens. In essence, deportation would be eliminated and combined with exclusion in a single removal process. Appeal of removal orders now would be limited. A 90-day deadline was set for removal following a removal order, and aliens ordered removed faced mandatory detention. Discretionary relief from removal orders became strictly limited.

In addition, asylum claimants would have a one-year filing deadline. Also, the conference agreement stated that asylum was not permanent, so that if country conditions changed, the alien would lose asylee status. Hatch won his exception to the deadline for "extraordinary circumstances" involved with the filing delay, and "changed circumstances" relating to eligibility also would waive the time limit.

For aliens removed and seeking reentry, the House generally gave in to the Senate. For those just arriving without proper documents, the bar on readmission became five years. The ten-year bar in the Senate bill won out for aliens ordered removed. The immigration lawyers' groups were furious about these provisions and pledged to pressure for their repeal.

Employer Sanctions and Verification in Conference

Both House and Senate bills established pilot programs to develop and test electronic verification systems. The key difference was that the House's version left employer participation voluntary, but contained incentives to encourage participation, such as presumption that the participating employer was fully in compliance with relevant immigration laws. The Senate legislation allowed the attorney general to require participation.

Furthermore, the House version called for a single system to be tested in five of the seven states with the most illegal aliens. The Senate bill provided for at least three different systems—one verifying Social Security numbers by telephone; one based on state-issued identification cards, such as driver's licenses, that include machine-readable Social Security numbers; and one checking on the immigration status of noncitizens.

Staff proposed that the two chambers' provisions be merged, keeping the House's voluntary basis for participation and incentives, and retaining the Senate's three types of systems. The voluntary participation language would meet small-business concerns, expressed through the National Federation of Independent Business. In preconference negotiations, this recommendation was generally acceptable to Republicans. Besides the NFIB, other GOP-leaning organizations weighed in favoring voluntary participation, including Grover Norquist's Americans for Tax Reform, the U.S. Chamber of Commerce, and a coalition known as Employers for Responsible Immigration Reform. Compared with the Gallegly Amendment and asylum reforms, the employment eligibility pilot programs were relatively easy to agree upon.

Most Republican conferees supported the change in the standards required for proving discrimination, which would grant employers protection against unfair immigration-related employment practice lawsuits. Employers would be able to ask new employees for additional documents in order to verify identity and employment eligibility. No longer would that request constitute a discriminatory practice. For a request to be discriminatory under the new law, it would have to be made with the intent to discriminate on the basis of immigration status. Republican conferees were willing to accept this higher standard. And the Employers for Responsible Immigration Reform coalition, among other business groups, favored the Senate provision. The Senate language appeared in the conference report.

GOP deals were easily struck regarding employment verification and the discrimination standard, but Simpson's provisions mandating federal standards for driver's licenses and birth certificates were more controversial. House Republicans, who had fought unfunded federal mandates, opposed the Senate requirements on those grounds. They also objected because of federal involvement in a matter of state jurisdiction, as well as for privacy concerns associated with the display of Social Security numbers. By mid-June, the National Conference of State Legislatures (NCSL) had written to express its concerns. Paramount was the driver's license and birth certificate mandate. NCSL voiced the same concerns as some GOP conference staff—unfunded mandates, federal preemption of state laws, Social Security number-related fraud, and privacy concerns—and wanted the Senate provisions eliminated.

On June 27, 15 Republican House Members, mostly freshmen, wrote to Speaker Newt Gingrich (R-GA) urging the removal of this Senate provision. Their letter read in part:

> It is a mark of just how odd the Senate scheme is that under Section 118, no state or local government agency could accept a valid driver's license issued by its own state for any evidentiary purpose whatsoever, unless the state kowtows to unspecified and unlimited requirements to be promulgated by bureaucrats at the Department of Transportation after consultation with the American Association of Motor Vehicle Administrators! What's next, a national Bureau of Motor Vehicles?

House Republican conferees were willing to discuss ways to modify the Senate language, rather than strike the provision outright. They recognized the rampant problems of document fraud related to these state-issued documents. The question became one of balancing interests, as well as preserving state flexibility.

Some GOP conference staff recommended removing the birth certificate and driver's license mandates on states, but retaining a birth certificate grant program. The grant program was designed to encourage states to develop a system for matching birth and death records nationwide. The program was directed at the problem of illegal residents buying the identity of deceased individuals. Clearly, discovering someone living under the assumed identity of an actual person poses a much tougher challenge for authorities than those assuming a fabricated identity. Therefore, if somehow birth and death records could be matched, it would become harder for identity thieves to perpetrate their crime.

Simpson's sticking point remained the Social Security number and the need for anticounterfeiting standards. The compromise set birth certificate guidelines for states, but retained state design flexibility. It allowed states to place Social Security numbers on driver's licenses or otherwise to verify the validity of an applicant's Social Security number. Federal grants would help defray states' costs of complying with these requirements. The compromise also kept the grant program for matching birth and death records. This compromise arguably addressed the "unfunded" part of the unfunded mandate objection, though it remained a mandate; it preserved flexibility for states to meet the federal standards; and it achieved the protection of Social Security number privacy while requiring the confirmation of a Social Security number's validity. This compromise is what appeared in the conference report.

Deeming and Sponsorship in Conference

The proposal on sponsor income level went through several drafts before conferees arrived at an acceptable compromise. Most House GOP conferees preferred the 200 percent of the poverty level income requirement as added protection against sponsors shirking their obligations. However, several Senate Republicans, including Specter (R-PA), viewed the House income requirement as a remaining bar to legal immigration in a predominantly illegal immigration reform package. The business coalition supported the lower Senate level (25 percent above poverty level). But that level was unacceptably low for House conferees.

The working proposal would merge the House and Senate provisions. The immigrant sponsor would still have to earn 200 percent of the designated poverty income, but if his household income fell between 125 percent and 200 percent, the petitioning sponsor could find a cosponsor with income meeting the 200 percent requirement. Both sponsor and cosponsor would be jointly and severally liable for the sponsored immigrant's illegal use of public benefits. Petitioners who served in the military and earned 100 percent of poverty income level could sponsor their spouses and minor children as immigrants. Also, sponsors would substantiate their income levels with three years of certified tax returns.

Republicans agreed to a two-tiered system. Sponsors would be required to earn 200 percent of the poverty rate or, if earning between 125 percent and 200 percent, find a cosponsor earning 200 percent of poverty in order to petition for most family immigrants. If the immigrant was a spouse or minor child of the sponsor, the income requirement dropped to 140 percent (with the 100 percent exception for active-duty U.S. military personnel sponsoring nuclear family members). Cosponsors would agree to the same financial obligations as primary sponsors in all instances, signing the legally enforceable affidavits of support.

Related to sponsor income requirements were the deeming requirements that had been the object of partisan attack on the Senate floor. To reiterate, under deeming, the sponsor's income would be deemed as available to the immigrant as equally to any member of the sponsor's household. That is why the income level was so important. Linking sponsor income levels with the principle of income deeming, as well as the public-charge prohibition, shows that Smith and Simpson were intent on framing legislation that would eliminate immigration's redistributive consequences. Previously, the law required deeming for only three assistance programs—Aid to Families with Dependent Children (or TANF for "Temporary Assistance for

Needy Families" as it came to be known following passage of the 1996 welfare reform law), Supplemental Security Income, and Food Stamps. Both the House and Senate immigration bills extended deeming to most federal programs and programs administered at the state level that received federal funds. Both exempted certain programs, made exceptions for battered women and children, and authorized states and localities to deem for their own benefits programs.

Several differences existed between the bills on deeming. The House bill prospectively applied deeming and sponsorship; the Senate version applied these requirements to immigrants already present in the country. The National Conference of State Legislatures took issue with the Senate provision, couching its objection in terms of an unfunded mandate and an administrative headache. Nevertheless, staff agreed to go along with the Senate version.

The Senate bill also applied deeming requirements to higher-education student loans and grants, while exempting recipients as of the date of enactment of the bill. The House exempted student loans and grants altogether. House GOP staff from the Economic and Educational Opportunities Committee said during preconference discussions that their committee's conferees would have problems with including higher education aid under deeming. They cited that only three percent of student loans go to immigrants, and these students have lower default rates than U.S. citizen aid recipients. In other words, the increased compliance costs to colleges and lending institutions would outweigh the savings to the federal government. Thus, conferees agreed to recede to the House provision.

Another difference was an amendment in the Senate bill authored by Charles Grassley (R-IA). This measure exempted nonprofit, charitable organizations from deeming requirements and stated that federal authorities could perform the eligibility checks on those participating in charitable programs. The House version contained no similar provision. Several organizations communicated support for the Grassley Amendment. These included the Human Services Forum, a coalition of social welfare groups including Catholic Charities USA, and the United Way, all of which contacted conferees directly. Republican staff proposed accepting the Grassley Amendment, but requiring the federal government to calculate the eligibility of aid recipients. Charitable organizations could distribute aid to individuals whom federal authorities had certified to be eligible.

This was generally how the provision appeared in the conference report. However, the final version required state or federal determination of one's eligibility and response to a charity's inquiry of an individual's status within ten days. It specified that after the ten days, the charity could go ahead and serve the person; also, deeming for charities only applied to public funds.

The Formal Conference Committee Meets

As Republicans continued to work out their own differences, the days slipped by. The Independence Day break came and went. Leadership in the House and Senate consulted Smith and Simpson, Dole and his advisers, and pressed on with budget and appropriations matters. Just before the August recess, Republicans finally struck agreements among themselves on most provisions. Smith sought to proceed with an expedited conference, naming House conferees, having them meet and hammer out a conference report, filing the report, and holding a floor vote on it all before the recess. Congressman Barney Frank (D-MA) threatened to pull out all procedural stops to delay the bill if Smith and the GOP leadership attempted to rush through a conference report before the August recess. By this time, Frank (D-MA), Berman (D-CA), and other committee Democrats were fuming about being excluded from the negotiation process. As Frank put it later:

> It [the conference negotiation] was a real disgrace under Lamar Smith. They ignored our input and totally froze us out. After House and Senate passage, the bill was totally rewritten. The Republicans acted despicably. Many of the full committee items were totally changed.
>
> We thought we could work with Lamar Smith but that turned out to be a sham. He totally ignored what we said. I've never seen a more blatant partisan performance. I'm not sure if Lamar was acting on Republican leadership orders or acting on his own, but it really doesn't matter because, if he was acting on orders, he certainly had no shame about executing them. (Frank interview 2/7/97)

In previous rounds of immigration reform, Democrats had included Republicans. One Republican aide involved in the process admitted that Frank had a point: "We should have given them a chance. We didn't even give them a chance to offer amendments. We had one five-hour meeting where the Democratic members were present." Others said that the exclusion of the Democrats was a practical necessity given that Republicans had a hard enough time reaching agreement among themselves.

It was not until September 11 that the House finally named conferees. On the evening of September 19, Speaker Gingrich (R-GA) convened a meeting of the GOP conferees. The Gallegly Amendment remained the sticking point. The question was whether to include the compromise version in the conference report. Six to 12 Republican Senators would vote against cloture (a motion to end debate and take up the bill, requiring 60 votes) along with most Senate Democrats, as long as the Gallegly language was included. That would be enough to kill the bill entirely.

Some proposed the idea of holding a separate vote on the Gallegly Amendment to please the Californians. One suggestion was to make it so watered down that it would be tough to vote against, such as to grandfather all current students. Another idea was to hold a Republican signing ceremony in San Diego, with Dole and California GOP members of Congress present while Speaker Gingrich signed the enrolled immigration bill.[2] This could be timed so as to let Republicans get credit for their bill and deny the president a White House Rose Garden signing ceremony just before the election. Simpson (R-WY) noted that, even without the Gallegly provision, H.R. 2202 was a tough reform bill.

Speaker Gingrich raised the idea of combining the immigration legislation with a continuing resolution, which would fund the government in case individual appropriations bills could not be finalized by September 30, the end of the fiscal year. Members agreed to proceed with a conference, leaving leadership the negotiating authority to determine how to dispose of the Gallegly Amendment and whether to combine the immigration bill with a spending package.

The formal House-Senate conference met September 24, and it ultimately amounted to a formality. Republicans found themselves backed into a corner, with time running out—given the widespread desire to adjourn in a week and go home to campaign. Most Democratic conferees were angered at having been excluded from the process. Some were perceived as unwilling to negotiate expeditiously; others were clearly not willing to negotiate in good faith at this point. They apparently recognized the time squeeze Republicans had gotten themselves into, and they sought to leverage their advantage to weaken the final bill substantially.

In the conference exchange, Democrats complained about being shut out of the process, how partisanship had driven the de facto conference procedure, and how they would never have countenanced such a closed process, especially for major legislation like this immigration bill. Edward Kennedy (D-MA) and Barney Frank (D-MA) made sanctimonious statements before the TV cameras, reporters, and congressional staff all jammed into a room in the Capitol. Yet the *Washington Post* published an editorial September 30 reminding Democrats that, under Democratic control, the conference report on the 1994 crime bill had been discussed in as closed a fashion as this legislation. "It's a terrible way to conduct the nation's business. But it's not the first time this has happened," the *Post* editorialized ("Pot and Kettle" 1996).

Dianne Feinstein (D-CA) was the only Democrat to make a plea for support of the legislation in spite of the closed conference process. She stated her intention to sign the conference report and that she would urge President Clinton to sign it. She reminded her colleagues that the public sentiment against illegal immigration remained strong and that immigration problems remained.

---

[2]The enrolled bill is the legislation signed by the House Speaker and presiding officer of the Senate, and sent to and signed by the president (Oleszek 1996).

The formal conference meeting lasted all morning, with conferees making statements one by one. By the time the conference meeting adjourned, no amendments had been allowed, and the conference report was essentially ready to be filed. It did not include the Gallegly Amendment, after all, nor a provision in both House- and Senate-passed bills to authorize new Labor Department workplace inspectors. Feinstein, the only Democrat to do so, signed the conference report along with all Republican conferees.

The House adopted the conference report of H.R. 2202 the next day by a vote of 305–123. All but five Republicans voted in favor of the report, and 76 Democrats also supported the measure.

The White House Responds

Headed toward adjournment and the end of the fiscal year, and with congressional Democrats effectively limited during the conference committee proceedings, the negotiating leverage shifted in the White House's favor. President Clinton pressed his advantage by placing new demands to modify the immigration bill (*CQWR* 9/28/96, 2755–2759).

Lobbyists from the White House conveyed these new demands to GOP negotiators September 26. The president demanded that the immigration provisions be included in the fiscal 1997 omnibus spending resolution. Clinton also insisted on dropping the bill's new employment discrimination standard and the new deeming and sponsor income requirements. Republicans had already agreed to remove the Gallegly Amendment, which disappeared at conference. Instead, the House voted on the Gallegly provision as a standalone bill, which passed 254–175, but stood no chance of Senate passage or presidential signature. GOP members were taken aback by the president's tough new posture.

Republican leadership in Congress worked toward bringing the H.R. 2202 conference report to a cloture vote in the Senate and negotiating inclusion of the immigration package in the omnibus spending bill (*CQWR* 9/28/96, 2755–2759). Even without the Gallegly Amendment, Republican leaders would have been hard-pressed to win 60 votes and invoke cloture on the conference report, at least in time to adjourn the session. Senator Simon (D-IL), a conferee, called it "bad legislation," though only three Senators opposed the bill when it originally passed the Senate (*CQWR* 9/28/96, 2755–2759). On September 26, GOP leaders acceded to Clinton's demand that the immigration bill be included in the spending package.

The night of September 26, Simpson and Smith, Kennedy and Berman met to work out a compromise. However, the next day, when the things agreed to the night before were committed to writing, the White House and Democrats found the legislative language unacceptable (*CQWR* 10/5/96,

2864–2866). Frustrations on both sides grew. Simpson said on the Senate floor, "The White House and Democrat allies have moved the goalposts" (*CQWR* 10/5/96, 2864).

Negotiations and strategizing continued throughout September 27. By 4:30 A.M. on September 28, the White House and Congress had struck a deal. Speaker Gingrich, in a meeting in his office, sat alone on one side of a long table, facing a number of White House, INS, and Justice Department political appointees. Although it was the middle of the night, politically it was high noon at the O. K. Corral. Administration officials one by one stated demands for changing the bill. One by one, Gingrich shot them down, just like Wyatt Earp. Gingrich used political bullets. He reminded the administration negotiators how each weakening proposal they demanded would play to voters, especially those in California, when GOP television ads explained it and laid the responsibility squarely on Clinton-Gore and Democratic candidates. Gingrich could not dodge every bullet, but he was still standing in the end. The Speaker accepted a set of White House demands and shook hands with the White House's chief lobbyist.

Smith and Simpson arrived at the end of the meeting in time to learn what had happened to their bill (*CQWR* 10/5/96, 2864–2866). The Speaker agreed to include the immigration bill in H.R. 3610, the omnibus fiscal 1997 spending package. He accepted lowering the sponsor income requirement to 125 percent of the poverty rate. He agreed to drop several provisions related to deeming and verification. No longer would participation in means-tested benefits programs for a year constitute a deportable offense. Nor would the length of time that sponsors are responsible for immigrants be increased. Naturalization would not be denied to an immigrant subject to deportation if that person had received public benefits for a year or if that immigrant's sponsor had not paid the costs for the benefits received. AIDS treatment couldn't be denied to illegal aliens. And there would be no mandatory verification to catch illegal aliens on welfare rolls, though to do so would now be at the discretion of the federal agency administering a given program (*CQWR* 10/5/96, 2864–2866).

Republican negotiators stood firm against President Clinton's efforts to remove the higher standard of proof for immigration-related discriminatory employment practices lawsuits. And, significantly, the exclusion and removal provisions remained intact. The House again passed the immigration bill, this time as part of a larger spending bill, on September 28. The Senate passed H.R. 3610 on September 30, and the president signed it that same day.

Immigration Provisions in the Welfare Reform Bill

A discussion of immigration legislation in the 104th Congress would not be complete without some mention of welfare reform. Although the president vetoed the original welfare reform legislation that had passed as part of the Contract with America, he eventually signed a compromise version that was included in the fiscal 1997 budget reconciliation bill. The welfare provisions limited the access of noncitizens to public welfare benefits. President Clinton signed the bill into law on August 22, 1996, just a month prior to approving the immigration legislation.

The immigration provisions in the welfare reform bill were not highly controversial among voters. The public does not approve of natives using welfare benefits, much less newly arriving immigrants. There is also a widespread public perception that government aid should not be redirected from needy citizens to the foreign-born. Under the new welfare reform law, legal immigrants faced stricter standards of eligibility for welfare programs. Illegal aliens and nonimmigrants became ineligible for most welfare benefits. Only refugees, asylees, and veterans would be covered by federal benefit programs. Also, sponsors of immigrants found themselves bearing greater responsibility for the immigrants for whom they had petitioned (Vialet and Eig 1996; Vialet et al. 1996; *CQWR* 8/3/96). Sponsor-to-alien deeming was expanded, so that needy immigrants would have to turn to the sponsors who brought them to America as a first resort. In other words, the welfare provisions sought to ensure that immigrants would be less likely to become public charges.

Sponsorship of immigrants now meant that sponsors would bear financial responsibility for the foreign-born family members they brought to the United States. Under deeming of sponsor income, when a noncitizen applied for a means-tested welfare program, the income of the noncitizen's sponsor would be considered as the noncitizen's, available to immigrants for ten years or upon naturalization with respect to most public benefit programs. Congress did include a number of exceptions, such as emergency medical services, public health assistance, Head Start, and some job training and educational assistance programs (Vialet and Eig 1996). States were allowed to deny legal immigrants access to some types of assistance, including Medicaid and TANF (formerly AFDC).

In summary, the welfare reform legislation set new, more restrictive standards of eligibility, whereas the immigration bill provided the enforcement mechanisms for those standards. The primary motive behind the immigration provisions in the welfare reform legislation was cost savings, plain and simple (Shaw interview 4/15/97). The Congressional Budget Office estimated that half of the budget savings from the welfare reform legislation—$23.7 billion of the estimated $54.1 billion to be saved over six years—would come from changing the immigrant eligibility criteria (Vialet and Eig 1996). "A billion here and a billion there and pretty soon you're talking about real money," it is said the late Senate Minority Leader Everett M. Dirksen (R-IL) once noted. Thus, even in Washington in 1996, $23.7 billion was considered real money.

Voting Divisions on the House Floor

The votes on the major amendments and on passage of the immigration reform bill reveal the nature of the political divisions on the House floor. We have argued throughout this book that immigration policy has grown both increasingly controversial and partisan. The Congress that sat between January 1995 and January 1997 was one of the most partisan in history. Predictably, most of the floor votes on immigration policy show strong lines of party cleavage even after other variables are taken into account.

The analysis of the House roll-call votes on immigration measures during the 104th Congress appears in Table 6.1 (see also Table A6.1 of the chapter Appendix). The most consistent division on these votes was between Republicans and Democrats. Even on the Chrysler-Berman-Brownback Amendment, where the business lobby had worked so hard to pull over GOP fence-sitters, an estimated 87 percent of Democrats voted yes, compared with only 39 percent of the Republicans. The Gallegly Amendment on education also split the parties, as 91 percent of Republicans voted in favor of it, compared with only one-fourth of the Democrats (see Table 6.1).

In spite of the fact that there were fewer Southern Democrats in the 104th Congress than ever before, divisions between Northern and Southern members were as strong as they have ever been. A lopsided majority of Southerners voted as a bloc in favor of the Gallegly Amendment to restrict education benefits, against the Chrysler-Berman-Brownback Amendment, and in favor of House passage of the final product. An estimated 85 percent of Southern members voted in favor of Gallegly's education amendment, compared with only 56 percent of Northern members (see Table 6.1). And on passage in the House, an estimated 92 percent of Southerners voted for the bill, compared with just 36 percent of Northern members (see Table 6.1).

Another important division in these votes occurred along racial and ethnic lines. The black, Hispanic, and Asian members voted cohesively against the Gallegly education amendment, and in favor of the Chabot Amendment to strike voluntary verification and the amendment to strike the legal reforms. Constituency characteristics were also influential. Those with significant black, Hispanic, and Asian constituencies were especially likely to vote to weaken Lamar Smith's bill by striking the provisions cutting legal immigration. Those with large foreign-born constituencies did not support final passage of the bill. The border state members showed considerable heterogeneity of opinion within their ranks. They voted as a solid majority bloc only in favor of the McCollum Amendment to develop a tamper-proof social security card.

Members from agricultural districts showed no overwhelming tendencies, except at the end of the debate, where they voted against striking the legal reform language and in favor of the Pombo guest-worker program and for final passage of the bill.

Table 6.1   Estimated Probability of Voting Yes on Immigration Amendments and Final Passage of House Bill, 104th Congress, U.S. House of Representatives

Variables	Vote on Rule	McCollum Amendment on Tamper Proof ID Card	E. Bryant Amendment on Hospital Identification	Gallegly Amendment on Public Education	Chabot Amendment to Strike Voluntary Verification	Chrysler Amendment to Strike Legal Reform	Pombo Amendment on Guest Workers	House Passage	Conference Report
Democrat	.07	.57	.06	.24	.33	.87	.11	.24	.48
Republican	.99	.38	.70	.91	.44	.39	.64	.83	.99
White member	.87	.48	.36	.72	.35	.59	.38	.55	.92
Nonwhite member	.66	.38	.08	.25	.61	.93	.12	.69	.61
Non-South	.79	.48	.23	.56	.40	.75	.25	.36	.86
South	.94	.45	.56	.85	.34	.40	.56	.92	.95
Nonborder state	.84	.43	.31	.68	.42	.69	.35	.57	.89
Border state	.88	.58	.29	.63	.29	.56	.28	.59	.93
Not Judiciary	.84	.45	.31	.68	.39	.67	.34	.56	.90
Judiciary Committee	.94	.67	.32	.52	.33	.53	.21	.69	.82
Foreign born = .22	.91	.45	.38	.76	.42	.59	.48	.80	.95
Foreign born = 58.5	.09	.59	.06	.09	.18	.94	.01	.01	.09
Agriculture = .17	.85	.48	.36	.63	.42	.73	.22	.53	.85
Agriculture = 24.7	.82	.36	.06	.88	.14	.06	.99	.89	.99
Black = .13	.90	.50	.31	.71	.36	.60	.32	.83	.91
Black = 74.0	.32	.32	.30	.36	.49	.87	.37	.01	.84
Asian/other = .37	.81	.50	.25	.67	.33	.65	.26	.57	.90
Asian/other = 87.5	.98	.21	.84	.64	.79	.72	.91	.56	.86
Percent unemployment = 2.5	.81	.61	.26	.72	.23	.67	.34	.24	.94
Percent unemployment = 41.3	.95	.08	.54	.40	.93	.62	.30	.99	.45

Values represent the estimated probability of a Yes vote at the lowest and highest value of the independent variables, with all other variables held constant at their sample means.

The conference report was voted on in September absent the Gallegly Amendment and most of the legal immigration reforms, which by that time had been stripped from the legislation (see discussion below on conference report). It passed on a solid 305–123 vote that divided the chamber primarily by party and race. Among those in opposition were the overwhelming majority of the black, Hispanic, and Asian Caucus members. Those in urban areas outside the South with a high proportion of foreign-born residents were also opposed to the conference report, particularly members from California and New York. Republicans opposing the conference report included the Floridians of Cuban ancestry—Lincoln Diaz-Balart and Ileana Ros-Lehtinen.

Of the votes included in our analysis, these results show that partisanship decisively split the chamber. Still, conservative Democrats did cross party lines on a number of votes. A strong consensus emerged between conservative Democrats and Republicans on many issues in the 104th Congress. Recall that we have argued all along that the costs imposed by legal and illegal immigration had been the persistent source of redistributive cleavage producing sharp disagreements between Republicans and Democrats in recent Congresses. The 1994 elections, including the vote on Proposition 187 in California, served as a wake-up call to many Democrats who had followed their party's traditional line on many redistributive themes. In addition, the 1994 elections were especially worrisome to Southern Democrats. Democratic incumbents who lost their seats that year were mostly from Southern states (Gimpel 1996). Democrats who survived but who represented moderate and conservative districts could see that a close identification with their liberal party leadership could endanger their longevity if the electorate continued to express conservative preferences as it had in 1994. The result of this kind of thinking on the part of cautious Democrats is evidenced by a study of the vote on the Gallegly Amendment to give states the option of denying education benefits to the children of illegal aliens. Only 19 Republicans voted against this amendment, compared with 49 Democrats who supported it. Only about half of these Democrats were from Southern states. Seventeen of the yes votes came from the industrial heartland states of Pennsylvania, Ohio, Indiana, and Illinois. In Pennsylvania, the seven Democrats representing districts outside of Philadelphia and Pittsburgh voted with Gallegly.

Conclusions

The restrictions and strengthened measures of the final bill attested to the fortitude of Smith and Simpson, as well as to the fact that the original bills had been so broad and strong. Business opposition to the bill was largely neutralized after Senate floor action. Once legal reform was dead, business groups lost interest. This left their liberal colleagues in the left-right coalition unable to gain entree with Republican legislators. The liberal advocacy groups had never established strong relationships with GOP lawmakers and, in fact, had figured that Republicans had no chance of ever holding a majority in Congress (Gimpel 1997).

The final version of the 1996 immigration reform legislation was not nearly as broad as either Smith or Simpson had intended. Many of the original provisions, most notably those restricting legal immigration levels, were scrapped, and significant parts of the bill had been weakened. Simpson and Smith were disappointed about the failure on legal immigration. They continued to believe that those holding expansionist views on immigration were naive. Nevertheless, the new immigration law was much tougher than President Clinton, liberal Democrats in Congress, or the ethnic interest groups desired.

Lessons from the 104th Congress

In retrospect, the House and Senate sponsors of the legislation learned some valuable lessons from the experience. The strength of the business coalition had been completely underestimated. While he had considerable Hill experience, Alan Simpson did not anticipate how influential the business groups would be with his fellow Republicans. In the early 1980s, when he had chaired the immigration subcommittee, few businesses were involved in the immigration debate. In 1990, they were more involved, but not well organized to influence a Congress controlled by liberal Democrats. By 1995, the business community both was well organized and had open access to congressional leadership offices in both chambers. It was no great surprise that they won the concessions they demanded, yet the sponsors of the legislation had no precedent from which to predict how powerful these groups would be. When the Republicans had last controlled both chambers, in the early 1950s, there were few businesses dependent upon foreign labor, and there was no high-technology business sector.

Other observers placed the blame on Simpson's management of the legislation in the Senate. "Simpson played too much the lone ranger last year," recalled one lobbyist for a pro-restriction group. "He didn't work with others. He figured they would give one to ole Al as his swan song." Some chided Simpson for being arrogant, temperamental, and dismissive of his junior colleagues. Simpson truly had expertise in this area, but politicians do not always respect expertise. On Capitol Hill, even experts must play Congress's political games with skill and finesse.

For their part, the interest group community learned that they did not need to influence the entire Congress to defeat legal reform. Just a few swing voters, perhaps 50 to 60, made the crucial difference between splitting legal from illegal reform or keeping the two together. The voting studies we have done suggest that the Republicans most likely to defect were those in the Northeastern and Midwestern states in districts on the urban fringe or in older suburbs.

Table 6.2   Provisions of the Illegal Immigration Reform and Individual
Responsibility Act of 1996, as Enacted

Border Enforcement

- **Border Patrol:** Authorized funding for hiring 1,000 new Border Patrol agents each year for five years; authorized funding to hire 300 new support staff each year for five years for work at the border; ordered INS to relocate agents to border areas with the most illegal aliens; ordered INS to coordinate agent relocation efforts with local law enforcement; ordered INS to report to Congress on these actions within six months.
- **INS agents:** Authorized funding for 900 new INS investigators for alien smuggling and harboring of illegal aliens cases; authorized funds for hiring 300 new INS agents to investigate visa overstayers.
- **San Diego border fence:** Authorized $12 million to add two additional fences and road construction at a 14-mile segment of the U.S.–Mexico border near San Diego, California; exempted the fence project from the Endangered Species Act and the National Environmental Policy Act; allowed the Attorney General to use condemnation to acquire land for the fence.
- **Entry-exit database:** Required the Attorney General to create a database of information on aliens from their entry and exit documents; the database, which will aid INS in identifying visa overstayers, is to be created within two years.
- **Preinspection stations:** Required INS to establish preinspection stations at five of the 10 foreign airports from which the most inadmissible aliens come, in order to screen those aliens with improper documentation.
- **State/local law enforcement cooperation:** Allowed INS to make cooperative agreements with state and local law enforcement agencies to assist in the investigation, arrest, transportation and detention of illegal aliens.
- **Checkpoint flight penalty:** Created a penalty for fleeing through an INS checkpoint, punishable by up to five years in prison and making flight a deportable offense.
- **Tamper-proof border crossing cards:** Required INS to develop border crossing identification cards for aliens, using a machine-readable biometric identifier, such as a fingerprint, to make the ID cards more counterfeit-resistant.

Alien Smuggling and Document Fraud

- **Alien smuggling penalties:** Established felonies for smuggling aliens, up to 10 years in prison for the first two offenses, 15 years for further offenses; created a criminal penalty for knowingly hiring 10 or more smuggled aliens, up to five years in prison.
- **Involuntary servitude penalty:** Doubled the penalty to 10 years for employers who keep smuggled illegal workers in a state of involuntary servitude.
- **Document fraud penalties:** Raised the penalty for document fraud offenses from five years to 10 or 15 years in prison; for document fraud affecting drug trafficking, the penalty becomes 20 years, and 25 years if it involves terrorism.

(Continued)

Table 6.2   Continued

- **Document fraud assistance penalties:** Established a civil penalty for assisting someone to make a false application for public benefits; made it a criminal penalty for "knowingly and willingly" not disclosing having given such help, with up to 15 years in prison.
- **False citizenship claim penalty:** Created an up to five-year prison penalty for falsely claiming to be a U.S. citizen.
- **Unlawful voting penalty:** Established a criminal penalty for illegally voting in a federal election, punishable by up to a year in prison.
- **Federal prosecutors:** Authorized 25 additional Assistant United States Attorneys to prosecute alien smuggling and document fraud cases.
- **Wiretap authority:** Authorized use of wiretaps in investigations of immigration document fraud cases.
- **Undercover investigations:** Granted INS authority to operate undercover investigations into illegal immigration rings; INS may use front companies.
- **Asset forfeiture:** Extended forfeiture of assets used in committing an immigration-related offense or bought with the proceeds of such a crime as part of the sentence, should the court choose to allow asset seizure.
- **Subpoenas and video testimony:** Authorized INS agents to subpoena witnesses and use videotaped testimony in removal proceedings.

Removal and Detention

- **Inadmissibility and expedited exclusion:** Declared aliens arriving at U.S. ports of entry without documentation or with false documents to be inadmissible, and detained and removed without a hearing unless they can demonstrate a credible fear of persecution in their home country; an asylum officer will screen such claims; if the officer determines that no credible fear exists, the alien is deported; however, the alien may request a review within seven days by an immigration judge; the review may be conducted by teleconference or telephone.
- **Removal (formerly deportation) proceedings:** Combined exclusion and deportation proceedings into one removal process; removal hearings may take place by teleconference or, with the alien's consent, by telephone; 10 days' notice of a removal hearing is required; removal orders may be canceled if the alien has continuously lived in the U.S. for 10 years, is of "good moral character," or if removal would cause exceptional hardship on immediate family members in legal status.
- **Judicial review:** Review petitions must be filed within 30 days of the final administrative order and will not automatically stay removal, which must be specifically granted by a court.
- **Judicial removal:** Allowed judges to issue orders of deportation as part of probation or a plea bargain agreement.
- **Removal sanctions:** Established criminal penalties for failing to leave after ordered removed; authorized the State Department to stop granting visas to countries that refuse to receive their removed nationals.
- **Departure:** Required removal of aliens within 90 days of a removal order; aliens ordered to be removed must be detained; violent criminal aliens must complete their prison sentences before removal; certain nonviolent criminal aliens may be removed from the country before their prison term expires.

Table 6.2 Continued

- **Detention:** Required the detention of most criminal illegal aliens upon completion of their prison terms; granted the Attorney General discretion to release certain illegal aliens if there is insufficient detention space, aliens who are not a security risk or a risk of fleeing or whose countries will not take them back.
- **Prisoner transfer treaties:** Urged the President to negotiate bilateral treaties to transfer prisoners so criminal aliens may serve their sentences in their home countries; required the Secretary of State and the Attorney General to report to Congress by April 1, 1997, on the potential for such treaties.
- **Local law enforcement in emergencies:** Authorized the Attorney General to delegate authority to local law enforcement to perform immigration-related duties during mass immigrant influxes.
- **Military base detention program:** Established a pilot program to examine use of closed military bases as INS detention areas.
- **Barred readmission of deported aliens:** Barred previously deported aliens from readmission to the U.S. for five years; if an alien left while deportation proceeding were in progress or attempted to re-enter illegally, the bar on admission is 10 years; repeat offenders and aggravated felons are barred for 20 years.
- **Illegal aliens' status:** Declared anyone illegally residing in the U.S. from 180 days to one year ineligible for legal status for three years; those illegally present for more than a year were denied status for 10 years; exceptions to the time limits are asylum applicants and minors; also exempt are battered women and children, and the spouses and minor children of amnestied aliens while their applications for legal status are pending.
- **"Benedict Arnold" re-entry bar:** Barred permanently from re-entry anybody who has renounced his citizenship in order to avoid taxes.
- **Additional deportable crimes:** Made stalking, child abuse and domestic violence crimes for which one is deportable.
- **Criminal alien tracking system:** Authorized $5 million to create a criminal alien tracking center; required that a criminal alien database authorized in the 1994 crime bill help local governments identify deportable criminals.
- **Vaccination requirements:** Deemed aliens without proof of vaccinations inadmissible.

Employer Sanctions

- **Employment verification pilot programs:** Required the Attorney General to develop three pilot programs to test various employment verification methods; first, in five of the seven states with the most illegal aliens, employers may voluntarily verify a new employee's immigration status electronically with an INS database; all federal agencies in the test states must take part in the test; the INS must respond to employers within three days; if the initial response is that the employee is undocumented, the INS has 10 days to confirm that fact.

(Continued)

Table 6.2   Continued

- **Citizenship attestation pilot program:** Called for testing of a second pilot program to allow U.S. citizens to attest to their citizenship in lieu of going through the employment verification system; employer participation in the program is voluntary; all federal agencies within test states must participate; this project is to work in conjunction with the new false claim of citizenship crime.
- **Machine-readable document pilot program:** Created a third pilot program in which voluntarily participating employers may scan a state-issued identification card into a machine, which will verify the card holder/employee's Social Security number through the INS database; this project will take place in states that include Social Security numbers in machine-readable form on driver's licenses or other state-issued documents; all federal agencies in test states must take part in the pilot program.
- **Immigration-related employment discrimination standard:** Required the government to prove an employer's intent to discriminate against a worker on the basis of his immigration status as the reason the employer requested additional identification documents or took other steps to comply with employment verification requirements.

Benefit Eligibility

- **Immigrant sponsor requirements:** Set minimum household income level for sponsors of immigrants at 125 percent of the poverty level, except active-duty military personnel, who may petition for family members with only 100 percent of poverty income; required sponsors to sign a legally enforceable affidavit pledging to assume financial responsibility for their sponsored immigrants— mean-tested benefits agencies of the federal and state governments may sue sponsors, and sponsored immigrants may sue sponsors for failing to provide the support pledged.
- **Social Security benefits:** Specified that illegal aliens are ineligible for Social Security benefits.
- **Subsidized housing assistance:** Required the HUD Secretary to deny subsidized housing assistance to families in which all members are illegal aliens; for families with some members legal immigrants and others illegal, HUD would adjust the financial benefit to the percentage matching the number of legally present family members.
- **Battered women and children exception:** Created an exception to the 1996 welfare reform law to allow victims of domestic violence to receive public benefits even though they are illegal aliens; the exception required the battered women and children to be in the same household as the perpetrator, and that the domestic violence and the need for public benefits be linked.
- **Deeming exception for nonprofit charities:** Excepted nonprofit charities from the requirement to verify the immigration status of aid recipients in order to determine benefit eligibility.
- **Food stamps:** Extended food stamp benefits to legal immigrants, who would become ineligible under the 1996 welfare law, until at least April 1, 1997, and as long as August 22, 1997, to allow time to complete the process of certification.

Table 6.2 Continued

- **False application for benefits penalty:** Allowed judges to triple the prison term and double the fine in cases of forging or counterfeiting official U.S. seals for the purpose of falsely applying for public benefits.
- **Hospital reimbursement:** Authorized federal reimbursement, subject to the amount appropriated, of emergency medical treatment of illegal aliens if the care is not otherwise federally reimbursed.
- **Public charge visa denial:** Let consular officers deny immigrant visas to individuals determined likely to become a public charge.
- **State driver's license pilot programs:** Authorized states to develop pilot programs to test ways to deny illegal aliens of driver's licenses; directed the Attorney General to issue a report to Congress on these projects in three years.
- **GAO student aid study:** Directed the General Accounting Office to study and report to Congress illegal alien's use of student aid; report due within a year.
- **GAO welfare study:** Ordered a GAO study of unlawful means-tested public benefits usage by illegal aliens; report due within six months.

Miscellaneous Provisions

- **Asylum:** Required those already present in the U.S. to file an asylum application within a year of entry; most cases must be heard within 45 days and a ruling issued within 180 days; if the ruling is appealed, the appeal must be filed within 30 days; asylum may be denied if the alien can be sent to a safe third country, the individual had previously been denied asylum, the applicant failed to file an application within a year of arrival; the Attorney General's determination that an alien is ineligible for asylum is not subject to judicial review; if home country conditions change, one's asylum may be rescinded.
- **Forced population control basis for asylum:** Added having undergone forced abortion or forced sterilization, or fleeing persecution for resisting coercive population control policies as a reason one may be eligible for asylum; adopted an annual cap of 1,000 people admitted on this basis.
- **Parole authority:** Limited the INS's ability to use parole authority to facilitate the mass immigration of detainees, as occurred in 1994 with Cuban detainees at Guantanamo Bay; made such usage of parole authority to count parolees toward legal immigration caps.
- **Location of visa processing:** Authorized the State Department to determine the procedures for processing immigrant visa applications and where the processing will occur; this addressed a federal appeals court decision in *LAVAS v. Department of State*, on appeal before the Supreme Court, that requiring Vietnamese monks and nuns to return to Vietnam from Thailand to apply for U.S. visas was discrimination based on nationality.
- **Public education:** Denied visas to immigrants intending to attend a public primary or secondary school for over a year.
- **Temporary visas:** Clarified that a nonimmigrant visa is immediately void should a person overstay its term; directed that a new visa must be obtained in the alien's home country, rather than in Mexico or Canada or another close country.

(Continued)

Table 6.2   Continued

- **Genital mutilation:** Made performing genital mutilation on a female 18 years old or older a crime punishable by a five-year prison term.
- **State-issued documents:** Called for the establishment of national standards for state-issued identification documents; mandated that driver's licenses and state ID cards must have Social Security numbers, or a state agency must verify the Social Security number with the federal government; states must apply the standards to birth certificates issued after Oct. 1, 2000, and to driver's licenses and state ID cards issued or renewed after that date.
- **Counterfeit-resistant Social Security cards:** Directed the Social Security Administration to develop a tamper-resistant Social Security card.
- **Report on temporary agricultural workers:** Directed the INS to report to Congress on whether adequate numbers of temporary agricultural workers will be available in the future; the report deadline was the end of 1996.
- **Mail-order brides:** Required international matchmaking businesses to give clients information on U.S. immigration laws; failure to inform clients will result in a $20,000 fine; directed the Attorney General to report within a year on the mail-order bride business.

(Sources: *Congressional Quarterly Weekly Report* 11/16/96, 3287–3289; INS *Congressional Legislative Resource Guide* February 1997)

The high-technology businesses and their allies in the immigrants' rights, ethnic, and religious communities are now braced to fight future battles on legal reform. They learned that they could work together in spite of having incongruent views on most other issues. The leaders of the ethnic and immigrants' rights groups are convinced that the Republican sponsors of restrictions harbor a genuine animosity toward immigrants. Liberal Democrats viewed the attempts by Simpson and Smith as part of the GOP's old "Southern strategy" whereby you woo white voters by stressing racially divisive issues. Asians and Latinos look different, so they make an easy target for exclusion.

Those in the religious community involved with refugee resettlement resented the GOP focus on the costs of immigration. As one lobbyist put it, "I think its disgraceful that it became an issue of costs and numbers. We are talking about people, not costs." To these groups, immigration is a matter of human rights, of morality, not of an accountant's balance sheet. The religious groups learned that effective arguments could be hung on stories about the human beings affected by immigration policy. This was a powerful advantage. Smith and Simpson could make abstract arguments about what was in the national interest, but their opponents could put faces on their arguments. The religious groups could show how someone's life would be changed if the immigration laws were altered. These advocates fought anecdote by anecdote.

Libertarian Republicans viewed attempts to restrict immigration as small-minded policy inspired by populists who have little understanding of economics. They learned that they could work in combination with liberal Democrats with whom they have almost nothing else in common. They could also sense that for all the negative opinions being expressed about immigration, there were some consequential voices that favored it. "The libertarians won the op-ed war," said one House aide who had worked to pass Smith's bill. "A majority of the intellectuals were on the other side. And this stuff is influential with members. They read it, especially when it's in their districts. Most editorials were full of this immigrant romance—vague feelings that we can't cut immigration because this is a nation of immigrants." The libertarian members could also see that, from an electoral perspective, the public sentiment against immigration was rather shallow, at least in their districts, and that they would not be punished for their votes against Smith and Simpson (see Chapter 2).

Arguably, the new law would have been more restrictive had Republican lawmakers not run out of time. It took months of negotiation to reconcile differences among House and Senate Republicans, especially given the sheer complexity of the two bills. The unskillful use of time represented a strategic blunder, although it was not the first time the clock ran out. Republicans were still learning to run Congress, and massive immigration reform bills had failed to pass in previous Congresses under far more experienced leadership.

APPENDIX TO CHAPTER 6

Table A6.1 Logistic Regression Estimates of a Yes Vote on Amendments and Final Passage of House Immigration Bill, 104th Congress, U.S. House of Representatives

Variables	Vote on Rule	McCollum Amendment on Tamper-Proof ID Card	E. Bryant Amendment on Hospital Identification	Gallegly Amendment on Public Education	Chabot Amendment to Strike Voluntary Verification	Chrysler Amendment to Strike Legal Reform	Pombo Amendment on Guest Workers	House Passage	Conference Report
Party (0 = D, 1 = R)	8.10**	-.79**	3.55**	3.44**	.46**	-2.34**	2.72**	2.74**	4.30**
	(1.22)	(.24)	(.38)	(.36)	(.24)	(.30)	(.33)	(.36)	(.63)
Minority member	-1.26	-.38	-1.84**	-2.05**	1.07**	2.31**	-1.49**	.57	-2.01**
	(1.06)	(.47)	(.79)	(.74)	(.47)	(.87)	(.71)	(.75)	(.71)
Judiciary Committee	1.13	.91**	.06	-.64	-.26	-.59	-.70	.53	-.74
	(.94)	(.39)	(.51)	(.61)	(.41)	(.52)	(.49)	(.62)	(.76)
Southern state	1.44**	-.11	1.48**	1.48**	-.28	-1.52**	1.33**	3.05**	1.15**
	(.71)	(.27)	(.40)	(.44)	(.29)	(.38)	(.37)	(.51)	(.51)
Border state	.39	.60**	-.09	-.20	-.55*	-.58	-.32	.08	.57
	(.79)	(.31)	(.42)	(.50)	(.33)	(.42)	(.40)	(.51)	(.59)
Percent foreign born	-.08**	.01	-.04*	-.06**	-.01	.04	-.08**	-.14**	-.09**
	(.04)	(.02)	(.03)	(.03)	(.01)	(.03)	(.03)	(.04)	(.03)
Percent black	-.04	-.01	-.001	-.02	.01	.02	.002	-.001	-.007
	(.03)	(.01)	(.02)	(.02)	(.01)	(.02)	(.01)	(.03)	(.01)
Percent Asian/other	.04	-.02	.04	-.002	.03	.004	.05**	-.002	-.01
	(.03)	(.02)	(.03)	(.03)	(.02)	(.02)	(.02)	(.02)	(.02)
Percent agriculture	-.01	-.02	-.09	.06	-.06	-.14**	.25**	.08	.20**
	(.10)	(.05)	(.06)	(.07)	(.05)	(.05)	(.07)	(.06)	(.08)
Percent unemployment	.08	-.15**	.06	-.07	.19**	.01	-.01	.36**	-.15
	(.15)	(.06)	(.08)	(.09)	(.06)	(.08)	(.08)	(.09)	(.10)
Constant	-10.78	2.13	-6.54	-3.61	-2.29	4.43	-5.27	-5.03	-3.24
% Correctly classified	60.5	61.9	79.7	86.9	68.0	76.5	76.5	84.0	71.3
Null model	95.8	54.0	60.0	61.0	62.0	57.0	57.0	58.0	87.4
χ^2 =	413.7	38.8	212.8	273.2	46.8	186.4	192.5	254.5	293.8
Significance	p < .0001	p < .0001	p < .0001	p < .0001	p < .0001	p < .0001	p < .0001	p < .0001	p < .0001
N =	385	412	420	420	419	421	422	412	428

Source: Congressional Quarterly Almanac and *Congressional District Databook,* various years. Dependent variable: 0 = No vote; 1 = Yes vote. MLE Coefficients; standard errors in parentheses; *p < .10; **p < .05 two-tailed tests.

CHAPTER 7

CONGRESS AND THE FUTURE
OF IMMIGRATION POLICY

Throughout this book, we have presented the major issues of U.S. immigration policy as they have been taken up by Congress since passage of the 1965 Immigration and Nationality Act. Understanding the growing controversy over immigration and the political sources of that controversy not only shows where immigration policy has been, but also lends some insight as to where it is likely to go.

In vast areas of the country, the public is ambivalent about immigration matters. And members of Congress representing ambivalent districts can afford to ignore the issue for reelection purposes. Even by the late 1990s, there were many areas of the country where recent immigrants had not settled, or had settled in small enough numbers that they were unnoticed. The majority of new arrivals continue to cluster in just a few states, contributing to the high salience of the issue in places such as Texas and California, but the comparatively low salience of the issue in the Midwest. Even so, the areas where immigrants have concentrated are so politically important to the control of Congress and the presidency that immigration cannot be ignored by national party leaders.

The Partisan Reaction: Redistribution

We have argued that immigration has been translated into a redistributive issue such that votes for and against immigration policies can be predicted by reference to political partisanship. As the immigrant-related costs to society through government expenditures have increased, the immigration issue has become more partisan. The redistributive character of immigration policy has been accentuated by budgetary constraints. As the number of immigrants has risen, immigrant use of welfare programs, entitlement programs, and other federally funded benefits has also risen. Dollars allocated for these programs take money away from other budget priorities. As federal spending has steadily risen, deficit spending has been the rule, and the portion of the budget that goes to pay interest on the national debt has grown. Entitlement programs, such as Social Security and Medicare, are expanding on autopilot as the population ages. Moreover, once eligibility for various government programs has been extended to various classes of immigrants, Congress's choices become even more limited. The country consequently finds it more difficult to meet these obligations it has accepted. With respect to entitlement programs, where all eligible comers are entitled to certain benefits, the costs are counted in the billions and grow by billions. Immigrant participants and the standards for their qualification naturally have drawn increased scrutiny from both policymakers and the public.

Second, immigration's redistributive aspect has been highlighted by the public's resistance to higher taxes (Jacobson 1993). As the costs associated with immigrants have gone up, politicians and taxpayers have questioned the contributions of immigrants to the economy. Increasingly, Americans resent the ability of immigrant sponsors to shirk their pledged responsibility to provide for the financial well-being of the immigrants they bring into the country. This side of the redistribution issue involving taxes paid and services consumed has primed the debate between Democrats, whose constituencies have often favored more government spending for social programs, and Republicans, who desire cuts in these program areas.

Third, the redistributive aspect of the immigration issue can be seen in the preoccupation with its disproportionate impact in some geographic areas. Certain states and localities have seen the costs of providing services to immigrants shoot off the charts. In addition to state-administered federal programs, states and localities have borne the economic impact of immigrants with respect to education, law enforcement, and a host of other public services within their jurisdictions. Because immigrants tend to settle in certain states and localities, such as California, New York, and Florida, those places that feel the economic impact of immigrants the most (as well as the impact of illegal entrants) have pressed for a national redistribution of resources from nonimmigrant areas to immigrant-receiving areas. Given immigrant settlement patterns, federal reimbursement of the costs of immigration involves redistribution.

The evidence for the increasing partisan cleavage in Congress on immigration matters appears in Figure 7.1. Here we have examined the extent to which recorded votes in the U.S. House of Representatives since 1965 have been divided by the party affiliations of members. Figure 7.1 clearly shows that recorded votes on immigration policy have become more partisan over time, even after controlling for alternative influences on congressional decision making such as region and constituency characteristics. Divisions between Republicans and Democrats have been on a steady upward climb since the 96th Congress (1979–1980), when the Democratic majority first introduced a generous resettlement assistance program for refugees.

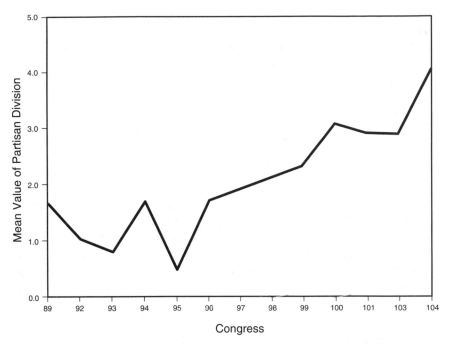

Values Based on Logistic Regression Coefficients for All Roll-Call Votes

Figure 7.1 Partisanship on Immigration Votes in the U.S. House of Representatives, 89th–104th Congresses

Of course the question that immediately arises is whether the increase in partisanship observable in Figure 7.1 is really the result of policy evolution, as we have argued, or some other force, such as the shrinking number of Southern Democrats. The differences in the regional and partisan composition of each Congress needs to be considered. In 1965, for instance, Democrats held a lopsided 294–141 majority. Of the 112 Southern seats, only 17 of them were in Republican hands. By 1996, the Republicans held the majority, and the number of Southern seats had increased to 125, of which 69 were in Republican control. Suppose that Southern Democrats occupied the same proportion of seats in the 104th (1995–1996) Congress that they did in the 89th (1965–1966). Would not these changes in legislative composition have made the difference between the nonpartisan voting on the 1965 Act and the highly partisan voting on Lamar Smith's restrictions in 1996? To investigate this possibility, we examined the proportion of Democratic seats in each of the Southern state congressional delegations in 1965 and, upon determining that proportion, reclassified the party identification of the Southern members of the 104th Congress to match the proportion of Republicans and

Democrats in the 89th Congress. For Texas, Louisiana, and Arkansas, the reclassification was straightforward. These delegations had no Republicans in 1965, so we reclassified all of the Republican seats as Democratic seats for our simulation. For the other Southern states, the recoding was more difficult. District boundaries had been reconfigured, and in some states such as Florida and North Carolina, there were many more districts than in the past. Our judgment was to reclassify the Republican seats as Democratic if the district's economic and social profile positioned it in approximately the same position on the relevant distributions as it occupied in 1965. The result of our reclassification was an increase in the proportion of Southern seats held by Democrats in the 104th Congress from 44.8 percent (the actual proportion) to 85.6 percent (roughly the same proportion held in 1965). Since the alternative hypothesis is only about the changing composition of the Southern congressional delegation, we did not alter the Northern seats.

The next step was to reevaluate the key votes in the 104th Congress using the reclassified data on Southern partisanship, that is, running the same statistical models we ran in Chapter 6 but substituting the new partisanship data for the old. By comparing the results of the simulated Congress to those of the actual 104th Congress, we could learn whether changes in the partisan divisions on immigration policy were purely a matter of the partisan realignment of the Southern congressional delegation. We would expect that the simulation would greatly diminish the effect of partisanship on immigration votes in the 104th Congress if the changes observable in Figure 7.1 were entirely the product of the replacement of Southern Democrats with Southern Republicans.

In fact, we discovered that partisanship remains a statistically significant explanatory variable for most of the immigration votes in the 104th Congress. We have presented a comparison of voting on two key measures by the actual and the simulated 104th Congress in Table 7.1. Counting many of the Southern Republicans as if they were Democrats makes only a modest difference to the partisan divisions on the House floor. In the actual Congress, an estimated 24 percent of Democrats voted in favor of passage of Smith's bill following the March floor debate, compared with 31 percent of Democrats in the simulation. Republicans still overwhelmingly favored the bill, and Democrats were only slightly more supportive. As for the conference report, 48 percent of Democrats favored passage in the actual 104th, compared with 57 percent in the simulated Congress (see Table 7.1 for comparisons). The difference between Republican and Democratic voting on these measures once the Southern Republicans are recoded as Democrats is still highly significant. The idea that the trend in Figure 7.1 can be explained entirely by the partisan changes in the Southern congressional delegation holds very little water. Even if many of the Southern Republicans had been Democrats, the votes on immigration measures would have divided the House chamber along party lines. Partisan conflict on immigration policy is largely a Northern phenomenon.

Table 7.1   Estimated Probability of Voting Yes on Final Passage of House Bill and the Conference Report, 104th Congress, U.S. House of Representatives

Variables	House Passage Actual 104th Congress	House Passage Simulated 104th Congress	Conference Report Actual 104th Congress	Conference Report Simulated 104th Congress
Democrat	.24	.31	.48	.57
Republican	.83	.87	.99	.99
White member	.55	.55	.92	.91
Nonwhite member	.69	.74	.61	.68
Non-South	.36	.30	.86	.82
South	.92	.96	.95	.97
Nonborder state	.57	.57	.89	.89
Border state	.59	.58	.93	.92
Not Judiciary	.56	.57	.90	.90
Judiciary Committee	.69	.70	.82	.81
Foreign born = .22	.80	.79	.95	.94
Foreign born = 58.5	.01	.01	.09	.20
Agriculture = .17	.53	.52	.85	.83
Agriculture = 24.7	.89	.93	.99	.99
Black = .13	.83	.85	.91	.85
Black = 74.0	.01	.01	.84	.01
Asian/other = .37	.57	.60	.90	.60
Asian/other = 87.5	.56	.43	.86	.43
Percent unemployment = 2.5	.24	.27	.94	.95
Percent unemployment = 41.3	.99	.99	.45	.21

Values represent the estimated probability of a Yes vote at the lowest and highest value of the independent variables, with all other variables held constant at their sample means.

Another alternative explanation for the trend in Figure 7.1 is that many issues have become more partisan in the 1980s and 1990s than in previous decades and that there is nothing special about immigration, per se. The increasingly partisan immigration voting patterns are simply part of a broader trend chronicled by other scholars (Rohde 1991; Poole and Rosenthal 1985; Poole and Rosenthal 1984). This explanation cannot be dismissed easily. American politics has been increasingly polarized since the mid-1960s (Poole and Rosenthal 1984). Immigration is not the only policy area that has evolved in a redistributive direction as the result of increasing budgetary pressure. Arguably, we could duplicate much of the analysis contained in this book for a number of other issues, showing how they are increasingly easy to understand in redistributive and partisan terms.

Where does this alternative explanation leave us with respect to our central thesis: that changes in the quantity and quality of immigration have been responsible for the diminishing consensus on immigration policy? Throughout, we have argued that changes in the nature of the immigrant population have made a critical difference to the debate. Beginning with the large-scale admission of refugees in the late 1970s, members began to argue about the cost of resettlement assistance. When the number of immigrants on Social Security, welfare, and other entitlement programs began to rise, programs for which middle- and upper-income voters bore a large share of the tax burden, Republicans such as Alan Simpson (R-WY) and Lamar Smith (R-TX) began to question the wisdom of the 1965 Act. Democrats, who had always defended entitlement spending as a means of aiding society's poor and underprivileged—many of whom could be counted upon as loyal Democratic constituents—naturally took a more pro-immigrant viewpoint.

Cultural Reaction

The influx of immigrants has been accompanied by a focus on their consumption of resources redistributed to them from middle- and upper-income taxpayers via government programs. But other concerns have been voiced as well. Protest has arisen over the extent to which immigrants contribute to changes in traditional values and mores, ranging from objections to multicultural curricula to complaints about Hollywood and Madison Avenue elitists reshaping advertising and entertainment to suit the tastes of a new population (Schlesinger 1992). The unprecedented levels of immigration from just a few nations has created large and lasting ethnic subcultures. By virtue of the size of these communities, immigrants living within them do not have the same incentives to Americanize, or to become enculturated. The slow pace of assimilation among the newer arrivals has engendered the resentment of the native-born against segments of the immigrant population. Many citizens and legal residents resent the proliferation of neighborhoods where only Spanish (or another foreign language) is heard. Many members of Congress routinely receive letters complaining about foreign-language signs, phone books, and automatic teller machines. The pervasive subculture makes it seem to these constituents as though they were living in a different country altogether.

Cultural distinctions have long manifested themselves in congressional voting behavior by virtue of regional differences in the reaction of members to certain issues. The primary division between those who favored repeal of the National Origins Quota System in 1965 and those who did not was between North and South, not between Republicans and Democrats (see Chapter 4). Divisions of this kind reflect rival cultural orientations. While the South is changing, Southern political culture was once rooted in the stability of thick kinship ties, firmly rooted communities, institutionalized segregation, few immigrants, and the slow pace of rural and small town life. Northern culture, on the other hand, was accustomed to faster population growth, large industrial cities, more mobility, weaker kinship ties, and more immigrants. The North was not always less racially segregated than the South, as residential patterns even in the 1990s clearly indicated. But segregation was never institutionalized there.

We have examined trends in the regional cleavages between Northern and Southern members on House roll calls since the mid-1960s. This trend is charted in Figure 7.2. The average division between the two regions in Congress diminished from the 89th (1965–1966) to the 93rd Congress

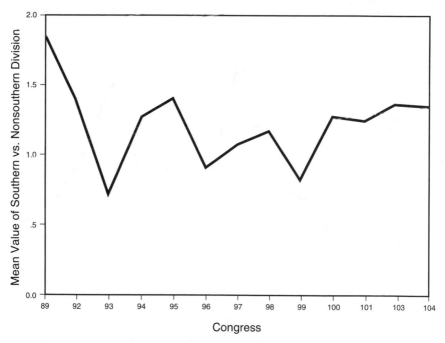

Values Based on Logistic Regression Coefficients for All Roll-Call Votes

Figure 7.2   North vs. South Division on Immigration Votes in the U.S. House of Representatives, 89th–104th Congresses

(1973–1974), and has been rather erratic since then. The cleavage between North and South peaked in the 95th (1977–1978) and 98th (1983–1984) Congresses and has remained high since the 100th Congress (1987–1988). Southern opposition to the extension of refugee assistance benefits probably accounts for the peak in the 95th Congress. Southern members, after all, had few immigrant constituents pushing for the entry of more refugees. As one Southern congressman put it in a 1997 interview, "I dare say we don't get any mail that says, 'Make the immigration laws more relaxed.'" Southerners and Northerners were in sharp disagreement in the 98th Congress until the inclusion of an agricultural guest-worker program brought conservative Democrats on board in the 99th Congress for passage of the 1986 Immigration Reform and Control Act. The steady opposition of the Southern delegation to liberalized immigration policies since the late 1980s can be accounted for on ideological grounds associated with the South's traditional culture.

Another chart (Figure 7.3), indicating the influence of multiculturalism on voting in the House, plots the impact of a foreign-born vs. native-born

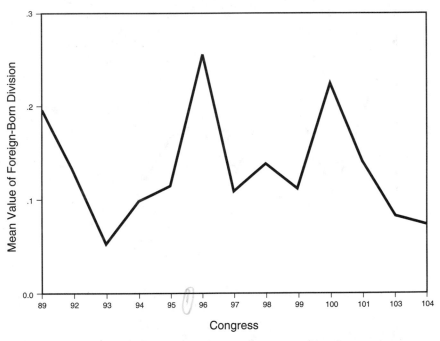

Values Based on Logistic Regression Coefficients for All Roll-Call Votes

Figure 7.3   Foreign-Born vs. Native-Born Divisions on Immigration Votes in the U.S. House of Representatives, 89th–104th Congresses

constituency on immigration votes. Legislators with immigrant constituencies were especially likely to vote against those with native-born constituencies in the 96th Congress (1979–1980) and the 100th Congress (1987–1988). The 100th Congress was unremarkable except that House Democrats tried to push for an extension of the amnesty deadline and for the extended voluntary departure of Central American refugees. These efforts were apparently greeted with unusual hostility by those from districts with predominantly native-born populations. In the 104th Congress, having an immigrant constituency was surprisingly inconsequential once other influences on congressional behavior had been accounted for. Partisanship dominated the debates in the 104th, minimizing the influence of other member or constituency traits.

Class and Racial Reactions

Yet another factor fueling controversy over the immigration issue is economic fear (Citrin, Green, Muste and Wong 1997). In times of economic uncertainty, many Americans understandably fear the loss of their livelihoods. This seems to be especially the case with union laborers and low-skilled workers, including many ethnic minorities. When the economy sours or undergoes dramatic shifts, these Americans fear the loss of jobs and wage depression due at least in part to the presence of immigrants, illegal aliens, and temporary foreign workers.

In the 1970s, stagflation coincided with mass opposition to the large refugee influx. In the early 1990s, a recession and corporate downsizing shook the U.S. economy simultaneously with a high immigrant inflow. The consequences of the amnesty program, high legal immigration levels, and the troublesome presence of illegal residents have often contributed to the insecurity of many native-born Americans in the past quarter century. Interestingly, our findings in Chapter 2 indicated that those workers who are better educated and highly paid do not share the same level of hostility to open immigration policies. They are more tolerant of immigration—not only because they have a broader range of life experience given their education, but because they can afford to be.

Strangely, we did not find in our study of immigration policymaking that district economic conditions had much impact on the way in which members voted on immigration policy once other district characteristics were taken into account. In the cases when economic conditions did have a clear impact, it was often in the direction opposite the one we had hypothesized. Those representing areas of high joblessness often voted for open immigration policies and against restrictions. We suspect this is because those districts with the highest unemployment rates were in urban areas where immigrants often settled. Ironically, the labor market position of many ethnics may be eroded by the liberal immigration policies that their representatives support. But in the clear choice between family reunification or economic advancement, many immigrants prefer family reunification first and foremost.

Nor did we find that the size of a legislator's black constituency had any relevance to his or her voting on immigration legislation. Blacks often view themselves as a deprived group and resent the use of affirmative action programs by Hispanics and Asians. In Chapter 1, we suggested that because the labor market position of blacks may be threatened by new arrivals, members representing largely black constituencies would favor immigration restrictions. In fact, the opposite is usually true. Those with black constituencies often vote for expansive immigration policies. That may be due to the fact that most districts with large black populations also have large immigrant populations. Blacks and immigrants are competing for housing and jobs in the very same neighborhoods. A member of Congress trying to represent both interests is therefore cross-pressured. Inasmuch as immigrants outperform blacks in urban labor markets, earning more money and holding better jobs (Waldinger 1996), the legislator may respond to the more prosperous and politically active group within the district—immigrants—therefore voting against restrictions most of the time.

Even African American legislators vote against restrictions and against the ostensible economic interests of the black populations they represent. Clearly the ideology of civil rights and equal opportunity is informing their votes in favor of expansive immigration and refugee policy. Black, Hispanic, and Asian leaders frequently view immigration policy through the lens of a minority rights framework. To maximize their political clout, they band together in Congress to work for policies they believe benefit all ethnic and racial minorities. The fact that certain policies may disadvantage one ethnic or racial minority constituency among their coalition appears not to enter the political equation.

When they do not explain their votes in terms of minority rights, often black legislators will justify voting with their Asian and Hispanic colleagues by appealing to arguments originating out of the new labor movement. In the 1980s, labor union leaders began to argue that it was the fault of employers that immigrants and blacks often wound up in competition for low-skill jobs. Hiring the newest wave of immigrant arrivals is a means employers use to pit worker against worker in keeping wages low and preventing the organization of labor unions (Torres interview 5/17/97). Minority legislators, so it is argued, understand that manipulation and, rather than turning against one another, instead coalesce to fight for workers' rights, regardless of the workers' skin color or national origin.

The modern view within the labor and civil rights communities is that workers' rights and civil rights are indistinguishable. Before the 1980s, labor leaders had little interest in fighting for civil rights. The changing demography of labor union membership is responsible for this historymaking combination. The AFL-CIO, under the leadership of John Sweeney, has focused renewed efforts on organizing ethnic minorities and women. In the past, labor's strength was based on traditional economic sectors such as manufacturing and construction—employment sectors where few minorities were employed. With economic restructuring has come a smaller, but very different labor movement. Service workers are the source of most of the union movement's new growth, and these employees consist largely of women, Hispanics, Asians, and African Americans. Unions are increasingly hiring organizers who speak and look like the people they are trying to organize.

Because workers' rights and civil rights have become intertwined in the 1990s, both black legislators and their Hispanic and Asian colleagues from districts with large immigrant populations see business as their common enemy. The Black, Asian-Pacific, and Hispanic Caucus organizations in Congress can therefore justify a united front, voting cohesively in favor of efforts to increase the availability of immigrant visas for purposes of family reunification, in favor of amnesty for illegals, and against efforts to restrict immigration.

Ideological Orientations and Immigration Attitudes

Aside from redistribution and ethnic group rights, political leaders may turn to other philosophical justifications for their positions on immigration policy. Policymakers construe the role of government in the economy either broadly or narrowly. Valuing a broad role for government naturally leads to the view that the government should have a substantial role in taking care of the needy. Those holding a broad view of government's role, with respect to immigration policy, would likely favor heavy government involvement in refugee admission and refugee assistance, for example. They might set a low threshold for immigrant eligibility for public benefits. Those who value a narrow role for government would place a premium on individual responsibility. They would say that beyond an individual's own responsibility lies the immigrant sponsor's primacy for the immigrant's well-being, and beyond that, private entities should provide for the welfare of immigrants. To them, the government is the last resort for provision of assistance. Clearly, these values are related to the redistributive questions involved in formulating immigration policy.

Another perspective focuses on which set of rights should take precedence. In this vein, individual rights are pitted against community rights. Those who place the higher value on the rights of individuals will believe that every individual possesses the right to immigrate, the right to asylum, and the right to due process in the deportation process. In opposition to this view are those who argue that a regard for the rights of the majority should guide policy decisions. This perspective does not devalue individual rights; it simply values the rights of the community of people to bind together in a society, to agree on their own rules to govern that society, and to require newcomers to abide by the rules of the group. When rules need changing or new rules are necessary, the group's corporate decision takes precedence over the individual rights of dissenters. These competing values do not represent a clearcut either/or choice. Usually, these two values operate on a continuum.

Some hold religious presuppositions that lead them to base immigration policy on a broad concern for human rights. They believe in corporate compassion. A guiding principle may be thought of as, "To whom much is given, much is required." Presuppositions of this kind lead one to conclude that a wealthy and well-blessed nation such as the United States bears a great responsibility to the less fortunate of the world. It is easy to follow the rationale moving from these presuppositions to a belief in a broad role for the government.

On the opposite side is a belief rooted in individual duty and personal responsibility. The guiding principle is to count the costs beforehand. Rather than corporate compassion, this view believes in individual compassion. It would be wrong for another (including the government) to commit someone else's resources to obligations with which he disagrees, perhaps on the grounds that those to be assisted have not exhausted more immediate alternatives. In the immigration context, one would view the country's first obligation as the welfare of its citizens, then to the immigrants already here. Afterwards, if the nation can afford it, the country may admit and aid other immigrants. This perspective may be thought of in terms of concentric circles. It begins viewing one's responsibility from oneself outward to one's family to one's neighbors to one's community and so on. It would be seen as immoral to shirk one's immediate responsibilities in order to accept and try to meet more distant obligations. And it certainly would be immoral to an individual holding these presuppositions for the government to do likewise. One may understand how such presuppositions lead to a view of limited government.

At heart, these ideological divisions derive from the ongoing debate of what America and American culture are all about. They are bound up with tradition and history, with the story of the nation and the countless stories of individuals and families. In a country that perceives itself metaphorically as a great melting pot, as a nation of immigrants, these philosophical differences are far from secondary. Rather, they are central to the nation's self-image and weave a rich intellectual fabric stretching back generations.

Looking to the Next Century

The temporary charter of the U.S. Commission on Immigration Reform expired in 1997. To the very end, the commissioners held hearings hoping to influence the direction of the policy debate. In its final report issued September 30, 1997, the Commission reiterated its call for cutting legal immigration. The Commission's efforts continued to focus attention on the growing backlog in the immigrant visa queue. In its final report, the Commission called for legal immigration cuts, dismantling part of the INS bureaucracy, renewing an emphasis on "Americanization," and simplifying the temporary visa system. The report also took issue with some of the new immigration law's reforms (CIR Report 1997).

Only time will tell if this Commission will be as instrumental to changing immigration law as the Hesburgh Commission was. The Hesburgh Commission had issued equally controversial recommendations but was not as subject to attack as the Jordan Commission had been. The difference is due partly to the fact that pro-immigrant interest groups had grown much stronger in the 15 years between the commissions. An additional blow to the Jordan Commission's influence was the death of Barbara Jordan early in 1996. She was a person of integrity and strong views. President Clinton could not as easily have abandoned the Commission's proposals on legal reform had Jordan survived. The Jordan Commission suffered a related weakness in that none of its appointees were sitting members of Congress. The Hesburgh Commission's recommendations could be easily advanced into legislation because leading members of the Judiciary Committees, including Alan Simpson, served as commissioners. While the Jordan Commission's members were clearly distinguished, hardworking people, this commission had no direct connection to Capitol Hill in the manner of the earlier commission.

The debate over the direction of immigration policy continued in the 105th Congress (1997–1998). Congressional committees held oversight hearings to ensure that the 1996 Act was being implemented properly. Agricultural interests, led by the American Farm Bureau Federation, were back arguing for a new and improved guest-worker program. Proposed legislation, including constitutional amendments, would deny birthright citizenship to the children of illegal entrants (H.J. Res. 26, H.J. Res. 60, H.R. 346). The House immigration subcommittee, still under the chairmanship of Lamar Smith (R-TX), held a hearing in the summer of 1997 on such a bill (H.R. 7) sponsored by California Congressman Brian Bilbray (R-CA) (*CQWR*, 6/25/97). Bilbray argued that granting citizenship rights for children of illegal immigrants rewards those who have broken the law. The Clinton administration fiercely opposed such a plan, arguing that denying automatic citizenship to U.S.–born children counters a basic constitutional guarantee. The Orange County, California, Board of Supervisors voted July 1, 1997, to endorse federal legislation to end automatic citizenship at birth, reflecting the lingering intensity of the immigration issue in California (Grad 1997).

Other proposed legislation offers to change the conditions of temporary worker programs, improve the integrity of Social Security cards and provide for criminal penalties for work-authorization document fraud, provide for stricter citizenship checks for prospective voters, impose a moratorium on most immigration, loosen the standards for naturalization, and not count the work experience of illegals for U.S. admission purposes.

The bills to require stricter checks on citizenship arose in response to a fall election in which Southern California Congressman Robert Dornan (R-CA) was defeated by political neophyte Loretta Sanchez by only 984 votes. Dornan disputed the results of the election on the ground that noncitizens had voted for his opponent. A follow-up investigation revealed that 227 noncitizens had indeed voted fraudulently and that they were encouraged to do so by an immigrants' rights group, Hermandad Mexicana Nacional, which had been sponsoring citizenship classes (Warren and Reza 1997; Warren, Filkins, and Reza 1997). Further investigations failed to uncover enough fraud to warrant overturning the election results in the Dornan-Sanchez race. After a year-long congressional investigation, the House voted to dismiss the challenge to Sanchez's election. The House Oversight Committee reported finding evidence of hundreds of ballots cast by noncitizens, but could not document enough illegal ballots to invalidate the election's results (Wilgoren 1998). Additional controversy was fueled by the revelation that INS officials knew that private agencies had been assisting noncitizen registration and voting, but had done nothing. Republicans inferred from these investigations that the Clinton administration had relaxed the rules on voter registration before the 1996 election in order to expand the pool of Democratic voters.

A similar case of immigration-related voting fraud was under investigation in Texas. Federal prosecutors in Dallas voiced frustration that INS headquarters in Washington was apparently hindering the investigation of alleged noncitizen voting in the November 1996 and May 1997 elections. While the U.S. attorney and the district INS office sought to run computer records checks of the local elections against the INS computer files in Washington, INS in Washington seemed to quash efforts at interagency cooperation. The Federal Bureau of Investigation assumed control of the investigation after INS headquarters stopped the Dallas district INS office from proceeding (Mittelstadt 1997a).

Alarming problems with alien smuggling and exploitation came to light in 1997. Authorities cracked a smuggling ring that brought deaf Mexicans to the United States and used them to sell trinkets on the street. The exploitation of these helpless immigrants ignited outrage throughout the country (Moore and Kasindorf 1997).

Cross-border shootings plagued the southern border. U.S. Border Patrol agents were fired upon on several occasions (Sanchez and Green 1997). U.S. troops were increasingly deployed along the border, primarily to combat drug trafficking (Mittelstadt 1997b). Troop deployment won congressional support, despite an incident in which U.S. Marines shot dead a teenager who appeared to threaten them with a firearm.

One interesting study also revealed that tightened border enforcement may have aggravated the problem of illegal immigration since the crackdown kept illegal aliens already in the country from going home (McDonnell 1997a). The Border Patrol attributed bolder, more outrageous means of alien smuggling to its effectiveness at tightening the border. And effective border enforcement had driven up the fees smugglers charge. One weekend in late January 1998, the Border Patrol caught three separate smuggling attempts that used tractor-trailer trucks. Alien smugglers, trucking their human cargo on routes farther east from San Diego in the desert, each carried more than 100 illegal aliens. One of the trucks held 177 people. Border Patrol officials learned that the aliens had paid the smugglers from $800 to $1,000 apiece for the desperate attempt to break U.S. immigration law. That fee two years earlier was $200 (Reza 1998).

The judicial branch shared a role in the immigration policy debate as the Supreme Court refused to take up lower-court rulings related to state efforts to obtain federal reimbursement for expenses due to illegal immigration. Arizona and California had advanced a novel legal theory in lawsuits against the federal government. The theory, that the federal government had failed to protect those states against invasion when it failed to keep illegal aliens from overrunning the borders, was rejected by separate lower courts. The courts ruled that the states' immigration disputes were political questions and not "justiciable"—subject to resolution by the judiciary (Carelli 1997). And a federal judge in California ruled November 14, 1997, that Proposition 187 was unconstitutional. Notably, the judge's opinion rested largely on the 1996 welfare reform law, not the Constitution. The ballot initiative's supporters had charged the judge as exhibiting bias in the case because she had taken three years to issue a ruling—widely viewed as a delay tactic. At least now Prop. 187 supporters could proceed with an appeal. The state attorney general— one Dan Lungren, formerly of the House Judiciary Committee—said, "I find that Judge Pfaelzer's interpretation of Congress' intent when drafting the federal welfare law defies all logic." Many expected the case ultimately to be decided by the U.S. Supreme Court (McDonnell 1997b).

Meanwhile, *National Review* senior editor Peter Brimelow, an ardent restrictionist, made the case against mass immigration on the basis of electoral politics (Brimelow and Rubinstein 1997). He argued in a feature article, "Electing a New People," that the demographics of modern immigration are transforming American electoral politics against Republicans and in favor of Democrats. Evidence from the 1996 elections seemed to prove him right. Election Day polls indicated that Asian and Hispanic support for Republicans had dropped from previous years, leading many Republicans to worry that the party was being typecast as anti-immigrant.

Based on the GOP's political fear of alienating Asians and Hispanics, the 105th Congress backtracked on certain provisions in the immigration and welfare reforms passed in the 104th Congress. One of the leaders of this reversal was Senator Spencer Abraham (R-MI). Proponents of immigration restrictions were discouraged to see Abraham succeed Alan Simpson (R-WY) as chairman of the Senate immigration subcommittee. Abraham began his tenure as chair by holding hearings highlighting the contributions immigrants have made to the country. He hired as his chief committee aide Stuart Anderson, the CATO Institute's immigration specialist who helped cement the coalition against legal immigration reform in 1996. Abraham prosecuted his campaign so forcefully that the National Council of La Raza honored him with an award, praising Abraham as "a guardian of the melting pot" (Freedberg 1997).

As congressional leaders and the White House agreed to a blueprint to achieve a balanced federal budget by 2002, they revisited provisions in the 1996 welfare reform bill that restricted eligibility requirements for immigrant participation in welfare programs. The pressure grew to restore those benefits for certain legal immigrants (*CQWR* 5/17/97; "Former DOL Official...", 6/6/97). Republican governors from states with large immigrant populations, including George Pataki (R-NY), Jim Edgar (R-IL), and Lincoln Almond (R-RI), lobbied Congress to revisit aspects of the legislation. Democratic governors pressured the Clinton administration for changes. Realizing that considerable savings came out of the new changes in the welfare law, Republican congressional leaders initially refused to reopen the welfare issue. "The word is out that it is easy to come to America and go on welfare," said House Ways and Means Chairman Bill Archer (R-TX) on a national television news program. "That's not what America is all about and we were elected to protect the taxpayers from this kind of abuse" (Cimons 1997).

In spite of Archer's intransigence, immigrants' rights advocates mobilized and won a policy reversal in the Balanced Budget Act that the White House and Congress hammered out. In the deal, elderly and disabled noncitizens had their eligibility for Supplemental Security Income (SSI) benefits restored. As the new immigration and welfare reform provisions began to take effect, most states maintained immigrants' eligibility for welfare benefits. In some cases, they were forced to use state funds to support their generosity (Meckler 1997). Among the most generous states were those with the largest immigrant populations—California and New York. The robust national economy eased the decision to pick up the tab for immigrant welfare because state tax revenues were higher and welfare rolls were smaller than in years past.

Meanwhile, more facts were coming to light about the costs associated with a nettlesome welfare situation—mixed households, with illegal parents and citizen children. As part of the 1996 welfare reform, Congress had called for the General Accounting Office to study how much in welfare payments went to illegal alien families through their eligible children by virtue of the children's U.S. citizenship. The GAO found that in 1995, legal children of illegal parents collected in excess of $1 billion in public assistance. While the children qualified for benefits such as AFDC, Medicaid, Food Stamps, and SSI, the illegal aliens in their households were ineligible. However, welfare payments to the minor children also benefit the illegal parents in these households. The GAO study illuminated the extent to which illegal adults in mixed households use their children's citizenship to collect taxpayer-funded benefits for which they themselves don't qualify (GAO 1997; Love 1997).

The restoration of SSI benefits encouraged the pro-immigration lobby to press for more reversals (Healy 1997). In the face of interest group pressure, Congress backed down on deporting hundreds of thousands of Central American refugees. When President Clinton paid a state visit to Latin America in May 1997, Mexican officials voiced concerns over America's new immigration law (Kitfield 1997). Mexican and Central American countries were concerned that massive deportations would suddenly flood their labor market with unskilled workers, perhaps leading to economic and political chaos. Even House Speaker Newt Gingrich (R-GA) voiced support for blocking their deportation, based on the Reagan administration's foreign policy in Central America during the 1980s, which had resulted in the refugee influx in the first place.

The emboldened lobbyists and ethnic advocacy groups applied political pressure to loosen up federal rules for immigrant eligibility for food stamps; for extension of Section 245(i), which allows immigrants—including illegal aliens—to remain in the country and adjust their status; and for additional funds to clear the backlog in naturalization petitions (Healy 1997). Marchers in Manhattan called for a mass amnesty for all illegal aliens present in the United States.

Section 245(i), added in 1994, allowed illegal immigrants to pay the INS a $1,000 penalty and adjust to legal status while remaining in the country. This provision was set to expire on September 30, 1997. During the 1996 round of immigration reform, Congress had decided to let 245(i) die. Illegals would then have to return home and petition for a valid visa from abroad. However, because 245(i) had raised millions of dollars for the INS, the agency supported permanent extension. The issue boiled down to continuing 245(i), with illegal aliens paying the government, or letting it expire and forcing illegal immigrants to go home (Edwards 1997). Congress temporarily extended the measure in short-term spending bills.

As 1997 closed, new immigrant sponsorship requirements began to take effect. INS drafted regulations to enforce these changes in the law, drawing criticism from all sides (Branigin 1997). Nevertheless, the tighter requirements adopted in the 1996 law meant that it would be tougher for family-based immigrants to gain admission because their sponsors would have to meet an income threshold. The reforms gave teeth to the public charge provisions of U.S. immigration law, and those teeth were about to take their first bite.

At the borders, the INS continued to pour its windfall of congressionally mandated resources into the effort to prevent illegal entry. Arrest statistics remained as high or higher along the southern border as they had in previous years, leading observers to doubt whether enforcement was stemming the tide. Presumably, a decline in the number of arrests is an indication that illegal immigrants have given up on their attempt to enter the country. But along the southern border, arrest is followed by release back into Mexico, whereupon many illegals only repeat the attempt.

The INS stepped up deportation of illegal immigrants and legal immigrants who had committed crimes. INS agents began routinely checking jails and prisons to ensure that, once deportable aliens had served their sentences, they could be removed from the country. In the summer of 1997, the INS launched "Operation Global Reach" to crack down on alien smuggling rings in foreign countries. Under this new plan, 13 overseas offices would be opened, and criminal investigators and intelligence officers would be posted abroad to help stem the traffic in human cargo (McDonnell and Bass 1997). Because it is much cheaper to prevent illegals from entering the country than it is to find them once they have settled here, the INS is expected to continue these efforts.

Congress and the executive branch will have to balance domestic and foreign-policy interests in the coming years, as enforcement efforts have been greatly increased and as activists push and pull political strings. In Washington, issues rarely ever go away. They recur according to changing circumstances and in connection with events that capture the public's focus.

Future research would do well to investigate the sources of public opinion on immigration (see Citrin, Green, Muste and Wong 1997). Racial attitudes and economic fears are important, as we noted in Chapter 2, but peoples' attitudes may be crystalized by non-economic and non-racial factors. Particularly important, but difficult to measure, are attitudes toward cultural differences among groups that are separable from racial attitudes. Some may oppose high immigration levels because they doubt the capacity of certain groups to assimilate well, or because they may sense among recent arrivals a growing group rights or entitlement mentality they judge to be alien to American values of individual rights and self-effort (Citrin, Reingold and Green 1990). Also, more investigation is warranted into why some groups continue to be less favorably received by natives than others. A negative attitude toward one group is not necessarily racism, per se, but could be formed on a legitimate basis. Someone may have firsthand awareness of undesirable conduct of members of a particular group in the community. Often, research in this area has dismissed perceptions of the negative conduct of certain groups as a function of prejudicial stereotyping based on limited exposure to one or two instances of the negative behavior (Henderson-King and Nisbett 1996; Hurwitz and Peffley 1997). But very little research has been done to verify whether peoples' judgments about the behavior of certain groups has any basis in reality, or could reflect more than hearsay or the experience of rare and isolated instances.

Immigration policy debates will ebb and flow both in the short term and over the long term. Members of Congress will weigh these issues in light of constituency demands as well as their own desire to produce good policy. Perhaps increased mass immigration and concomitant social and political changes will motivate the electorate to call for cuts in legal immigration. Whatever the future may hold concerning immigration policy, the political factors linking immigration to redistributive issues will probably continue to divide the House and Senate along partisan and ideological lines. And of course, regional factors reflecting cultural predispositions can be expected to enter the equation, as well.

In the absence of a truly national outcry demanding restrictions on legal immigration, the future of policy in this area rests largely in the hands of the Washington interest group community. The congressional politics of immigration reform in 1996 proved that the forces combating restrictions had developed a formidable network that could not be taken for granted. The interest groups favoring restriction would not have the energy and organization to match their opposition anytime in the foreseeable future. With Alan Simpson gone, Lamar Smith and his staff settled back to prepare longer-range plans for advancing their ideas on legal immigration.

In the coming years, the entire basis for the current immigration system requires careful reevaluation and debate. Even in 1996, there were few questions raised about the fundamental constitution of the system of preferences and quotas. Congress has seemed mostly content to operate under a tweaked version of the 1965 law. For example, why should countries have the same visa allotment? There was no examination of this basic question. Familiar questions about the true economic impact of legal immigrants remain the subject of hot debate. While Congress awaits its next opportunity to reform the immigration system, the academic studies of the impact of immigrants will continue to pile up. Perhaps the findings of economists, sociologists, and demographers will eventually point in one obvious direction. But when and if they do, the congressional politics of immigration reform will still pave the path toward change.

SOURCES

The following abbreviations have been used throughout the text as shortened citations:

CR: Congressional Record, published daily while Congress is in session.

CQWR: Congressional Quarterly Weekly Report, published weekly. CQWR sources listed by reporter's name.

CIR Report: Reports of the U.S. Commission on Immigration Reform, also known as the Jordan Commission.

CQ Almanac: Congressional Quarterly Almanac, published annually.

INS Statistical Yearbook: U.S. Immigration and Naturalization Service *1994 Statistical Yearbook.*

Congressional Task Force Report: Report of the Congressional Task Force on Immigration Reform.

Judiciary Committee Activities Report: *Report on the Activities of the Committee on the Judiciary of the House of Representatives During the 104th Congress.*

Elliott Abrams and Franklin S. Abrams. 1975. "Immigration Policy—Who Gets in and Why?" *Public Interest*, 3–29.

B. E. Aguirre, Rogelio Saenz, and Brian Sinclair James. 1997. "Marielitos Ten Years Later: The Scarface Legacy," *Social Science Quarterly* 78:2:487–507.

Richard Alba and Victor Nee. 1997. "Rethinking Assimilation Theory for a New Era of Immigration" *International Migration Review* 31:4:826–874.

Stuart Anderson. 1995. "An Analysis of H.R. 2202: The Immigration in the National Interest Act of 1995," working paper (Arlington, VA: Alexis de Tocqueville Institution).

R. Douglas Arnold. 1990. *The Logic of Congressional Action* (New Haven: Yale University Press).

Associated Press. 1996. "Arizona-Mexico Border Crackdown: Arrests Rise 34 Percent in Past Year." October 14.

Thomas Bailey. 1987. *Immigrant and Native Workers: Contrasts and Competition* (Boulder, CO: Westview Press).

Susan Gonzalez Baker. 1997. "The 'Amnesty' Aftermath: Current Policy Issues Stemming from the Legalization Programs of the 1986 Immigration Reform and Control Act," *International Migration Review* 31:1:5–27.

Edith J. Barrett and Fay Lomax Cook. 1991. "Congressional Attitudes and Voting Behavior: An Examination of Support for Social Welfare," *Legislative Studies Quarterly* 16:3:375–391.

Ann P. Bartel. 1989. "Where Do the New U.S. Immigrants Live?" *Journal of Labor Economics* 7:4:371–391.

Elizabeth B. Bazan. June 11, 1996. Memorandum. Removal of Alien Terrorists: A Side-by-Side Comparison of the Removal Provisions of H.R. 2202, As Passed by the House and the Senate (Washington, DC: Congressional Research Service, Library of Congress).

Howard Berman, Member of Congress, et al. June 24, 1996. Letter to the Honorable Orrin Hatch, Chairman, U.S. Senate Judiciary Committee, and the Honorable Henry Hyde, Chairman, U.S. House Judiciary Committee.

Marion T. Bennett. 1963. *American Immigration Policies: A History* (Washington, DC: Public Affairs Press).

Norman E. Binder, J. L. Polinard, and Robert D. Wrinkle. 1997. "Mexican-American and Anglo Attitudes toward Immigration Reform: A View from the Border," *Social Science Quarterly* 78:2:324–337.

Joan Biskupic. 1990. "Employer Sanctions Draw Fire after Report on Job Bias," *Congressional Quarterly Weekly Report.* March 31: 1005–1006.

Joan Biskupic. 1990. "House Panel Begins Markup of Visa-Allotment Bill," *Congressional Quarterly Weekly Report.* April 7: 1075–1076.

Joan Biskupic. 1990. "Anger Grows Over U.S. Limit on Visitors With AIDS Virus," *Congressional Quarterly Weekly Report.* April 14: 1138–1139.

Joan Biskupic. 1990. "House Subcommittee Approves Visa-Allocation Revision," *Congressional Quarterly Weekly Report.* April 21: 1200.

Joan Biskupic. 1990. "Diversity Is One Principal Goal in Deciding Whom to Let In," *Congressional Quarterly Weekly Report.* August 4: 2519–2520.

Joan Biskupic. 1990. "House Bill Lifts Visa Levels, Aids Relatives, Skilled," *Congressional Quarterly Weekly Report.* October 6: 3225–3227.

Joan Biskupic. 1990. "Simpson Holds Bill Hostage, Demands Major Changes," *Congressional Quarterly Weekly Report.* October 13: 3424–3426.

Joan Biskupic. 1990. "Sizable Boost in Immigration Ok'd in Compromise Bill," *Congressional Quarterly Weekly Report.* October 27: 3608–3609.

Joan Biskupic. 1990. "Immigration Overhaul Cleared After Last-Minute Flap," *Congressional Quarterly Weekly Report.* November 3: 3753.

Joan Biskupic and Chuck Alston. 1990. "Fight Over Chinese Students First on Congress' Agenda," *Congressional Quarterly Weekly Report.* January 20: 193–195.

Brian Blomquist. 1996. "Dole Would Let States Refuse Illegals' Children in Schools," *Washington Times.* June 4: A4.

Brian Blomquist. 1996. "Congress Prepares for Showdown Over Provision in Immigration Bill," *Washington Times.* June 19: A4 .

Edna Bonacich. 1972. "A Theory of Ethnic Antagonism: The Split Labor Market," *American Sociological Review* 37:547–559.

Edna Bonacich. 1976. "Advanced Capitalism and Black/White Race Relations in the United States" *American Sociological Review* 41:34–51.

George J. Borjas. 1990. *Friends or Strangers: The Impact of Immigrants on the U.S. Economy* (New York: Basic Books).

George J. Borjas, Richard B. Freeman, and Lawrence F. Katz. 1992. "On the Labor Market Effects of Immigration and Trade," in George J. Borjas and Richard B. Freeman, eds., *Immigration and the Workforce* (Chicago: University of Chicago Press), pp. 213–244.

Brady, David W. and Charles S. Bullock, III. 1980. "Is there a Conservative Coalition in the House?" *Journal of Politics* 42:549–559.

David Brady and Barbara Sinclair. 1984. "Building Majorities for Policy Change in the House of Representatives," *Journal of Politics* 46: 1033–1060.

William Branigin. 1997. "Income, Support Requirements Imposed on Immigrant Sponsors," *Washington Post*. October 21:A3.

Vernon M. Briggs, Jr. 1992. *Mass Immigration and the National Interest* (Armonk, NY: M. E. Sharpe).

Vernon M. Briggs, Jr., and Stephen Moore. 1997. "Still an Open Door? U.S. Immigration Policy and the American Economy," in Nicholas Capaldi, ed., *Immigration: Debating the Issues* (Amherst, NY: Prometheus Books), pp. 161–187.

Peter Brimelow. 1995. *Alien Nation: Common Sense About America's Immigration Disaster* (New York: Random House).

Peter Brimelow and Ed Rubinstein. 1997. "Electing a New People," *National Review*. June 19. Internet edition.

Cassandra Burrell. 1997. "Farmers Claim Labor Shortage," Associated Press. September 24.

Steven A. Camarota. 1998. *The Wages of Immigration*. Center for Immigration Studies, Paper No. 12 (Washington, D.C.: Center for Immigration Studies).

Richard Carelli. 1997. "Court Nixes Two Immigration Appeals," Associated Press. October 6.

Alvar W. Carlson. 1994. "America's New Immigration: Characteristics, Destinations and Impact 1970–1989," *Social Science Journal* 31:3:313–236.

Edward G. Carmines and James A. Stimson. 1989. *Issue Evolution: Race and the Transformation of American Politics* (Princeton, NJ: Princeton University Press).

Dan Carney. 1996. "Republicans Agree on Measure To Combat Illegal Aliens," *Congressional Quarterly Weekly Report*. September 7: 2531.

Dan Carney. 1996. "Scaled-Back Bill Moves Ahead As GOP Considers Options," *Congressional Quarterly Weekly Report*. September 28: 2755–2759.

Dan Carney. 1996. "As White House Calls Shots, Illegal Alien Bill Clears," *Congressional Quarterly Weekly Report*. October 5: 2864–2866.

Dan Carney. 1996. "Law Restricts Illegal Immigration," *Congressional Quarterly Weekly Report*. November 16: 3287–3789.

Dan Carney. 1997. "Republicans Feeling the Heat As Policy Becomes Reality," *Congressional Quarterly Weekly Report*. May 17: 1131–1136.

Ruben Castaneda. 1997. "Banking on Advocacy," *Hispanic* (October): 24–30.

Steve Chabot, Member of Congress, et al. June 26, 1996. Letter to the Honorable Newt Gingrich, House Speaker.

Barry Chiswick. 1986. "Is the New Immigration Less Skilled than the Old?" *Journal of Labor Economics* 4:1: 192–196.

Phyllis Pease Chock. 1995. "Ambiguity in Policy Discourse: Congressional Talk About Immigration," *Policy Sciences* 28:2:165–184.

Marlene Cimons. 1997. "GOP Leader Vows Fight on Immigrant Aid," *Los Angeles Times.* February 10.

Jack Citrin, Donald P. Green, Christopher Muste, and Cara Wong. 1997. "Public Opinion Toward Immigration Reform: The Role of Economic Motivations," *Journal of Politics* 59:3: 858–881.

Jack Citrin, Beth Reingold, and Donald P. Green. 1990. "American Identity and the Politics of Ethnic Change," *Journal of Politics* 52:4: 1124–1153.

Rebecca Clark, Jeffrey S. Passel, Wendy N. Zimmerman, and Michael E. Fix. 1994. "Fiscal Impacts of Undocumented Immigrants." *Government Finance Review* 11:1:20–23.

Aage R. Clausen. 1973. *How Congressmen Decide: A Policy Focus* (New York: St. Martin's Press).

Nancy Cleeland, Peter M. Warren, and Esther Schrader. 1997. "Investigators Search Hemandad Offices," *Los Angeles Times.* January 15.

Nadine Cohodas. 1985. "Status of Salvadorans Debated on Capitol Hill," *Congressional Quarterly Weekly Report.* April 27: 787–788.

Nadine Cohodas. 1985. "New Immigration Bill Introduced in Senate," *Congressional Quarterly Weekly Report.* May 25: 1024.

Nadine Cohodas. 1985. "Swift Senate Action Sought on Immigration Reform Bill," *Congressional Quarterly Weekly Report.* July 6: 1332.

Nadine Cohodas. 1985. "Action Starting on Immigration Legislation," *Congressional Quarterly Weekly Report.* July 20: 1420–1421.

Nadine Cohodas. 1985. "Senate Passes Immigration Bill; Action Moves to House," *Congressional Quarterly Weekly Report.* September 21: 1859–1861.

Nadine Cohodas. 1985. "Admission of 70,000 Refugees Proposed," *Congressional Quarterly Weekly Report.* September 28: 1950.

Nadine Cohodas. 1985. "Markups to Begin on House Immigration Bill," *Congressional Quarterly Weekly Report.* November 16: 2364.

Nadine Cohodas. 1985. "House Panel Approves Immigration Measure," *Congressional Quarterly Weekly Report.* November 23: 2441–2442.

Nadine Cohodas. 1986. "Immigration Bill Halted Again by Dispute on Farm Workers," *Congressional Quarterly Weekly Report.* May 3: 989.

Nadine Cohodas. 1986. "Immigration Markup Delayed so Negotiations can Continue," *Congressional Quarterly Weekly Report.* June 14: 1337.

Nadine Cohodas. 1986. "Immigration Bill Stalls over Farm Labor Issue," *Congressional Quarterly Weekly Report.* June 21: 1411–1412.

Nadine Cohodas. 1986. "House Panel Breaks Deadlock, Sends Immigration Bill to Floor," *Congressional Quarterly Weekly Report.* June 28: 1479–1480.

Nadine Cohodas. 1986. "Rules Ponders Immigration Bill Procedures," *Congressional Quarterly Weekly Report.* September 13: 2129.

Nadine Cohodas. 1986. "House Kills Immigration Bill, Little Chance for Resurrection," *Congressional Quarterly Weekly Report.* September 27: 2267.

Nadine Cohodas. 1986. "House Approves Package of Immigration Bills," *Congressional Quarterly Weekly Report.* October 4: 2363.

Nadine Cohodas. 1986. "Congress Clears Overhaul of Immigration Law," *Congressional Quarterly Weekly Report.* October 18: pp. 2595–2596.

Nadine Cohodas. 1988. "Senate Blocks House Move to Extend Amnesty for Aliens," *Congressional Quarterly Weekly Report.* April 30: 1164.

Congressional Quarterly Almanac. Various years (Washington, DC: Congressional Quarterly Press).

Congressional Record (CR) (Washington, DC: U.S. Government Printing Office, various dates).

Congressional Task Force on Immigration Reform. June 29, 1995. Report to the Speaker, the Honorable Newt Gingrich.

William F. Connelly, Jr., and John J. Pitney, Jr. 1994. *Congress' Permanent Minority? Republicans in the U.S. House* (Lanham, MD: Rowman and Littlefield Publishers).

Arthur F. Corwin. 1978. "A Story of Ad Hoc Exemptions," in Arthur F. Corwin, ed., *Immigrants-and Immigrants: Perspectives on Mexican Labor Migration to the United States* (Durham, NC: Duke University Press), pp. 136–175.

Arthur F. Corwin. 1984. "The Numbers Game: Estimates of Illegal Aliens in the United States, 1970–1981," in Richard R. Hofstetter, ed., *U.S. Immigration Policy* (Durham, NC: Duke University Press), pp. 223–291.

Amanda Covarrubias. 1996. "Smugglers and Their Human Cargo Join Forces in Deadly Game," Associated Press Wire Story. May 6.

Richard B. Craig. 1971. *The Bracero Program: Interest Groups and Foreign Policy* (Austin: University of Texas Press, 1971).

John S. Cummins, Chairman, National Conference of Catholic Bishops Committee on Migration. September 24, 1996. Letter to U.S. Representatives.

Scott Cummings and Thomas Lambert. 1997. "Anti-Hispanic and Anti-Asian Sentiments Among African-Americans," *Social Science Quarterly* 78:2: 338–353.

Donald A. Danner, Vice President of Federal Government Relations, National Federation of Independent Business. March 18, 1996. Letter to the Honorable Lamar Smith, Chairman, U.S. House Subcommittee on Immigration and Claims.

Robert A. Divine. 1957. *American Immigration Policy, 1924–1952* (New Haven: Yale University Press).

Katharine M. Donato. 1994. "U.S. Policy and Mexican Migration to the United States, 1942–92," *Social Science Quarterly* 75:4:705–729.

John W. Donohue. 1982. "The Uneasy Immigration Debate," *America.* March 20: 206–209.

Marion Moncure Duncan. 1997. "National Origins Quotas Should Be Retained," in Nicholas Capaldi, ed., *Immigration: Debating the Issues* (Amherst, NY: Prometheus Books) pp. 117–123.

Helen F. Eckerson. 1966. "Immigration and National Origins," *Annals of the American Academy of Political and Social Science* 367: 4–14.

James R. Edwards, Jr. 1997. "Congress Winks at Illegal Immigration," *Investor's Business Daily.* October 23: A34 .

Larry M. Eig. June 11, 1996. Memorandum. Exclusion and Deportation: A Side-By-Side Comparison of the Removal Provisions of H.R. 2202 (Washington, DC: Congressional Research Service, Library of Congress).

Larry M. Eig and Joyce C. Vialet. May 16, 1996. Memorandum. Alien Eligibility For Public Benefits, "Public Charge," and Related Provisions: A Side-By-Side Comparison of H.R. 2202, as Passed by the House and Senate (Washington, DC: Congressional Research Service, Library of Congress).

Employers for Responsible Immigration Reform. September 20, 1996. Letter to U.S. Representatives.

John Engler, Chairman, Republican Governors Association. July 10, 1996. Letter to the Honorable Trent Lott, U.S. Senate Majority Leader.

Thomas J. Espenshade. 1994. "Does the Threat of Border Apprehension Deter Undocumented U.S. Immigration," *Population and Development Review* 20:4:871–891.

Thomas J. Espenshade and Charles A. Calhoun. 1993. "An Analysis of Public Opinion Toward Undocumented Immigration," *Population Research and Policy Review* 12: 189–224.

Thomas J. Espenshade and Haishan Fu. 1997. "An Analysis of English-Language Proficiency Among U.S. Immigrants," *American Sociological Review* 62: 288–305.

Thomas J. Espenshade and Vanessa E. King. 1994. "State and Local Fiscal Impacts of U.S. Immigrants: Evidence from New Jersey," *Population Research and Policy Review* 13:1: 225–256.

C. Lawrence Evans. 1989. "Influence in Congressional Committees: Participation, Manipulation and Anticipation," in Christopher J. Deering, ed. *Congressional Politics* (Pacific Grove, CA: Brooks Cole).

Robert D. Evans, Director, American Bar Association. June 20, 1996. Letter to the Honorable Lamar Smith, Chairman, U.S. House Subcommittee on Immigration and Claims.

Dianne Feinstein, U.S. Senator. September 9, 1996. Letter to the Honorable Trent Lott, U.S. Senate Majority Leader, and the Honorable Newt Gingrich, Speaker of the House.

Randall K. Filer. 1992. "The Effect of Immigrant Arrivals on Migratory Patterns of Native Workers," in George J. Borjas and Lawrence F. Katz, eds., *Immigration and the Workforce* (Chicago: University of Chicago Press), pp. 245–269.

Morris P. Fiorina. 1974. *Representatives, Roll Calls and Constituencies* (Lexington, MA: Lexington Books).

Keith Fitzgerald. 1996. *The Face of the Nation: Immigration, the State and National Identity* (Stanford, CA: Stanford University Press).

Michael Fix, Jeffrey S. Passel, and Wendy Zimmerman. 1996. "The Use of SSI and Other Welfare Programs by Immigrants," Testimony before the U.S. Senate Subcommittee on Immigration. February 6.

Michael Fix and Wendy Zimmerman. 1994. "After Arrival: An Overview of Federal Immigrant Policy in the United States," in Barry Edmonston and Jeffrey S. Passel, eds. *Immigration and Ethnicity: The Integration of America's Newest Arrivals* (Washington, DC: Urban Institute Press).

"Former DOL Official Offers Thoughts On Revamping U.S. Immigration System," 1997. *Bureau of National Affairs* April 9: A31.

James J. Fotis, Executive Director, Law Enforcement Alliance of America. June 27, 1996. Letter to the Honorable Elton Gallegly.

John Fox. 1997. *Applied Regression Analysis, Linear Models and Related Methods* (Beverly Hills, CA: Sage).

Louis Freedberg. 1997. "Republican Relishes Role as Champion of Legal Immigration," *San Francisco Chronicle*. July 8.

Edward Funkhouser and Stephen J. Trejo. 1995. "The Labor Market Skills of Recent Male Immigrants: Evidence from the Current Population Survey," *Industrial and Labor Relations Review* 48:4:792–811.

Michelle Gahee. 1995. "Measure Heightens Border Vigilance," *Congressional Quarterly Weekly Report*. June 17: 1752.

Roberto Garcia de Posada, Executive Director, Hispanic Business Roundtable. July 17, 1996. Letter to Conferees.

Phil Garlington. 1997. "Crossing the Border: Illegal and Dangerous," *Orange County Register*. January 19.

General Accounting Office. 1990. *Immigration Reform: Employer Sanctions and the Question of Discrimination* (Washington, DC: Government Printing Office).

General Accounting Office. 1994. *Illegal Aliens: Assessing Estimate of Financial Burden on California* (Washington, DC: Government Printing Office).

General Accounting Office. 1997. *Illegal Aliens: Extent of Welfare Benefits Received on Behalf of U.S. Citizen Children* (Washington, DC: Government Printing Office).

James G. Gimpel. 1996. *Legislating the Revolution: The Contract with America in its First 100 Days* (Boston: Allyn and Bacon).

James G. Gimpel. 1997. "Grassroots Organizations and Equilibrium Cycles in Group Mobilization and Access," in Paul S. Herrnson, Ronald Shaiko, and Clyde Wilcox, eds., *The Interest Group Connection* (Chatham, NJ: Chatham House Publishers), pp. 100–115.

Nathan Glazer and Daniel Patrick Moynihan. 1970. *Beyond the Melting Pot*, 2nd ed. (Cambridge, MA: MIT Press).

Jamie S. Gorelick, Deputy Attorney General. March 13, 1996. Letter to the Honorable Newt Gingrich, House Speaker.

Jamie S. Gorelick, Deputy Attorney General. May 31, 1996. Letter to the Honorable Lamar Smith, Chairman, U.S. House Subcommittee on Immigration and Claims.

Shelby Grad. 1997. "Orange County Supervisors Back Citizenship Denial," *Los Angeles Times*. July 2.

Bob Gravely. 1997. "Lamar Smith Backs Bar on Citizenship for Offspring of Illegals," *Congressional Quarterly Weekly Report*. June 25. Internet edition.

Guillermo Grenier and Alex Stepick. 1992. *Miami Now! Immigration, Ethnicity and Social Change* (Gainesville, FL: University of Florida Press).

John Mark Hansen. 1991. *Gaining Access: Congress and the Farm Lobby, 1919–1981* (Chicago: University of Chicago Press).

Edwin Harwood. 1983. "Alienation: American Attitudes Toward Immigration," *Public Opinion*. June/July: 49–51.

Edwin Harwood. 1986. "American Public Opinion and U.S. Immigration Policy," *Annals of the American Academy of Political and Social Science* 487:201–212.

Melissa Healy. 1997. "Immigrant Advocates to Test Clout," *Los Angeles Times*, September 1.

David Heer. 1996. *Immigration in America's Future* (Boulder, CO: Westview Press).

Eaaron I. Henderson-King and Richard E. Nisbett. 1996. "Antiblack Prejudice as a Function of Exposure to the Negative Behavior of a Single Black Person." *Journal of Personality and Social Psychology* 71:4: 654–664.

John Higham. 1955. *Strangers in the Land: Patterns of American Nativism, 1896–1925*. (New Brunswick, NJ: Rutgers University Press).

Gladwin Hill. 1953. "The Wetbacks: McCarran's Immigrants," *Nation*. August 22: 151–152.

Bill Ong Hing. 1993. *Making and Remaking Asian America Through Immigration Policy, 1850–1990* (Stanford, CA: Stanford University Press).

Melvin J. Hinich and Michael C. Munger. 1997. *Analytical Politics* (New York: Cambridge University Press).

Michael D. Hoefer. 1991. "Background of U.S. Immigration Policy Reform," in Francisco L. Rivera-Batiz, Selig L. Sechzer, and Ira N. Gang, eds., *U.S. Immigration*

Policy Reform in the 1980s: A Preliminary Assessment (New York: Praeger), pp. 17–44.

Scott P. Hoffman, Director of Operations, Americans for Tax Reform. June 20, 1996. Letter to Conferees.

Scott P. Hoffman, Director of Operations, Americans for Tax Reform. June 24, 1996. Letter to Conferees.

Richard R. Hofstetter. 1984. "Economic Underdevelopment and the Population Explosion: Implications for U.S. Immigration Policy," in Richard R. Hofstetter, ed., *U.S. Immigration Policy* (Durham, NC: Duke University Press), pp. 55–79.

Richard R. Hofstetter, ed., 1984. *U.S. Immigration Policy* (Durham, NC: Duke University Press).

M. V. Hood and Irwin L. Morris. 1997. "¿Amigo or Enemigo?: Context, Attitudes and Anglo Public Opinion toward Immigration," *Social Science Quarterly* 78:2: 309–323.

David Hosansky. 1996. "Long Line of Complaints," *Congressional Quarterly Weekly Report.* September 28: 2758.

Michael Hout. 1988. "More Universalism, Less Structural Mobility: The American Occupational Structure in the 1980s," *American Journal of Sociology* 93: 1358–1401.

Gregory A. Huber and Thomas J. Espenshade. 1997. "Neo-Isolationism, Balanced-Budget Conservatism, and the Fiscal Impacts of Immigrants," *International Migration Review* 31:4: 1031–1053.

Donald Huddle. 1993. *The Costs of Immigration* (Washington, DC: The Carrying Capacity Network).

Jon Hurwitz and Mark Peffley 1997. "Public Perceptions of Race and Crime: The Role of Racial Stereotypes," *American Journal of Political Science* 41:2 375–401.

Edward P. Hutchinson. 1981. *Legislative History of American Immigration Policy 1798–1965* (Philadelphia: University of Pennsylvania Press).

Holly Idelson. 1995. "Immigration: Bridging Gap Between Ideas and Action," *Congressional Quarterly Weekly Report.* April 15: 1065–1071.

Holly Idelson. 1995. "Influx of Newcomers to U.S. Puts Pressure on Politics," *Congressional Quarterly Weekly Report.* June 10: 1648–1649.

Holly Idelson. 1995. "House Panel Bill Cracks Down on Legal and Illegal Entry," *Congressional Quarterly Weekly Report.* July 15: 2073–2074.

Holly Idelson. 1995. "New Immigration Restrictions Easily Clear First Hurdle," *Congressional Quarterly Weekly Report.* July 22: 2187–2188.

Holly Idelson. 1995. "House Panel Opens Debate on Major Restrictions," *Congressional Quarterly Weekly Report.* September 23: 2912–2914.

Holly Idelson. 1995. "Panel Makes No Big Changes to Overhaul Bill—Yet," *Congressional Quarterly Weekly Report.* September 30: 3010–3011.

Holly Idelson. 1995. "Smith Keeps Overhaul on Track Through Complex Markup," *Congressional Quarterly Weekly Report.* October 14: 3147–4148.

Holly Idelson. 1995. "Panel Focuses on Benefits, Temporary Workers," *Congressional Quarterly Weekly Report.* October 21: 3211–3212.

Holly Idelson. 1995. "House Judiciary Approves Sweeping Restrictions," *Congressional Quarterly Weekly Report.* October 28: 3305–3308.

Holly Idelson. 1996. "Lawmakers Split on Including Legal Aliens in Overhaul," *Congressional Quarterly Weekly Report.* March 2: 556–557.

Holly Idelson. 1996. "Opponents Win Concessions During Senate Markup," *Congressional Quarterly Weekly Report.* March 9: 621–623.

Holly Idelson. 1996. "Economic Anxieties Bring Debate On Immigration To a Boil," *Congressional Quarterly Weekly Report.* March 16: 697–699, 701.

Holly Idelson. 1996. "House Votes To Crack Down On Illegal Immigrants," *Congressional Quarterly Weekly Report.* March 23: 794–796, 798.

Holly Idelson. 1996. "Panel Opts for Modest Changes In Level of Legal Entrants," *Congressional Quarterly Weekly Report.* March 30: 882–884.

Holly Idelson. 1996. "Election-Year Skirmishes Divert Senate Action," *Congressional Quarterly Weekly Report.* April 20: 1051.

Holly Idelson. 1996. "Senate Rejects Two Attempts To Cut Legal Immigration," *Congressional Quarterly Weekly Report.* April 27: 1173–1174.

Holly Idelson. 1996. "Bill Heads to Conference After Senate Passage," *Congressional Quarterly Weekly Report.* May 4: 1221–1224.

Holly Idelson. 1996. "Conferees Prepare for Clash On Welfare Proposals," *Congressional Quarterly Weekly Report.* July 6: 1922–1924.

Immigration and Nationality Act, 10th ed. 1995. Committee Print of the Committee on the Judiciary, U.S. House of Representatives. Serial No. 1 (Washington, DC: U.S. Government Printing Office).

Immigration Control and Financial Responsibility Act of 1996. Report of the Committee on the Judiciary, U.S. Senate, on S. 1664. 1996. S. Rpt. 104–249 (Washington, DC: U.S. Government Printing Office).

Immigration in the National Interest Act of 1995. Report of the Committee on the Government Reform and Oversight, U.S. House of Representatives, on H.R. 2202. 1996. H. Rpt. 104–469, Part 2 (Washington, DC: U.S. Government Printing Office).

Immigration in the National Interest Act of 1995. Report of the Committee on the Judiciary, U.S. House of Representatives, on H.R. 2202. 1996. H. Rpt. 104–469, Part 1 (Washington, DC: U.S. Government Printing Office).

Immigration in the National Interest Act of 1995; Temporary Agricultural Worker Amendments of 1996. Report of the Committee on Agriculture, U.S. House of Representatives, on H.R. 2202. 1996. H. Rpt. 104–469, Part 3 (Washington, DC: U.S. Government Printing Office).

Immigration in the National Interest Act of 1995; Temporary Agricultural Worker Amendments of 1996. Report of the Committee on Agriculture, U.S. House of Representatives, on H.R. 2202. 1996. H. Rpt. 104–469, Part 4 (Washington, DC: U.S. Government Printing Office).

Gary C. Jacobson. 1993. "Deficit-Cutting Politics and Congressional Elections," *Political Science Quarterly* 108:3: 375–403.

J. Craig Jenkins. 1978. "The Demand for Immigrant Workers: Labor Scarcity or Social Control?" *International Migration Review* 12:4:514–535.

Kevin R. Johnson. 1995. "Civil Rights and Immigration: Challenges for the Latino Community in the 21st Century," *La Raza Law Journal* 8:1:42–89.

R. Bruce Josten, Senior Vice President, U.S. Chamber of Commerce. March 20, 1996. Letter to the Honorable Ed Bryant.

Fred Kammer, President, Catholic Charities U.S.A. June 10, 1996. Letter to Conferees.

Jeffrey L. Katz. 1996. "An Unusual Immigration Alliance," *Congressional Quarterly Weekly Report.* March 16: 700.

Charles B. Keely. 1971. "Effects of the Immigration Act of 1965 on Selected Population Characteristics of Immigrants to the United States," *Demography* 8:2:157–169.

Sarah M. Kendall. 1996. "America's Minorities Are Shown the 'Back Door'...Again: The Discriminatory Impact of the Immigration Reform and Control Act," *Houston Journal of International Law* 18: 900–933.

Edward M. Kennedy. 1966. "The Immigration Act of 1965," *Annals of the American Academy of Political and Social Science* 367: 137–149.

Edward M. Kennedy, U.S. Senator, et al. May 20, 1996. Letter to Conferees.

Nancy Mohr Kennedy, Senior Director of Government Relations, United Way of America. June 10, 1996. Letter to the Honorable Ed Bryant.

John W. Kingdon. 1981. *Congressmen's Voting Decisions* (Ann Arbor: University of Michigan Press).

Dick Kirschten. 1995. "Second Thoughts," *National Journal.* January 21: 150–155.

James Kitfield. 1997. "Mexico's Turn," *National Journal.* May 31: 1085–1087.

Sherrie A. Kossoudji. 1992. "Playing Cat and Mouse at the U.S.-Mexican Border," *Demography* 29:2:160–180.

Augustine J. Kposowa. 1995. "The Impact of Immigration on Unemployment and Earnings Among Racial Minorities in the United States," *Ethnic and Racial Studies* 18:3: 605–627.

Michael Kranish. 1997. "Clinton Policy Shift Followed Asian-American Fund-Raiser," *Boston Globe.* January 16. A1.

Michael Kranish. 1997. "Policy Shift Over Fund-Raiser Is Denied," *Boston Globe.* January 17: A1.

William J. Krouse. May 21, 1996. Memorandum. Strengthening Immigration Enforcement and Facilitating Legal Entry: A Comparison of House and Senate Provisions in H.R. 2202 (Washington, DC: Congressional Research Service, Library of Congress).

Joseph B. Kruskal and Myron Wish. 1978. *Multidimensional Scaling* (Beverly Hills: Sage).

James H. Kuklinski. 1979. "Representative-Constituency Linkages: A Review Article," *Legislative Studies Quarterly* 4:1:121–140.

James J. Lack, President, National Conference of State Legislatures. June 14, 1996. Letter to U.S. Representatives.

Margaret Mikyung Lee. May 20, 1996. Memorandum. Alien Smuggling and Document Fraud Provisions: A Side-By-Side Comparison of H.R. 2202, as Passed by the House and Senate (Washington, DC: Congressional Research Service, Library of Congress).

Margaret Mikyung Lee. May 28, 1996. Memorandum. Deterrence of the Transportation of Illegal Aliens and Miscellaneous Provisions on the Enhancement of Immigration Law Enforcement: A Side-By-Side Comparison of H.R. 2202, as Passed by the House and Senate (Washington, DC: Congressional Research Service, Library of Congress).

Michael C. LeMay. 1987. *From Open Door to Dutch Door* (New York: Praeger).

Linda Levine. 1995. "Immigration: The Effects on Native-Born Workers" CRS Report for Congress. March 30: 95–439 E.

Frank Levy. 1995. "Incomes and Income Inequality," in Reynolds Farley, ed., *State of the Union–America in the 1990s, Vol. 1: Economic Trends* (New York: Russell Sage), pp. 1–18.

Edgar Litt. 1970. *Ethnic Politics in America* (Glenview, IL: Scott, Foresman and Co.)

Alice Ann Love. 1997. "Immigrants' Kids Get $1 Billion in Welfare." Associated Press. November 22.

B. Lindsay Lowell, Frank D. Bean, and Rodolfo O. de la Garza. 1986. "The Dilemmas of Undocumented Immigration: An Analysis of the 1984 Simpson Mazzoli Vote," *Social Science Quarterly* 67:1: 118–127.

Karin MacDonald and Bruce E. Cain. 1998. "Nativism, Partisanship and Immigration: An Analysis of Prop. 187" in M. B. Preston, B. E. Cain, and S. Bass, eds., *Racial and Ethnic Politics in California, Vol 2*. (Berkeley, CA: Institute for Governmental Studies).

Forrest Maltzman and Steven S. Smith. 1994. "Principals, Goals, Dimensionality and Congressional Committees," *Legislative Studies Quarterly* 19:4: 457–476.

Karl Manheim. 1995. "State Immigration Laws and Federal Supremacy," *Hastings Constitutional Law Quarterly* 22:239–1018.

Jeffrey R. Margolis. 1995. "Closing the Doors to the Land of Opportunity: The Constitutional Controversy Surrounding Proposition 187," *University of Miami Inter-American Law Review* 26: 363–401.

Philip L. Martin. 1990. "Harvest of Confusion: Immigration Reform and California Agriculture," *International Migration Review* 24:69–95.

Philip L. Martin. 1996. "California's Farm Labor Market and Immigration Reform," in B. Lindsay Lowell, ed. *Temporary Migrants in the United States* (research papers of the U.S. Commission on Immigration Reform).

Philip L. Martin and Maron F. Houstoun. 1984. "European and American Immigration Policies," in Richard F. Hofstetter, ed., *U.S. Immigration Policy* (Durham, NC: Duke University Press), pp. 29–54.

David J. Masci. 1990. "Groups Line Up on Both Sides of Border Fee Proposal," *Congressional Quarterly Weekly Report*. December 1: 4003.

David J. Masci. 1995. "Panel OKs Restrictions On Legal Immigrants," *Congressional Quarterly Weekly Report*. December 2: 3657–3658.

David J. Masci. 1996. "Immigration Draft OK'd by Panel," *Congressional Quarterly Weekly Report*. March 23: 797.

Douglas Massey. 1995. "The New Immigration and Ethnicity in the United States," *Population and Development Review* 21:3:631–652.

David R. Mayhew. 1974. *Congress: The Electoral Connection* (New Haven: Yale University Press).

Patrick J. McDonnell. 1997a. "Border Crackdown Paradox Studied," *Los Angeles Times*. October 10.

Patrick J. McDonnell. 1997b. "Prop. 187 Found Unconstitutional by Federal Judge," *Los Angeles Times*. November 15.

Patrick J. McDonnell and Dina Bass. 1997. "INS Expands its War on Smuggling of 'Human Cargo'," *Los Angeles Times*. June 20.

Lawrence Mead. 1992. *The New Politics of Poverty* (New York: Basic Books).

Laura Meckler. 1997. "States Keep Immigrants' Benefits." Associated Press. October 19.

Michelle Mittelstadt. 1997a. "INS Investigated for Slowing Probe." Associated Press. September 19.

Michelle Mittelstadt. 1997b. "Congress Faces Immigration Issue." Associated Press. October 17.

John Mollenkopf and Manuel Castells, eds. 1991. *Dual City: Restructuring New York* (New York: Russell Sage).

Martha T. Moore and Martin Kasindorf. 1997. "Latest Arrests Highlight Growing National Problem," *USA Today.* July 28: 1A , 2A .

Thomas Muller. 1993. *Immigrants and the American City* (New York: New York University Press).

Thomas Muller. 1996. "Nativism in the mid-90s: Why Now?" in Juan F. Perea, ed., *Immigrants Out! The New Nativism and the Anti-Immigrant Impulse in the United States* (New York: New York University Press), pp. 105–118.

Thomas Muller and Thomas J. Espenshade. 1985. *The Fourth Wave: California's Newest Immigrants* (Washington, DC: The Urban Institute Press).

David Nather. 1997. "Congress Ready to Clear Budget Plan As Work Begins on Health Legislation," *Bureau of National Affairs* June 6: A49–A50.

Gerald L. Neuman. 1993. "The Lost Century of American Immigration Law," *Columbia Law Review* 93:8:1833–1901.

Josephine Nieves, Executive Director, National Association of Social Workers. September 16, 1996. Letter to Conferees.

Karen O'Connor and Lee Epstein. 1984. "A Legal Voice for the Chicano Community: The Activities of the Mexican American Legal Defense and Education Fund, 1968–1982," *Social Science Quarterly* 65:2:

Walter Oleszek. 1996. *Congressional Procedures and the Policy Process*, 4th ed. (Washington, DC: Congressional Quarterly Press).

Susan Olzak. 1992. *The Dynamics of Ethnic Competition and Conflict* (Palo Alto, CA: Stanford University Press).

Gary Orfield. 1975. *Congressional Power: Congress and Social Change* (New York: Harcourt Brace Jovanovich).

Jeffrey S. Passel. 1994. *Immigrants and Taxes: A Reappraisal of Huddle's "The Costs of Immigrants"* (Washington, DC: The Urban Institute).

Ed Pastor, Member of Congress, et al. June 20, 1996. Letter to the Honorable Ed Bryant.

Juan F. Perea. 1996. *Immigrants Out! The New Nativism and the Anti-Immigrant Impulse in the United States* (New York: New York University Press).

Rosanna Perotti. 1994. "Employer Sanctions and the Limits of Negotiation," *Annals of the Academy of Political and Social Science* 534: 31–43.

Michael J. Piore and Charles F. Sabel. 1984. *The Second Industrial Divide: Possibilities for Prosperity* (New York: Basic Books).

Mary E. Pivec. 1996. "Immigration Reform Targets Employers' Role as Gatekeepers," *Legal Times.* June 10: S27, S43–S45.

"Plans Laid To Curb Immigration." 1995. *Congressional Quarterly Almanac* (Washington, DC: Congressional Quarterly), pp. 6-9–6-18.

Keith T. Poole and Howard Rosenthal. 1984. "The Polarization of American Politics," *Journal of Politics* 44: 1061–1079.

Keith T. Poole and Howard Rosenthal. 1985. "The Unidimensional Congress, 1919–1984." Graduate School of Industrial Administration, Working Paper no. 44-84-85. Carnegie Mellon University.

Keith T. Poole and Howard Rosenthal. 1991. "Patterns of Congressional Voting," *American Journal of Political Science* 35:1: 228–278.

Keith T. Poole and Howard Rosenthal. 1997. *Congress: A Political-Economic History of Roll Call Voting* (New York: Oxford University Press).

Michael Posner and Elisa Massimino. Lawyers Committee for Human Rights. September 17, 1996. Letter to Conferees.

"Pot and Kettle." 1996. Editorial. *Washington Post.* September 30: A22.

Miriam Potocky. 1996. "Refugee Children: How Are They Faring Economically as Adults?" *Social Work* 41: 364–373.

William T. Pound, Executive Director, National Conference of State Legislatures. September 13, 1996. Letter to Representatives.

David M. Reimers. 1992. *Still the Golden Door: The Third World Comes to America*, 2nd ed. (New York: Columbia University Press).

David M. Reimers. 1996. "The Emergence of the Immigration Restriction Lobby Since 1979," Paper prepared for the annual meeting of the American Political Science Association, San Francisco. August.

Report on the Activities of the Committee on the Judiciary of the House of Representatives During the 104th Congress. 1997. H. Rpt. 104–879 (Washington, DC: U.S. Government Printing Office).

H. G. Reza. 1998. "417 Immigrants Found in 3 Big Rigs Crossing Desert," *Los Angeles Times.* January 31.

Fred W. Riggs. 1950. *Pressures on Congress: A Study of the Repeal of Chinese Exclusion* (New York: King's Crown Press).

Francisco L. Rivera-Batiz, Selig L. Sechzer, and Ira N. Gang, eds. *U.S. Immigration Policy Reform in the 1980s: A Preliminary Assessment* (New York: Praeger), pp. 17–44.

David W. Rohde. 1991. *Parties and Leaders in the Post Reform House* (Chicago: University of Chicago Press).

Elizabeth S. Rolph. 1992. "Immigration Policies: Legacy from the 1980s and Issues for the 1990s" (Santa Monica, CA: RAND Corporation).

Philip J. Romero, Andrew J. Chang, and Theresa Parker. 1994. *Shifting the Costs of a Failed Federal Policy: The Net Fiscal Impact of Illegal Immigrants in California* (Sacramento: California Governor's Office of Planning and Research).

Peter I. Rose. 1997. *Tempest-Tossed: Race, Immigration and Dilemmas of Diversity* (New York: Oxford University Press).

Myron Rothbart and Oliver P. John. 1993. "Intergroup Relations and Stereotype Change: A Social Cognitive Analysis and Some Longitudinal Findings," in P. Sniderman, P. Tetlock, and E. Carmines, eds., *Prejudice, Politics and the American Dilemma* (Stanford: Stanford University Press).

James W. Russell. 1994. *After the Fifth Sun: Class and Race in North America* (Englewood Cliffs, NJ: Prentice Hall).

Denyse Sabagh, President, and Jeanne A. Butterfield, Associate Director of Advocacy, American Immigration Lawyers Association. September 18, 1996. Letter to Members of the U.S. House of Representatives.

Peter D. Salins. 1997. "Toward a New Immigration Policy," *Commentary* 103:1: 45–49.

Leonel Sanchez and Stephen Green. 1997. "Border Agents Shot at Again; Alarm Rises," *San Diego Union-Tribune.* July 1.

Save Our State, Save Our Sovereignty. September 16, 1996. News Release. "Immigration Reform Groups Oppose Gallegly Amendment."

Raymond C. Scheppach, Executive Director, National Governors Association. September 23, 1996. Letter to Conferees.

Allen Schick. 1995. *The Federal Budget: Politics, Policy, Process* (Washington, DC: The Brookings Institution).

Phyllis Schlafly, President, Eagle Forum. July 12, 1996. Letter to Conferees.

Arthur M. Schlesinger, Jr. 1992. *The Disuniting of America: Reflections on a Multicultural Society* (New York: W. W. Norton).

Robert F. Schoeni, Kevin F. McCarthy, and Georges Vernez. 1996. *The Mixed Economic Progress of Immigrants* (Santa Monica, CA: RAND Corporation).

Peter H. Schuck and Rogers M. Smith. 1985. *Citizenship Without Consent: Illegal Aliens in the American Polity* (New Haven: Yale University Press).

Donna E. Shalala, Secretary of Health and Human Services, Robert B. Reich, Secretary of Labor, and Shirley S. Chater, Commissioner of Social Security. June 19, 1996. Letter to the Honorable Alan K. Simpson, Chairman, U.S. Senate Immigration Subcommittee.

Louis P. Sheldon, Traditional Values Coalition. June 28, 1996. Letter to Conferees.

Rita J. Simon. 1985. *Public Opinion and the Immigrant: Print Media Coverage 1880–1980* (Lexington, MA: D.C. Heath).

Rita J. Simon and Susan H. Alexander. 1993. *The Ambivalent Welcome: Print Media, Public Opinion and Immigration* (Westport, CT: Praeger).

Alan K. Simpson, U.S. Senator. 1996. "The Immigration Bills: Facts vs. Fantasies," *Washington Post*. June 17: A17.

Peter Skerry. 1993. *Mexican-Americans: The Ambivalent Minority* (New York: The Free Press).

Christopher H. Smith, Member of Congress, et al. June 7, 1996. Letter to Conferees.

James P. Smith and Barry Edmonston, eds. 1997. *The New Americans: Economic, Demographic and Fiscal Effects of Immigration* (Washington, DC: National Academy Press).

Stephen S. Smith and Christopher J. Deering. 1984. *Committees in Congress* (Washington, DC: Congressional Quarterly Press).

Joseph J. Spengler. 1958. "Issues and Interests in American Immigration Policy," *Annals of the American Academy of Political and Social Science* (March): 43–51.

Danielle Starkey. 1993a. "Immigrant Bashing: Good Policy or Good Politics," *California Journal*. 24:15–19.

Danielle Starkey. 1993b. "Return to Sender: Deporting Illegal Aliens Convicted of Felonies," *California Journal*. 24:21–23.

Barry N. Stein. 1979. "Occupational Adjustment of Refugees: the Vietnamese in the United States," *International Migration Review* 13:1:25–45.

Dan Stein, Executive Director, Federation for American Immigration Reform. June 21, 1996. Letter to the Honorable Ed Bryant.

Robert M. Stein, Stephanie Shirley Post, and Allison L. Rinden. 1997. "The Effect of Contact and Context on White Attitudes Toward Immigrants and Immigration Policy," Paper presented at the 1997 Annual Meeting of the American Political Science Association, Washington, DC, August 28–31.

Alex Stepick. 1984. "Haitian Boat People: A Study in the Conflicting Forces Shaping U.S. Immigration Policy," in Richard R. Hofstetter, ed., *U.S. Immigration Policy* (Durham, NC: Duke University Press).

Subcommittee on Immigration and Claims, U.S. House Committee on the Judiciary. 1995. Hearing. February 8. *Management Practices of the Immigration and Naturalization Service* (Washington, DC: U.S. Government Printing Office).

Subcommittee on Immigration and Claims, U.S. House Committee on the Judiciary. 1995. Hearing. February 24. *Foreign Visitors Who Violate the Terms of Their Visas by Remaining in the United States Indefinitely* (Washington, DC: U.S. Government Printing Office).

Subcommittee on Immigration and Claims, U.S. House Committee on the Judiciary. 1995. Hearing. March 3. *Worksite Enforcement of Employer Sanctions* (Washington, DC: U.S. Government Printing Office).

Subcommittee on Immigration and Claims, U.S. House Committee on the Judiciary. 1995. Hearing. March 10. *Border Security* (Washington, DC: U.S. Government Printing Office).

Subcommittee on Immigration and Claims, U.S. House Committee on the Judiciary. 1995. Hearing. March 30. *Verification of Eligibility for Employment and Benefits* (Washington, DC: U.S. Government Printing Office).

Subcommittee on Immigration and Claims, U.S. House Committee on the Judiciary. 1995. Hearing. April 5. *Impact of Illegal Immigration on Public Benefit Programs and the American Labor Force* (Washington, DC: U.S. Government Printing Office).

Subcommittee on Immigration and Claims, U.S. House Committee on the Judiciary. 1995. Hearing. May 17. *Legal Immigration Reform Proposals* (Washington, DC: U.S. Government Printing Office).

Subcommittee on Immigration and Claims, U.S. House Committee on the Judiciary. 1995. Hearing. June 29. *H.R. 1915, Immigration in the National Interest Act of 1995* (Washington, DC: U.S. Government Printing Office).

Subcommittee on Immigration and Claims, U.S. House Committee on the Judiciary. 1995. Hearing. December 7. *Guest Worker Programs* (Washington, DC: U.S. Government Printing Office).

Subcommittee on Risk Management and Specialty Crops, U.S. House Committee on Agriculture, and Subcommittee on Immigration and Claims, U.S. House Committee on the Judiciary. 1995. Hearing. December 14. *Agricultural Guest Worker Programs* (Washington, DC: U.S. Government Printing Office).

James L. Sundquist. 1983. *Dynamics of the Party System* (Washington, DC: The Brookings Institution).

Roberto Suro. 1996. *Watching America's Door: The Immigration Backlash and the New Policy Debate* (New York: Twentieth Century Fund Press).

Raymond Tatalovich. 1995. *Nativism Reborn: The Official English Language Movement and the American States* (Lexington: University Press of Kentucky).

Lonnie P. Taylor, Vice President, U.S. Chamber of Commerce. July 30, 1996. Letter to the Honorable Ed Bryant.

Daniel J. Tichenor. 1994. "The Politics of Immigration Reform in the United States, 1981–1990," *Polity* 26:3:333–362.

Daniel J. Tichenor. 1997. "Political Regimes and Policy Change: Immigration Reform in American Political Development." Paper presented at the annual meeting of the American Political Science Association, Washington, DC, August 28–31.

Martin Tolchin. 1982. "Immigration Bill Has Personal Roots," *New York Times.* August 11: A18.

Robert H. Topel. 1994. "Regional Labor Markets and the Determinants of Wage Inequality," *American Economic Association Papers and Proceedings.* May: 17.

John Hayakawa Torok. 1995. "'Interest Convergence' and the Liberalization of Discriminatory Immigration and Naturalization Laws Affecting Asians, 1943–1965," *Chinese America: History and Perspectives* (San Francisco: Chinese Historical Society of America), pp. 1–28.

Julius Turner. 1951. *Party and Constituency: Pressures on Congress* (Baltimore: The Johns Hopkins Press).

U.S. Commission on Immigration Reform. 1994. *U.S. Immigration Policy: Restoring Credibility* (Washington, DC: U.S. Government Printing Office).

U.S. Commission on Immigration Reform. 1995. *Legal Immigration: Setting Priorities* (Washington, DC: U.S. Government Printing Office).

U.S. Commission on Immigration Reform. 1996. Research papers edited by B. Lindsay Lowell. *Temporary Migrants in the United States* (Washington, DC: U.S. Government Printing Office).

U.S. Commission on Immigration Reform. 1997. *Becoming an American: Immigration and Immigrant Policy* (Washington, DC: U.S. Government Printing Office).

U.S. Immigration and Naturalization Service. 1997. *Congressional Legislative Resource Guide*. February.

U.S. Immigration and Naturalization Service. 1996. *Statistical Yearbook* (Washington, DC: U.S. Government Printing Office).

U.S. Select Commission on Immigration and Refugee Policy. 1981. *U.S. Immigration Policy and the National Interest* (Washington, DC: House and Senate Judiciary Committees).

Peter Van Doren. 1990. Can We Learn the Causes of Congressional Decisions from Roll Call Data?" *Legislative Studies Quarterly* 15:311–340.

Georges Vernez and Allan Abrahamse. 1996. *How Immigrants Fare in U.S. Education* (Santa Monica, CA: RAND Corporation).

Joyce C. Vialet. September 7, 1994. "Immigration: What Is PRUCOL?" CRS Report for Congress 94–710 EPW.

Joyce C. Vialet. May 29, 1996. Memorandum. Worksite Enforcement: Verification Systems and Employer Sanctions—A Side-by-Side Comparison of H.R. 2202, as passed by the House and Senate (Washington, DC: Congressional Research Service, Library of Congress).

Joyce C. Vialet. December 3, 1996. "Immigration Fundamentals." CRS Report for Congress 95–56 EPW.

Joyce C. Vialet. February 12, 1997. "Immigration: Reasons for Growth, 1981–1995." CRS Report for Congress 97–230 EPW.

Joyce C. Vialet and Larry M. Eig. October 16, 1996. "Alien Eligibility for Benefits under the New Welfare and Immigration Laws." CRS Report for Congress 96–617 EPW.

Joyce C. Vialet and Molly R. Forman. July 23, 1996. "Immigration: Numerical Limits on Permanent Admissions." CRS Report for Congress 94–146 EPW.

Joyce C. Vialet, William Krouse, Ruth Ellen Wasem, and Larry M. Eig. November 22, 1996. "Immigration Legislation in the 104th Congress." CRS Reports for Congress 95–881 EPW.

Maurilio Vigil. 1990. "The Ethnic Organization as an Instrument of Political Change: MALDEF, A Case Study," *Journal of Ethnic Studies* 18:1: 15–31.

Carmen Delgado Votaw, Chair, and Janne G. Gallagher, Counsel, Human Services Forum. June 12, 1996. Letter to the Honorable Ed Bryant.

Roger Waldinger. 1996. *Still the Promised City: African-Americans and New Immigrants in Post-Industrial New York* (Cambridge, MA: Harvard University Press).

Fang Wang. 1996. "Voting on Proposition 187: Nativistic Sentiment and Ideology Split." Paper presented at the annual meeting of the Midwest Political Science Association, Chicago. April.

Peter M. Warren, Dexter Filkins, and H. G. Reza. 1997. "Records Show Orange County Vote Inquiry's Broad Scope," *Los Angeles Times*. February 1.

Peter M. Warren and H. G. Reza. 1997. "Investigators Say Group Helped Noncitizens Vote," *Los Angeles Times*. February 5.

Ruth Ellen Wasem. May 21, 1996. Memorandum. Miscellaneous Immigration Provisions: A Side-By-Side Comparison of H.R. 2202, as Passed by the House and Senate (Washington, DC: Congressional Research Service, Library of Congress).

Michael J. White and Gayle Kaufman. 1997. "Language Usage, Social Capital and School Completion among Immigrants and Native-Born Ethnic Groups," *Social Science Quarterly* 78:2: 385–398.

Jodi Wilgoren. 1998. "House Dismisses Dornan Challenge of Sanchez's Win," *Los Angeles Times*. February 13.

Roger P. Winter, Executive Director, Immigration and Refugee Services of America. September 23, 1996. Letter to Members of Congress.

Raymond E. Wolfinger. 1965. "The Development and Persistence of Ethnic Voting," *American Political Science Review* 59:4: 896–908.

John R. Wright. 1996. *Interest Groups and Congress: Lobbying, Contributions and Influence* (Boston: Allyn and Bacon).

Philip Q. Yang. 1995. *Post-1965 Immigration to the United States: Structural Determinants* (Westport, CT: Praeger).

Forrest W. Young. 1987. *Multidimensional Scaling—History, Theory and Applications* (Hillsdale, NJ: Lawrence Erlbaum Associates).

John Zaller. 1990. "Political Awareness, Elite Opinion Leadership and the Mass Survey Response," *Social Cognition* 8: 125–153.

John Zaller. 1992. *The Nature and Origins of Mass Opinion* (New York: Cambridge University Press).

Min Zhou. 1997. "Segmented Assimilation: Issues, Controversies and Recent Research on the New Second Generation." *International Migration Review*. 31:4: 975–1003.

Norman L. Zucker and Naomi Flink Zucker. 1987. *The Guarded Gate: The Reality of American Refugee Policy* (San Diego: Harcourt Brace Jovanovich).

Norman L. Zucker and Naomi Flink Zucker. 1992. "From Immigration to Refugee Redefinition: A History of Refugee and Asylum Policy in the United States," *Journal of Policy History* 4:1:54–70.

Personal Interviews

The following list is of those interviewed who wished to be acknowledged as sources:

Gary Ackerman (D-NY), 4/8/97.

Stuart Anderson (CATO Institute), 1/16/97.

Wright H. Andrews (Federation for American Immigration Reform), 2/5/97.

Bob Barr (R-GA), 4/8/97.

Ken Bentsen (D-TX), 5/17/97.

Howard Berman (D-CA), 3/25/97.

Jeanne Butterfield (American Immigration Lawyers Association), 2/13/97.

Randy "Duke" Cunningham (R-CA), 4/15/97.

Jennifer Denson (Federation for American Immigration Reform), 2/5/97.
Paul Donnelly (U.S. Commission on Immigration Reform), 6/17/97.
Cal Dooley (D-CA), 4/24/97.
Bob Ehrlich (R-MD), 4/29/97.
Jennifer Eisen (Intel Corporation), 2/20/97.
Bob Filner (D-CA), 2/27/97.
Matthew Finucane (Asian Pacific American Labor Alliance), 2/24/97.
George Fishman (House Subcommittee on Immigration and Claims), 1/18/97.
Floyd Flake (D-NY), 4/17/97.
Barney Frank (D-MA), 2/7/97.
George Gekas (R-PA), 2/27/97.
Bob Goodlatte (R-VA), 2/13/97.
Ed Grant (House Subcommittee on Immigration and Claims), 1/10/97.
Michael Hill (U.S. Catholic Bishops Conference), 2/21/97.
Steve Horn (R-CA), 3/3/97.
Raymond Kethledge (Legislative Counsel, Senator Spencer Abraham (R-MI)), 2/25/97.
Jay Kim (R-CA), 2/27/97.
Peter King (R-NY), 4/8/97.
Daphne Kwok (Organization of Chinese Americans), 2/4/97.
David Lehman (Legislative Counsel, Bob Goodlatte (R-VA)), 1/10/96.
Peter Levinson (House Judiciary Committee), 1/10/96.
Bryan Little (American Farm Bureau), 1/17/97.
Zoe Lofgren (D-CA), 2/27/97.
Susan Martin (U.S. Commission on Immigration Reform), 6/17/97.
Bill McCollum (R-FL), 5/16/97.
Richard Mereu (Legislative Counsel, Elton Gallegly (R-CA)), 2/20/97.
Patsy Mink (D-HI), 5/23/97.
Stephen Moore (CATO Institute), 1/16/97.
J. Michael Myers (Minority Staff, Senate Subcommittee on Immigration), 5/29/97.
Ed Pastor (D-AZ), 5/14/97.
Kyle Rogers (U.S. English), 1/16/97.
Frank Sharry (National Immigration Forum), 2/13/97.
E. Clay Shaw (R-FL), 4/15/97.
Lamar Smith (R-TX), 2/26/97.
Mark Souder (R-IN), 4/24/97
Cordia Strom (House Subcommittee on Immigration and Claims), 1/28/97.
Linda Chavez Thompson (AFL-CIO), 3/7/97.
Esteban Torres (D-CA), 5/17/97.
Georgina Verdugo (Mexican American Legal Defense and Education Fund), 1/28/97.
Lisa Zachary (Council of Jewish Federations), 5/1/97.

INDEX

Note: *Italicized* page numbers indicate profiles of members of Congress.

340

Schiff, Steve, 233
Schroeder, Patricia, 163, 234
Schumer, Charles, 171, 173, 175, 177, 188, 190, 234, 236
Scott, Robert, 237
Scott, William, 121
Select Commission on Immigration and Refugee Policy (Hesburgh Commission), 83, 135–36, 217, 309
Sensenbrenner, James, 127, 128, 159, 174
Sharry, Frank, 225
Shaw, E. Clay, 159, 163, 166, 174
Sierra Club, 51
Simon, Julian, 53
Simon, Paul, 170, 240, 242–43, 248, 264, 265, 267, 268, 282
Simon, Rita, 41
Simpson, Alan K., 19, 26, 110, 134–37, 154–56, 168, 169, 175, 180, 183, 186–87, 191–96, *192*, 215, 217, 220–21, 238–44, 247–48, 252–53, 261, 264, 265–67, 272, 278, 280–83, 287–88, 294–95, 302, 312, 315
Simpson-Mazzoli Act. *See* Immigration Reform and Control Act (1986)
Slavery, 10, 11
Smith, Lamar, 1–4, 19, 22, 26, 104–5, 110, 185–86, 188–94, 213, *214*, 216, 220–23, 226, 228, 229, 230, 232, 234, 237, 239, 240, 254–57, 259–61, 263, 265–66, 272, 274, 278, 280, 282, 285, 287–88, 294–95, 299, 302, 309, 315
Smith, William French, 137
Smuggling, 12, 13, 71, 226, 310, 314
Social Security benefits, 162, 298, 302, 309–10
Social Security identification, 89, 260, 276, 277–78, 285
Souder, Mark, 261
Southeast Asian refugees, 32–33, 52, 119–20, 130–31, 144
Southern Democrats
demise of, 26
immigration policy and, 20, 22, 108, 130, 131, 139, 143, 299–300
Southern Republicans
immigration policy and, 300
rise of, 26, 117–18
Soviet refugees, 73, 74, 185
Special agricultural workers (SAW), 173–74
Specter, Arlen, 250, 253, 272–73, 278
Sponsorship, 79–80, 220, 227, 250–52, 265–66, 270–71, 278–79, 283, 284, 313–14
Stagflation, 305
Summary exclusions, 76, 267, 274–76
Supplemental Security Income (SSI), 10, 32, 220, 312, 313
Supreme Court, U.S.
illegal immigration, 311
immigration as federal responsibility, 16
state control over immigration policy, 11
Sweeney, John, 243–44, 307
Swindall, Pat, 182

Symington, Fife, 17

TANF (Temporary Assistance to Needy Families), 15
Tanton, John, 50, 255
Telephone verification system, 235
Temporary workers, 80–81, 83–84, 227–28, 242, 253, 309–10
Texas
attitude toward immigration, 16–17
California versus, 16–17, 219
immigrant settlement in, 14–17, 22, 28, 53–54, 106, 143, 194, 200
immigration-related voting fraud and, 310
lawsuit seeking federal reimbursement, 16
reclassification and, 300
relationship with Mexico, 219
Think tanks, 53, 66, 220, 244
Thurmond, Strom, 110, 134, 155, 187
Tiahrt, Todd, 261
Torres, Esteban, 177, 180–82
Tower, John, 139
Truman, Harry S, 11–12, 60, 96, 97, 100
Turkey, 94

Urban Institute, 10, 15
U.S. Immigration Policy and the National Interest, 135

Vietnamese refugees, 52, 119–20
Amerasians, 66
public opinion concerning, 32–33, 40, 41, 73, 134

Visa overstay, 12–13, 81, 217, 223, 267–68
Visa preference system. *See* Immigration preferences
Voting
immigration-related voting fraud, 310
Voting Rights Act, 219

Waiting lists, 2, 63, 179, 219, 227
Waldinger, Roger, 116
Walker, Robert, 143
Wallop, Malcolm, 260
Warrantless searches, 265
Washington, Asian immigrants and, 98–99
Watt, Mel, 231, 237
Weber, Vin, 143
Welfare programs, 21, 78–80, 155, 250, 283–84, 302, 312–13
White, Richard, 116
Wilson, Pete, 16, 43, 157, 159, 170, 174, 201, *203*, 204, 241
Worldwide quotas, 65–66, 123–24, 154
Wright, Jim, 163

Zachary, Lisa, 233, 241
Zero Population Growth (ZPG), 50, 246, 255

ABOUT THE AUTHORS

James G. Gimpel, associate professor of government at the University of Maryland, has published two books and numerous articles on Congress, political behavior and public opinion. Before joining the university faculty, Gimpel worked as a legislative assistant in both the U.S. House and U.S. Senate. Gimpel earned his doctorate at the University of Chicago in 1990 and his master's from the University of Toronto in 1985, both in political science.

James R. Edwards, Jr., communications manager at the Healthcare Leadership Council in Washington, D.C., handled the Judiciary Committee assignment of Congressman Ed Bryant (R-Tenn.) in the 104th Congress. Edwards staffed the Immigration Conference Committee and served on the Majority Leader's Immigration Reform Working Group. Edwards holds a Ph.D. in communications from the University of Tennessee, awarded in 1992. He earned a master's degree in 1983 and a bachelor's in 1980, both in speech communication from the University of Georgia.